Most Popular Search Tools on the Web

Name	URL
AltaVista	www.altavista.com
Excite	www.excite.com
HotBot	www.hotbot.com
Infoseek	www.infoseek.com
Ask Jeeves	www.askjeeves.com
Lycos	www.lycos.com

Banks on the Web

Name	URL
Security First Network Bank	www.sfnb.com
NetB@nk	www.netbank.com
CompuBank	www.compubank.com
Wingspan Bank (division of FCC National Bank)	home.wingspanbank.com

Stock Sites on the Web

Name	URL	Comments
Motley Fool	www.fool.com	Make the Fool your first stop for stock information. The site contains links to information, trends, articles, and message boards.
Quote.com	www.quote.com	Read the latest financial news, get quotes, charts, and research at this massive site.
Reuters Moneynet	www.moneynet.com	You'll find all the information you need packed into a tight, easy to follow format.

Shop at a Cybermall

Mall Name	URL	Order Method	Comments
Internet Plaza	internet-plaza.net/	online, email, fax, or phone	Over 200 establishments are located under one cyber-roof!
Web Warehouse	www.webware	online, email, fax, or phone	In addition to hip brands, you can buy insurance, event tickets, and even peruse real-estate listings.
Shops.Net	shops.net	online, email, fax, or phone	Shops.Net is made up of links to other sites.
eMall	emall.com/	online, email, fax, or phone	Shop here for mainly specialty gourmet and garden items.
Shop.com	www.shop.com	online, purchase order, phone, fax, or mail	Shopping at Shop.com is as easy as 1-2-3.
iMall	www.imall.com	online	Take advantage of iMall's unique search tool that lets you look through each merchant's inventory for a specific item.

Attend an Online Auction

Auction Site	URL	Payment	Comments
eBay	www.ebay.com	Money order or cashiers check	eBay's pages are accessed 1.5 billion times per month.
uBid Online	www.ubid.com	Credit card	Owned by America Online, Auction uBid has some great name-brand merchandise for sale.
Amazon.com	www.amazon.com	Credit card	The Amazon auction is an addition to their regular business of books, CD's, and videos.

Play Games with Others on the Web

Name	URL	Cost	Games	Comments
2AM	www.2am.com	Free	Various, including Chain of Command, Total War, Poker, Chess, and Backgammon	2AM is part of the AltaVista network. You'll need to obtain the software and register before you can play.
HEAT	www.heat.net	Free for perimeter service, $5.95 for Premium	Various action games	A must see for the serious action gamer.
Imagic	www.imagicgames.com	Free for basic service with other pricing plans available	Free for players of Backgammon, Checkers, Chess, and a scaled-back version of the Kingdoms of Drakkar	One stop gaming for everyone.

Download Software from the Web

Site Name	URL	Description
Tucows	www.tucows.com	Links to most of the most popular shareware on the Web.
Download.com	www.download.com	Reviews of programs, along with the top, popular, and new software titles.
File Mine	www.filemine.com	Prospect File Mine for the files you want.
Softseek	www.softseek.com	Organized by categories.
Jumbo! The Download Network	www.jumbo.com	With 250,000 titles, you're sure to find the program you want.
Microsoft	www.microsoft.com/downloads/search.asp	Free software that can be used with Internet Explorer and other Microsoft products.

PRACTICAL

Internet

Barbara Kasser

Contents
at a Glance

que®

A Division of Macmillan Computer Publishing, USA
201 W. 103rd Street
Indianapolis, Indiana 46290

Practical Internet

International Standard Book Number: 0-7897-2226-7

Library of Congress Catalog Card Number: 99-65658

Printed in the United States of America

First Printing: **October 1999**

01   00   99   4   3   2   1

Trademarks

Warning and Disclaimer

Publisher
John Pierce

Development Editor
Susan Hobbs

Managing Editor
Thomas F. Hayes

Project Editor
Leah Kirkpatrick

Copy Editor
Victoria Elzey

Indexer
Rebecca Salerno

Proofreader
Tricia Sterling

Technical Editor
Bill Bruns

Team Coordinator
Lori Morgan

Interior Designer
Anne Jones

Cover Designer
Dan Armstrong

Copy Writer
Eric Borgert

Production
Dan Harris
Heather Moseman
Darin Crone

Contents

About the Authors

Barbara Kasser is a network administrator and software trainer. She has been involved with teaching people to use computers for her entire career. Barbara considers the Internet as her personal playground and the first place to look for information. She is usually online and logged in. Barbara has written training manuals on the Internet, Internet conferencing, and creating Web sites. In addition to *Practical Internet*, Barbara authored *Using the Internet, Fourth Edition, Netscape Navigator 4, Browsing and Beyond* and co-authored *Internet Explorer 4, One Step at a Time*.

Barbara lives in South Florida with her husband Bill, teenage son, two cats, and a dog. Barbara is very concerned about keeping kids safe on the Internet. You can contact Barbara via email at barbara@kasser.com.

Dedication

To Richard Kasser, my son, who shared his summer with me and performed admirably as an editorial assistant, technical consultant, and general helper. Richard, thanks so much for all your time and hard work.

Acknowledgments

It takes a lot of people and effort to produce one book. My deepest thanks to the wonderful team at Macmillan who worked so hard behind the scenes to transform my text and screen shots into a finished product. To John Pierce, thanks for providing the focus for *Practical Internet*. To Susan Hobbs, a fabulous development editor who always managed to be cool, collected, and funny; I send my heartfelt appreciation. Special kudos to Bill Bruns, making a return appearance as the tech editor on another of my projects.

I would also like to thank the folks at Waterside Productions, especially David Fugate, who worked tirelessly on my behalf. A big hug goes to Bea Ensign, my friend and reader, who looked over my shoulder and read each chapter to find my typos and make sure my words made sense. And finally, to Dr. Carla Haddix, the best veterinarian in the world, whose calm and caring manner kept both me and my dog Duffy on track during the writing of this book.

I would also like to thank all of the nameless and faceless people who produce each and every site on the Web. Some of those folks, like Anton Skorucak of PhysLINK.com, use their own money and resources just to provide you and me with information. Thanks for making the world a better place for all of us.

Tell Us What You Think!

As the reader of this book, *you* are our most important critic and commentator. We value your opinion and want to know what we're doing right, what we could do better, what areas you'd like to see us publish in, and any other words of wisdom you're willing to pass our way.

As a Publisher for *Que*, I welcome your comments. You can fax, email, or write me directly to let me know what you did or didn't like about this book—as well as what we can do to make our books stronger.

Please note that I cannot help you with technical problems related to the topic of this book, and that due to the high volume of mail I receive, I might not be able to reply to every message.

When you write, please be sure to include this book's title and author as well as your name and phone or fax number. I will carefully review your comments and share them with the author and editors who worked on the book.

Fax: 317.581.4666

Email: `office_que@mcp.com`

Mail: John Pierce
Que
201 West 103rd Street
Indianapolis, IN 46290 USA

introduction

Who Should Read This Book?

You should read *Practical Internet* if you want to know more about the Internet. If you're already using the Internet, *Practical Internet* will take you places you haven't been to yet and show you faster, easier ways to get to places you know. If you're new to the Internet and tired of feeling left out because everyone's talking about being online, you'll find all the information you need to get started. Internet veteran or novice, you'll discover exactly what you need to take control of your Internet sessions and make the Internet work to your advantage.

You should be a Windows user who's familiar with some simple Windows concepts, like dialog boxes and menus, and how to work with your mouse. You should also have some basic understanding of how the files and folders are arranged inside your computer.

If you don't yet have an Internet service provider, you'll be able to select one that's right for you based on the information that's provided. If you don't have the programs you need to work with the Internet, or you're using an older version of Internet Explorer or Netscape Navigator, you'll learn how to download and install the latest and greatest versions of the software.

What Makes This Book Different?

With so many books available about the Internet, why should you select *Practical Internet*? Well, for one thing, this book speaks to you. I share your excitement at being part of the Internet community, your concerns about security, and your fears that the whole thing will be over your head. I wrote this book to get you up and running on the Internet as quickly and painlessly as possible.

In addition to being an author, network administrator, wife, and mother, I'm also an Internet user. We use the Internet for just about everything at my house, from finding information about the latest computer products to looking up phone numbers. My son uses the Internet to get help with his schoolwork and stay in touch with his friends. Because I turn to the Internet whenever I need help, want to find some information, or to communicate with my friends and colleagues, I understand the kinds of things you're looking for. I also understand that you're short on time and patience, so I promise not to bog you down with unnecessary steps or technical jargon.

On a daily basis, I work with both Internet Explorer and Netscape Communicator. Both software products are tools to help you accomplish your Internet objectives—such as looking at pages on the World Wide Web, sending and receiving email, and communicating in real-time. Accordingly, *Practical Internet* includes step-by-step instructions for both programs, in addition to simple explanations about Internet concepts. No matter which program you're using, you'll find the steps you need to get the job done.

Also included in the book are listings of the sites that you might want to visit. I've done lots of research to find Web sites that you might like to visit or that illustrate a particular section in the book. The list includes site titles, Web addresses (URL's), and descriptions. That way, when you read about a topic, you can visit a related site immediately. Use the listed sites as the starting points of your Web experience.

Everyone has different reasons for using the Internet. Some people use it for research and others to have fun. Many businesses use the Internet as a way to transact business and communicate with customers and employees. The beauty of the Internet is that it provides so much information and opportunities for communication.

My job is to tell you about many of these opportunities and show you the fastest way to take advantage of them. I take that job seriously. When you're through reading *Practical Internet*, I want you to be able to understand most of the Internet's facets and use them with ease. Most of all, I want you to love using the Internet as much as I do.

How to Use This Book

You can start at page 1 and read straight through. You can also turn to the index for an explanation and instructions for a particular task. Either way you'll find the information you need.

Although you don't need to start with the first chapter, each chapter is designed to build on the knowledge you gained in the previous chapters. If you're an Internet "newbie," begin with Chapter 1 and work through each successive chapter.

Practical Internet will help you accomplish just about anything that can be done on the Internet. The step-by-step exercises in the book walk you through exactly what you need to know to accomplish a task. I'll tell you if you need to be connected to the Internet to perform the steps. I've included loads of illustrations that will help you follow the examples. I've also shared some of my personal experiences—some good, some bad—to let you know what you might expect.

When you're finished with the book, don't tuck it away on a shelf. Instead, keep it handy so you can reference it whenever you need some help. Also, use the book as a directory to many different Web sites.

How This Book Is Organized

I've broken down the Internet into sections that make sense. There are six parts:

Part 1: Internet Basics

This is the place to learn what the Internet is, who owns the Internet, and who makes the rules. You'll find a section about how to get connected, with lots of advice to help you choose the service that's right for you. Information about commercial service providers, like America Online and Compuserve is contained in this section. You'll also learn about the most popular browsers, Microsoft Internet Explorer and Netscape Navigator. When your browser is set up, you'll take a brief trip out onto the World Wide Web. You'll also address some Internet privacy issues and find out what you can do to make your Internet experience secure.

Part 2: Taking Control of the Internet

Now that you've gotten a basic understanding of the Internet, it's time to learn how to navigate through Web pages. You'll learn about

Web addresses, called URL's, and how to move from page to page. You'll jump to new pages with hyperlinks and learn what to do if a link doesn't work. You'll also learn how to search for the Web documents you want to find with site directories and search engines. Since setting up effective queries is the way to find specific documents, you'll get lots of tips to help you design your queries. The Internet is a great place to obtain new software for your computer; you'll learn how to download and install new programs. You'll also learn where to go to get new software.

Part 3: Contacting the World

Reach out to the world through the Internet. You'll learn how to set up your browser's mail program to send and receive email. You'll find out how to create messages to one person or a group. You'll also learn how to file you email messages and the best way to create a personal filing system. You'll experience the exciting world of newsgroups and mailing lists, where you can find a group that shares your interests, broadens your horizons, or just offers some support and help. From there, you'll move into chatting across the Internet. You'll learn how to send instant messages to other folks who are online. In no time, you'll find ways to stay in touch with friends and family. You might even make some new friends, or re-establish communication with people who you haven't heard from in ages.

Part 4: Putting the Internet to Work for You

Harness some of the Internet's power and channel it to your computer. Get the latest news and information from the many sources on the Internet. Want to read your hometown newspaper? Chances are, it's on the Web. You'll learn how to stay on top of all the current and late-breaking news. You'll also learn how to manage your money with some online assistance. Everybody's talking about making investments on the Internet. You'll learn about online banking and enter the exciting world of financial planning and investing. Whether you're writing a research paper, a thesis, or you just need to find out information, you'll find how to use the World Wide Web as an educational resource. If you're looking for career assistance, you'll discover how the Internet can offer assistance in finding your dream job. You'll also learn how to create an electronic résumé and visit a few of the Web's best job banks.

Part 5: Let the Fun Begin

Now that you've covered the serious stuff, it's time to turn to the Internet for fun! Toddlers to teenagers will find sites and help specifically designed for them. Additionally, you'll learn how to implement measures to keep your kids safe when they're online. Shopping on the Web is fun and easy. You'll visit a few of the Web's best shopping sites and attend an Internet auction. Once you've got the hang of Internet shopping, you'll learn how to use the Web to search for cars, homes, and even mortgages. Feel like you need a vacation? No problem— you'll discover how to get a great deal on a trip that's tailor-made for you. If your computer is equipped with a sound card, speakers, and a microphone, you'll learn how to find and play CD-quality music on your computer. Even the busiest people need a break sometimes, so you'll have the opportunity to tickle your fancy with all different types of Internet games. Finally, after you've learned what the Internet offers, it's time to put your own information there for the world to see. You'll learn how to create some fabulous-looking Web pages, without knowing anything about Web languages or programming.

Part 6: Appendixes

Practical Internet contains a glossary and two appendixes. Use the glossary to find words that are highlighted in the chapters. Appendix A, "Employer Sites from A to Z," provides an alphabetical listing of some of the Web's best sources for employment. Appendix B, "The Best Buying Sites on the Web," is a shopper's delight. You'll find a wide variety of sites that can help you buy books and CDs to a new puppy or kitten.

Special Book Elements

Commands, directions, and explanations in this book are presented in the clearest format possible. The following items are some of the features that will make this book easier for you to use:

- *Menu and dialog box commands and options.* You can easily find the onscreen menu and dialog box commands by looking for bold text like you see in this direction: Open the **File** menu and click **Save**.

- *Hotkeys for commands.* The underlined keys onscreen that activate commands and options are also underlined in the book as shown in the previous example.

- *Combination and shortcut keystrokes.* Text that directs you to hold down several keys simultaneously is connected with a plus sign (+), such as Ctrl+P.

- *Cross-references.* If there's a related topic that is requisite to the section or steps you are reading or a topic that builds further on what you are reading, you'll find the cross-reference to it after the steps or at the end of the section like this:

  SEE ALSO
  ➤ *You learn all about real-time chatting on page 286*

- *Glossary terms.* For all the terms that appear in the glossary, you'll find the first appearance of that term in the text in *italic*, along with its definition.

- *Side notes.* Information related to the task at hand, or "inside" information from the author, is offset in sidebars as to not interfere with the task at hand and to make it easy to find this valuable information. Each of these sidebars has a short title to help you quickly identify the information you'll find there. You'll find the same kind of information in these that you might find in notes, tips, or warnings in other books, but here the titles should be more informative.

From Here

You're ready to begin your Internet journey. Be prepared to find information about anything, communicate with the world, and make new friends. You're sure to find whatever you're looking for on the Internet. In fact, the Internet's blend of information, communication tools, and fun stuff might make you see the world in a whole new way. Don't be nervous: I'll be with you every step of the way! Have a wonderful time.

part

I

INTERNET BASICS

chapter

1

What Is the Internet?

The Internet is the name given to a vast and wonderful system that connects people and information through computers. The Internet can be considered as the world's largest wide area network, because it accesses computers from all over the world. By using the Internet, you can look up information on any subject you might imagine or send and receive messages through email. If you have a hobby, favorite television show, or special interest, you can join a newsgroup and share your views with common-minded people. One of the newest advances enables you to participate in a real-time conversation across the Internet—without incurring a penny in long distance charges. Even more exciting advances are waiting on the horizon.

The best way to approach the Internet is to choose something you want to find. However, sometimes the sheer volume of information can seem overwhelming. Chances are, though, that whatever you want to find is out there. Airline prices, current events, career information, games, recipes, and menus all vie for your attention. You can even listen to live broadcasts or your favorite music. One of the hardest decisions you'll need to make on the Internet is when to stop your journey. Even the shortest visit can turn into an hours-long trip.

Most people connect to the Internet from their homes or offices. Many public libraries and universities offer Internet access—sometimes for free. Traditionally, you have needed a computer and a telephone line to access the Internet. New technologies make connecting even easier. You can even connect your computer to the Internet with a special modem utilized by your cable television company or the provider of your satellite dish. You might consider subscribing to a service that enables you to use your television set to get connected. After you're connected, you can switch back and forth between your favorite television show and the Internet. If you're a busy executive on the run, you can connect to the Internet with a small, hand-held device.

SEE ALSO
➤ *You can find more information about WebTV on page 40*

The most exciting aspect of today's Internet is the empowerment it offers. Knowledge is power. By finding information about topics that you feel are important, you gain the upper hand in many situations.

My good friend's 10-year-old daughter, Roxanne, suffers from epilepsy. Last year, her doctors agreed that Roxanne would grow out of it and provided little support for the family. When it seemed like Roxanne's condition was growing worse, my friend, Virginia, logged on to the Internet. Within a few days, Virginia discovered an online support group for parents of epileptic children. She found pages and pages of medical information. Best of all, she discovered information about a doctor who had successfully treated cases that sounded like Roxanne's. Virginia sent the doctor an email message and received an answer the next day. Although the doctor was located on the other side of the world, he sent Virginia a list of his colleagues in the United States. Roxanne got a new doctor, and her condition improved dramatically. The Internet played a major role in helping a young girl live a normal, happy life.

Rob, another friend of mine, lost his job when the company where he'd worked for 15 years went through a downsizing phase. Rob was shattered. He had kids in college and a mortgage. Unemployment hadn't been part of his plans. After exhausting all of the usual job search techniques, Rob concentrated on finding a job through the Internet. User groups pointed him to the best Internet job listings. Rob found a listing that matched his qualifications and sent a message to the prospective employer. In a short time he was asked to first email his résumé, and then email a list of references. The next day a message appeared in Rob's email Inbox, asking when he would be available for an interview. Happily, Rob got the job, and the Internet scored another success.

SEE ALSO

➤ *If you're interested in making a career or job change, see page 381*

Today's Internet enables people from all over the world to share ideas and knowledge. The Internet has established itself as a permanent member of our society and economy. It won't take long for you to make the Internet part of your daily life!

Who Owns the Internet?

No one "owns" the Internet.

Even the provider that you or your company pays for access doesn't own the Internet. Instead, the access provider functions like a gatekeeper—they let you in, and then let you out. However, the access providers don't own the road you use to get there.

Your local phone and cable company owns the telephone lines you use to connect to the Internet. The regional Bell operating companies and long distance carriers own the leased lines that connect most of the network. These phone lines are tied into several high-speed links, each called a backbone. Major communications companies—like Sprint and MCI—own or rent the backbone links.

The Internet is simply too big to be owned by a single person or a conglomerate. Whether you're part of a company who owns the equipment or a user who posts a page to the World Wide Web, you're a partial owner of the Internet.

A few years ago, the phrase "Information Superhighway" could be heard everywhere. The Information Superhighway is considered the Internet backbone because it's responsible for transporting masses of data back and forth across long distances by way of fiber optic cable that criss-crosses countries around the globe. Several companies share the ownership and maintenance of the Internet backbone.

An Internet History Lesson

The amazing thing about the Internet is how quickly it has exploded into our daily lives. When you think about the history of flight, the Wright brothers in Kitty Hawk, North Carolina in the early 1900s probably comes to mind. The history of the automobile goes back even further. Unlike these, the history of the Internet began back in the 1960s. However, it's only been since the early '90s that the Internet has evolved into what we see today.

In its infancy, the Internet was created to carry governmental and military information in case of an atomic blast. Fortunately, the nuclear "event" never materialized. But the fledgling information system surpassed its developer's wildest dreams.

In 1957, the Soviets put a satellite called Sputnik into orbit. The launch surprised the world and shocked the American scientific community. The President of the United States, Dwight D. Eisenhower, hurriedly put together a team of the brightest scientific minds in America. The resulting organization, run by the Department of Defense and called the Advanced Research Projects Agency, or ARPA, worked to protect American defense information from a nuclear explosion.

Sputnik and the subsequent Cold War caused a real panic among the U.S military. Nuclear attacks on American cities suddenly seemed possible. One of ARPA's missions was to create a network of linked computers which each stored security data and could be accessed by Defense personnel from many different locations. In the event of a nuclear strike, the network would still be able to function even if some of the computers were damaged.

The Birth of ARPAnet

In the mid-'60s a test network was assembled. At the same time, the United States government began to take a look at the impact computers could have on the private sectors of education and business. The Pentagon funded ARPA to produce a network of "super-computers" (primitive by today's standards) that would be linked and could easily communicate with one another.

The autumn of 1969 saw the first super-computer installed at UCLA in Los Angeles. Three months later, four computers, called nodes, were linked together on the network, which was nicknamed ARPAnet, after its founders. In 1971 there were 15 nodes in the ARPAnet and by 1972, over 30 more. By connecting to the ARPAnet, researchers and scientists could share one another's computer facilities.

One of the biggest advances of the ARPAnet project was the development of a common language that computers connected to the network could use to talk with one another. This language, called TCP/IP (Transmission Control Protocol/Internet Protocol) network protocol, became the standard protocol for the ARPAnet. Because all of the ARPAnet's computers used TCP/IP to communicate, the details of each node's brand and type were unimportant.

Bigger and Better

Because it was so easy to use TCP/IP, more and more computers joined ARPAnet. In addition to ARPAnet, other, smaller computer networks appeared. In turn, many of these smaller networks linked themselves to ARPAnet. Individuals or companies who did not adhere to ARPAnet's tight standards ran many of the smaller networks. Instead of exchanging information about scientific research

Storing bits of data in packets

During the panic following the Sputnik launch, researchers at the RAND Corporation came up with a revolutionary system that enabled computers to talk to one another. Their idea was to break up large computer transmissions into several smaller pieces. These pieces, called packets, would be sent out through a network of telephone lines connecting numerous computers. The pieces would be reassembled into the original transmission after they arrived at their destination.

Using packets was an ingenious way to transport data. Each packet would begin at some specified source node, and end at a specified destination node. The packets would be able to make their way through the maze of the network of phone lines on an individual basis. If the first destination node was blown to bits, the packet would continue on to another node on the network. Because all of the computers on the network were equal to each other, it didn't really matter where the final transmission was reassembled.

Fortunately, the nuclear war never materialized. However, the packet idea, designed to prevent the loss of key data, forms the basis of Transmission Control Protocol and is still in use today.

and military secrets, the information sometimes took a more folksy, conversational tone.

The nodes on the network were often used for the exchange of ideas and gossip. News and personal messages were commonly transmitted to users thousands of miles apart. The ARPAnet became a social haven as well as a scientific one. Mailing lists, a type of broadcasting technique in which one message could be sent automatically to large numbers of network subscribers, sprang up. The most popular mailing list was called "SF-LOVERS" and contained postings about science fiction.

In 1983, the military portion of ARPAnet splintered off and became MILnet. Without any military influence, ARPAnet grew rapidly. There were no membership restrictions; anyone with a computer, a phone line, and a simple knowledge of TCP/IP could connect. However, because computers were mostly found in colleges and universities, most of the growth took place in the educational sector. Instead of being known as the ARPAnet network, the collection of linked computers was dubbed the "Internet," short for inter-network.

The National Science Foundation Steps In

The '80s brought some key changes to the Internet. In 1984, the National Science Foundation set up a network. The NSFnet provided some great technological advances, including faster and more powerful super-computers to store information. The NSFnet upgraded and expanded every two years after its founding. In addition to the NSFnet, the National Institutes of Health, NASA, and the Department of Energy each set up and maintained their own networks.

The NSF decided to link five super-computing centers together to make research easier to complete. Although the NSF tried to enlist ARPAnet's help for the project, ARPAnet was unable to contribute any assistance. Instead, the NSF built their own network based on standards set by ARPAnet. After the new network was built, the NSF linked colleges and universities in one region, and then linked each of the regional networks to the super-computing network. In a short time, the heavy network "traffic" generated by all of the computers using the new network slowed the response time to a crawl.

As soon as they realized that the new network was too slow, the NSF commissioned an agreement with Merit Corporation, an outside consortium of Michigan educational institutions to upgrade the physical system. Additionally, Merit Corporation was asked to maintain the administration for the NSFnet. The NSF network soon became the fastest and most reliable network on the Internet. Merit asked for permission to include commercial traffic on the Internet. Although the NSF disagreed at first, after much deliberation they agreed to allow commercial traffic.

In 1989, the funding for ARPAnet expired and the ARPAnet network disappeared. Few people noticed. Almost the entire Internet community had moved to the network run by the NSF.

The Name Game

From the early days of the Internet, keeping track of the aliases of each of the computers connected to a network was a problem. With so many networks and so many computers accessing the networks, the problem of tracking which computer was which rapidly escalated into a nightmare. For example, as far back as the early 1970s, a computer that was called PITT at one location might be called PITT-U at another and PITT-37 at another. Although it was clear that a list of distinct names needed to be maintained, no one would agree what the list should contain and who should control it. Different Internet factions suggested different types of lists—each getting a more hostile response.

Finally, after the bickering became intolerable, the Network Information Center (NIC) stepped in to take control. NIC announced that each site could determine the names of their computers, also called hosts. NIC would step in only if a duplicate name was requested. The warring Internet factions agreed to a truce, and NIC began its involvement in the registration of hostnames. In fact, NIC still is an active participant in registering Internet names.

The first naming system that NIC developed was labor-intensive and low tech. All of the information for each hostname was maintained in a file called hosts.txt. Each time a change was made to the file, all of the users were expected to obtain and install the updated version on each of their systems. After a short while it was apparent that the name system needed to be revamped.

The earliest plans for the present day Domain Name System appeared in 1981. After several revisions, the plan to use top-level domain names that identified the specific network to which the host belonged was implemented in 1984. So, for example, PITT became PITT.ARPA. Now, two host computers that were part of different networks could have the same "first" name. Considering that a little over 1,000 host computers existed, using a standard naming convention simplified the process of finding the host computer to which to connect.

Pretty soon, it became apparent that the naming system needed to be tweaked. A major change was instituted. Instead of using the network names like ARPA or NASA, the names were divided into more basic varieties. Most computer names were assigned on the basis of six Internet "domains": edu, gov, mil, org, net, and com. Edu, gov, and mil represented educational institutions, government sites, and military installations. Names that ended in "org" meant that the host computer belonged to a non-profit organization. Net in a domain name indicated the host was a gateway between networks. The most common domain name, "com," stood for a commercial institution.

The History of Browsers

In the Internet's earliest days, only real "techies" were able to access it. Users needed to type in commands from an onscreen command prompt and interpret what appeared back on their screens. All the information appeared in text format; no colors, pictures, or sounds livened up the display.

The World Wide Web changed all that. The advent of the Web made it easy to get around. Instead of typing in a series of commands to move from one Web location to another, users could click a hyperlink to jump from page to page. A Web browser (technically known as a client) is a software package you use to view information from the Internet. A browser program, like Internet Explorer or Netscape Navigator, acts as the go-between for your computer and the Web. Although such programs have only existed for a short time, they have an interesting history.

Tim Berners-Lee and his colleagues at the CERN European Laboratory for Particle Physics conceived the first Web browser. In 1993, a new browsing program called Mosaic was introduced by the NCSA (National Center for SuperComputing Applications) at the University of Illinois. The inventor of Mosaic was a 22-year-old student named Mark Andreessen. Unlike the old CERN browser, the new client program (Mosaic) featured a graphical user interface. Instead of a plain background and a box in which to type text, Mosaic featured buttons to which users could point and click to move around.

Mosaic was an instant success. In fact, using Mosaic was so simple that thousands of new users used it to visit the Web. Soon after the introduction of Mosaic, Cello, another GUI browser, appeared. In 1994, most users visited the Web with either Mosaic or Cello. When Windows 95 was introduced, Cello quickly disappeared from the market. Another browser called Winweb came and went around the same time period. In fact, a few scant years later, few people knew that Cello or Winweb ever existed. Although Mosaic is still available, its popularity has declined rapidly.

Mark Andreessen and his friends left the NCSA and started Netscape Communications Corporation. In short order, their new browser stunned the Internet community. Netscape introduced a list of new Web browser features, including added support for displaying graphic images, advanced security for Web-based business transactions, the ability to open more than one Web site at a time, and much, much more. Additionally, Netscape featured mail and news client programs along with its Web browser. Netscape was free for educational and non-commercial use; other users could download and preview it for free for an indefinite time. In a short time, Netscape became the undisputed star of the Web browser world.

Microsoft Corporation got into the browser market with the introduction of Internet Explorer. The first version of Internet Explorer caused few ripples in Netscape's pond. The Microsoft browser had only basic features and caused general protection fault errors on many computers. However, over a very short time, Microsoft introduced upgrades to the original Internet Explorer program that made it almost as powerful as Netscape. At one point, the war between the two browsers was so intense that upgrades to each program were introduced within a week of each other. Microsoft was quick to point out that Internet Explorer was completely free with no strings attached. The gap in popularity between the two programs narrowed.

In 1997, Netscape introduced Netscape Communicator and Microsoft introduced Internet Explorer 4. Both packages are rich with new and exciting features and offer much more than basic Web browsing. Microsoft Internet Explorer quickly gained the greater percentage of users to become the number one browser. Although Netscape still holds the lead in popularity, Microsoft has made serious inroads on the quest to becoming the number one browser. Both rival companies have promised even bigger and better features in the near future.

You're probably wondering who runs the Internet. Read on.

Who Makes the Rules?

The wild, Wild West

Today's Internet has been compared to the Wild West because for the most part, the Internet is an uncharted frontier. Many of the Internet governing bodies consist of volunteers. Groups like the Internet Society, Internet Engineering Task Force, and Internet Architecture Board work to further the development of the Internet and keep it running smoothly.

Just like Internet ownership, you won't find a specific group or person that governs the Internet. This lack of rules and regulations makes the Internet more interesting, but occasionally results in strange or unusual content. Right now, what appears on the Internet is determined by the person who puts it there. So, valuable information co-exists with pornography, skinhead sites that preach hate and violence, and information (usually bogus) on how to cure diseases. Fortunately, you can spend your whole life on the Internet and never encounter items you feel are objectionable, or in bad taste.

Although no board of directors or fat-cat bosses make the rules, several organizations share Internet administration responsibilities.

Who Pays for the Internet?

Remember the old song that went something like, "The music goes round and round...?" Well, understanding who pays for the Internet is something like understanding the song. The National Science Foundation currently subsidizes a portion of the costs. The users, like you or your company, pay Internet service providers (ISPs) or Commercial Online Services like America Online or CompuServe for Internet access. In turn, these providers pay inter-network providers for connection to their servers.

Although commercialization is relatively new, advertisers pay a huge chunk of money to support the Internet. Their money pays for better equipment and lines. Like television, the fees that advertisers pay to hawk their products across the Internet underwrite many of the costs that you'd have to pay otherwise. Of course, the flip side of Internet commercialization is that you're barraged with non-stop advertising at many Web sites.

Where Is the Internet?

Unlike a library or shopping mall, the Internet does not have a set geographic location. You can't go to the Internet or watch all of the computers in action. Because the Internet is merely a collection of linked computers, it's physical location can't be tied down to one place.

If your computer accesses the Internet, then a portion of the Internet is in your den or office. The computer of your access provider also holds a piece of the Internet. Additionally, the computers that hold the Web sites you visit are also Internet owners.

Who Uses the Internet?

It seems like everyone uses the Internet these days. Actually, Internet users come from every age and income bracket. Users connect from home, school, or work. Ask your friends and colleagues if they've used the Internet. You'll probably be surprised at how many people you know are happily using the Internet right now.

The Internet is the fastest growing market in the world. Although it's hard to get an exact count, it's safe to say that there are currently 60-70 million users, and about 1 million new users are added each month. Over 125,000 companies are currently conducting business on the Internet. At least 73 new Web sites are added to the World Wide Web, a portion of the Internet, each day.

What Can You Do on the Internet?

The Internet has changed the way Americans shop, obtain information, and have fun. Just a few short years ago, primarily government

Patronize Internet merchants

Think about supporting Internet advertisers by buying their products. At the least, take the time to view some of the ads you come across. The ads are usually entertaining and informative, and help to defray some of the costs that you'd have to pay otherwise.

personnel and college educators used the Internet. Now, you can't go through a day without hearing the Internet mentioned at least once—through the media, at work or school, or from friends and colleagues. "Send me an email," has practically replaced the phrase "Call me."

For starters, the first thing you can expect to find on the Internet is information. In fact, information is still the Internet's main product. Information is available in many formats. Most of the information you see is contained on the World Wide Web, although it can still be obtained from other, older sources traditionally used for educational purposes.

The type of information you find is largely dependent on what you're looking for. If you're a student and need to do research on a topic, the Internet is a great place to start. If you're using the Internet to track your investments and investigate new financial opportunities, you're at the right place. Want to buy a new computer or appliance? How about finding the phone number of an old friend that you haven't seen in years? You could find recipes for leftover turkey or low-fat fried chicken. Want to read your hometown newspaper right from your computer? All these, and more, await you on the Internet.

See and say

For about $100, you can buy a camera that attaches to your computer and sends images of you while you're chatting. Just be sure that you have a fast Internet connection or the images will seem jerky and disjointed.

Second only to information are the opportunities for communication provided by the Internet. Electronic mail—or email, for short—offers you the opportunity to exchange messages with people all over the world. You can attach computer files, like letters and memos, to messages that you send. If you'd like to find a group of people who share your interests, you can join a newsgroup. Messages posted to a newsgroup, unlike email, are posted to an electronic bulletin board so that all the users can read and reply.

If you prefer communication in real-time, you can visit a Chat server. Even though the discussion in chat rooms is textual—you need to type your comments and then send them—the conversation moves along so quickly that you can easily forget that you're typing. (My sister likened it to watching a foreign movie with subtitles.) And of course, if your computer is equipped with a sound card and a microphone, you can engage in a long-distance conversation with anyone, anywhere, without paying a penny in long-distance charges.

After you've become comfortable with the Internet, you might decide to create your own presence by creating a page that will be placed on the World Wide Web. You can design your page to display photos and other graphic images about you, your family and your interests, or you can just use unadorned text. You can add sounds, music, and of course links to other Web sites you like.

SEE ALSO

➤ *Learn more about how to create Web pages on page 491*

The page you design can be fun or it can serve an important purpose. Grade school classes are creating their own Web pages. This year, instead of a traditional birthday gift, my son is giving his friends their own Web pages. On a more serious side, many people are putting résumés and other job-search–related material on the Web.

SEE ALSO

➤ *Learn how to create a résumé for the Web with Netscape Composer on page 387*

Pages on the Internet are designed in a special language called *HyperText Markup Language* or *HTML*. Just a few years ago, you needed to know HTML if you wanted to create content for the Web. Now, however, many programs enable you to type text and drag and drop images while the programs create the underlying code for you. Using one of these programs, you can create an exciting Web page without knowing a drop of HTML.

The Internet is so vast and its options are so varied that before long you'll wonder how you ever lived without it. In fact, you'll find yourself preaching information about the Internet to your friends. Just wait!

Putting Your Business on the Internet

If you are the owner or operator of a small business, have you considered putting your business on the Internet? Whether you have a product to sell or want to be able to communicate with your employees who are scattered in several locations, the Internet is a great way to get quick results.

A Web site for your company instantly makes your business a global presence. Your page is accessible to anyone who's using the Internet anywhere in the world. International exposure, which used to cost thousands of dollars, is yours at a very small price.

You can use the Internet to tell people about your company and what it has to offer. With one page or a collection of linked pages, you can show your company's hours, product line, location, and contact information. You can even use your site to offer other information or advice. For example, one janitorial supply company I work with includes floor care tips on their site.

If you are selling a product, think about selling it over the Internet. People can visit your site and order your product. With minimal investment on your part, you can reap the benefits of having a global business that never closes. If you're concerned about security issues for your customers, you can take steps to make your site more secure.

Setting up an intranet is another way to use the Internet for your small business. An intranet is a site to which only your employees have access. An intranet is beneficial to companies that have employees in many different locations. The site can work as an employee bulletin board. You can post memos, letters, spreadsheets, or other pertinent facts your employees need to see.

SEE ALSO

➤ *Learn about intranets on page 58*

Clients and servers make it work

At this point, you're probably wondering how the Internet works. What element enables all of the computers, not to mention the thousands of miles of telephone cabling, to work together to bring you the Internet. The answer is simple—clients and servers.

Servers are the programs that provide resources. Clients, on the other hand, are the programs that you use on your computer to tap into the resources. The purpose of the computers, cabling, and all the other equipment is to let the servers and clients talk between each another.

Looking at Standard Internet Components

Fortunately, the Internet is broken into distinct segments to help you get around. One segment, the World Wide Web, is the fastest growing area on the Internet. Your tour of the Web involves visiting Web sites. (Touring the Web is sometimes called "surfing.") Email and newsgroups are other commonly used Internet factions.

The World Wide Web

The World Wide Web is where you'll spend much of your Internet time. (The Web is the nickname most people use for the World Wide Web.) The Web is one of the newest and most popular Internet services. Prior to the development of the Web, you had to type a series of complicated commands to navigate through the maze of information on the Internet. If you didn't know what you were looking for, it was very easy to get lost or hung up.

The Web was developed by CERN (the European Laboratory for Particle Physics) to enable anyone to access and view documents that were stored on servers anywhere on the Internet. Although the World Wide Web originated as a program for use by only CERN researchers, its appeal quickly overwhelmed the Internet community. Special client applications, called browsers, were developed to take advantage of the Web's amazing capabilities.

Web sites are the pages you visit as you travel around on the World Wide Web. Every Web site consists of one or more documents, called pages. A *home page* is the first page of a Web site that serves as a cover or index by introducing and organizing the material at the site. Even if a site has only one page, the first page is called the home page. Figure 1.1 shows the home page for Macmillan Computer Publishing.

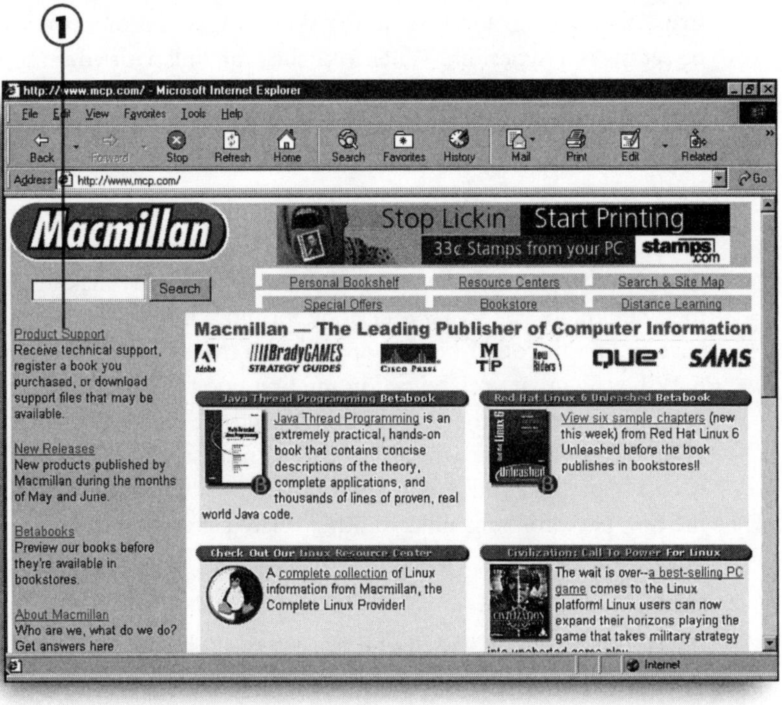

They mean the Web

When people talk about looking at sites on the Internet, most of the time they're talking about the World Wide Web.

FIGURE 1.1
The Macmillan home page has links to other pages.

① Click one of the links to move to another page.

Pages on the World Wide Web are different from the pages you find in books. For one thing, a Web page doesn't have a set page size and can be short or long. When you print one Web page, you could end up with several sheets of printed material. Also, instead of page numbers, every page on the Web has its own address, called a Uniform Resource Locator (URL).

SEE ALSO

➤ *Learn about URLs on page 112*

The Web pages you visit might be simple, with only a few lines of text, or they can be elaborate documents, filled with colors, different typefaces, and graphic images. Some of the images might move or change when you pass your mouse over them. In addition, Web pages can contain sound and other multimedia effects, such as animation. Some pages are so well-designed that they look like something out of a Hollywood studio.

Although looking at a visual feast is exciting, what makes Web pages so special is their capability to contain *hyperlinks*. A hyperlink is a link to another page or location on the Web. Either text or graphics can be set up as a hyperlink. When you click the link with your mouse, you're whisked to another related site that might actually be located on a server halfway around the world. By using hyperlinks, you can move quickly from site to site.

The value of hyperlinks can't be overstated. For example, let's say you go to your local public library to do some research for a science project. After you get the volumes you need and start making notes, the book refers you to another book for more information. Now you have to find the other book (hopefully, it's there in the library) and find the page that's referenced in the first book. And, of course, the second book refers you to a third book and the whole process starts again. Hyperlinks bypass most of this painful process. When you click a hyperlink, you're whisked to the new site in a few seconds. If the new page contains links to other related sites, you can click these links to move rapidly through the material.

SEE ALSO

➤ *Learn to travel through the World Wide Web with hyperlinks on page 119*

Electronic Mail (Email)

Email is everywhere! You might already have an email address at work or at school. If you already have Internet access, you probably have an email address from your provider. It's funny to think that email was invented as a diversion for the original users of the ARPAnet. Now, instead of a diversion, email plays an important part in how you communicate.

The mechanics of email are similar to sending regular mail, called "snail mail". You type a message using your email client (see Figure 1.2) and then click **Send**. The message is then transmitted across the Internet by means of various gateways and ends up in the addressee's Inbox. If the addressee is unavailable when the message is delivered, the message remains as an unopened piece of mail until it has been read. Because email follows a standard format, it doesn't matter if you and the addressee are using the same mail client program.

Plain text or HTML

Older mail packages sometimes use plain text that doesn't contain formatting or colors. Newer mail programs, like Outlook Express and Messenger, support "rich text" that can contain different fonts, formatting, and colors. Sending formatted email messages to someone who's using an older mail program can result in headaches.

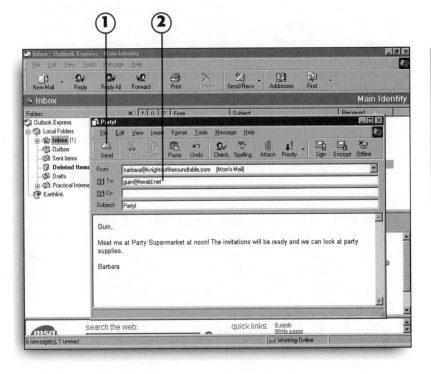

FIGURE 1.2
Composing a message using Microsoft Outlook Express.

① Click here to send the message.

② The address of the recipient goes here.

The major differences between email and snail mail are obvious. For one, you don't need to turn over couch cushions looking for a stamp before you can send your email. The second difference is even more exciting—email is usually delivered in a matter of minutes, rather than days. This means that you can exchange several messages over the course of a day without racking up postage charges or waiting for replies.

Email is rapidly becoming a business standard. Because you can attach computer files to the messages you send, email is an excellent way to share information with your business associates and colleagues. However, there is a down side to such rapid delivery. Because email deliveries generally take minutes, the turnaround time on a project speeds up. (When I was writing this book, I'd submit my manuscript files in the morning and have corrections back by lunchtime!)

Although email is a great business tool, it can also be used for more pedestrian reasons. My family is scattered all over the world, but we regularly keep in touch via email. Friends who hadn't spoken for years are now exchanging family gossip by email.

Newsgroups

Internet newsgroups conduct online discussion on just about any topic you can imagine. These discussions work like the bulletin boards that you see at the supermarket or the library—someone posts a message or question and then anyone who wants to posts a comment or reply below the original message (see Figure 1.3). The original message is called a *thread*.

Most of the Internet newsgroups are part of a network called Usenet (short for User's network). Over 30,000 Usenet groups exist on the Internet. Your Internet provider may have its own groups as well. Additionally, you might be able to participate in regional discussions or discussions that concern only employees of your company or students at your school.

Internet discussions can be moderated or unmoderated. Moderated discussions are usually more serious because the moderator has the right to refuse to post any message that doesn't conform to the rules of the group. Unmoderated discussions often get heated and exciting.

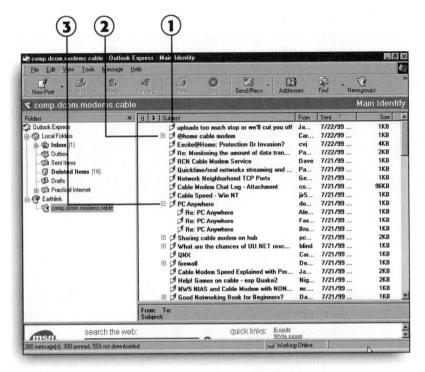

FIGURE 1.3

Messages have been posted to a newsgroup about modems.

1. Message headers (subjects) are shown here.

2. The plus sign indicates that more messages pertaining to this subject have been posted but are not currently displayed.

3. The minus sign indicates that additional messages pertaining to the original subject are visible.

Online discussions are very popular. A discussion group that talks about a popular Tuesday-night police show receives almost 300 postings every day. You can follow the postings of the groups that interest you without ever posting your own comments, or you can become an active participant.

Because newsgroup postings look and act very similar to email messages, your news client (the program you use to view newsgroups) might be integrated into your email program.

SEE ALSO

➤ *Learn all about newsgroups on page 255*

Where Does the Internet Go from Here?

You don't need a crystal ball to tell you that the Internet will continue to grow and have a major impact in our lives. Right now, the Web contains millions of Web sites with hundreds of millions of

Web pages. More pages appear daily. Currently, millions of people from hundreds of countries have access to the Internet. That number is expected to triple or even quadruple in the next few years.

The Internet of the future will be tightly integrated into many people's lives. For one thing, students will use the Internet as an educational tool. The United States hopes to have all classrooms connected to the Internet by the end of 2000. Students will use the Internet as a research tool, finding answers and solving problems. Homework assignments will be submitted via email. ("My dog ate my homework," just won't fly anymore.) Teachers will conduct online conferences with parents when it's convenient for both parties.

E-commerce will become more important. Although you can currently shop on the Web, a combination of more merchants and tighter security measures will make buying easier. You'll be able to buy anything from a new car to prescription medicines, knowing that you've gotten the best deal in the world.

Doctors will turn to the Internet to help patients. The collective knowledge of doctors around the world will be available to help patients anywhere. Online conferencing and email will keep doctors in touch with one another.

In the very near future, you'll be able to watch most of your favorite television programs on your computer screen. Screenings of the latest movies will be available on the Internet. Some movies may even work like video games, with you as an active participant in the plot and outcome of the story.

While computers are now the primary means of accessing the Internet, more Internet-enabled devices, such as pagers and cell phones, will send and receive email and access the Web. Everything from your car to your refrigerator will be connected to the network. Sound too good to be true? Electrolux has developed the Screen-Fridge, a 21st century Internet icebox that manages your pantry, among other things. It can email a shopping list to your cyber-supermarket and coordinate a convenient delivery time with your schedule. The ScreenFridge can even contact the parent company and effect emergency repairs, if needed. Other appliance manufacturers are also developing Internet-aware appliances.

The best part of the Internet of the future is that it will be faster and cheaper. Modems and direct connections will help to speed up the loading of Web pages on your computer. Cable companies are currently entering the Internet connection market, driving down prices in many areas. You may have a wireless connection, enabling you to move your computer from room to room.

Welcome to an exciting new frontier!

chapter 7

Get Ready for the Connection

Now that you've gotten a feel for what the Internet is all about, you're ready to get connected. How do you do it? What hardware do you need? Relax! When you're done with this chapter, you'll know everything you need to connect to the Internet and begin your journey.

Basic Equipment You Need

First off, you need a computer to connect to the Internet. Minimum system requirements for spending time on the Internet require that the computer needs to have a Pentium processor with 16 megabytes of Random Access Memory (RAM). Your monitor should support VGA (Video Graphics Array) or SuperVGA. If you're connecting to the Internet through a phone line, you need a modem. (You learn all about modems later in this chapter.) The information in this book assumes you're running one of the later versions of Windowsor NT.

Your computer also needs several megabytes of free space to install helper applications and the plug-ins needed to bring you movies, graphics, and sounds. Although neither is mandatory, a sound card and speakers help you to take advantage of the sound effects and music added to many Internet sites. You also need a mouse or other pointing device.

SEE ALSO
➤ *You learn about helper apps and plug-ins on page 199*

Keep in mind that the minimum requirements are exactly that—the bare bones minimum you need to get connected. If you have a faster processor, preferably a Pentium or a comparable processor with a speed of 166 megahertz or higher, or even a newer, faster chip, and more than 64 megabytes of RAM, your computer will provide a smoother ride to the Internet. Slower, older equipment will really detract from your Internet experience.

More Hardware Can Optimize Your Internet Experience

A few extra or upgraded pieces of equipment can turn your Internet experience into an extra-special time. Keep in mind that everything on the list is optional; for example, you don't need a larger monitor or a microphone to have a great time on the Internet. Unless you have loads of extra money, pick and choose the pieces that fit in with the way you plan to use the Internet. You can always wait and buy additional hardware whenever you feel you need it. The following list shows items you might consider adding to your system later on.

- *19- or 21-inch monitor.* The larger the monitor, the more you see! (However, make sure your desk or computer cart can accommodate a larger monitor before you bring it home.) Prices on big monitors fall all the time. If you're buying a new computer, you can generally upgrade to a 19-inch monitor for a few hundred dollars more. If you really want to splurge, get a 21-inch monitor. Best of all, take a look at the newest flat panel-style monitors.

- *32-bit sound card.* The best cards are 32-bit models with wavetable synthesis and are fully duplexed. Most sound cards produce sound by a process called FM synthesis. Wavetable synthesis is superior to FM because it uses actual recorded samples of the sound that are manipulated by MIDI commands. (Even if you don't understand how this works, take my word that the sound produced by a card with wavetable synthesis sounds live, not tinny or machine-like!)

- *The best computer speakers.* The best speakers utilize a subwoofer system and produce rich bass tones and symphonic sound. The very best speakers are capable of surround sound. Make sure you use computer speakers. Never attach your home stereo speakers to your computer. For one thing, the sound will be awful because stereo speakers need more power than your computer's sound card amplifier can produce. Also, home stereo speakers aren't magnetically shielded. If you use stereo speakers with your computer, you run the risk of damaging your monitor so that part of the display looks dark, called *warping*, as well as damaging the data on your hard drive or floppies.

- *Color printer.* It's great to be able to produce a hard copy of a Web site that looks as good on paper as it did on your monitor. Color laser printers are expensive. Color inkjet printers are very reasonable in price and produce dynamite looking output.

- *Computer microphone.* If you plan to participate in an Internet conference, get a computer microphone. The mike plugs into the sound card and enables you to talk over the Internet. (Make sure you have a sound card before you buy a microphone.) Internet microphones are very inexpensive.

Whenever you have some free time, cruise down to your local computer store or flip to the back portion of a computer magazine and look at the ads. The equipment shown here, and other hardware additions, like cameras and scanners, can pay for itself in enjoyment.

Modem Mastery

Inside or outside

Modems come in two "flavors"—external or internal. External modems sit outside of your computer or, if you're using a laptop, come on a card that's inserted into a special slot. Internal modems are installed inside the computer and can't easily be unplugged or transferred to another computer.

External modems are generally contained in their own casing and attach through a serial port located in the back of your computer. External modems need to have their own power supply.

Internal modems are standard issue on most newer computers. However, if your computer doesn't have a modem, or you're looking for a modem that can be attached to more than one computer (although not at the same time), an external modem may suit your needs.

After you determine that your computer has the horsepower and a few extra options to take you to the Internet, you need to consider how you're going to connect. Right now, most people connect to the Internet through a modem. (You'll learn alternative ways to connect later in this chapter.)

Why is a modem so important? Most telephone lines are designed as POTS (Plain Old Telephone Service) lines and cannot support data transmissions. Therefore, your *modem*, an acronym for MOdulator-DEModulator, is the bridge device that your computer needs to connect to other computers through the phone lines. Your modem performs two crucial functions:

- Modulates outgoing computer data by converting them into digital signals which can be transmitted via a phone line.

- Demodulates incoming analog signals by transforming them into their digital equivalents so they can be read by your computer.

Modems Do It in Modulation

You've already learned that modems translate outgoing and incoming data into a language computers can understand. Just listen to the screeching, whistling, and tweeting sounds a modem makes when it's connecting to the Internet. Those sounds are modulation—your modem is "speaking" to the modem at the other end.

Your modem has a data transfer rate, which is measured in bps (bits per second) increments. The maximum speed of the data transfer rate is pre-determined by the specific *modulation protocol* of the modem. Think of modulation protocol as a standard that enables two modems to communicate in the same language. Modems need to share the same standard language to understand one another.

During the late 1990's, several different manufacturers produced new fast modems that offered speeds of up to 56,000 bits per second, or Kbps, for short. The two most common types of these modems were the X.2 and K56Flex. Since a standard for the new fast modems had not yet been determined, the technology behind both types was considered proprietary.

The International Telecommunications Union (ITU), a part of the United Nations, set the standard for 56Kbps modems in early 1999. The new standard was called *V.90*. Although most service providers currently support X.2 and K56Flex, support for these types will diminish in the future. If you're planning to buy a new modem, make sure that you get one that conforms to the V.90 standard.

Checking Your Modem Configuration

It's easy to check what type of modem you're using. If you find that your modem's maximum speed is slower than 56Kbps, you might want to check out a new one. When you view the information about your modem, be sure and make a note of the settings you find; you might need to know the information when you set up an account with an Internet service provider.

If you're using Windows or NT, perform the following steps to check the configuration of your modem:

Modem configuration

1. Double-click the **My Computer** icon on your Windows desktop.
2. Double-click the **Control Panel** folder. The Control Panel opens and displays several icons.
3. Double-click the **Modem** icon, which looks like a telephone. (If you don't see the Modem icon when you first open the Control Panel, use the scrollbars to move down through the rows of icons that appear in Control Panel.) The Modem Properties dialog box appears, as shown in Figure 2.1.

Shaking hands

When modems first establish communications, they perform a peculiar modem ritual called handshaking to determine each other's speeds. If one modem has a faster speed than the other, the speedier modem "bumps down" to the lower speed. Even if your computer is equipped with a 56Kbps modem, your Internet connection may be considerably slower if your service provider has slower modems.

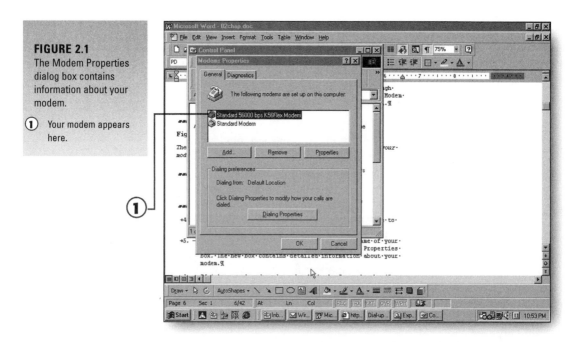

FIGURE 2.1

The Modem Properties dialog box contains information about your modem.

① Your modem appears here.

4. Click the modem name that's shown in the box to select it and then click **Properties**.

5. A new Modem Properties box that displays the name of your modem appears, layered over the original Modem Properties box. The new box contains detailed information about your modem.

6. If it's not already selected, click the **General** tab. (See Figure 2.2.)

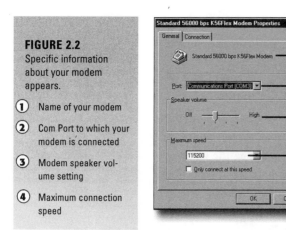

FIGURE 2.2

Specific information about your modem appears.

① Name of your modem

② Com Port to which your modem is connected

③ Modem speaker volume setting

④ Maximum connection speed

7. Click **OK** to close the Modem Properties dialog box that contains specific information about your modem. When that box closes, click **OK** to close the Modem Properties dialog box and return to the Control Panel.

8. Click the **Close (X)** button on the Control Panel title bar.

There are additional settings about your modem contained within the Modem Properties dialog box. Although it's unlikely that you'll be asked about those settings, you can access the information by clicking the **Dialing Properties** button and the **Connection** tab.

Two Phone Lines?

If your modem is a standard model, a telephone cord is plugged into the modem at one end and the telephone line at the other. Currently, when your modem is in use, you can't make or receive calls.

Since I hate talking on the phone, I've never minded that my line is inaccessible when my modem is in use. However, my teenage son flipped out when his friends couldn't get through. Finally, I restored peace in my family by having a second phone line installed for my modem. My only regret is that I didn't anticipate that my son would connect to the Internet on one phone line while talking to his friends on the other!

Actually, if you connect to the Internet by modem, a second phone line makes sense. The cost of a second phone line is not terribly expensive. The second line frees up your primary line and makes it easy to call tech support or a hotline if you need help while you're connected to the Internet. If you have a business, a second phone line is almost a necessity. Contact your phone company for monthly charges and installation costs.

Other Connection Choices

Although most people connect to the Internet with a computer and a modem, you've got a wide range of alternatives from which to choose. Exciting new technologies match your needs and your budget with various connection options.

What is baud?
When people talk about modem speeds, they often incorrectly use the term baud in reference to the transmission speed of data. The term "baud", named after the 19th century French inventor Baudot, originally referred to the speed a telegrapher could send Morse Code. When people use the word baud, they're really referring to bits per second (bps).

In one way and out the other
Before you run out and sign up for one of the more expensive connection options, keep in mind that some of the fast speeds only work when the modem is sending information to your computer. When your computer sends information back, you'll still need a standard modem. The combination of fast and slow data transmissions may make your Internet connection appear only slightly faster. Check with your provider before you sign on.

Table 2.1 shows you these options and gives you the high and low points of each service. The first service, Dial-up, uses a standard modem like the one we've already discussed.

Table 2.1 Internet connection options

Service	Availability	Standard Cost Per Month	Typical Connection Speed	High Points
Dial-up	almost everywhere	$20	56Kbps/ 28.8Kbps/ 33.6kbps	Modem is inexpensive, service is available anywhere
WebTV	most U.S. states	$22	56Kbps/ 28.8Kbps/ 33.6Kbps	Use it instead of a computer
ISDN	almost everywhere	ranges from $50 to $130	128Kbps	Fast, proven technology
Satellite	almost everywhere	$55 for 100 hours	400Kbps	Fast, easy to hook up if you already have a TV dish
Cable	limited but growing rapidly	$35 to $70	1.5Mbps	Fast connection
DSL	limited but growing rapidly	$50 to $1,000	1.5Mbps	Fast connection, always connected
Frame relay and T1/T3	almost everywhere	$300 to $5,000	1.5Mbps	High speed, direct connection

WebTV Combines the Internet with Your Television

If you're connecting to the Internet from home, WebTV provides an interesting way to access the Internet, as shown in Figure 2.3. After the installation of a WebTV unit, your television screen functions like a computer monitor. Your TV remote becomes your mouse. You can even watch your favorite television program while you're looking at Web pages with WebTV's WebPIP™ feature.

Sound exciting? If you're planning to limit your Internet experience to looking at Web pages and sending out email messages, WebTV may be for you. Microsoft has a big interest in WebTV and has pumped money and resources into the WebTV technology. Still, WebTV is a bit player in the companies that provide Internet access.

For optimum viewing, your TV should have a fairly big screen. You'll need to purchase a WebTV unit before you can use the service. Once you're connected, the tiny keyboard makes typing a chore. Since the WebTV service is proprietary, you'll be limited in which Internet services you can choose—chatting and instant messaging aren't available to WebTV subscribers. Additionally, printing and sending attachments to email messages can be problematic.

WebTV's latest offering is a service called WebTV Plus Service for Satellite. This service requires a DISH player and a subscription to the corresponding DISH network. WebTV Plus Service for Satellite brings the Internet and satellite television together in one service. It adds a new dimension to your satellite programming with features for playing games, pausing and recording a satellite broadcast, and searching through programs.

Fast ISDN

ISDN, short for Integrated Services Digital Network, is an ITU-defined telephone standard that is used for "noise-free" phone communication and Internet access. ISDN works with most standard phone wiring. ISDN provides Internet access at 128Kbps.

A few years ago, ISDN was touted as the future of fast-speed connections. Newer technologies, like cable modems and DSL, have pushed ISDN to the back burner. However, ISDN still is a viable option to connect to the Internet. It's available in most areas and the service is generally reliable and trouble-free.

Contact your ISP

Don't wait until after your ISDN line is installed to make sure that your Internet service provider supports ISDN connections. Expect to pay double or triple the standard monthly charge to an Internet provider for ISDN service.

The biggest advantage to ISDN service is that it's available in most locations. However, ISDN service is more expensive than standard telephone service. Since it's not usually a flat-rate service, the more you use, the more you pay. Contact your telephone company for more information about ISDN.

The Dish on Satellite

Satellite service requires a major component: a satellite dish with a clear view of the sky. Satellite dishes are expensive and require costly installation and fine-tuning. With most satellite Internet service providers, the satellite works only for downloading information to your computer. You'll require a modem and telephone line to do any real Internet browsing or send email.

Want to know more about DirecPC

Visit the Hughes site at www.direcpc.com to find out more about DirecPC service. You'll find out where the service is available, how much it costs, and how you can subscribe.

Most satellite subscribers live in rural or remote locations and don't have any other connection options. Like with other satellite services, rough weather can play havoc with a connection to the Internet. However, both WebTV and Hughes DirecPC hope to make their services more appealing to regular, urban users.

Tap Into Cable Modems

Several cable TV companies are now providing Internet access for their subscribers. In fact, many industry analysts predict that cable modems are the connection choice of the future. Unfortunately, cable modem service is available in limited areas, although the service is growing.

Cable modems aren't really modems. Instead, they offer a digital connection, very similar to ISDN service. Currently there are two types of cable modem services available:

- **Dual path asymmetric** is an older technology and requires a modem and a phone line. The cable modem transmits data from the Internet to your computer, while the modem connected to your phone line transmits data back. Dual path asymmetric connections are faster than standard Internet connections but are probably not worth the time and investment.

- **Single path symmetric** connections require only a cable modem and can affect two way communication between your computer and the Internet. If your company offers a single path symmetric connection, find out if you can get connected.

Even though cable modems provide a great way to access the Internet, they have a dreadful reputation for failure. The installation process is expensive and can take a while to complete. Many cable companies are simply not staffed to provide technical service or support. My friends have told me horror stories of waiting weeks for a repair technician or dealing with incompetent tech support personnel. Still, as more and more cable companies offer the service, these kinks should be ironed out.

Since each cable company uses their own modems, you can't go to the cable modem store and buy the one you want. Depending on the company, the modem and installation can be quite pricey. Before you sign up, check out all the costs and find out how much down time, if any, the service has experienced in the last few months. If possible, talk with a few existing subscribers to find out if they're satisfied.

Lightning Fast DSL Service

DSL service, cable modems' chief rival, is a relatively new kid on the block. DSL, an acronym for **Digital Subscriber Line**, provides a direct connection to the Internet without a phone line. (Whenever your computer is turned on, you're instantly connected to the Internet!) DSL service is fast and convenient. Best of all, you don't need a second phone line.

Right now, DSL service is available in very limited areas. Installation costs approximately $200 and monthly charges can be high. Most DSL connections include an Internet service provider. Although you won't have to pay additional ISP charges, you'll have to change your email address if you already have an established account with another provider.

Is DSL really faster than other Internet connections? Yes! Here's an example: using a 56Kpbs modem, a two megabyte video clip takes around five minutes to download and play on your computer. With a DSL line, you see the clip in five seconds. With DSL service, most Web pages load almost instantly on your computer screen.

Direct T1 and T3 Connections

Tiny computers

Small, pocket-sized computers can also be used to connect to the Internet. Although these devices, generally called handhelds, are convenient, they are usually too small and under-powered to do any real amount of Internet surfing. However, in the near future, handheld devices are expected to gain more than a foothold in the marketplace.

Many companies and educational institutions connect directly to the Internet backbone with T1 and T3 lines. This type of service is very expensive and requires some high-tech hardware. It also requires some very technical knowledge to get it up and running.

If you're a home or small business user, connecting to the Internet with a backbone connection is probably not a viable option. Of course, if you've just won the lottery or have lots of extra money, you can always call your local phone company and find out what it will take to get this type of connection.

Accessing the Internet

Now that you know more about the computer hardware you need and are mulling over which connection option to choose, you're probably wondering what type of magic takes place when you click the **Connect** button. Actually it's not magic at all. Instead, TCP/IP takes the lead in easing your computer out onto the Internet. Take a few minutes to understand how the pieces fit together.

Using TCP/IP

TCP/IP stands for Transmission Control Protocol/Internet Protocol and is the protocol responsible for making sure that your computer can communicate with all of the other computers it encounters on the Internet. TCP/IP and its companion, an IP Address, go hand-in-hand in getting you connected to the Internet. Although you needn't trouble yourself with all of the technical details of TCP/IP, use the following analogy to understand how it works.

Let's say that you meet up with a long-lost cousin who lives across the world. Even though you look alike and share a lot of the same genetic makeup, you can't communicate because you both speak different languages. Can you imagine how happy you'd be if there was a simple language that enabled you to speak like cousins who had grown up together? In computerese, TCP/IP is that universal language. TCP/IP enables computers, no matter which brand or type, to communicate with one another.

Understanding IP Addressing

The whole concept and use of IP numbers can be incredibly technical, but there's only a small bit of information you need to understand.

In order to connect to the Internet, every computer, including yours, must be identified by a unique number, called an *IP address*. IP addresses are written as a series of four numbers, separated by periods. For example, the following is an example of an IP address:

`159.97.5.185`

Your Internet service provider leases a bank of these IP numbers. When you connect to the Internet, you're assigned a unique IP number that identifies your computer. When you disconnect, the number is returned to the pool and assigned to another subscriber. If you're connecting to the Internet from the office or school, you may have a specific IP number that's assigned to your computer.

DNS hovers in the background

Think of Web addresses as "handles" or aliases. The real Web address is always an IP number. The Domain Name System (DNS) provides updated lists of domain names and corresponding IP numbers. Although you probably don't know it, your access provider maps you to one or more DNS servers to get the latest translations.

Most everything on the Internet is driven by IP numbers. When you click a link or type the address of a Web page, the URL (Web address) is translated into an IP address, so the computer can read it. Even email addresses are translated into IP numbers. For example, when you want to see the Web page at http://www.mcp.com, or send an email to your buddy, freddy@freeloader.com, your computer must break down the Web or email address into an IP address.

This all happens through an amazing process called *name resolution*, which occurs behinds the scenes most of the time that you're on the Internet. When you type a Web address, the necessary portion of text is translated into an IP address and sent along. Email addresses require even more translation. It's a whole lot easier for you to remember an email address like kingarthur@camelot.com, than kingarthur@ 159.62.172.12!

SEE ALSO
➤ *You learn more about Web addresses on page 112*

In the following exercise, you obtain the IP address that's assigned to your computer. Unless you've got a direct Internet connection, you need to be already connected to the Internet for the steps to work. Additionally, you must be using Windows 95 or 98.

Finding your IP number

1. Click the **Start** button and choose **Run** from the **Start** menu. The Run dialog box appears.

2. Type winipcfg in the **Open** text box and click **OK**.

3. In a moment, the IP Configuration dialog box appears, displaying your IP number, as shown in Figure 2.4. If you were planning to use a program like Microsoft NetMeeting for Internet conferencing, you'd need to know this number to continue.

4. Click **OK** to close the IP Configuration dialog box.

NT or Windows 2000 users

If you're using Windows 2000 or NT, you can check your IP address from a command prompt. Click the **Start** button, point to **Programs**, and choose the **Command** prompt. You'll be whisked to a dark screen. Type **ipconfig /all** and press **Enter** to see your number. To exit the Command prompt, type **exit** and press **Enter**.

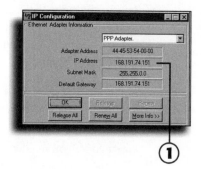

FIGURE 2.4
The IP Configuration dialog box displays information about your Internet connection.

① The IP number assigned to your computer

Making the Connection

Now that you've got all the theory behind you, it's time to actually make the connection and jump onto the Internet with both feet. There are a few different ways to access the Internet.

If your office or school has an Internet connection, there's a good chance that you can get access without having to pay a dime. Check with the folks that run the computer department, usually called Information Technologies (IT). Of course, if you visit the Internet from your desk at work, you'll probably be subject to some restrictions, like the types of sites you can visit and what kind of messages you can send. Additionally, the places you access from your work computer might be monitored.

A good solution for the home user is to connect to the Internet through an *Internet service provider*, or ISP for short. Depending on your geographic area, you can probably open a phone directory and find listings for several Internet providers. Most ISPs grant you Internet access, include an email address, and the ability to connect to a Usenet (newsgroups). Additionally, some ISPs enable you to store personal Web pages on their server.

Another route to the Internet is offered by several commercial online services. America Online is the best known of this type of service. Commercial online services, sometimes called COSs, provide email, news, electronic shopping, chat, and original content, as well as access to the Internet. Unfortunately, Internet access is generally secondary to the list of other services provides by an online service.

Connecting to the backbone

To connect to the Internet, you need to attach to the Internet "backbone," a superhighway of cabling that enables massive amounts of voice, data, and video to be combined and transmitted at extremely high speeds. Very few computers have direct access to the backbone. Your Internet service provider leases a high-speed line, called a T1 or T3 connection, and then, for a fee, provides you with a gateway (or bandwith) to the Internet backbone.

How Do I Choose a Provider?

Choosing the right ISP is a primary step in getting connected. Every day, more and more new providers are competing for your business. There are local and national ISPs, each with different service options and payment schedules.

Before you select an ISP, be sure you know what you need:

- If you travel frequently and need to be able to connect to the Internet from hotels and conference rooms far from your local area code, you need a provider that offers national or even international access as part of the package.

- How many hours a month do you intend to be connected?

- Do you need just one account or multiple accounts for other family or your staff members?

After you've jotted down your conditions, you can match them to the services offered by an ISP.

Start your search by asking your friends and colleagues which service providers they use. Take advantage of their experience. Most people who are already connected will be happy to share their provider's name. Check the business section of your local newspaper and look in the Yellow Pages. Speak to the people in the computer department at your company.

When you've decided on a provider, call and ask a few questions before you commit. Don't feel strange or shy about calling first. After all, your ISP is going to be your lifeline to the Internet. If the service fails, you're left with a computer, modem, and no place to go. If you're using the Internet for business, down time can mean lost money to you.

Use the questions shown here as a springboard. If you can think of additional questions, ask them too!

1. How long have you been providing access to the Internet and how many subscribers do you have?

2. How many of those subscribers can be connected to the Internet at one time?

3. What services and software will I receive if I subscribe to your service?

4. What is the cost of your service? Are there any hidden costs like a setup fee, a charge for calling technical support, or extra costs if I have my own Web site? Do you offer different service options or pricing plans?

5. Do you give discounts to groups like students or employees of a company? If so, am I entitled to the discount?

6. Do you charge monthly, quarterly, or annually? Is it less expensive if I choose to subscribe for a longer time period?

7. Can I call tech support if I have a problem with your service? What are tech support's hours?

8. Do you provide outside training or give me detailed instructions on setting up the connection?

9. Do you have local access numbers for my calling area?

10. During the last three months, how many hours was the service unavailable? What caused the outages and what was done to correct the problem from occurring in the future?

Every Business Needs a Good ISP

If you're setting up your business on the Internet, your choice of ISPs becomes much more important. Your ISP is your lifeline to the Internet. As a casual home user, changing ISPs generally means giving out your new email address and maybe missing a few messages. As a business user, changing ISPs can result in a disastrous loss of valuable time and revenue.

Connecting your small business to the Internet is more than simply plugging a couple of cables together. There are a lot of points you need to consider in your search for an ISP. Make sure that the ISP has an unblemished record of connection time. If the ISP has had more than one or two outages in the last three months, think seriously before you make a commitment. After all, every time someone can't find your Web page or send you email, you could be losing money.

SEE ALSO

➤ *You learn more about intranets on page 58*

49

Select an ISP that can provide your company with business-oriented features. For example, if you need to develop a Web site, choose an ISP that offers both expert Web page design and hosting services. You might need to interface your inventory to an Internet information browser. Or, perhaps you plan to create an intranet, a "mini" Internet that is accessible only to your employees. Setting up these types of services demands an ISP with an in-depth knowledge of both Internet technology and computer systems integration. Be sure that the provider you select for your business service has knowledge in all these areas and can help you to make your company's "net presence" profitable and productive.

National or Local ISP?

Open your local phone directory to "Internet" and, most likely, you'll see ads for several local ISPs. When it's time to choose a provider, you can opt to connect via a local ISP or choose a big, well-known national provider. Which should you choose?

Depending on the geographic area in which you live, the choice might be simple. One or the other provider might not offer a local telephone number for you to call. (If you're going to have to make a long distance call every time you access the Internet, you can rack up some huge phone charges in a hurry.)

Choosing a national ISP makes good sense if you travel or if you're new to the Internet. Many of the long distance services offer national Internet access, in addition to their telephone services, as shown in Figure 2.5. Generally, these companies offer their Internet service separately from their long distance service. You can sign up with EarthLink/Sprint or AT&T to provide your Internet access, even if you don't use the company as your long distance carrier.

Because most national ISPs are backed by big networks with extensive resources, you can expect reliable service. Sometimes, national ISPs are a bit more expensive than local ISPs. However, most national ISP's have local access numbers in most national and many international locations. (I was able to connect to EarthLink for the cost of a local call in both London and Paris.)

FIGURE 2.5
EarthLink offers
subscribers a wide
range of services.

Local ISPs, on the other hand, might offer more personalized service. If something goes wrong, you might find it's easier to get through quickly to the tech support people to resolve the problem. If you're setting up your business on the Internet, your local ISP might have a representative who can meet you personally. The differences between local and national ISPs can be compared to shopping in a big brand-name supermarket or buying your groceries from the small market across from your house. Both have distinct advantages; it's up to you to decide which provider best meets your needs.

Table 2.2 shows the top five national ISP's.

Table 2.2 Top national Internet providers

Name	Comments
EarthLink/Sprint www.earthlink.net	Fast and easy set. Excellent tech support. In addition to standard Internet access, EarthLink offers a free monthly magazine called bLink and other fun perks.

continues...

Table 2.2 Continued

Name	Comments
AT&T Worldnet www.att.com	Easy to set up. Service is consistently reliable. May be hard to get through to tech support if you need assistance.
IBM Internet Connection www.ibm.net	Very simple installation. However, service only covers 100 connection hours.
Concentric www.concentric.net	Reliable service with many international access numbers.
Mindspring www.mindspring.com	Easy to connect, with lots of free tech support. Downside: a surcharge of $7.50 per hour if you need to connect to one of their 800 numbers.

In addition to national service providers, there are some excellent regional providers as well:

- **Northeast** providers include RCN at www.rcn.com and Bell Atlantic Internet Solutions at www.bellatlantic.com.
- **Midwest** providers include Voyager at www.voyager.net and Ameritech at www.ameritech.net.
- **South** providers include Cybergate at www.gate.net and BellSouth at www.bellsouth.net.
- **West** providers include SBC/Pacific Bell Services at www.pacbell.net and GST Whole Earth Network at www.wenet.net.

What Are Commercial Service Providers?

America Online, CompuServe, and the Microsoft Network are popular commercial service providers. Although these providers grant you Internet access, the type of service they offer is different from a standard ISP. Instead of giving you the means to connect to the Internet, email, and newsgroup accounts and possibly a browser, commercial service providers offer a graphical interface that's packed with the provider's own content. They put you in a point-and-click world where you don't need to know about operating systems or the pros and cons of different Web browsers.

SEE ALSO

➤ *You find out about the function of a browser on page 64*

Although these services do possess an appeal for novices and Internet beginners, many people quickly grow tired of the graphical interface that attracted them at first. Becoming Internet savvy doesn't take all that long. After you've got a little Internet experience under your belt, you might not appreciate all the coddling that commercial online services have to offer. Instead, you might choose to go to the Web with a sophisticated browser, like Internet Explorer or Navigator, and search for your own information.

Looking at America Online

The America Online service, often called AOL, is the world's most popular Internet online service, with more than 10 million subscribers worldwide. The service provides subscribers with a variety of interactive features, including email, news, sports, weather, financial information and transactions, electronic shopping, and more. Additionally, AOL provides World Wide Web access.

Many new users are introduced to the Internet as AOL subscribers. AOL aggressively markets their service and sends out thousands upon thousands of America Online setup CD's and disks. With a whopping 50 or so free hours the first month you install the service, AOL may be a good way for you to start your Internet journey.

AOL catalogues its various services under channel headings, as shown in Figure 2.6. When you click one of the channel headings, you're presented with another set of set of choices that relate to the channel you selected. Each time you click a new choice, a window with related information appears layered on top of the windows on the America Online screen. If you find a spot on AOL that you'd like to return to, you can simply click the red heart on the title bar to add the spot to AOL's favorite places. If you don't want to move through a series of menus to find a specific topic, you can use a keyword search. AOL looks through its network and presents links to all of the references to the keyword you entered.

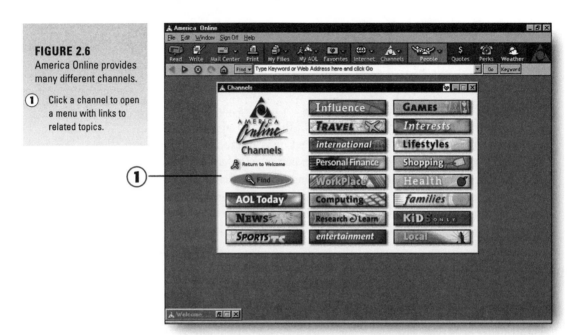

FIGURE 2.6
America Online provides
many different channels.

① Click a channel to open
a menu with links to
related topics.

Although AOL has a wealth of information in its own database, the service offers some standard Internet components, such as access to the World Wide Web and email. If you know the URL of a Web site you'd like to visit, type it in the box in the AOL Browser toolbar. AOL also offers email; your new mail is placed in your mailbox and held until you read it (see Figures 2.7 and 2.8).

The pricing structure of America Online has been changed to make the service more competitive with most ISPs. America Online now offers unique "tiered" pricing, which is structured to appeal to a broad range of consumers with different interests, needs, and budgets. You can choose between unlimited use for a flat monthly rate or pay by the hour. If you already have an account with an ISP, you can access AOL for unlimited hours for a small amount per month, using AOL's TCP/IP pricing option.

Instant Messenger

AOL offers a service called Instant Messenger that enables people to chat across the Internet. The service is free and can even be used by non-AOL subscribers. You'll learn more about Instant Messenger in Chapter 17.

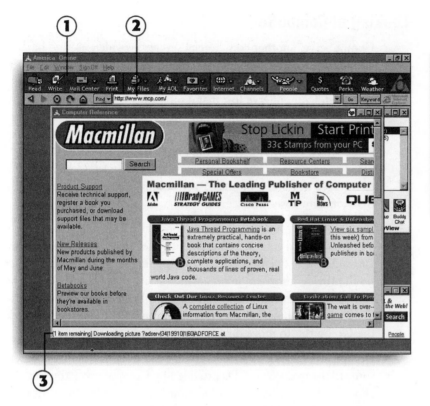

FIGURE 2.7
America Online's Web browser toolbar.

① Browser navigation buttons

② Type a URL in the box.

③ Status bar informs you of progress

FIGURE 2.8
The America Online New Mail window.

① Unread messages

Looking at CompuServe

CompuServe, another commercial service provider, used to be considered the best online service and bulletin board for computer professionals and others in the technical field. As other services appeared, CompuServe lost many subscribers. Recently, CompuServe was acquired by America Online. Since then, CompuServe has added many new services and features aimed at the home-based Internet user. CompuServe has a vast library of organized business and educational information. In fact, CompuServe is recognized more of a business, professional and technical service than a family-based service.

If you select CompuServe as your commercial service provider, you'll get the standard Internet components, including Web browsing and email. You'll also have access to CompuServe forums, which are set up to provide information on a wide variety of topics. Most forums consist of three parts: Message Boards, Library Files, and Conference Rooms. It's easy to move around in CompuServe; click the **Go** button to move directly to a service.

CompuServe is easy to install. You'll need to install the CompuServe software from disks or CDs provided by CompuServe. You can choose between a Typical installation (recommended for most users) or a Custom installation (an option for users who already have connections to the Internet).

Payment plans for CompuServe include both a standard unlimited service and an hourly rate. CompuServe subscribers are given the first month of service for free.

The Main menu screen reflects CompuServe's professionalism. The screen is never flashy and is easy to look at, as shown in Figure 2.9. The Main menu is made up of links to related channels and forums. Click a link to move to the related page.

One of CompuServe's biggest problems remains its mail system. Members are provided with numeric identifications (IDs), such as 120987,661. It's hard to remember your own numeric ID, let alone someone else's. Sending email to a numbered box is sometimes an exercise in futility. Fortunately, CompuServe wised up; now members have the ability to change their numeric ID's to text.

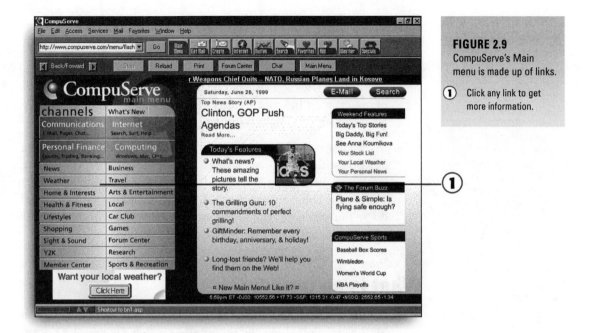

FIGURE 2.9
CompuServe's Main
menu is made up of links.

① Click any link to get
more information.

Comparing Online Providers

With so many providers and so many different service options, you
might feel unsure about which one to choose. Use Table 2.3 to con-
trast and compare the options provided by each provider.

Table 2.3 Comparison of service providers

Name/Type	Level of Internet Access	Web Browser	Allow Personal Web Page	Provide Installation Software	Offer Technical Support
Local or national	Full Internet access	Depends on ISP	Usually	Usually	Optional
America Online (COS)	Full Internet access	AOL's own browser	Yes	Yes	Yes
Compu-Serve	Full Internet access	CompuServe's own browser	Yes	Yes	Yes (excellent support options)

Connecting to the Internet from Work

Millions of people now have Internet access from the workplace. If you've got a connection to the Internet at your desk, chances are that the sites you visit can be tracked by the person in charge of maintaining Internet security. (Forewarned is forearmed—don't go anywhere you might be ashamed of later!)

Many companies provide Internet access to their employees in conjunction with a corporate *intranet*. Unlike the Internet, which covers the world, an intranet is designed to be viewed by the employees of a particular company or group. However, similar to the Internet, it doesn't matter if the employees are located in the same building or scattered across the globe.

What Is an Intranet?

An intranet uses the same tools and techniques as the global Internet to provide information and services, but within a company or organization. An intranet can work equally well within the confines of a small company with a few employees scattered in different locations or within a large, global corporation. If you've got an intranet at your office or school, you view documents that look just like the ones on the Web. An intranet can be up and running without any connection to the outside world. An intranet has three basic uses:

- *Internal bulletin board*. Delivers corporate information, such as telephone and email directories, human resource databases, forms, meeting schedules, and discussion threads.
- *Communications delivery*. A cost-effective mechanism for transporting information. Employees send email instead of sending a fax or making expensive telephone calls for interoffice communications. Additionally, file transfer protocol (FTP) replaces expensive express mail or overnight delivery, whether at the same location or your company's other locations.
- *Day-to-day business functions*. Such as order processing, sales tracking, inventory control, and delivery status. By placing documents like company policy manuals and employee phone listings on the intranet, a company can save thousands of dollars in both printing and distribution costs.

A sample of an intranet page is shown in Figure 2.10.

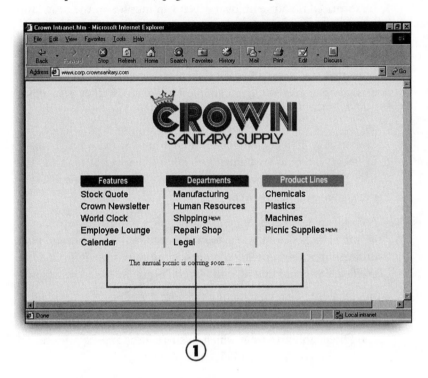

The benefits of intranets are being discovered everyday as more
companies integrate them into their workplaces. One of the most
significant and noticeable benefits is the increased productivity that
results from quick company-wide communications and data sharing.

The cost of an intranet is very inexpensive compared to the resulting
long-term savings. Most companies already have most of the hardware resources required, such as computers, modems, and phone
lines. The other equipment needed is readily available and relatively
cheap compared to putting together, and then maintaining, a straight
local or wide area network.

Employees usually have rights to view most of the documents on an
intranet. However, the network administrator can set up a *firewall,*
which prevents employees from using their browsers to access documents on the World Wide Web. Some intranets require employees
to log in with a name and password, and others pass employees
through to the intranet opening page.

If you work for a company with more than a few employees, don't be surprised if your employer sets up an intranet in the near future.

Extending the Intranet to an Extranet

Now that you know all about intranets, the next logical step to explore is an *extranet*. In its simplest form, an extranet is an expanded intranet that can include customers, clients, suppliers, and almost anyone else who has contact with your business on a daily basis. You actually give people outside your company (who relate to your business) access to your intranet using Internet technology. Extranets help businesses improve customer service, increase revenue, and save time, money, and resources.

A company that supplies janitorial supplies to other companies, for example, might allow its customers to browse its catalog and place orders online, eliminating the need for sales representatives. Or a travel agent could link up with several cruise lines and others in the vacation field. Other uses for an extranet include:

- Providing training programs or other educational material
- Discussion groups in which to share ideas and experiences among colleagues and clients
- Furnishing schedules of company hours and holidays

An extranet can allow access to all of the sites on the intranet, or it can restrict users to only certain areas. For example, a travel agent that books group tours might be allowed to see different pages than an individual who's looking for a weekend getaway for his family. The login method to an extranet needs to be set up carefully to ensure that external visitors to the intranet stay only in the pages to which they have access.

Building an extranet is hard work; even harder than building an intranet! Many issues—compatibility, access, and security—need to be worked out before the external users are provided access. An extranet requires more planning than an intranet and costs more, too. Costs need to be built in for training, security, additional firewalls, and ID/password controls.

What Is a Freenet?

A *Freenet* provides free, public access to the Internet. Freenets are often sponsored or supported by local library systems. Most of the time, users must go to the library and use the Freenet there. Although they don't usually offer all of the tools provided by an ISP, Freenets give email services and limited access to the World Wide Web. Additionally, some Freenets provide access to community and government databases. Even though there are many Freenets around the world, each one is tailored to meet the needs of the local community. No two Freenets are identical.

You can compare a Freenet to a large online encyclopedia that contains information about a metropolitan area. The information is placed on a large, dedicated computer, hooked up to the phone system, and made available to the general public, free-of-charge. Most Freenets can support hundreds of users simultaneously, but the number of local users that can use the Freenet at one location depends on the number of phone lines purchased and dedicated to Freenet use.

Volunteers, local government, and corporations provide the information you view on a Freenet. These information providers are the Freenets lifeblood. They work together to keep the information on the Freenet current, and they ensure that the information keeps pace with the community's information needs. (No one wants to read about the Fourth of July parade at Christmas-time.) Freenets invite information providers from all sectors of the community to supply information for placement on the system. See Figure 2.11 for an example of a Freenet page.

Many Freenets have Usage Policies that spell out what a user can do and where he or she can go on the network. Even though Freenet users have access to the Internet, Web usage is not intended to be recreational. For example, a Freenet user isn't supposed to use the service as a way to find the latest gossip about her favorite television star. Instead, Freenet users are expected to look at only the documents on the Web that deal with educational or community issues.

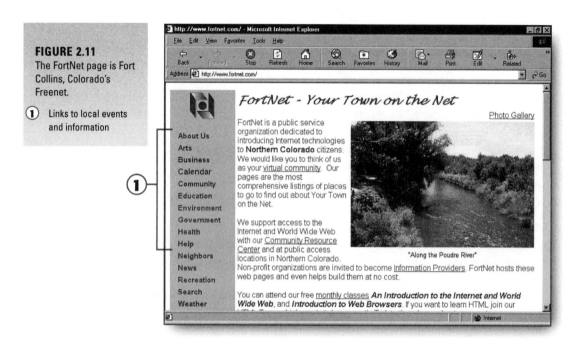

FIGURE 2.11
The FortNet page is Fort Collins, Colorado's Freenet.

① Links to local events and information

Freenets usually provide free email accounts to their users. The mail system of most Freenets isn't very sophisticated, and only allows short text messages. You can't attach a document or include graphic images in a Freenet mail message. Still, Freenet mail services make email available to many people who otherwise wouldn't have access to an electronic mailbox.

SEE ALSO

➤ *Read about other ways to get free email on page 230*

A few years ago, Freenets could only be accessed with programs like Telnet and other older Internet programs. Now, with the explosion of the World Wide Web and the popularity of browser programs like Internet Explorer or Netscape, most Freenet sites offer a Web version with color and pictures in addition to the text-only version.

If you're planning to become an Internet "power" user, a Freenet isn't for you. However, if you don't have a way of getting Internet access (for example, you don't own a computer), check with your local library to see if you can get a Freenet account.

Meet Your Best Friend— Your Browser

Understanding what a browser does   •

How do you get a browser?   •

Looking at Netscape Navigator   •

Working with Internet Explorer   •

After you've established your connection to the Internet, you need a client program called a *browser* to bring the pages of the World Wide Web to your computer. The name "browser" is descriptive, because the program lets you browse through all of the pages on the Web. Think of the browser as your passport to visit the Web. Although there are older browsers, like text-based Lynx that's used by many vision-impaired computer users, we'll concentrate on the latest versions of the most popular browsers available to you. Currently, the two most common and powerful browsers are Netscape Navigator (the main component of the Netscape Communicator suite) and Microsoft Internet Explorer.

What Does a Browser Do?

It's a GUI world

Both popular browsers feature a graphical user interface, or *GUI* (pronounced goo-ey), that sets up a colorful onscreen way for you to interact with a software program on your computer. In addition to using your keyboard, you can use a mouse or other pointing device to make choices from drop-down menus and buttons.

Browsers perform many functions. The first and most important thing your browser does is communicate with the server that stores the page you want to see. To understand why this job is so important, you need to first understand that the World Wide Web provides the global environment for the information you want to access. This information is stored on Web pages that contain many different elements, such as text, image, audio, and video. A Web page can be located on a server anywhere in the world. When you request a page, your browser first needs to determine on which server the page is stored, ask the server for permission to fetch it, and then load the page on your computer. All of this is truly amazing when you realize that the entire process takes seconds, instead of minutes or hours!

The responsibility doesn't stop after the page is loaded. Your browser works to manage your entire Web experience. Navigation aids are provided, such as the capability to move back and forth between pages you've viewed during the current session. A history of the pages to which you've navigated is maintained. Your browser also lets you keep a record of the pages you want to return to later on, so you can return with one simple click. The correct display of fonts, colors, and images is another task for the browser. Want to print a page or save it to the hard drive of your computer? Your browser handles these jobs, too.

How Do You Get a Browser?

Netscape Navigator, the browser component of Netscape Communicator or Microsoft Internet Explorer, are the two most popular browsers. (A text-based browser, called Lynx, is used by many vision-impaired Internet users.) Most times, you don't have to do anything special to obtain one or the other. If your computer is a newer model, there's a good chance that a browser was pre-installed. If you're running Windows 98 or Microsoft Office, the Internet Explorer browser was installed as part of the software package.

If you're accessing the Internet from your work or school, the folks that handle the computer network have already made that decision for you, and one of the programs is already installed for your use. If you're using an ISP to connect, the provider probably furnished one to you when you signed up. For example, EarthLink provides Internet Explorer as part of their service.

Or, you might be just getting started with the Internet and need to obtain a browser. If a browser isn't already installed on your computer, furnished to you by your ISP, or you decide you want to change, both Netscape Navigator and Internet Explorer are easy to obtain. You'll find Netscape at www.netscape.com and Microsoft at www.microsoft.com. Follow the instructions shown on the Netscape or Microsoft page to download the programs. You can also obtain the browsers from one of these sources:

- Copies of Netscape Communicator, the complete suite that includes many Internet features including the Navigator browser, Messenger for Mail and Newsgroups, and Netscape Composer can be ordered from the Netscape Sales Center at 1-800-278-1015.

- Microsoft Internet Explorer's suite of Web-related programs can be ordered by calling the Microsoft Sales Department at 1-800-426-9400.

- Alternatively, check out some of the computer and Internet magazines at your local bookstore. Many times one or the other browser is included on a giveaway CD included with the magazine.

Browser minimalists

Although most people prefer Netscape Navigator or Internet Explorer, some Web users feel that both browsers are top heavy with unused features. These "minimalists" prefer the Opera browser. Actually, while Opera browser performs basic Web functions, its clean look and feel can be attractive. You can read more about the Opera browser at www.opera.com.

Which Browser Is Right for You?

Using betas

Beta software is a pre-release of a program that's distributed prior to its final, commercial release. Beta software is often incomplete and can cause errors or even crash your computer.

Both Netscape and Microsoft usually make available several versions of their newest browsers in beta format as the final products are being developed. The beta software is available for downloading.

If you decide to use a beta browser, back up your important files so that, if the beta crashes your system, you'll be able to restore your computer.

Unfortunately, no set formula can determine which browser is better. Both Netscape Navigator and Microsoft Internet Explorer perform most of the same Web functions on your computer. (I use both of them interchangeably.) Both offer online technical support. Each browser claims to be the biggest and best. How do you decide?

One or the other browser might not run on your computer. Usually, the instructions for installation are very specific about types of computers that can be used with the browser. However, if you're not sure if a particular browser will work on your computer, read the requirements on the CD cover or the browser's Web site before you go through an installation process. If your ISP offers technical support, call their "hot line" and ask for advice.

SEE ALSO

➤ *You'll learn about downloading files on page 179*

It's important to understand that both Web-browsing software programs are part of a suite of products in which each separate program performs another Internet-related function. Table 3.1 shows the main components of both Netscape Communicator and Internet Explorer. Because both Microsoft and Netscape periodically release upgraded versions, additional features might be available when you set up your browser software.

What we're using

This book references Netscape Communicator 4.61 and Internet Explorer 5.0. If your browser is a different version, you might notice a slight difference in the appearance of the screen and a few program features might work a little differently. However, as long as you're using version 4.0 or higher in either suite, most features will work the same.

Table 3.1 Components of the Internet Explorer and Netscape Communicator suites

	Microsoft Internet Explorer	Netscape Communicator
Browser	Internet Explorer	Navigator
Desktop Integration	Active Desktop	None
Electronic Mail	Outlook Express	Messenger
Newsgroups	Outlook Express	Messenger
Chatting	Chat	AOL Instant Messenger
HTML Authoring	Front Page Express	Composer
Security	Security Zones	Certificate Management

Browser Upgrade Considerations

If an older version of Navigator or Internet Explorer is installed on your home computer, consider upgrading to the newest versions. Install the browser according to the directions provided with the documentation that comes with your browser or from your ISP. When the procedure is complete, you'll have the latest and greatest version.

If you're connecting to the Internet from your office or school, check with your network administrator before you begin the browser upgrade. Some companies have very specific reasons for using an older version and will frown on your attempts to make a change. Worse, since many large companies and educational institutions run software from a server on a *LAN*, short for Local Area Network, and your upgrade attempts might make a muddle. Play it safe and ask first.

As a rule, installing one browser version over another goes without a hitch. If you're already using Netscape or Messenger Mail or Microsoft Internet Mail or Outlook Express, the installation procedure should incorporate any of your saved messages and your address book into the new program. Additionally, your Bookmarks or Favorites should be visible in the new browser.

However, be aware that strange things sometimes happen when you install a newer program over an older one. Depending on the other software that you have installed on your computer, the installation process might not recognize your mail or your bookmark (favorites) files. Protect yourself. Print out the mail messages you want to save, or save each of them to a file. Make a note of the bookmarks you really want to keep. Most importantly, back up your computer before you begin, including the Windows registry.

If the worst happens and the installation doesn't go quite as smoothly as you planned, just restore your computer files from your backup. Even if you don't have a backup, you won't lose all browser settings if you've taken a few minutes before the installation to jot them down.

Grab an update

If you're upgrading Netscape from a previous version, click the **Help** menu and chose **Software Updates**. Follow the prompts to download and install the latest version of Communicator. Alternatively, go to www.netscape.com and click the link for the latest version of the Communicator suite.

Microsoft Internet Explorer's can click a link on the MSN page (www.msn.com). The upgrade to Internet Explorer may take a few hours to download and may need to be restarted several times if you are downloading the upgrade during peak hours.

Perform the upgrade during a time when your computer isn't being used for something important. (Upgrading your browser while finishing a big sales presentation spells disaster!) Both browsers have clear instructions about the upgrading process. If necessary, print them out and keep them close at hand during the upgrade. Be sure and follow the instructions to restart your computer after the upgrade is complete.

Version Mania

At present, both Netscape and Internet Explorer have several different versions available. Some versions are designed to run on a particular system, such as Unix or the Macintosh. (Netscape even has a version defined to run under OS/2, a now nearly defunct platform developed by IBM several years ago.) Some of the older versions were designed to run on Windows 3.x, and don't have many of the latest features, such as support for Java or ActiveX controls.

If you want to know which version of the browser is currently installed, click the **Help** menu and choose **About...** while the browser is running. A window that displays the version number appears, as shown in Figure 3.1. Or, pay attention to the version number that's displayed as your browser loads.

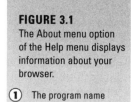

FIGURE 3.1
The About menu option of the Help menu displays information about your browser.

① The program name and version number are shown here.

Both Netscape and Microsoft give their browser products away for free. Since everyone wants the latest and greatest, you might think it's a good idea to upgrade every time a new release is announced. However, installing the latest version of your favorite browser can be a big mistake.

Sure, each new version adds features. Generally speaking, each new version requires more hard drive space and memory than its predecessor does. If your computer is an older model, or your hard drive is crammed with programs, make sure that you've got the hardware power to run the latest browser version before you install it.

Looking at Netscape Navigator

Netscape Navigator is the browser component of the Netscape Communicator suite. Navigator is a widely used Web browser. Because Netscape offers versions of Navigator for most types of computers, such as Macintosh, Unix, and Sun workstations, many corporations and schools choose it for large, cross-platform networks. Although it initially charged customers for its browser product, Netscape is now offering the entire Communicator suite for free. Your ISP might include Netscape Communicator or Navigator as part of your installation package.

The first time you open Navigator, you're asked to register the software and get your own custom home page. Don't shy away from registering. Registration takes only a few seconds and gives you free access to Netscape Netcenter, a free service that offers software and information on all types of news and commerce. Additionally, Netscape provides registered free email and a customizable start page.

In this exercise, you register your software and set up your own My Netscape page. The whole process takes only a few minutes and, best of all, you'll only need to do this one time. If you're already a Navigator user and you'd like to create your My Netscape page, click the **Help** menu and choose **Register Now** when Netscape is open. Then follow the steps shown in the exercise, starting with step 3.

Signing up with Netscape

1. Click the **Start** button on the Windows taskbar to open the **Start** menu.

2. Click **Programs**. Choose **Netscape Communicator** and then slide across to Netscape Navigator. The **Netscape Communicator** submenu appears.

3. Click the **Netscape Navigator** menu selection. In a few seconds, the Welcome to Communicator Page appears. Click the button marked **Click here to Register Now**!

4. The New Member Sign Up page appears. Type the information in the appropriate boxes, similar to the illustration in Figure 3.2.

> **Deciphering version code**
>
> Upgrades to both browsers appear frequently. You can tell which version of browser software you're running by its number. For example, Netscape Communicator 4.61 is newer than 4.0. The first number is the series (obviously 4.0 followed the 3.0 series). The first number to the right of the decimal point indicates if the version is brand new (0) or an upgrade to the existing release. Finally the third number indicates if the release is slightly upgraded with patches and bug fixes.
>
> Interim releases generally add a few minor features and fix problems. Additionally, interim releases generally supercede the previous release and make betas for the older release obsolete.

FIGURE 3.2
Get registered with Netscape.

① Fill in the blanks.

② Asterisks indicate the field must be completed.

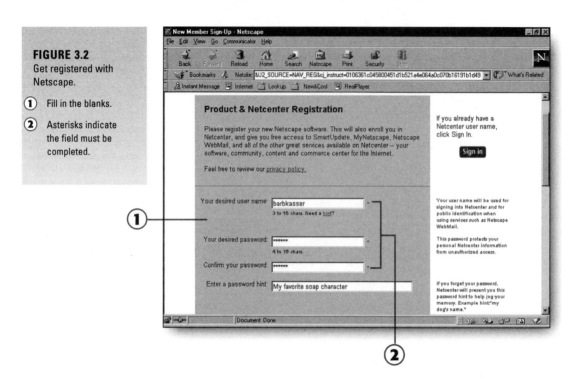

5. Three check boxes appear at the bottom of the form, as shown in Figure 3.3, asking if you would like to be included in the Member Directory, if you'd like email notification of new services featured by Netscape Netcenter, and if you'd like Netscape Netcenter to provide your information to selected companies. The options are selected by default. If desired, uncheck the box next to each option you don't want. When you're through, click the **Next** button at the bottom of the page to continue.

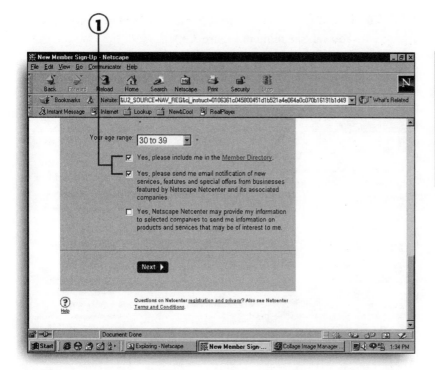

FIGURE 3.3
The options at the bottom of the form are selected by default.

① Click a check box to remove the check and de-deselect the option.

6. If the name you selected is available, the next box to appear displays your new username and asks you to reply to an email that will be sent within 48 hours. Make a note of the username you selected and click the **Next** button. (If the name you chose is in use, you'll be returned to the New Member sign up page and will have to select a new name.)

7. You're ready to build your own Start page. Take a few minutes to choose the items that you'd like to see when you first open Navigator. Check the boxes for categories and items that interest you. Scroll down the page and select your time zone. When you're all done, click the button marked **Build My Page!**

8. Your very own customized Netscape Netcenter page appears. (You can see mine in Figure 3.4.)

FIGURE 3.4
The My Netscape Netcenter page contains only what you want.

① Click here to change the content on the page.

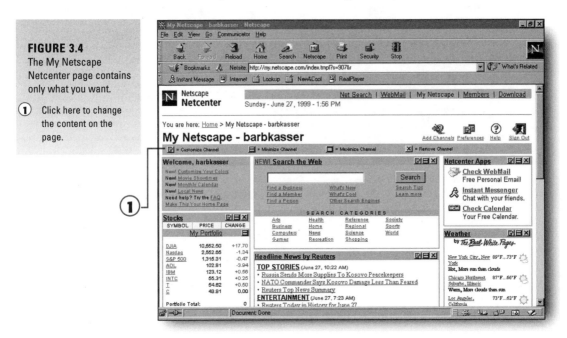

Good work! You've ready to move on to your first real visit to the World Wide Web.

Navigating the Navigator Screen

The Navigator screen contains many elements. Figure 3.5 shows a Web page and illustrates Navigator's individual components.

FIGURE 3.5
The Kings Road home page
is displayed on the Netscape
screen.

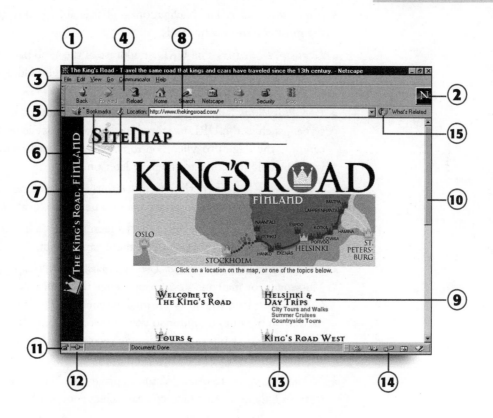

① Title bar
② Netscape icon
③ Menu bar
④ Navigation toolbar
⑤ Location toolbar
⑥ Bookmarks icon
⑦ Page Proxy/Link icon
⑧ Location/Netsite box

⑨ Hyperlinks
⑩ Scrollbar
⑪ Security information
⑫ Online/Offline connection
⑬ Status bar
⑭ Communicator Component bar
⑮ Communicator Component bar

The following describes each element on the Navigator screen:

- *Title bar.* The title bar displays the title of the page that's displayed.

- *Navigation toolbar.* The Navigation toolbar enables you to access the most common commands.

- *Location/Netsite box.* The URL or address of the Web page that's on the screen appears here. You can type a different address to move to another page.

- *Page Proxy/Link icon.* Information about the page that's on the screen, such as the URL, is stored in the Page Proxy icon. You can drag the Page Proxy icon on top of the Bookmarks icon so you'll be able to return to the page later on.

- *Hyperlinks.* Click a hyperlink to move to the place referenced by the link, either on the same page or a new Web location.

- *Bookmarks icon.* Click the **Bookmarks** icon to open a list of sites you've referenced so that you find them easily again.

- *Online/Offline Connection icon.* Used primarily in Netscape Messenger for mail and newsgroups, click the **Online/Offline Connection** icon to copy your mail and news folders to the hard drive of your computer so you can work without being connected to the Internet. When you reconnect, Messenger automatically synchronizes any changes you made when offline.

- *Menu bar.* Similar to other Windows programs, Navigator features a menu from which you can select commands.

- *Location toolbar.* The Location toolbar displays the Web address of the page that's displayed on the screen and provides you with quick access to your bookmarks.

- *Netscape icon.* The icon that displays the logo of Netscape Communications Corporation serves two purposes. First, the icon shows a meteor shower when Navigator is fetching a page you requested. Second, you can move to the Netscape home page when you click the **Netscape** icon.

- *Security information.* The lock icon represents the security of the page that's on the screen. When the lock handle is closed, the page is secure.

- *Component bar.* This bar offers speedy access to some of the other programs in Netscape Communicator. In Figure 3.5, the bar is docked, or anchored, at the bottom-right corner of the screen. The bar can also "float" on top of the Navigator screen so you can move it around.

- *Status bar.* Information about the current page is displayed here.

- *Scrollbar.* The vertical bar that appears on the right side of the window and contains arrows at either end, a gray or colored area in the middle and a scroll box that reflects your vertical position on the page. Drag the scroll box up or down within the scrollbar to move through the page.

- *What's Related icon.* Click the **What's Related** icon to see sites that offer products, services, and information that are similar or connected to those offered by the site that you're currently on! You can go directly to a related site by selecting one of the links in the drop-down menu, or select **Detailed List** to see a Web page with a list of related sites.

On the Web with Navigator

Navigator makes it easy to navigate through the page that's on the screen. In this exercise, you use some of Navigator's special tools as you move through the Web and look at some different Web pages.

Using Navigator's tools to move around the Web

1. Navigator should be open from the last exercise. If it's not already open, open Navigator by clicking the **Start** button and choose **Netscape Communicator** and then **Netscape Navigator**. In a few seconds, a Web page appears on the Navigator screen.

2. (Optional) The Component bar, a bar that contains shortcuts to other Communicator programs, appears on the screen. If it's in your way, click the **Close (X)** button on the bar. If you're using an older version of Communicator, you can click the **Communicator** menu and choose **Dock Component Bar**. Either way, the bar becomes smaller and anchors to the right bottom corner of the Navigator window.

3. Position your mouse arrow in the Netscape icon (the big N) and click once. Stars and comets flare around the Netscape "N" as Navigator moves you to the Netscape home page. Additionally, as the page is accessed, several messages flash across the status bar. In a moment, Netscape's home page appears.

4. Locate the words **Document:Done** on the status bar, and click in the **Location** box. The Web address that's currently displayed in the box appears highlighted, as shown in Figure 3.6.

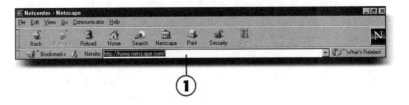

5. Type the following Web address carefully in the box; `www.mcp.com`. (It's not necessary to delete the text that's already on the box, because the new text overwrites the old text.) After you've made sure you haven't made any typos, press **Enter**.

6. The stars and comets flash in the Netscape icon as Navigator accesses the Macmillan home page. When the page is finished loading, the words **Document:Done** appear in the status bar. Place your mouse pointer over each of the buttons on the Navigation toolbar.

7. Each button appears outlined as your mouse passes over it. After a second, a screen tip appears in a yellow balloon, showing you the button's function. Figure 3.7 shows the Navigation toolbar displaying a screen tip. The screen tip also appears on the status bar located at the bottom of the screen.

8. Move your mouse arrow around the text and graphics on the Macmillan page. The mouse arrow changes to the shape of a hand as it passes over underlined and different colored text, called hyperlinks, on the page.

SEE ALSO

➤ *You learn more about hyperlinks on page 119*

9. The Macmillan page is too long to fit on your computer screen. Drag the right scroll box down slowly to view the lower portions of the page.

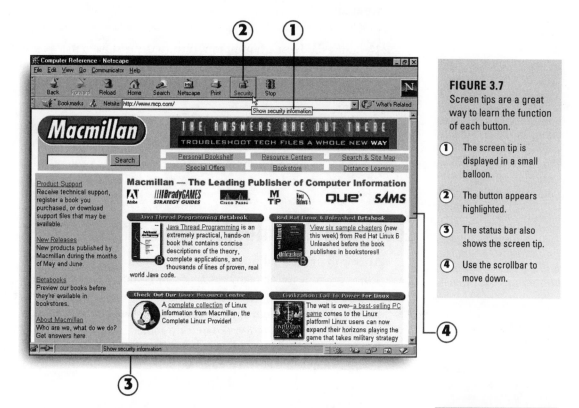

FIGURE 3.7
Screen tips are a great way to learn the function of each button.

① The screen tip is displayed in a small balloon.

② The button appears highlighted.

③ The status bar also shows the screen tip.

④ Use the scrollbar to move down.

10. Click the **Reload** button on the Navigation toolbar. The Macmillan home page is redrawn on the screen.

11. Click inside the **Location/Netsite** box. When the current URL appears highlighted, type **www.mrshowbiz.com** and press **Enter**. When the Mr. ShowBiz page appears, take a moment and explore the page.

12. Click the **Back** button on the Navigation toolbar. The Macmillan page reappears. Each time you click the Back button you move backward through one previously viewed site.

13. Click the **Forward** button on the Navigation toolbar. After a brief moment, the Mr. Showbiz page appears again on your screen. You click the Forward button to move ahead after you've

A shortcut for the Back and Forward buttons

Click the right mouse button on the **Back** or **Forward** button to view the page titles of sites you've seen during the present session. Now you won't have to cycle back through each individual page you visited during your online session because you can move to it immediately by clicking the page title.

used the Back button. You know that you've moved to the beginning or end of the sites you've already seen when either the Back or Forward button is dimmed.

SEE ALSO

➤ *You'll learn how to change the Web page you see when you open Navigator on page 138*

14. Click the **Home** button to return to the first page that you see when you open Navigator for a browsing session.

SEE ALSO

➤ *You'll learn how to change the Web page you see when you open Navigator on page 138*

15. Because Navigator is a Windows program, you close it as you would any other Windows program. Click the **Close** box (the box with the X on the Navigator title bar). The program closes and you're returned to your Windows desktop.

Looking at Internet Explorer

Microsoft introduced Internet Explorer 4.0 in late summer of 1997. This version featured many exciting new components and included the option to change the way you work with your Windows files and folders. Although Netscape Navigator had been the most popular browser, Internet Explorer 4.0 quickly gained a large percentage of users. With the release of Internet Explorer 5, Microsoft added some new, exciting features and eliminated some older, under-utilized program features that slowed the previous version.

Today, Internet Explorer has emerged as the top dog in the browser world. Internet Explorer is interwoven into Windows 98. If you use mostly Microsoft software, like the Microsoft Office suite of products, making Internet Explorer your Web browser makes good sense. The browser is tightly integrated with other Microsoft software. For example, if you need online help with Word or Excel while you're connected to the Internet, you can click **Help, Microsoft on the Web** to launch Internet Explorer and move to the appropriate technical support site. (If you're a Netscape user, the technical support page will appear in Navigator but some of the site's features may not be available.)

Internet Explorer has some exciting features. The *Intellisense* feature has expanded automation in many areas allowing you to take advantage of *Autosearch*, which enables you to search from the Address bar. Additionally, Intellisense offers support for *AutoComplete*, which provides a drop-down list of sites you have already visited or fills out forms automatically, and *AutoCorrect* which corrects typos that would otherwise prevent you from going directly to the page you want.

SEE ALSO

➤ *You'll learn about searching the Web on page 137*

One of Internet Explorer's most popular features is its capability to integrate the Web with your Windows desktop. You can turn the *Active Desktop* feature on or off when you install Internet Explorer. If you turn it on, the Active Desktop changes the way Windows looks and works; Internet Explorer becomes the Windows Explorer, making working with the files and folders on your hard drive just like navigating the Web. You also have the option of changing the way you open programs, folders, and files to single-clicking instead of a double-clicking. (If you're an established Windows user, you can turn off the single-click feature if you can't get used to it.) The Active Desktop streamlines working with the Web and your computer into one process, but it might take some getting used to.

Internet Explorer 5.0, the version we're referencing in this book, is designed to work in Windows 95, 98, or NT. If you're not using Windows 95 or NT 4.0, you need to contact Microsoft or visit their Web page and find out if Internet Explorer can successfully run on your computer. The Microsoft technicians will also be able to tell you where you can obtain the version that's right for you.

Exploring the Internet Explorer Screen

The Internet Explorer browser screen is made up of many elements. Figure 3.8 shows a Web page and illustrates Internet Explorer's individual components.

FIGURE 3.8
The Crown Sanitary home page is displayed in Internet Explorer.

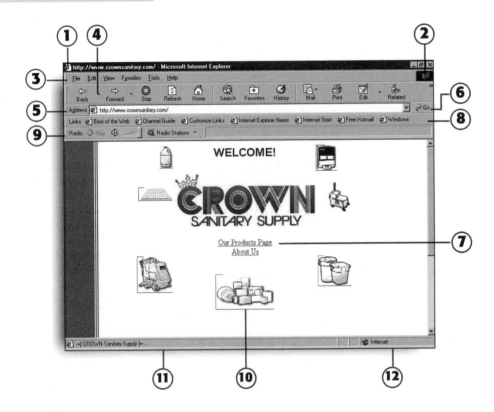

(1) Title bar

(2) Internet Explorer icon

(3) Menu bar

(4) Standard buttons bar

(5) Address bar

(6) Go button

(7) Page icon

(8) Links toolbar

(9) Radio toolbar

(10) Hyperlinks

(11) Status bar

(12) Security zone information

The following describes each element shown in Figure 3.8:

- *Menu bar.* Similar to other Windows programs, Internet Explorer features a menu from which you can select commands.

- *Standard Buttons toolbar.* The Standard Buttons toolbar contains commands you'll use as you tour the Web.

- *Address bar.* The Address bar shows the Web address of the page that's displayed on the screen. You can also use the Address bar to search for another site.

- *Go button.* After you've typed a URL in the Address bar, click the **Go** button to move to the new page. The Go button is a new feature in Internet Explorer 5.0.

- *Links toolbar.* Links on this bar provide a quick way to move to the site. The Links toolbar can be customized to add the links to sites you like.

- *Radio toolbar.* The Radio toolbar allows you to select an Internet radio station. Choose a radio station from the Radio Station Guide and listen to Internet-based programs.

- *Page icon.* When you're viewing a page you want to revisit, drag the link icon into the Favorites folder.

- *Internet Explorer icon.* The box that displays the Internet Explorer icon animates while Internet Explorer is fetching a Web page for you.

- *Hyperlinks.* Click a hyperlink to move to the place referenced by the link, either on the same page or a new Web location.

- *Security zone.* The security zone displays the level of security of the Web site that appears on the screen. You can set the security zone levels for the pages you view.

- *Status bar.* Information about the current page is displayed here.

- *Title bar.* The title bar displays the title of the page that's displayed.

No Radio bar

If you don't see the Radio bar on your Internet Explorer screen, click the **View** menu, choose **Toolbars**, and then **Radio**. If Radio isn't a submenu selection, you'll need to install the latest Windows Media Player.

Similar features

You might notice that Netscape Navigator and Internet Explorer look very similar. Both browsers share many common components and features. In fact, both browsers do a great job of bringing Web pages to your computer screen.

An Internet Explorer Experience

Now that you've had the opportunity to look at a picture of the components that make up the Internet Explorer browser screen, you're ready to do some of your own exploring. In this exercise, you launch the Internet Explorer browser and take a look at some of its unique features as you visit some Web pages. Make sure you're connected to the Internet before you begin the first step.

Taking a tour of the Web with Internet Explorer

1. Starting Internet Explorer is easy! As part of the installation process, Internet Explorer places a Quick Launch toolbar next to your Windows **Start** button. Click the icon that looks like a low-ercase E with a ring around it. Alternatively, click the **Start** button, slide up to **Programs**, and then point to the Internet Explorer Program group and then Internet Explorer.

2. The first Web page to appear could be the Welcome Internet Start page or your ISP's home page. Unless you change it, this page will appear each time you launch Internet Explorer. Click inside the **Address** box. When the URL in the Address box appears highlighted, type `www.conspire.com`. (Don't worry about deleting the text that's already in the box, because the new text will overwrite the old text.) After you've made sure you haven't made any typos, click the **Go** button or press **Enter**.

SEE ALSO
➤ *Information on changing your Internet Explorer Start page is shown on page 138*

3. The Internet Explorer icon becomes animated as the server that stores the Conspire home page is contacted. In a moment, the Conspire page appears on your screen.

4. With the Conspire home page on your screen, move your mouse pointer slowly across the buttons on the Standard Buttons toolbar, noticing that the each button appears in color and becomes raised when the pointer passes over it.

5. Move your mouse arrow around the text and graphics on the Conspire Page. (The page has links to the 60 greatest conspiracy theories of all time.) The mouse arrow changes to the shape of a hand as it passes over hyperlinks on the page. You'll learn more about hyperlinks later in this chapter.

6. Any toolbar that's displayed on the browser screen can be hidden when you're not using it. For now, hide the Links toolbar by positioning your mouse pointer to the right of the buttons on

the Links toolbar (so it's in a blank spot) and clicking the right mouse button. A shortcut menu, shown in Figure 3.9, appears.

FIGURE 3.9
A check mark means the toolbar is visible.

7. Click the **Links** item on the shortcut menu. The menu closes and the Links toolbar is removed from the screen. Anytime you want to redisplay a toolbar you've hidden, click the **View** menu and choose **Toolbars** and then the name of the toolbar you want to show (in this case, **Links**).

8. Repeat step 5. When the shortcut menu appears, click **Radio** to close the Radio toolbar. Any time you want to redisplay the toolbars, repeat the steps and check the hidden toolbars.

9. Click inside the **Address** box and type the following Web address carefully in the box: `www.skeptic.com`. After you've made sure that you've typed the address correctly click the **Go** button or press **Enter**.

10. Position your mouse pointer in the menu bar on the right of the screen and move up and down the menu. Notice that as your mouse passes over each item, a colored arrow appears to the left of the text. Additionally, the mouse pointer takes the shape of a hand as it passes over certain items on the page.

11. Click the **news** menu selection. Although the menu on the left remains constant, a new page appears in the center of the screen. The new page contains links to many related sites.

12. Click an item that interests you on the News page. The new page appears in a few seconds.

13. Click inside the Address box. The current URL appears highlighted. Type `www.usatoday.com` and press **Enter**. In a moment or two, the USA Today Web page appears on your screen. Take a moment and read the latest "real" news.

14. Click inside the Address box, type `www.tvguide.com`, and press **Enter**. Now you're looking at the television news! After you've looked around, click the **Back** button on the Standard Buttons toolbar to open the page you were viewing previously.

15. Click the **Back** button again. You're stepped back one more page that you've visited.

16. The **Forward** button on the Standard Buttons toolbar contains an arrow pointing to the right. Click the arrow to display a list of sites you've seen in the current session and select one from the list to return to that site.

    Each time you click the **Back** or **Forward** buttons, you're returned to the site you viewed previously during your current browsing session. If you want to get back to a site that you visited awhile ago, clicking the arrow on the button to display the list of sites helps you get back to where you want to go without having to revisit many sites. Alternatively, right-click the buttons to see a list of the most-recently visited sites and select the site to which you want to return from the list.

17. Click the **Home** button on the Standard Buttons toolbar. The page you saw when you first opened Internet Explorer appears on the screen. You've come full-circle; you're back home again.

    Now you've taken a brief tour of several different Web sites. It's really easy to move around from site to site.

Just for now

The browsing history stored in the **Back** and **Forward** buttons is erased when you close Internet Explorer. You'll find out how to view your browsing history for a chronological period in Chapter 6, "Making Your Way on the Web."

---

chapter

4

Maintaining Your Privacy on the Internet

Identifying privacy and security issues ●

Understanding cookies ●

Purchasing safely on the Web ●

Looking at Internet fraud ●

Privacy was the number one concern reported by Internet users, according to a recent survey conducted by Georgetown University. Privacy and related security issues are important to everyone on the Internet, from users like you and me to large corporations and Web merchants. Internet privacy and security have many varied facets.

The media has sensationalized the dangers of the Internet—young women running away with men they've met in Internet chat rooms, youngsters getting information about bomb building and weapons, and unscrupulous Web merchants who don't deliver what they promise. You've probably heard about one or more similar Internet horror stories in the last few months. Yet, as you sit at your computer and click links, the Internet seems like a safe place.

Should you be concerned? The answer is both no and yes. The Internet is probably safer than the media has made it out to be. Still, you need to practice some Internet safety measures. There are some pretty shady characters on the Internet, just as there are in your town. If you're not careful, there's a chance your identity and personal information could be compromised.

You're not anonymous

You're never totally anonymous on the Internet. Your ISP can tell what time you logged in and how long you spent online.

Privacy and Safety Versus Security

There are worlds of difference between Internet privacy and safety, and Internet security.

Internet privacy should give you the right to prevent anyone from obtaining any information about you and your Web habits, including when you log on and which sites you visit. Additionally, no unauthorized individuals should have access to your buying patterns or financial information, including credit card numbers and other important financial data. Your privacy on the Internet keeps you safe from unsolicited communication and misuse of your personal information.

Most Internet privacy concerns are simple to understand. You'd probably hate to walk down a busy street in a large city wearing a huge nametag that displayed all your personal information. Why should you have to wear a cyberspace equivalent? The same privacy afforded to you in the real-world should be assured on the Internet.

Internet security is largely the bailiwick of corporations and government and financial institutions. The chief reason for Internet security measures is to prevent access to data that is confidential or private. Furthermore, Internet security guards against intentional vandalism, such as the deliberate changing of records or sabotaging computer systems.

Blurring the Lines

The lines between Internet privacy and security are easily blurred. When governments and corporations set up security measures, individual's privacy can suffer. For example, the company I work for develops chemical formulas and other highly confidential data. To prevent competitor espionage and information leaks, many security measures are in place. All employees have access to the Internet but the company uses a firewall to prevent them from visiting non-business sites. Additionally, employees cannot utilize Java applications because the company honchos won't allow direct contact with another server. Anyone who violates the policy or tries to get around the company firewall loses Internet privileges. Reports of each employee's Internet history are maintained.

SEE ALSO
➤ *You can read more about intranets and firewalls on page 58*

If you have email at work, there's a good chance that your messages are not totally private. Someone in the IT department, usually the Mail Administrator, can look at your outgoing and incoming messages. If you're sending company secrets to the chief competitor through the company email system, you'll probably be summoned to the boss's office before too long.

Sometimes, total Internet privacy might not be the best idea. Should anonymity protect a terrorist who uses Internet resources to plan an attack on a crowded government facility, or shield underage buyers who illegally purchase firearms and other weapons online? Right now, there's no real mechanism in place for Internet wiretapping where law enforcement officials would need to show cause and get warrants.

Who's Watching You?

Is there anyone out there, looking in on you as you blithely click links and access information? Probably not. However, the following list shows some typical cyberspace bad guys that you might encounter.

- **Snoopers** take advantage of files called *cookies* on the hard drive of your computer. (You'll learn all about cookies in the next section in this chapter.) Without your knowledge, some Web sites use your cookies file to collect your Web browsing patterns.

- **Thugs** are Internet gangsters who obtain information illegally or hold other users, corporations and governments hostage. By misusing a program called a *sniffer*, some thugs can scan all messages routed through a particular server to search for passwords or credit card numbers. Other thugs write computer viruses that are generally spread through the exchange of files attached to email messages. These viruses can range from mildly annoying, like the virus that plays Yankee Doodle through your computer's speakers every day at 5:00, to dangerous programs capable of wiping out the hard drive of your computer.

- **Spoofers** operate by first luring you to a Web site and then getting you to divulge your credit card information by fraudulent means. Most *spoofer* sites take you to a U.S. site first, but automatically redirect you to an international site without your knowledge. Once they've got your card number, spoofers are off to the mall with the bill sent to you.

- **Predators** are the scariest folks of all. Internet predators stalk other Internet users by faking an identity and gaining their victim's trust. Most predators prey upon children. Although some predators get their kicks from simply corresponding and chatting, most predators try to escalate the relationship to an exchange of pictures (usually sexually explicit) or, worse, a face to face secret meeting.

SEE ALSO
➤ *You'll see some strategies on how to protect kids against predators on page 412*

Surprisingly enough, your worst enemy on the Internet isn't any of the criminals discussed here. Most times, it's you! Giving out personal data indiscriminately or shopping with no-name Web merchants who offer deals too good to be true, means that you're setting yourself up for trouble. Additionally, if you violate company policy and visit adult or hard-porn sites from the office, you might get yourself fired.

Cookies, Cookies, Cookies

As you know, some Web shopping sites ask you to register before you can look at the available products and services. Later on, when you return to the site, the site recognizes you and might even send out a personal greeting.

For example, I buy books at Amazon.com almost every week. When I visit the Amazon.com site, my name appears—almost by magic—on the Amazon home page, as displayed in Figure 4.1. You might find that sites you re-visit display your name or show a personalized greeting.

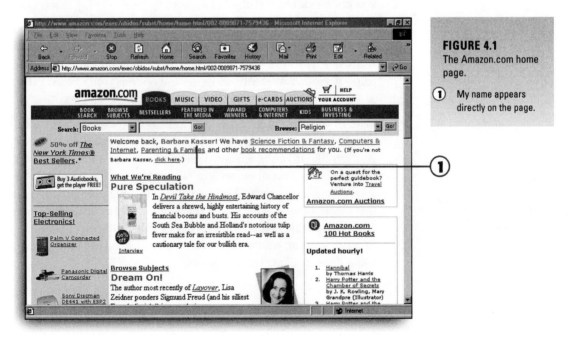

FIGURE 4.1
The Amazon.com home page.

(1) My name appears directly on the page.

Why is it called a cookie?

Even though many people think otherwise, there's nothing sinister or amusing about the term "cookie". For years, computer programmers and other techno-types have used it to describe data that's held by an intermediary as a cookie. The specification for cookies was included in the first version of Netscape Navigator.

Even if you don't register at a site, your browser passes information to some of the Web sites you visit. When you visit a page on the Web, that site can record a lot of information about you, including your name, your company name, your location, the type of computer you're using, your operating system, the type and version of your browser, and what Web pages you've looked at. This exchange of information is called a *cookie*.

Cookies are stored on the hard drive of your computer. Most of the time cookies are used for innocent purposes. For example, if you customize your My Netscape or MSN Start page, the customization information is stored in a cookie. When you access the page, the cookie tells Netscape or Microsoft what you've chosen to include on your page.

Other times, cookies might have a more sinister use. Even though you haven't granted permission, your movements on the Web might be tracked by the cookies your browser exchanges with Web servers. Some unscrupulous sites could build a database of your viewing habits and sell it to Web advertisers. If you're concerned about your privacy or don't want anyone to know what sites you've accessed, you can block the exchange of cookies.

Unfortunately, a browsing session without cookies has drawbacks. For one thing, you might not be able to access some of the sites you really like. If you've set up some customization options in a starting page or another Web site, those special options won't be available.

Cookies are actually simple text files that are stored on the hard drive of your computer. Internet Explorer stores individual cookies in a folder generally called Cookies in your Windows directory or in your profile. If you're a heavy Web user or browse to a lot of sites, the files inside that directory can occupy a lot of space on your hard drive. Navigator stores all of the cookies in a file called cookies.txt that's stored in the same folder that holds other information about your user profile (generally c:\Program Files\Netscape\Users\ default). You can delete the cookie folder or files, but your browser will automatically create a new one.

Managing Your Cookies

Should you worry about cookies? Many seasoned Web users say no. They reason that cookies are part of the necessary exchange of information on your Web excursion. Of course, most of these users are careful which sites they access and what information they provide. Other Web users take the opposite approach and take steps to deal with cookies as they're passed to and from their browser.

The Anonymizer Web page at www.anonymizer.com, as shown in Figure 4.2, offers a service that can give you the capability to make sure that you're completely anonymous on the Web. The Anonymizer acts as an agent between you and the site you want to view. Instead of accessing the page from your browser, you provide the URL to the Anonymizer. In turn, the Anonymizer accesses the page and provides it you. You can use the service for free, but expect a delay as the page is accessed. For around $15 per quarter, the Anonymizer ensures that the page it accesses for you will appear with no discernible delay.

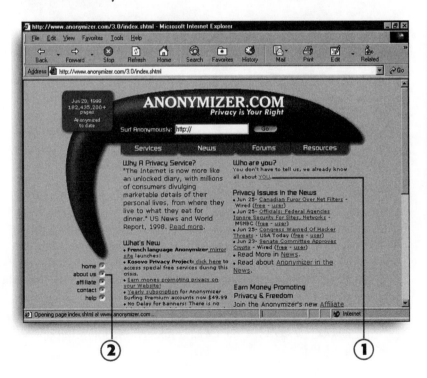

FIGURE 4.2
The Anonymizer Home Page contains links to many different pages dealing with Internet privacy.

(1) Click the link to discover what the Anonymizer can tell about you.

(2) Click here to learn more about the service.

If you don't want to look at sites through a third party, but are concerned about cookies, you can change some of the settings in your browser. Internet Explorer and Navigator enables you to monitor when and where cookies are passed between your browser and a Web server. Many users opt for their browser to let them know when cookies are being passed back and forth. The choice is yours.

I think of cookies as a device like caller ID that's attached to some telephones. I know that sometimes the pages I visit know information about me and therefore, I'm careful where I go and what information I submit to insecure sites. However, I understand that someone, somewhere might recognize who I am; my possible lack of anonymity is a small cost to pay for using the Internet.

Changing the way Internet Explorer handles cookies

1. From within Internet Explorer, click the **Tools** menu and select **Internet Options**. The Internet Options dialog box appears.

2. Click the **Security** tab and then click the **Custom Level** button, as shown in Figure 4.3.

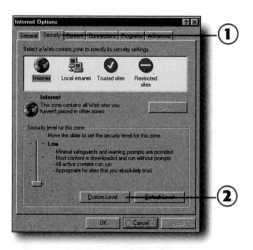

It's a trade-off

If you opt to be notified each time your browser deals with cookies, you'll be kept busy choosing to accept or reject each one. This can get annoying. On the other hand, you'll know exactly what information is being transmitted between computers. Try it both ways before you decide.

FIGURE 4.3
Set Internet Explorer to alert you when cookies are passed to and from your computer.

① Security tab is selected

② Click the **Custom** Level button to display the available options.

3. Scroll down the Security Settings dialog box until you reach the section on Cookies. The Cookies section has two categories: *Allow cookies that are stored on your computer* and *Allow per-session cookies (not stored)*. Under each category, the following options are available:

- *Enable (the system default)*. This means that Internet Explorer will send information about you whenever asked. Additionally, Internet Explorer will store information about your Web sessions.

- *Prompt*. This means that whenever a Web server attempts to send you a cookie, you'll be notified via dialog box and can accept or reject it. You'll see the first few characters of the cookie (although sometimes the information is coded) before you make your decision.

- *Disable*. This means that you won't be able to access many of the sites on the Web. You'll be anonymous as you go from site to site. However, any site that requires information from you, like a customized Start page or a site that provides a custom stock portfolio, won't be available to you.

4. In both categories, click the **Option** button next to **Prompt**, as illustrated in Figure 4.4, and click **OK**.

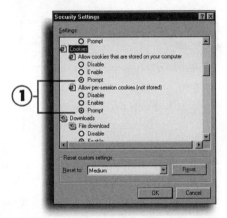

FIGURE 4.4
Take control of cookies in Internet Explorer.

① Choose **Prompt** in both categories.

5. Click **OK** to close the Security Settings dialog box. A Warning! dialog box appears, asking if you're sure you want to change the security settings. Click **Yes**.

Click **OK** to close the Internet Options box and return to the main Internet Explorer screen. The changes you made won't take effect until the next time you enter Internet Explorer.

6. If you're not already connected to the Internet, connect now. Click inside the Address box and type **www.dailyfix.com**. Visit some other Web sites. As you move to a new Web page, you'll see a Security Alert dialog box advising you that a cookie is about to be passed.

When the Security Alert dialog box is on the screen, click **More Info** to display what information is contained in the cookie. Figure 4.5 shows an example of a Security Alert dialog box, similar to the one you see.

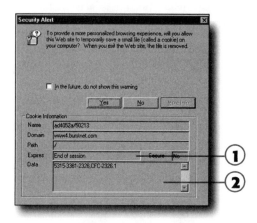

FIGURE 4.5
Read what will be placed on your computer.

① Date the information will be deleted

② Coded information

7. Each time a Security Alert box appears, click **Yes** if you'll accept the cookie and **No** to reject it. If you click **No**, you'll still be able to access the site but the page might not display correctly.

8. Reverse the steps by repeating steps 1 through 3 and choosing the **Enable** option in both Cookies categories. Click **OK** to close the Security Settings dialog box and then **OK** again to close the Internet Options dialog box and return to Internet Explorer.

Setting cookie options in Navigator

1. From within Navigator, click the **Edit** menu and select **Preferences**. The Preferences dialog box appears with a list of Categories on the left side.

2. Click the **Advanced** category to display the options shown in Figure 4.6.

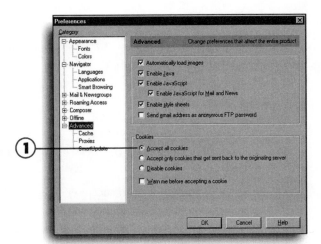

FIGURE 4.6
The Advanced tab enables
you to change how
cookies are handled.

① Default choice is
  already selected

3. The following options are available:

   ■ *Accept all cookies.* The Navigator default, cookies will pass
     freely between your computer and Web servers.

   ■ *Accept only cookies that get sent back to the originating server.*
     Some cookies will get through.

   ■ *Disable cookies.* No information will pass between you and
     the Web server. Some Web pages may not be available and
     others might not display properly if you choose this option.

   ■ *Warn me before accepting a cookie.* Check this option if you
     want to make a choice each time a cookie is about to be
     passed.

4. Click the option button next to **Accept only cookies that get
   sent back to the originating server** and check the option to
   Warn me before accepting a cookie. Click **OK** when you've
   made your selections, and close the Preferences dialog box.

5. Click inside the Location/Netsite box, highlight the existing
   text, and type www.tvguide.com. Press **Enter** when you're done
   typing. As the TV Guide site is accessed, you'll be offered the
   choice to accept the cookie, as shown in Figure 4.7. Click **OK**
   to accept the cookie or **Cancel** to reject it.

Cookie warnings

If you set Navigator to
warn you each time a
cookie is passed between
your browser and a Web
page, you'll be amazed at
how many times the warn-
ing box appears. If you find
you're overwhelmed with
cookie warnings, change
your settings to Accept all
cookies.

FIGURE 4.7

Navigator asks how you'd like to proceed.

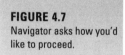 Information about the cookie, including its expiration date

If you choose **Cancel**, the new page will appear but might not display correctly.

6. Since you'll be asked to accept cookies for almost every site you attempt to visit, you may wish to set the Navigator to enable cookies without prompting you. If so, repeat steps 1 through 4, unchecking the box next to **Warn me before accepting a cookie** and checking the option button next to **Accept all cookies**. Click **OK** to close the Preferences dialog box and return to the Navigator screen.

Are Cookies Really Monsters?

Cookies are one of the Internet's most maligned features. Many people don't know whether they should disable or limit the cookies passed by their browsers. Use the answers to some commonly asked questions to put your mind at ease.

Q. Are cookies dangerous to my computer?

A. No. Your cookies file is actually made up of text. Cookies cannot be used to take a snapshot of your hard drive or pass viruses.

Q. If I visit a lot of Web sites, will the cookies file grow and eventually take over my computer?

A. Cookies files are really tiny. To put the file in perspective, you'd need about 60 million cookies to fill up a 6 gigabyte hard drive. Even if you were connected to the Internet 24 hours a day, it would be highly unlikely that you'd amass a cookie file even a fraction of that size.

Q. Both my browser at home and at work are set identically to handle cookies. The same sites that I access at home with no

problem send me error messages telling me to turn cookie on
when I try to get to them from the office. What gives?

A. In a corporate environment, your computer may be behind a firewall or *proxy server* that prevents cookie transmissions. Regardless of
how your browser is set, cookies won't be sent or received by your
browser.

Sign In, Please

Many pages on the Web require you to complete a form. Forms are
fill-in-the-blanks tools that help make the Web interactive by providing a method of communication between you and other points on
the Internet. Just like a paper form, a Web form is completed, and
then sent to another site for processing. If you think about it, you're
probably used to filling out forms for many different things. Your
income tax, a personal check, and even a lottery card are all examples
of different forms with which you're familiar.

Similar to a personal check that has an area for the amount, the payee,
and so on, Web forms contain distinct fields that ask for information.
You are required to complete some of the fields on the form in order
to submit it for processing, but often, forms will include fields that are
optional, which you can skip, if you prefer. After you complete the
form, you click a button to transmit it across the Internet.

The forms you encounter on the Web enable you to communicate
with someone at the other end to request or transmit information.
Although each form provides a different outcome, they all share
common characteristics. Follow these simple rules to navigate
through all types of Web forms.

- Click or press **Tab** to move from field to field. Don't press
  Enter.
- Complete all required fields, generally identified by an asterisk
  character. If you don't, the form will be kicked back to you or,
  worse, discarded at the other end.
- When you've filled in the form, click the appropriate button
  necessary to transmit it (generally labeled **Send** or **Transmit**).
  Otherwise, the information you filled in will go nowhere.

Forms that require you to fill in information are common on the Web. You'll encounter this type of form if you request information from a business or buy something online. Like the form shown in Figure 4.8, an information form you submit generally contains required and optional fields. Type the information in each field carefully, because after the form is transmitted you can't correct any typos. Figure 4.8 displays some of the questions on the form to set up a custom page and get personalized service at Yahoo!.

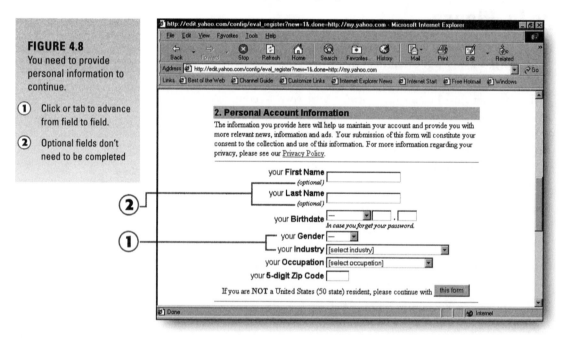

FIGURE 4.8
You need to provide personal information to continue.

(1) Click or tab to advance from field to field.

(2) Optional fields don't need to be completed

SEE ALSO

➤ *Curious about setting up a custom page at Yahoo!? You'll have the opportunity on page 140*

When you submit a form, the information you've entered, whether it's your name, a search request, or your credit card number, is transmitted across the phone line to another computer. Although your data is in the phone line, it can be intercepted and read by someone else.

Before you panic, please keep in mind that although theoretically the information can be intercepted, in all likelihood, it's probably

Just say no

Don't feel that you have to fill out every Web form or register for every service you encounter on the Web. Make sure that you are registering for services or premiums you want. If you aren't comfortable with some of the questions on a Web form, move on instead of completing the form.

not. Intercepting a telephone transmission and reading the information is a very difficult and complex task. The conversation you have on the telephone could be "tapped," or listened to by an unauthorized person. So could your Internet data. In either situation, it's highly unlikely that anyone else is listening or looking.

Still, it's best to play it safe. Protect your privacy. Apply the same rules to your Web usage that you apply to telephone transactions. You wouldn't provide detailed personal information to a stranger on the phone, so don't provide it to a stranger on the Web. Although it's the exception rather than the rule, some Web businesses sell your name or other information to mailing lists or other Web merchants. Do business with Web businesses that you know are reputable or have been recommended by a friend or colleague. Don't submit your credit card number or information unless you're sure the site is secure.

SEE ALSO

➤ *You'll learn more about buying on the Internet on page 427*

If you observe these simple rules, you won't have anything to worry about. Actually, many people and businesses on the Web are very concerned about Web security. The data you transmit can be encrypted or scrambled to prevent anyone from observing what you send. Additionally, many Web vendors provide a "secure buy" service that works with a secret personal identification number (PIN). Other companies provide certificates that lock the information you submit from prying eyes.

Check Out the Privacy Policy

Many Web sites take privacy concerns very seriously. If you're concerned that the information you submit to a site is going to be sold or misused in any way, check the page for a Privacy Policy. (The Amazon.com policy is shown in Figure 4.9.) You'll find a link to the site's privacy policy on the pages of many Web merchants. Read a site's privacy policy carefully. You need to feel comfortable while you're visiting a site, or you won't return.

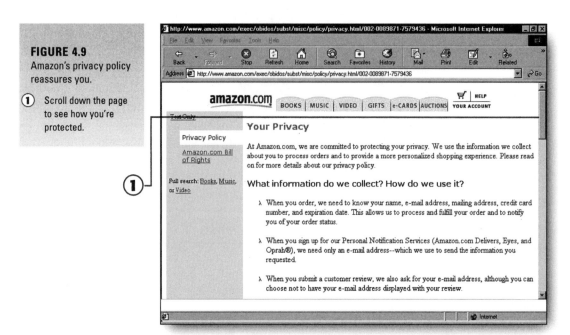

FIGURE 4.9
Amazon's privacy policy reassures you.

(1) Scroll down the page to see how you're protected.

Making a Buy

What is e-commerce?
E-commerce is a general term that refers to the buying and selling of goods and services across the Internet. Sometimes the term "e-business" is used interchangeably with e-commerce.

One of the Web's best advantages is that it you can shop for anything you can imagine. Internet shoppers have the world at their disposal, during any hour of the day or night. Sitting at your computer, you can find the product you want—at a price you can afford.

Shopping on the Web can violate your privacy. Both you, the buyer, and the Web merchant, each need to take steps to ensure the safety of the transaction. In fact, transaction security is a serious matter. The future of e-commerce depends on the capability to assure buyers and sellers that transactions between both parties are private. Internet Explorer and Navigator support security protocols and work, often behind the scenes, to keep your e-commerce transactions from the eyes of snoopers.

Many companies are working on new and improved ways to make Internet buying as safe as shopping at your local store. All the competition to develop better and better transaction security measures is good for the consumer. Several different companies are promoting the use of cyber-cash and smart cards. Soon, both terms will be common household words.

SEE ALSO

➤ *You'll find how to pay for Web purchases on page 442*

The most common protocol used in transaction security is called *SSL*, for Secure Socket Layers. SSL was developed by Netscape and has gone through a few upgrades to make it even more secure. Other protocols used are Secure Electronics Transaction, or SET, and Private Communications Technology, or PCT, for short. Both use the basic SSL model and add even more features for enhanced security.

Deciphering Secure Socket Layers

Netscape first developed the Secure Sockets Layer to create an environment for secure Web transactions. SSL uses some high-level technology to ensure that your transactions are secure. Let's briefly examine each of the elements that make up SSL.

Public Key Encryption

Your browser and a secure Web server exchange public keys. The *key* is actually the code used to scramble the information, like your credit card number and what you're ordering. As the information goes out across the Internet, only your browser and the Web server can read it. As an added security measure, the information can be unlocked with a private key when it reaches its destination.

The encoding and decoding is actually accomplished by the use of two random numbers. The first random number is the *public key* that's known by your browser and the secure server. The second random number is the *private key*, only known at one end of the transaction, or the other. Security is provided by the fact that the random numbers are very large. Because there are so many possible combinations, it would be impossible to work through every one.

Digital Certificates

Digital certificates provide an added measure of security. When you send the public key, a digital ID goes along as well. The digital ID works like your driver's license and identifies you. Because digital certificates are used for extra security, you don't need one to shop on the Web. However, if you're doing a lot of online shopping, you can obtain your own digital certificate.

> **Cracking the code**
>
> A few years ago, two University of California-Berkeley students and a researcher in France simultaneously announced that they'd cracked the code generated by Netscape. The Internet world was horrified. Since then, Netscape has taken steps to make it virtually impossible for anyone to decipher the code again.

Charge it to your phone bill

Online shoppers worried about sending their credit card details over the Internet will be able to charge Web purchases to their telephone bill instead, if software from a Hong Kong company takes off.

In the near future, a company named New Media plans to launch its NetCharger product in 40 countries, aiming to eliminate the security concerns associated with sending credit card numbers over the Internet.

Authentication

The third portion of SSL is called *authentication* and checks to make sure that you are who your certificate says you are. Authentication is handled behind the scenes when you transmit information in a message. Your computer creates a mathematically designed digest of the message called a *hash*. Each hash is unique. When the receiving computer receives your message, it runs the same hash function you used. If both hashes aren't identical, the message is rejected.

Viewing Secure Web Sites

Fortunately, most Web merchants take care of the advance work of making their sites secure. You don't need to do anything special to visit a secure site because all of the work is done for you, behind the scenes. Internet Explorer and Navigator both provide visual clues to let you know you're accessing a secure site:

- *Warning dialog box.* If you click a link or type in the URL to a secure site, your browser displays a dialog box, similar to the one shown in Figure 4.10, to let you know that the site you're accessing is secure.

FIGURE 4.10
Internet Explorer informs you that the site is secure.

① Check this box if you don't want to see this message again.

①

- *URL identification.* The URL in the Address box changes from `http://` to `https://`, as shown in Figure 4.11.

- *Security Padlock icon.* Internet Explorer and Navigator display a security icon, shaped like a padlock, on the status bar at the bottom of the page. When the icon looks like a closed padlock, you know the site is secure (refer to Figure 4.11). Navigator adds an additional visual clue by coloring in the padlock icon so it stands out.

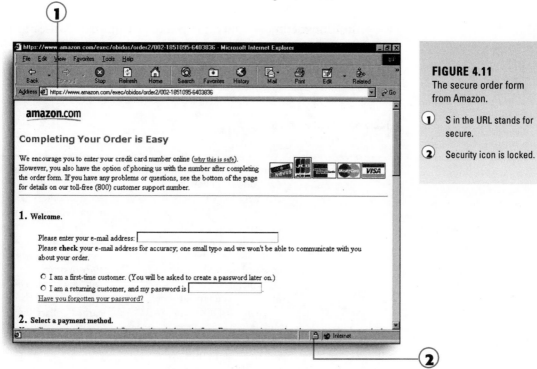

FIGURE 4.11
The secure order form
from Amazon.

(1) S in the URL stands for
secure.

(2) Security icon is locked.

For even more information about a secure document, you can
double-click the **Closed Padlock** icon on the status bar. A window
appears with categories of information about the security levels on
the page. When you're through reading the information, close the
window to return to the secure page.

It's important to remember that not all Web merchants offer secure
Web transactions. If you're worried about exchanging credit card
information on a non-secure site, don't complete the transaction.

Protect Against Fraud

Unfortunately, a new generation of con artists are using the Internet
for some old-fashioned fraud with a new twist. The scammers use
the Internet as a way to contact potential victims. Using slick,
professional-looking Web sites and a well-edited sales pitch, the
scammers can deceive even the most cynical Internet user.

Most Internet fraud centers get you to give up your hard-earned dollars. However, some Internet fraud is more malicious and can cost you your computer or, in extreme cases, your life. Table 4.1 shows some common Web fraud schemes and how to avoid them.

Table 4.1 Internet fraud

Scam Type	How It Works	How to Avoid
Pyramid scheme	You visit a slick Web site that shows you how you can make lots of money in a short time. The Web site displays testimonials from other "distributors", sometimes with phony email addresses beneath their pictures. For a sum of money, you buy into the company as a distributor and in turn you recruit other distributors who will pay you. In truth, you lose your investment and your pride.	Ignore solicitations to visit a Web site to see how others have made fast money. If you are tempted, check out the company with the Better Business Bureau or other consumer group before you flush your hard-earned dollars away.
Chain letter	An Internet chain letter is any email which encourages you to forward it indiscriminately to others. Some chain letters are fake virus warnings, stuff that's "cool" or "funny", or sad stories. Chain letters often contain file attachments which hold damaging programs. A recent Internet chain letter contained a file that claimed to be a "Happy Holidays" card. However, the file damaged the computers of those who opened it.	Don't open file attachments unless you've requested them and you know what they contain. Delete unopened files attached to messages from senders you don't know. Don't let your curiosity get the best of you.

Scam Type	How It Works	How to Avoid
Phony prizes and sweepstakes	You fill out a form to enter a contest or get information at a Web site. Later on, you're notified that you've won a prize. However, you'll have to pay shipping or other handling charges. The prize is usually non-existent or worth much less than the handling charges you paid to receive it.	Don't enter every Web contest you find. If you are notified that you're a winner, check out the company before you send a check or credit card information.
Bogus scholarship search services	Bogus scholarship first obtain the email addresses of graduating high school seniors and then contact them offering to find college scholarship dollars for a fee. In all but a few cases, the students (or their parents) are the big losers.	Scholarship brokers both on and off the Internet are pretty shady characters. If you decide to work with one, get the address and phone numbers of a few people for whom they actually obtained funds.
Stalkers	Pretending to be secret admirers, stalkers send their victims complimentary or romantic email or instant messages. Once the victim is comfortable with the secret love, the stalker escalates the online relationship. Eventually, the stalker arranges for a private, secret meeting.	Don't let yourself be flattered by messages from unknown senders. Don't respond to any "secret admirer" messages. If the messages contain threats or frightening language, contact your ISP and your local police.

Protect Yourself from Internet Fraud

Being aware of potential dangers on the Internet gives you a hard start on avoiding most unnecessary situations. Follow these steps to guard against trouble:

- **Don't judge reliability by a professional or flashy Web site.** Anyone with a few dollars can create, register, and promote a Web site. Remember that a Web site can be used as another form of advertising.

- **Remember that people in cyberspace may not always be what they seem.** That nice young man who encouraged you to pay to be a distributor in her company may, in fact, be a criminal with a long arrest record for fraud. Before you part with any money, make sure the company is for real.

- **Be careful with whom you share your financial or other personal information.** Don't provide your bank account, credit card, social security number, or other personal information unless you know the company is legitimate and the information is necessary for the transaction.

- **If a deal seems too good to be true, it probably is.** Some Internet marketers show pictures of expensive items like purses and watches, but send you a fake. You're not likely to spend $25 online for a "real" French designer bag that retails for $650 at the mall.

- **Pay for your Internet purchases with a credit card.** If a Web merchant asks for cash, think twice before sending the money. Most legitimate Web merchants offer secure buying sites so your credit card information is protected. If the merchandise turns out to be damaged or sub-standard, your credit card company may be able to help you go back against the merchant.

Groups on Your Side

The Internet is rapidly becoming a daily part of business, communications, and the transfer of information. In a very short time span, the Internet has become a part of daily life. If your Internet experience leaves you shaken and upset, you have several places to turn.

First, remember that your local police can provide invaluable assistance against Internet criminals. The police can't do anything until you contact them, so don't be afraid to let them know if you feel threatened. Even if they can't send a squad car to catch the criminal, most local law enforcement agencies have a good handle on Internet crime.

Your ISP can also be your best advocate on the Internet. If you feel you've been scammed or you're receiving harassing email, make sure your ISP knows about what's going on. Additionally, make sure that your ISP has a Privacy Policy that states clearly that they will not share your name and personal information with anyone.

The following Web sites are Internet powerhouses in the area of keeping you safe. Visit them for more information.

Call the cops

Many local law enforcement agencies have pamphlets and other information on Internet crime. Consider giving them a call to see what they might have available for you.

- The Better Business Bureau at www.bbbonline.org is always there for you, the consumer. Offered at the site are helpful consumer tips, advice for safe surfing, and a searchable of index of BBB Online Participants.

- The Americans for Consumer Privacy at www.computerprivacy. org has a wealth of information that can help keep you safe. You can even join their organization by filling out a form (secure, of course!) at the site.

- The Internet Fraud Watch (www.fraud.org/ifw.htm) is on patrol for you. The site, shown in Figure 4.12, has links to information, tips, statistics, and even a way to report Internet fraud. Best of all, you can call a toll-free number instead of sending an email.

FIGURE 4.12
The Internet Fraud Watch page provides valuable information.

① Click a menu link to find out more.

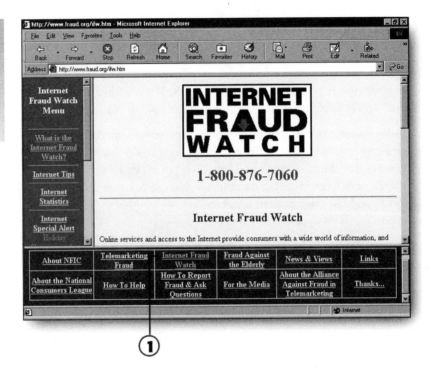

part

II

TAKING CONTROL OF THE INTERNET

5

Let the Browsing Begin

Learning about URLs •

Returning to sites you've viewed before •

Navigating through frames •

Printing and saving Web pages •

The Address Is Everything

Say what?

The term "URL" is usually pronounced by saying each letter. However, some people talk about Web addresses as "earls". Folks in the Midwest sometimes call it a "yurl". However, you pronounce it, a URL always means a Web address.

It seems like everyone has a Web site these days. Most major companies have a presence on the Web. Your favorite television news show or soap opera might have a site. Even your friends and relatives can have Web sites. Every site on the Web is identified by its own unique name.

The Web address of each site is called a *URL*, short for Uniform Resource Locator. A URL is broken up by periods, called dots, and can contain letters, slashes, and other punctuation. Although the characters in a URL might look like they've been placed in a hit-and-miss fashion, each and every symbol and group of letters and numbers has its own function.

The first page of a Web site is called its *home page*. A site can have just one page called the home page, or it can have many pages that are linked to the main (home) page. Think of a home page as a front door to the rest of the site.

SEE ALSO

➤ *Interested in creating your own Web site? You'll learn how on page 487*

When you're typing a URL, it's important to type it with every dot, slash, and colon in place. If one of the characters is typed incorrectly when you're entering a Web address in the Address box of your browser, you'll see the wrong page or, worse, an error message instead of the page you expected.

Breaking Down a URL

URLs can seem like a confusing blend of unpronounceable letters and punctuation. However, when you break down a URL into parts, it's easy to understand. Take the following URL:

```
http://www.mcp.com
```

The `http://` portion is called the *protocol type* and identifies the document as a Web site. (You probably haven't come across any yet, but other protocols on the Internet include `ftp://` or `telnet://`.) Protocol types define the ways computers communicate with one another. Fortunately, your Web browser does all of the work of setting up the appropriate method of communication after it reads the protocol type. In fact, when you're typing a URL, you can omit the http:// portion, as you'll find later in this chapter.

The `www` portion of the name indicates that this is the Web managing portion of the computer called `mcp.com` (the `http://` portion off the name already identified it as a Web page), which is the actual computer at the domain that's running the server.

The dot (.) character joins each element of the address. The dot character is pronounced *dot*.

The `mcp` portion of the name is unique and can be defined by the group or person who selected it. In the case of `mcp`, the letters stand for Macmillan Computer Publishing. The name can be short and abbreviated, or long and descriptive. For example, a friend of mine opened a Web business and used `candylandwarehouse` in this portion of the name. Depending on where the domain name is obtained, you might not be able to choose this portion. For example, if your ISP allows you to set up a personal Web page, your URL will probably be something like `www.myisp.com/~yourname`.

The `com` portion of the name is probably the most familiar; you've heard the phrase *dot com* before. `com`, the three letter extension called the top-level *domain*, indicates that the page is registered to a commercial user or that the Web host that stores the page is a commercial institution.

When you put all the elements together, the URL `http://www.mcp.com` makes sense!

What's in a Name

In the example of Macmillan Computer Publishing's URL, the `www`, `mcp`, and `com` portions combine to form a *domain name*. Customized names, like Macmillan's, need to be registered with a special Internet agency, after they've been researched to make sure that the name is unique. After they're registered, these names need to be paid for every year to keep them active.

Domain names are spoken just the way they're read. For example, because the letters `www` or `mcp` don't form a word that someone could say, the names of the letters are used instead. However, in my friend's case, the portion of the virtual domain name that reads candyland-warehouse is spoken as one, long word.

If you want to tell someone a URL, follow a few simples rule to say it correctly. Whenever you see a period (.), say the word *dot*. A forward slash (/) is referred to as slash, a colon character(:), as colon. If the letters in the name form a word that can't be pronounced, pronounce each letter name.

Com Is Only One of Many

The most common domain names end with .com (dot com). Although you're familiar with the domain name com, there are actually five more domain names. Table 5.1 lists each domain name and provides a little information about them.

Table 5.1 Common domain names

Name	What It Means
com	The site or the host of the site is a commercial enterprise.
net	Most .net sites are part of a network. Your ISP may use a .net domain name.
gov	The site is owned by a U.S. governmental agency.
edu	Educational institutions use .edu as their domain name.
mil	.mil is a tip that the site is owned by the U.S. military.
org	There's a good chance that the site is owned by a non-profit organization.

Also used, although less often, by state and local government agencies, libraries, museums, non-edu schools, and individuals is .us. When .us is the top-level domain, it is usually preceded by a state code—the same two-letter abbreviation used by the U.S. Post Office.

The three letters of the domain name can be followed by another dot (period) and then a two-letter country code. If you don't see a country code, the domain is probably located somewhere in the United States.

New Domain Names

Although there are six domain names, `com` is drastically overloaded. Because `com` denotes that either the owner of the name or the Web server that stores the Web page is a commercial enterprise, it's often difficult to determine who owns a page that uses a com domain. (For example, a service called Geocities provides free space for personal home pages to over one million users. Each of those pages uses the URL **www.geocities.com** as part of their address.) Additionally, there just aren't enough com names to accommodate all the requests for registration. Fortunately, seven new domain names are in the works.

The new top-level domain names will be as follows:

- *.web*. Web-related
- *.firm*. business
- *.arts*. art and culture-related
- *.info*. information services
- *.rec*. recreation and entertainment-related
- *.store*. a business offering goods for sale
- *.nom*. of personal or individual nature

In fact, the whole structure for assigning and registering domain names is changing. A company called Network Solutions, working from an exclusive contact from the National Science Foundation, was handling domain name registrations. Recently, the government opened up the Internet domain name registration business to competition. The first new registrar was Register.com, a New York-based division of Forman Interactive Corp. Other companies include America Online; CORE, a U.S.-based consortium of small international registry firms; Oleane, a subsidiary of France Telecom; and Melbourne IT of Australia.

Currently, the distinction between `.com`, `.net`, and `.org` names is fading. `.com` is still the most popular—in the first three months of 1999, Network Solutions registered over 1 million new `.com` names. Because `.com` is so overloaded, it's often impossible to get the name you want. However, that same name may be available with a different domain suffix.

Can't get enough

Country codes can be a little tricky to decipher if you're not a geography major or you don't have an atlas nearby. Here are a few of the country codes used in domain names: **au** for Australia, **ca** for Canada, **de** for Germany, and **iq** and **ir** for Iraq and Iran, respectively. The code **kp** indicates North Korea while **kr** denotes South Korea. The Scandinavian countries of Norway, Sweden, Finland, and Denmark ring in with **no**, **se**, **fi**, and **dk**. Finally, you might see **il** (Israel), **cn** (China), **jp** (Japan), or **uk** (United Kingdom).

Yours or mine?

In most of the exercises in this chapter, I suggest Web addresses that you can use to perform the steps. If you have other addresses you'd like to use, please feel free to substitute yours for mine. After all, I want you to feel comfortable using the Web, not hung up looking at sites you don't want to see.

Big business

Some forward-thinking business people registered as many domain names as possible when the Internet was in its infancy. Later on, companies like Coca-Cola were surprised to find that the domain names that matched their corporate or logo were already taken. The owners of the domain names were willing to sell their interests in the name, for a huge price.

A huge court battle ensued. Since Internet law is evolving and has few precedents, no one was sure how the courts would rule. Ultimately, the courts ruled that cybersquatter rights don't exist in cyberspace. The owners of registered trademarks were entitled to use those trademark names in their domain names. The individuals who had registered the names had to give them up to their rightful owners.

Still, domain name registration is a big business. Some organizations contain "think tanks" where workers are paid to come up with variations on every domain name under the sun. The buying and selling of those names has created a new niche in the business world.

In the future, three things are expected to simplify the registration of domain names and drive down the price. More places to register, the graying of distinction between the top three suffixes, and a set of new domain suffixes will make registration in the near future as easy as putting a name in a phone book.

Entering URLs

Typing URLs into the Address box of your browser is a common way of moving around the Web. Most big companies have recognizable domain names. If you're not sure about a company's Web address, you might try typing `www.companyname.com` and seeing what comes up. Odds are that you'll probably get lucky and find the site you're looking for at least 50% of the time.

Entering URLs

1. Connect to the Internet and open your browser.

2. When your start page appears, click inside the box at the top of the screen that displays a Web address. (the text will begin with `http://`). The address appears highlighted.

3. Type the following URL carefully, `www.bigbus.co.uk`, or another URL you know, and press **Enter**. (If you're using Internet Explorer 5.0, you can click the **Go** button instead of pressing **Enter**.) Your browser contacts the server that stores the page and, in a moment, a new Web page appears on the screen.

4. Look carefully at the URL in the Address box. Even though you didn't type the `http://` portion, your browser filled it in for you.

5. You can use menu commands to move to a new site. (You might want to use the menu method if the toolbar that displays Web addresses is hidden from view.) If you're using Internet Explorer, click **File** and choose **Open**. Navigator's command reads **Open Page**.

6. An Open dialog box, similar to the one shown in Figure 5.1, appears. (If you're using Navigator, your dialog looks slightly different, but contains the same basic components.) Type another URL in the Open text box. If you want, type `www.royal.gov.uk`.

FIGURE 5.1
The Open dialog box.

If the URL contains mixed case (upper- and lowercase) letters or punctuation, type it exactly as it appears. Depending on where the page is stored, you might not be able to access it otherwise.

7. If you're using the Internet Explorer browser, click **OK**. If you're using Navigator, click **Open**. The dialog box closes and, in a moment, a new Web page appears.

8. Both Internet Explorer and Navigator enable you to type a portion of the URL and let the browser search the Web for the page you want. Click inside the Address box and highlight the URL that's shown in the box.

9. Type `royalfamily` and press **Enter**. Although it takes a few seconds longer than if you had typed the complete URL, your browser displays the Royal Families of the World page.

   Keep in mind that this feature, although handy, can't always find the page you're looking for. Sometimes there are too many pages that match the letters you typed and, instead of the page you were expecting, you see a list of possible matches. Other times, the wrong page (usually one that holds no interest for you) is accessed. Play it safe. If you know the complete URL, type it to be assured of opening the exact page you want.

10. Your browser remembers the URLs of sites you visited previously and helps you return to those sites. As soon as the Royal Families of the World page is done loading, click inside the Address box. When the URL in the box appears highlighted, type about six characters of one of the URLs you typed previously, for example, `www.bigbus`, and wait for a few seconds.

    If you're using Navigator, your browser fills in the rest of the line with a URL that matches what you've typed so far.

> **Using the Stop button**
>
> If you change your mind after your browser begins to access the new page, or if you realize you've made a typo, click the **Stop** button on the toolbar to stop the transfer.

Internet Explorer users see a drop-down list of sites that match the letters you typed, as shown in Figure 5.2.

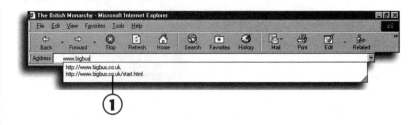

If the portion filled in by Navigator isn't correct or the site you want is not displayed on the Internet Explorer list, continue typing the URL letter by letter until your browser displays the URL you want, or you finish typing.

11. Navigator users press **Enter** to return to the Web page that matches the URL shown in the box. If you're using Internet Explorer, choose the site from the list of sites that match what you typed so far. In a moment, the page you want to see appears.

12. After you've looked around, click the **Back** button on the toolbar to open the page you were viewing previously.

13. Click the **Back** button again. You're stepped back one more page that you've visited.

14. Right-click the **Forward** button on the toolbar to display a list of sites you've seen in the current session and select one from the list to return to that site.

    Each time you click the **Back** or **Forward** buttons, you're returned to the site you viewed previously during your current browsing session. If you want to get back to a site that you visited awhile ago, clicking the arrow on the button to display the list of sites helps you get back to where you want to go without having to revisit many sites.

15. Click the **Home** button on your browser's toolbar to return to your starting page.

Working with Hyperlinks

So far, you've moved around the Web by typing the URLs of the sites that you want to see. While this navigation method has worked so far, it's not the most effective way to move around. As you saw in the previous exercise, some Web sites don't have straightforward, easy-to-remember addresses. If you were required to remember every URL you wanted to visit, your brain would become overloaded very soon. Fortunately, hyperlinks whisk you from place to place on the Web.

No matter which browser you use, you'll spend a lot of time moving around the Web with hyperlinks. Think of hyperlinks as the glue that connects Web pages. Your mouse pointer takes the shape of a hand when it passes over a hyperlink. Most of the time, hyperlinks, or links for short, appear in Web pages as underlined, colored text or graphics. Links are easy to follow; click one and you're moved to the linked site.

Links work the same way on every browser. Most text links are displayed in blue before you click them. As soon as you click a link, its color changes to purple, letting you know that you've already visited the linked site. Why is this important? When you've looked at one Web site after another as you search for a particular piece of information, it's helpful to know if the site is one you've already visited. (Sometimes, you can visit hundreds of sites in one Web session.) However, using the color method to track where you've been isn't always effective. Many Web designers override this feature and make sure that the color of visited links does not change from their original color.

Traveling with links

1. If you're not on the Internet, connect now and open your browser by clicking the **Start** button and opening it from the Windows Start menu.

2. When the browser is launched and displaying a Web site, click inside the box near the top of the screen that contains a Web address so that the text in the box appears highlighted.

SEE ALSO

➤ *To learn more about Web addresses, see page 112*

> **You "cache" on quick!**
> When you access a Web page by clicking the **Back** or **Forward** button, the page loads much faster than it did the first time you opened it. Called a *cache* (pronounced cash), your browser stores Web pages you've seen recently on the hard drive of your computer. Instead of actually going to the server and fetching the page again, the browser quickly brings it back from the cache when you click **Back** or **Forward**. If you think the page has changed since the last time you saw it, click the **Refresh** button in Internet Explorer or the **Reload** button in Navigator.

> **Find out where you're going**
> If you want to know where a link will take you, point to the link with your mouse and note the address of the Web site in the status bar at the bottom of the screen.

Watch what you type
You need to type carefully when you're typing a URL. Typing the wrong letters or the incorrect domain can bring a surprise to your screen. For example, typing **www.whitehouse. net** accesses a spoof site of the White House. The .com domain suffix would bring up a pornographic site totally unsuitable for children.

3. Type the following Web address in the box and press **Enter**:
   www.whitehouse.gov

4. Watch the status bar at the bottom left of the screen as the page is accessed. In a short time, the status bar displays a message indicating that the page is loaded on the screen.

5. Place your mouse pointer in the top-right corner of the browser window and slowly move the pointer around the screen. As you move the pointer down, notice that its shape changes to a hand, which signifies a link, as it passes over different parts of the screen.

6. Position the mouse over one of the graphic images on the page. The pointer assumes the shape of a hand, telling you that the image is a hyperlink. Additionally, a screen tip that describes the link appears, as shown in Figure 5.3.

FIGURE 5.3
Underlined, colored text generally indicates a hyperlink.

(1) The hand indicates that the text is a link.

(2) The location of the link is displayed in the status bar.

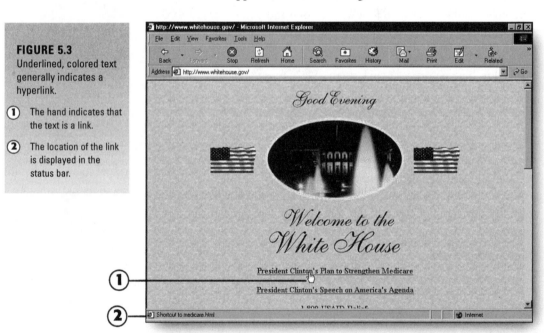

7. Place the mouse pointer over some colored, underlined text on the page so that the mouse pointer's shape changes to a hand.

8. Click the underlined text and, in a moment, a new page appears on the screen.

Clicking a Non-Working Link

It happens to everyone who spends any time on the Web. You click a link (generally to a site that really looks exciting) and, instead of seeing the new page on the screen, you see an error message. If you're like most people, you back up and try the link again, assuming that you've done something wrong.

Actually, invalid links are the closest thing to a Web epidemic. There are many reasons why clicking a link fails to bring up the expected page. The most common reason is that the page the link refers to has been taken off the Web or its been moved to a new location. Sadly, it happens all the time. If you click a link and see an error message instead of the linked page, don't be alarmed. It wasn't your fault. The Web needs to find a way to clean up after itself.

Table 5.2 contains a list of common error messages associated with invalid or failed links, what they mean, and what you can do.

Link anchor

Hyperlinks connect locations on the Web. The portion of the link that causes the mouse arrow to change shape is called a *link anchor*.

Table 5.2 Failed links

Error Message	What It Means	Possible Solutions
Error 404 or File not Found	The page has moved to a new location or has been removed from the Web.	There's not much you can do when you see this type of message. The link you clicked refers to a page that's been removed or relocated.
A connection to the server could not be established or Server not responding	The problem can be at your end or on the server that hosts the linked page.	Check to see if you've accidentally been disconnected from the Internet. If not, try clicking the link again. If you receive the same message, you know that the host server isn't available right now. Try the page later.
Unauthorized entry refused	You don't have permission to view the page.	Not all pages are open to all; maybe the page requires a username and password. If you're accessing the Internet from your office, the network administrator might have declared the site off-limits.

continues...

Table 5.2 Continued

Error Message	What It Means	Possible Solutions
Too many users, try again later. or Connection refused by host	Too many people are simultaneously trying to access the site.	Wait a bit and try again later.
Document contains no data or Protocol l in this address is invalid	The address you clicked is incorrect.	If the address has a specific page listed, remove the reference to that page and try again. For example, if the address in the Address box is something like http://www.barbaracom/books.htm, delete the books.htm portion and then try to connect.

Using Your Browser's History

Until now, you've moved around the Web by clicking links and typing URLs. In the last exercise, you visited several Web sites by typing their URLs. If you were asked to repeat the URLs you typed, you probably couldn't remember each one. Chances are, though, that you remember something about one of the sites that makes you want to go back and take a second look.

As you learned earlier in this chapter, you can use the **Back** and **Forward** buttons on the toolbar to return to sites you've visited during the current Web session. However, after you quit the browser, the history stored in the **Back** and **Forward** buttons is cleared. Unless you remembered the specific URL or the location of the link you clicked to find it the first time, a visited Web site would be difficult to return to.

Both browsers maintain a running tally of the last 15 or so URLs that you've typed into the Address box. (The URLs of pages you visited via hyperlink don't appear here.) To display the list, click the down arrow next to the right of the Address box. Click the URL you want to revisit from the list. Figure 5.4 shows the list of sites I visited by typing the URLs into my browser.

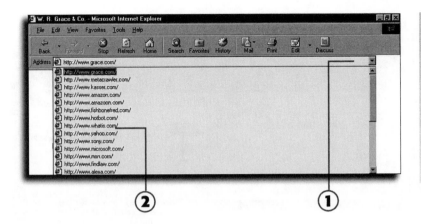

FIGURE 5.4
The last URLs you typed
are displayed.

① Click the down arrow
   to open the list.

② The last URLs, includ-
   ing ones with typo-
   graphical errors,
   appear in the list.

Fortunately, both Navigator and Internet Explorer store your complete browsing history for you. You can use the history to quickly
find and revisit sites that you've seen before, no matter how you
accessed them. Navigator provides a flat, text history that opens
in a separate window. Internet Explorer displays your history in
an Explorer bar that has a more graphical look.

Viewing a History of Links and Sites in Internet Explorer

Internet Explorer saves a list of the sites you visited previously. The
sites are arranged by date and then in folders arranged by domain
names. Individual pages are arranged in their respective folders.

SEE ALSO

➤ *Review information about domain names on page 113*

The Internet Explorer bars provide a way for you to look through a
page of links on the left side of the screen, like your History, while
displaying the links to which the pages refer on the right. You see an
Explorer bar when you click the **History**, **Search**, or **Favorites** buttons on the Standard Buttons toolbar.

When you display the History Explorer bar, shown in Figure 5.5, the
screen splits into two panes—the page you were viewing is shown on
the right and the History bar appears on the left. The bar holds folders that hold links to sites and individual pages visited in previous
weeks and days.

Resize the window

The History Explorer bar is
displayed in its own pane
on the Internet Explorer
screen. You can make the
bar bigger or smaller,
according to your needs
and preferences. Position
your mouse pointer on the
right edge of the bar so
that the pointer appears in
the shape of a double-
sided arrow. Click and drag
the two-headed arrow in
the direction you want to
resize the bar. Release the
mouse button and, voilà,
the Explorer bar has been
resized.

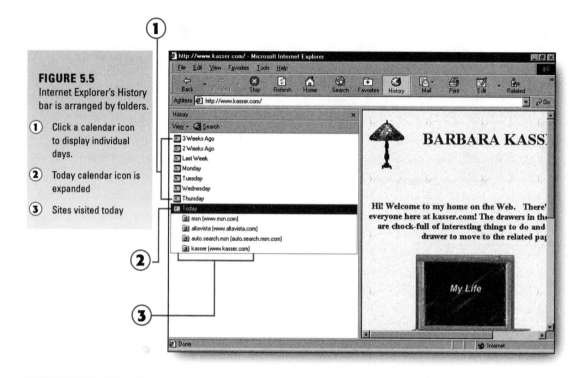

FIGURE 5.5

Internet Explorer's History bar is arranged by folders.

(1) Click a calendar icon to display individual days.

(2) Today calendar icon is expanded

(3) Sites visited today

Expand and contract

If you've visited a lot of Web sites, clicking one day's folder icon can fill the History pane and make the other days disappear. Simply click the day again to hide the pages beneath it. Both the calendar icons and Web folder icons work like a toggle switch. One click expands and a second click causes the folder to contract, or fold up.

The folders are arranged in a hierarchical structure of weeks and then top-level Web sites. Click a calendar icon to display individual days. Then click the day's calendar icon to display the Web sites you visited on that day.

When you click a Web folder, the individual pages you visited at the site are displayed by name, as shown in Figure 5.6. Internet Explorer displays the page name that's been assigned by the person who designed the page, so sometimes the names are not easy to decipher. For example, a search results page may show something like "detail.asp" followed by a series of letters. If you want to see the exact location of the page shown in your History, point to the link and hold the mouse still for a moment. A screen tip pops up, displaying the location in the status bar.

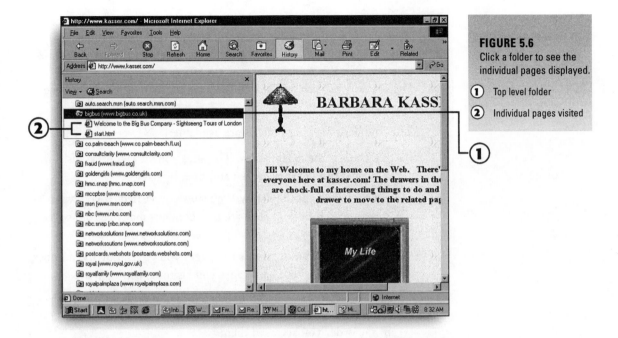

FIGURE 5.6
Click a folder to see the individual pages displayed.

① Top level folder

② Individual pages visited

If you want to know more about your previous visit, such as the time you accessed the page or graphic image, right-click it on the Explorer History bar. Choose **Properties** from the resulting shortcut menu. The Properties dialog box appears (see Figure 5.7) and displays the time and date the page was last accessed.

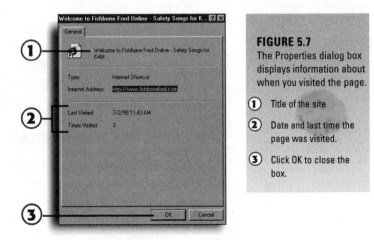

FIGURE 5.7
The Properties dialog box displays information about when you visited the page.

① Title of the site

② Date and last time the page was visited.

③ Click OK to close the box.

The History Explorer bar makes it easy to find sites that you've viewed previously. Internet Explorer makes the History bar even more user-friendly by providing you with some additional, customizable options. You can change how the sites are displayed on the History bar. You can also search through the listed sites for the one you want to find.

The following viewing options are available:

- **By Date** is the default view. The sites you viewed previously are arranged in folders by weeks and then by days.
- **By Site** arranges the list by Web sites you visited. If you want to find a specific page in a site that contains many related pages (like the Microsoft or Netscape sites), choose this view.
- **By Most Visited** organizes the pages you've seen by the number of times you visited. The pages you visited most often are displayed at the top of the list.
- **By Order Visited Today** shows the pages you visited today in the order you accessed them.

In addition to changing the view of History bar, you can search through the list of sites and pages you've seen. Click the **Search** icon on the History bar and type what you're looking for into the **Search for** text box. Enter a few words of the title of the Web page or its URL. Click the **Search Now** button to display a list of matching sites.

Whenever you find a page you want to return to, click the page on the History list. In a few seconds, the page you requested opens in the browser window on the right side of the screen. To close the Explorer History bar, click the **Close (X)** button on the right side of the bar.

No result

When you search through the list of sites you've seen, you'll need to know a portion of the URL or page title. Internet Explorer can't look through all the text and graphics on the pages you've seen before.

Change the Tracking Interval

Internet Explorer is set to track your browsing history for the last 20 days. Most folks won't ever need to change this interval. However, you can increase or decrease the period that Internet Explorer uses to track your browsing history. Here's how:

Adjusting Internet Explorer's history tracking interval

1. Click the Internet Explorer **Tools** menu and choose **Internet Options** to open the Internet Options dialog box. If the General tab is not selected, click **General**.

2. The History option, shown in Figure 5.8, is located in the third section of the dialog box. Click the spin arrows to change the number of days displayed.

Take control

You can open the Internet Options dialog box when you're not using Internet Explorer. Simply open the Windows **Control Panel** and choose **Internet Options** from the list.

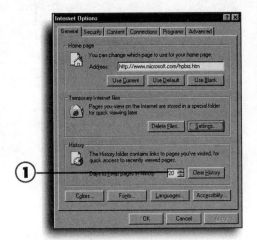

FIGURE 5.8
The Internet Options dialog box displays information about when you visited the page.

① Click these arrows to increase or decrease the time period that your browsing history is stored.

3. Click **OK** to save your changes and close the Internet Options dialog box.

Using Navigator's History Feature

When you access your Navigator History window, you're presented with the title, location (URL), dates visited, and other information about Web sites you've visited. Additionally, the Navigator History window enables you to search for a particular keyword or portion of a URL. The search function is especially helpful if your history is too large to look through or you don't want to spend time finding a particular site.

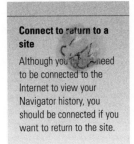

Connect to return to a site

Although you won't need to be connected to the Internet to view your Navigator history, you should be connected if you want to return to the site.

To open the History window, click the **Communicator** menu and then **Tools** and **History**. Your Navigator History list appears in a small window that's layered over the Navigator screen, as shown in Figure 5.9. Notice that in addition to opening on the screen, a History button appears on the Windows taskbar.

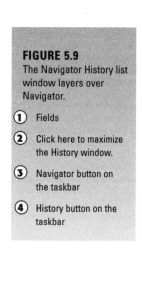

FIGURE 5.9
The Navigator History list window layers over Navigator.

① Fields

② Click here to maximize the History window.

③ Navigator button on the taskbar

④ History button on the taskbar

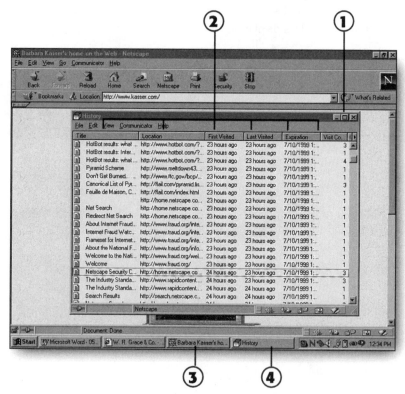

The small size of the Navigator History window makes it hard to read. You can maximize the window to make the History window fill the screen. Even when you maximize the window, the titles of the sites you've visited appear truncated and can be impossible to understand. If you can't see all the information in a field, hold your mouse pointer over the truncated information. In a moment, a *screen tip* appears that displays all the information in the field.

By default, the History list is arranged in last date visited order. However, you can rearrange the order of the list with a few mouse clicks. Click the **View** menu and choose from one of the options on the drop-down menu, as shown in Figure 5.10. Additionally, you can choose an option to sort by in ascending (the standard) or descending order.

FIGURE 5.10
Click a menu selection to change the organization of the History list.

(**1**) Bullet indicates current selection

Sooner or later, your memory will fail. Something about a site you've visited will haunt you, but you won't remember the location of the site or when you saw it. Fortunately, your Navigator History is searchable.

So long as you can remember a word in its title or a portion of its URL, you can search for a site on the History list. Click **Edit** and then choose **Search History List**. The Search History List dialog box appears, as shown in Figure 5.11.

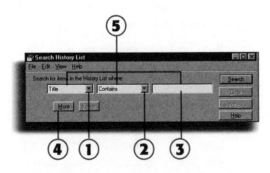

FIGURE 5.11
Use the Search History List dialog box to find a specific site on your History list.

(**1**) Click here to select another field.

(**2**) Click here to select another operator.

(**3**) Type the keyword here.

(**4**) Click here to add additional fields and operators to the search.

(**5**) Fields

The box currently reads "**Search in the History List where the Title Contains**". **Title** is the default field to be searched and the default operator is **Contains**. If you want to search for another field or use another operator, like **Doesn't contain, Is** or **Isn't**, click the down arrow next to the item you wish to change and choose a new one from the drop-down list.

Navigator opens in a separate window

If you're going back and forth between the Navigator and the History window, it's easy to lose your place. The **View** menu in the History window enables you to change the way the History list is displayed. If you click **View** and see choices like **Increase Font** or **Refresh**, you're in the Navigator window. Click the button labeled **History** on the Windows taskbar to make History the active window.

Computer slow-down

If Navigator is running in more than one window on your computer, such as when you open a site from the History list, you might notice that your system seems sluggish and non-responsive. Close one of the Navigator windows to conserve valuable system resources.

Type the keyword, such as a word you remember from the Web page title or a portion of the URL, in the empty text box next to the operator. If you want to add an additional field to look through, click **More**. When you've set up the boxes correctly, click **Search**.

Navigator looks through the History list. In a few moments, the Web sites that match the criteria you specified are displayed. When you've located the entry for the site you want to revisit, double-click its name or location. The corresponding page opens in a new Navigator window. Notice that two Navigator buttons now appear on the Windows taskbar.

If you searched for a site on your History list, you'll need to close the Search window by clicking the **Close** button located at the right of the History window title bar. Ditto for the History window; close the History list when you you're done looking through it.

Dealing with Frames

As you tool around the Web, visiting pages, you're bound to come across a page that contains *frames*. Frames enable a Web designer to split a page into multiple rectangular sections, each with its own function and look.

Both browsers support the use of frames. Frames can be used as menu bars, as a way to add visual excitement to a page, and as means for making a lot of different information available on one page. Because each frame is actually a separate Web page, you can move up and down in one frame while the other frames stay still.

Look at the example of a page with frames shown in Figure 5.12. Two Web pages, each with its own scrolling capability, are combined into one page. If you move through one of the frames with the vertical scrollbar, the other frame will remain constant. In this case, frames enable you to actually see two pages on one screen.

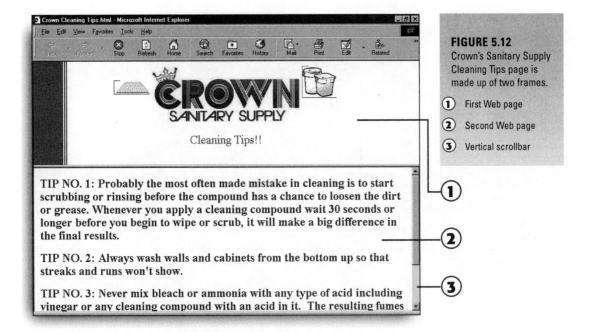

FIGURE 5.12
Crown's Sanitary Supply
Cleaning Tips page is
made up of two frames.

1 First Web page

2 Second Web page

3 Vertical scrollbar

Sometimes frames aren't obvious. In Figure 5.13, one frame holds a menu bar that provides links to related pages at the Palace Bleu Hotel's site, like Reservation or Amenities. When you click one of the links on the frame at the left, the larger frame to the right displays the content you requested.

Frame navigation can be tricky. Because each frame on a page acts as its own page, clicking the **Back** and **Forward** buttons might not take you out of the page that's on the screen. Instead, you cycle through the frames that make up the page.

If you feel like you can't get out of a page that contains frames, don't get frustrated. Position the mouse pointer in your browser's Back button and click the right mouse button to display a list of page titles you've visited. Choose the title of the page you want to revisit from the list.

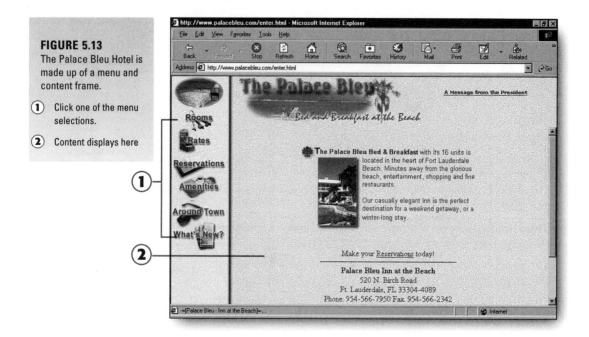

FIGURE 5.13
The Palace Bleu Hotel is made up of a menu and content frame.

① Click one of the menu selections.

② Content displays here

Completing Forms

SEE ALSO

➤ *You learn all about searching for Web sites on page 137*

Printing a Web Page

When the exact page you're looking for appears on the screen, you might want to print it. After all, what good is a recipe for ceviche with onions, pepper flakes, and cilantro if it's displayed on your computer screen and not in your kitchen? Fortunately, if your computer is connected to a printer, you can print any Web page you see.

Sometimes printing one Web page results in your printer spitting out sheet after sheet. That's because Web "pages" are not really pages, like the ones you create with your favorite word processing program. Instead, Web pages have no logical bottom. Remember how you've had to use your scrollbar to move to the bottom of a Web page? That page, and others like it, might translate to several printed sheets.

Your browser's print function runs through Windows. If you're familiar with printing from other programs within Windows, you'll find that the procedure for printing from your browser is very similar. Before you begin this exercise, your browser should be visible on the screen.

Printing what you want

1. Click the **File** menu and choose **Print**. The Print dialog box appears, similar to the one shown in Figure 5.14.

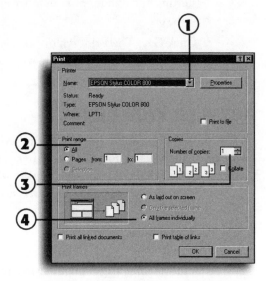

FIGURE 5.14
The Print dialog box provides many printing options.

(1) Name of your printer should be displayed here

(2) Select page range.

(3) Choose number of copies here.

(4) Frames section is only available if the page contains frames

2. If the current page contains Frames, Internet Explorer provides a **Print Frames** section in the Print dialog box that enables you to control which frames are printed. Click the **Option** button next to the selection that best describes the way you want the frames to appear: **As laid out on screen**, **Only the selected frame**, or **All frames individually**.

   For Navigator users, click inside the frame you want to print, and choose **Print Frame** from the **File** menu. (The Print option will not be available.)

3. Verify that the correct printer is selected in the **Name** box. If not, click the down arrow to open the list of installed printers and select the correct printer.

133

4. If you want more than one copy, use the spin controls to change the number of copies.

5. If you're printing more than one copy of a lengthy page, check the **Co̱llate** button to ensure that you'll get each set of copies in numbered page order. (Otherwise, you'll print all of the copies of page one, then all the copies of page two, and so on.)

6. Depending on what you want to print, click the **Option** button next to **A̱ll**, or **Pages**. If you choose the **Pages** option, fill in a starting and ending page number in the corresponding **f̱rom** and **ṯo** boxes.

7. Click **OK**. The Print dialog box closes and, in a moment, you have a printed version of the page on your screen.

Saving a Web Page

Both browsers allow you to save any Web page to the hard drive of your computer or to a diskette. After you've saved a page, you can open your browser and view the page while you're *not* connected to the Internet. Because a saved page is just like any other Windows document, you can move it, delete it, or store it indefinitely.

You need to understand how a page is constructed before you save it. Most of the pages you look at consist of text and graphic images, or pictures. Some pages might even have other elements, like sound clips. In order to reconstruct the page after you've saved it, you need to save not only the text portion of the page, but each other element as well.

Saving Web documents

1. Connect to the Internet and open your browser. Find a Web page that you want to save.

2. With the page you want to save visible on the screen, click the **F̱ile** menu and choose **S̱ave As**. (If you're viewing a page with frames in Navigator, select **Save F̱rame As** instead.) The Save Web Page dialog box appears, as displayed in Figure 5.15.

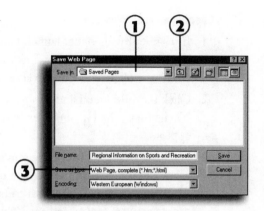

FIGURE 5.15
Save the page so you
can view it later.

① Save in box displays
the name of the cur-
rent folder.

② Up One Level button

③ File type is displayed
here.

3. Navigate to the folder in which you want to store your saved documents. (If you're using a folder on the desktop, click the **Up One Level** button on the Save As dialog box toolbar until desktop is visible in the **Save in** box. Find the folder you want, and double-click it to open it.)

4. Click in the **File name** box and type a descriptive name for the Web page. Alternatively, accept the page title that's already displayed in the box.

5. Make sure that the letters HTML appear in the **Save as type** box. If they don't, click the down arrow next to the file type that's currently showing and choose **HTML** from the list.

6. Click **Save**. You've saved the text portion of the Web page.

7. Now you need to save each graphic image. Position your mouse pointer on the first graphic image and right-click. Choose **Save Picture As** (Internet Explorer) or **Save Image As** (Navigator).

8. The folder in which you saved the text portion of the page should appear. If it doesn't, navigate to the folder by following the directions in step 3.

9. Because your browser identifies the filename and type, don't change the filename and file type. Click **Save**. The image is saved to your computer.

10. Repeat steps 7, 8, and 9 to save each graphic image on the page.

Opening a saved Web page

1. If it's not already open, launch your browser. (If you're not connected to the Internet, click the **Stop** button to prevent your browser from trying to access your home page.)

2. Click the **File** menu and choose **Open** (**Open Page** in Navigator). The Open (**Open Page** in Navigator) dialog box appears.

3. Navigate to the folder where you saved the Web page and related graphics with the Browse button and choose the file. Alternatively, type in the path to the file, such as C:\WINDOWS\ DESKTOP\SAVED PAGES\ and then type the filename. When you're through, the box that contains the filename and folder location should look similar to the one shown in Figure 5.16.

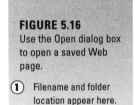

FIGURE 5.16
Use the Open dialog box to open a saved Web page.

① Filename and folder location appear here.

4. If you're using Internet Explorer, click **OK**. If you're using Navigator, click **Open**. In a moment, the saved page appears on your screen.

Making Your Way on the Web

Customizing your browser ●

Creating a custom Start page ●

Keeping a List of your favorite Web sites ●

Viewing related sites ●

Have It Your Way

Now that you've been using the Web for a bit, you'd probably like to be able to personalize your Internet experience. For one, you might want to change the first page that appears when you open your browser. Additionally, you might want to change the appearance of a page when it's displayed on the screen. The Web and your browser team up to make it easy for you to have it your way.

Changing the Start Page

Your *Start page* appears each time you open your browser. You also see your Start page when you click the **Home** button on the toolbar. In the Web's old days (a few short years ago) the Start page was simply considered your home base and wasn't very exciting. Now, however, Start pages are tailored to your personal needs and can be fully customizable. My personal EarthLink Start page is shown in Figure 6.1.

FIGURE 6.1
The EarthLink Start page displays links and customized information.

(1) Personal information

(2) Advertising

(3) Links

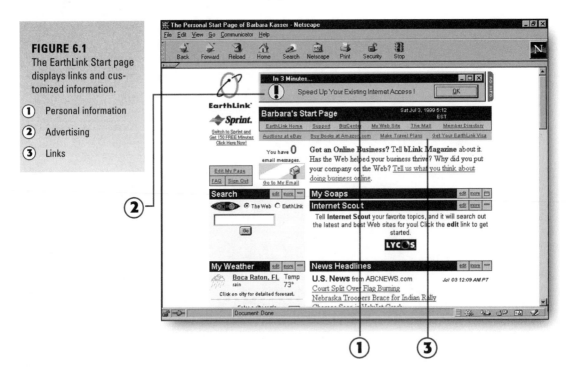

Start pages have become big business for many companies and ISPs. Most Start pages contain a wide variety of features, such as links to search engines, stock quotes, news and weather, and such other information. Many Start pages also display advertising in the form of *banner ads*. Start pages can be a source of revenue and advertising dollars. The fact that millions of people log into a particular site each day—like the My Netscape or MSN pages or the one offered by your ISP, offers the potential for a lot of exposure for advertisers.

SEE ALSO

➤ *Custom Start pages work by storing your preferences in the cookies file on the hard drive of your computer. Read more about cookies on page 89*

The term *portal* is used to describe pages with many links to advertisers and other useful features. You'll find portal sites all over the Web, both in customizable Start pages and at many search services and search engines.

Setting Up Your Own Custom Page

Why not customize your own Start page? Once you've gotten the page just the way you like it, you'll have a tailor-made way to view the information that's important to you whenever you open your browser. If your browser currently opens to the Microsoft or Netscape Start pages, click the link and follow the directions to personalize your page. Most of the larger ISP's also offer custom Start pages. If you don't see any instructions on your ISP's home page, contact the ISP's tech support department for instructions.

SEE ALSO

➤ *You'll learn the value of having another email address on page 230*

Another alternative is to build a Start page at Yahoo!. In addition to being a top search service, Yahoo! offers some great customizable features on their personalized pages. When you set up a Yahoo! page, you get free email, the Yahoo! Messenger with Voice Chat, and a range of other free services. All you need is a few minutes to build a dynamite My Yahoo! page. The service is completely free. Best of all, it's fun!

Only you

Although your custom Start page displays its own URL, most times only you or someone sitting at your computer can see it. Some customized Start pages are so private that they require you to enter a password before you can access the page.

Building a Custom Page at Yahoo!

1. Connect to the Internet and open your browser. Click inside the Address box, type **www.yahoo.com**, and press **Enter**. In a moment, the Yahoo! page appears, as shown in Figure 6.2.

FIGURE 6.2
The Yahoo! Home page.

① Click here to start building your page.

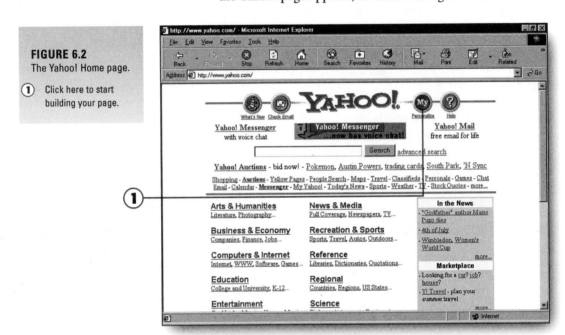

2. Click the link to **My Yahoo!** near the top of the page. When the next page appears, click the link to **Get My Own Yahoo!**

3. The Welcome to Yahoo! page appears, displaying a form for personal information. Click or tab to each mandatory field and type the required information such as your desired Yahoo! username and email address.

4. When you're finished filling out the form, click the link to **Terms of Service** at the bottom of the page. Although you're not required to read the Terms of Service, it's a good idea to know what Yahoo! will provide for you and what's expected of you in return.

   If you'd like, you can print the Terms of Service and then save it with your Yahoo! username and password. Click the **Back** button when you're done.

Only what's required

Whenever you fill out a form on the Web, look for the fields that are not mandatory. On the Yahoo! Sign Up form, for example, you needn't reveal your first and last name or your interests. Check for a site's Privacy Policy if you're uneasy.

SEE ALSO
➤ *Printing a Web page is discussed on page 132*

5. Click the **Submit this Form** button. In a moment, another page appears, welcoming you to My Yahoo!. If you've chosen a username that's already in use, you'll need to select another name and submit the form again.

6. Click the link to **My Yahoo!**. Your very own custom page appears. Now you can customize the page by clicking the **Personalize** button and following the easy-to-follow instructions provided by Yahoo!.

Your custom My Yahoo! page can be opened by you anytime you want. You can even make it your new Start page (see the next section in this chapter). If you try to access your My Yahoo! page from another computer, you'll be asked to log in and provide your password.

Modifying Your Browser's Start Page

Modifying your browser's settings to display a new Start page is a snap! It only takes a second or two to change the settings. Best of all, you can change your Start page again, anytime you want. If you created a My Yahoo! page in the last exercise, consider making that the first page you see when you open your browser. Of course, any other Web page will work equally as well.

Make sure that you know the URL of the page you want to open first before you begin the process of changing it. Or, go to the page before you begin the process.

Changing the Start page in Internet Explorer

1. From within Internet Explorer, click the **View** menu and choose **Internet Options**.

2. When the Internet Options dialog box appears, click the **General** tab and find the first section of the page entitled Home Page (see Figure 6.3).

No can do
If you're accessing the Internet from work or school, the folks who run the network may prevent you from changing your Start page. In fact, you may be denied access to creating a personal page at Yahoo! or anywhere. Check with your Network Administrator before you attempt any customization or special views.

FIGURE 6.3
Set your Internet Explorer Start page in the Internet Explorer.

① Tabs

② Home page section

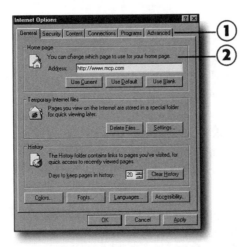

3. Set your page in one of the following ways:

- Click inside the **Address** text box and type the URL of the new opening page. (Type carefully!)

- If the page that's on the screen is the page you want to use, click the **Use Current** button.

- If you don't want any page to appear when you open Internet Explorer, click the **Use Blank** button.

4. When you're done, click **OK**.

Changing the Start page in Netscape Navigator

1. Navigator users should click **Edit** and then **Preferences** to display the Preferences dialog box.

2. Under the **Category** section on the left side of the page, click **Navigator**. Information about settings in Navigator appears, as shown in Figure 6.4.

3. Verify that the option button next to **Home page** is selected in the **Navigator starts with** section.

4. Move down to the middle section, called **Home page** and choose one of the following options:

- Click **Use Current Page**, if you have the page you want to use displayed onscreen.

- Click inside the **Location** text box and replace the URL that's currently displayed with the one you want. Check to make sure that there are no typos when you're finished typing.
- Click the **Browse** button to locate a file on your computer to use as your Start page.

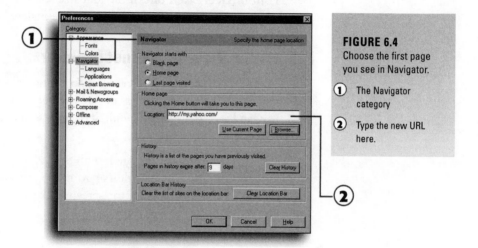

FIGURE 6.4
Choose the first page you see in Navigator.

① The Navigator category

② Type the new URL here.

5. Click **OK** to close the Preferences dialog box and return to the Navigator screen.

That's it! The next time your browser starts, you'll see the page you just entered.

Switching Fonts

You can change the appearance of the Web page that's displayed on your screen with a few simple mouse clicks. Why would you want to? Perhaps the font, or typeface, of a page is hard to look at. Or, if you've been staring at your computer for a long time, you might want to blow up the size of the letters to make them easier to read. Using your browser's tools, you can change the appearance of any displayed page to suit your needs. The new font size is in effect until you change it again during the current session or close your browser.

For Internet Explorer users, click the **View** menu and choose **Text Size**. A check mark appears next to the font size that's currently in effect. Click the new size you want to use. If you're not sure, try one level up or down from the font size that's in use now. When the menu closes, the page is redrawn.

For Navigator users, click the **View** menu and then choose **Increase Font** or **Decrease Font**. If the font size still isn't the size you wanted, repeat the step until the font size matches what you wanted.

Full Screen View in Internet Explorer

Internet Explorer has a secret weapon for use when you want to see more of a Web page and less of the browser. Instead of hiding toolbars and the status bar, use Full Screen view to use all your screen real estate to show the page.

Press **F11** to display the page in Full Screen. Only a small toolbar without text and your Windows buttons appear at the very top of the screen. Press **F11** to return the screen back to its previous size when you're done.

Keeping a List of Your Favorite Sites

You can visit personal favorites—such as cafés, shops, and resorts—again and again. You may even have the phone numbers and related information for the places you love saved in your address book, or taped to your refrigerator. The saved information makes it easier to find your way back.

Shortcuts

Think of Bookmarks or Favorites as Web shortcuts. They make it easy for you to get to your favorite sites without cluttering your mind (or your desk) with URLs.

As you make your way around the Internet, you're sure to find some favorite sites on the Web, too. Internet Explorer calls them *Favorites*. Navigator calls them *Bookmarks*. Both browsers enable you to group these favorite Web sites in a list so you can return to them again and again. After you've set up your list, the sites you like are never more than a few mouse clicks away.

Before too long, your list of Favorites (Bookmarks) grows so long that it becomes difficult to find the one you want. (When my sister first started using the Internet, she bookmarked more than 250 sites in less than three months!) Fortunately, you can create folders to organize and store your Favorites (Bookmarks). That way, if you're looking for the link to the Mr. Showbiz site, for example, you can find it easily in your Show Business folder.

Although Internet Explorer Favorites and Navigator Bookmarks do roughly the same thing, each browser works a bit differently. Follow the exercises that correspond with the browser you're using. Be sure you are connected to the Internet, and your browser is open before beginning the following step by step.

Setting Favorites in Internet Explorer

Creating Favorites with Internet Explorer

1. Click inside the Address bar and type a URL, for example `www.foodchannel.com` and press **Enter**.

2. When the new site appears, right-click on a blank spot on the page (not on a hyperlink) and select **Add to Favorites** from the resulting shortcut menu. The Add Favorite dialog box, shown in Figure 6.5, appears on the screen.

3. Click **OK**. The page on your screen is now added to your list of Favorites.

4. Verify that your Favorite is set up by clicking **Favorites** on the menu bar. The title of the onscreen page, shown on the Internet Explorer title bar, appears on the list.

Organizing Your Favorites Into Folders

Using a Favorite is a fast, easy way to return to a Web site. With one simple click, you are transported back to the site without needing to type or even remember its URL. However, if you add a lot of sites to Favorites, your Favorites list can grow unwieldy before too long. Your best bet is to organize your Favorites into folders.

Where did those other folders come from?

Don't be surprised if you see several folders in your Favorites list that you didn't create. Internet Explorer sets up a few folders filled with Favorites for you during the installation process. You can visit any of these sites by choosing **Favorites** on the Internet Explorer menu bar, then opening the folder and clicking the URL of the page you want to visit. If Microsoft Office is installed on your computer, you'll also see the Favorites you've added when you were using the programs in the suite.

FIGURE 6.5
Use the Add Favorite dialog box to store your favorite sites.

Using a folder structure for your Favorites makes good sense. You have the freedom to create a structure that works for you. Your filing system for Favorites can be as simple or elaborate as you like. If you are super-organized, you even create folders within folders, just as you do with the folders that store files on your computer.

The easiest way to organize your Favorites is to click **Favorites** on the menu bar and then **Organize Favorites**. The Organize Favorites dialog box appears, as shown in Figure 6.6. Since the picture was taken using the Favorites from my computer, my Favorites probably look differently than yours.

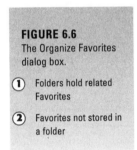

FIGURE 6.6
The Organize Favorites
dialog box.

(1) Folders hold related
Favorites

(2) Favorites not stored in
a folder

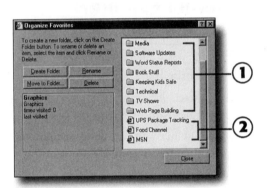

Click the **Create Folder** button to set up a new folder. A closed folder icon appears at the bottom of the Favorites list with the words New Folder selected. Type a descriptive name for the folder or one that will give you a clue what it contains. (My son created a folder called Richard's Favorites. Months later, he had no idea what types of pages it held.) The folder name can be anything you like, as long as the title does not exceed 256 characters. When you're through typing the folder name, click outside the folder name box.

To move a Favorite inside a folder, click it once to select it and then click **OK**. When the Browse for Favorites dialog box appears, click the folder that will store the Favorite and click **OK**. When you're all done, click the **Close** button to close the **Organize Favorites** dialog box. Whenever you want to return to the site that a Favorite points to, click **Favorites**, click the proper folder, and then click the Favorite.

Bookmarking Sites with Navigator

Netscape Navigator uses bookmarks to enable you to return to your Favorites sites. Bookmarks, like Favorites in Internet Explorer, can be added as you're touring the Web to help you return sites later on. When you install Netscape Navigator, you're provided with a list of several pre-set bookmarks that are arranged by categories in folders. Add your own bookmarks to the ones already provided for you.

Bookmarking sites with Navigator

1. Click in the **Location/Netsite** box (now reading Go To). When the present URL in the box appears highlighted, type a URL, such as **www.bocaratonnews.com**, as demonstrated in Figure 6.7, and press **Enter**.

FIGURE 6.7
Bookmarks QuickFile shows folders and Bookmarks.

2. When the new page appears, click the **Bookmarks QuickFile** icon, located at the side of Location toolbar. A list of folders and Bookmarks appears, with commands at the top of the list.

3. Choose **Add Bookmark**, as shown in Figure 6.8. (I've been using Navigator for ages, so my Bookmarks list is probably much more extensive than yours.) The list closes and the Bookmark to the Web page is added to the bottom of the list.

4. Type another URL, such as **www.computercoach.com**, in the Location/Netsite box and press **Enter**. The new page appears on your screen.

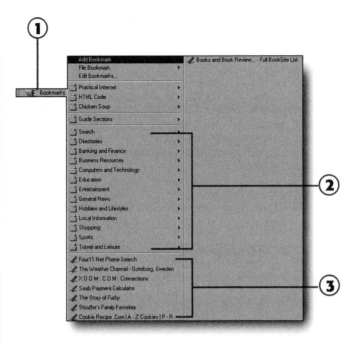

FIGURE 6.8
Highlight Add Bookmark
to bookmark the page
that's on the screen.

① Bookmark QuickFile
icon

② Folders hold related
bookmarks

③ Bookmarks not stored
in a folder

How Favorites work

Using Favorites can seem
like magic sometimes. You
click a Favorite and, almost
instantly, the corresponding
Web site appears. Actually,
Favorites aren't magic at
all. Like so much of the
interaction between
Internet Explorer and
Windows, files are the
source of the transaction.

Whenever you add a site to
your Favorites list,
Windows stores the URL in
a folder on the hard drive
of your computer (generally
something like
C:\Windows\Favorites).
When you click a site name
on the Favorites list,
Windows and Internet
Explorer open the file, read
the code, and show you the
content of the site.
Considering that the whole
procedure takes only a few
seconds, that's pretty
amazing!

5. To bookmark this site, place the mouse pointer on the Page
   Proxy icon 🔖 located next to the Location/Netsite box. As
   shown in Figure 6.9, the page icon changes to look like a page
   with a bookmark on top of it, and the mouse pointer assumes the
   shape of a hand. Additionally, a screen tip and information on
   the Status bar tell you to how to create the bookmark.

6. Without releasing the mouse button, drag the Page Proxy icon
   leftward to the Bookmarks. As it drags, the mouse pointer has a
   link icon with a small cross underneath attached 🔖.

7. Release the mouse button so that the tip of the mouse pointer is
   located in any portion of the word Bookmarks.

Good work! You've added two bookmarks. Practice adding bookmarks to sites you like.

Arranging your Bookmarks

1. Open the Bookmarks list by clicking the **Bookmark QuickFile**
   icon on the Location toolbar. Your Bookmark folders appear
   with the commands **Add Bookmark**, **File Bookmarks**, and **Edit
   Bookmarks** at the top.

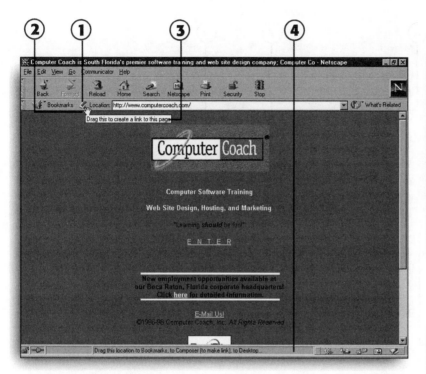

FIGURE 6.9
Drag the Page Proxy
icon to create a
bookmark.

① Page Proxy icon

② Mouse pointer takes
the shape of a hand

③ Screen tip

④ Status bar provides
instruction

2. Choose **Edit Bookmarks**. The Bookmarks list appears on top of
the Web page that's on your screen.

A plus sign (+) next to a folder indicates the folder is collapsed or
closed. A minus sign (-) next to a folder indicates that the folder
is expanded or open; you can see the bookmarks in the folder.
(See Figure 6.10.)

3. Move a bookmark into an existing folder by clicking the bookmark next to the bookmark title and dragging it on top of the
folder you want to move it to. When you release the mouse
button, the bookmark drops into the folder.

4. To create a new folder to store bookmarks, right-click on the
spot on the list where you want the folder to appear. Choose
New Folder from the shortcut menu.

5. The new folder is displayed on the list and the Bookmark
Properties dialog box appears, as shown in Figure 6.11.

Click and drag

To quickly place a Favorite
inside a folder, hold down
the left mouse button and
drag the Favorite on top of
the new folder. As you
drag, a shadow copy of the
Favorite's icon appears.
When you release the left
mouse button, the Favorite
is now placed in the folder.

**Displaying the Favorites
list**

Similar to how Internet
Explorer displays the
History list, if you click the
Favorites button on the
Standard Buttons toolbar,
the Favorites list opens in
an Explorer bar on the left
side of the screen. If you
click a Favorite on the list,
the site opens on the right
side of the screen.

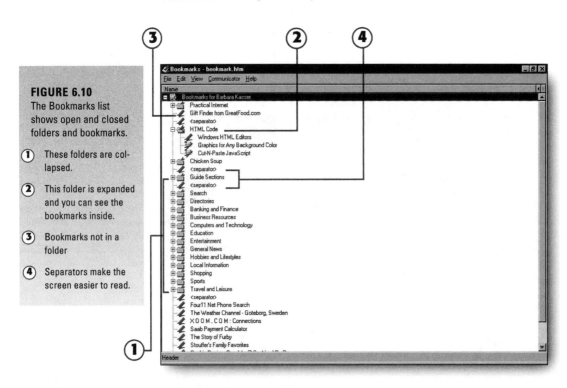

FIGURE 6.10
The Bookmarks list shows open and closed folders and bookmarks.

(1) These folders are collapsed.

(2) This folder is expanded and you can see the bookmarks inside.

(3) Bookmarks not in a folder

(4) Separators make the screen easier to read.

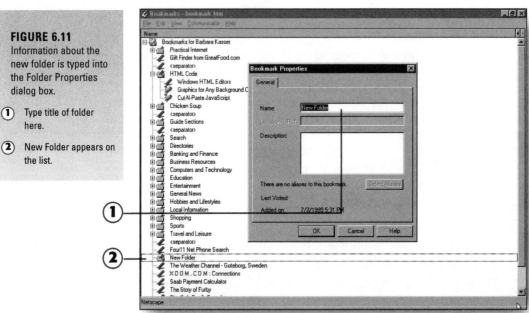

FIGURE 6.11
Information about the new folder is typed into the Folder Properties dialog box.

(1) Type title of folder here.

(2) New Folder appears on the list.

6. Type the name of the new folder in the **Name** text box and click **OK**. The dialog box closes and the folder on the list displays the new name.

7. Repeat step 3 to drag a bookmark into the new folder.

8. Separators make the screen easier to read, click the mouse on the line above where you want the separator to appear and click **File**, **New Separator**. A separator is added.

Find Related Pages

Everybody who's used the Web for awhile shares a common experience: As you journey through the Web, you encounter a page that almost matches what you're looking for, but it's not quite right. You can go back and search again, try another URL, or look for a link to a different site.

SEE ALSO

➤ *You'll learn all about searching on page 156*

Internet Explorer and Navigator recognize how frustrating it is to come so close to what you want, but be so far away. Accordingly, both browsers have incorporated a **Related** button into their latest versions. This new feature can save you lots of time and energy.

When you click the **Related** button, your browser sends the URL of the page you're using to a special search service. The service reviews the URL and responds with a list of several URLs of related sites. Before the list is sent back to your browser, the server filters out any non-working links.

The Related service is currently in its infancy. Although the Related list covers millions of URLs on the Web, there's a good chance that the service might not find any related sites when you click the button. However, Alexa Internet, the developer of the service is confident that, as the data collection process continues, more sites will be added on an ongoing basis.

If you're using Internet Explorer, click the **Related** button on the Standard Buttons toolbar or click the **Tools** menu and choose **Show Related Links**. The Search bar appears on the left side of the screen, similar to the History and Favorites Explorer bars you

---

Create a shortcut to your favorite page

In addition to the two methods you've learned to set bookmarks, Navigator takes advantage of the Windows shortcut menu to provide you with yet another way to navigate when you're viewing a Web site. Right-click the mouse pointer on an empty spot on the Web page. When the shortcut menu appears, click **Add Bookmark**. Take care not to position the mouse pointer on a link or graphics image when you access the shortcut menu.

Close the Bookmarks window

When you work with your Navigator bookmarks, the Bookmarks file opens in a separate window. Be sure and close the Window when you're done working with your bookmarks.

worked with earlier. The links to related sites are shown in the bar. Figure 6.12 shows the results of clicking the Related button when the Macmillan Computer Publishing home page is on the screen.

Once the Search bar with Related links for one site is displayed on the screen, the service will continue to access related sites while the bar is on the screen. Close the bar to stop the service.

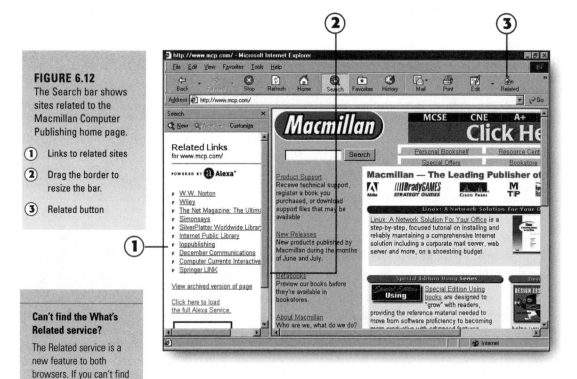

FIGURE 6.12
The Search bar shows sites related to the Macmillan Computer Publishing home page.

(1) Links to related sites

(2) Drag the border to resize the bar.

(3) Related button

Can't find the What's Related service?

The Related service is a new feature to both browsers. If you can't find the **Related** button in Internet Explorer or the **What's Related** button in Navigator, there is a good chance that the feature didn't come with your browser. Go to www.alexa.com and follow the links to download and install the Related software. You'll learn about downloading software in Chapter 8.

In Navigator, the related sites are shown in a drop-down menu under the What's Related button.

If you're using Navigator, click the **What's Related** button to send the first URL to the system. After you've clicked the button once, Navigator will also make a request for the next three new URLs (sites) for you to visit. This is done to speed up the response so you won't have to wait long if you are using the feature often. If you keep using the What's Related service (by clicking the button), Navigator will keep making the requests; if you stop using it, Navigator will stop making the requests after three more sites.

Figure 6.13 shows the What's Related links for the Macmillan Computer Publishing page. The links appear in a drop-down list underneath the What's Related button.

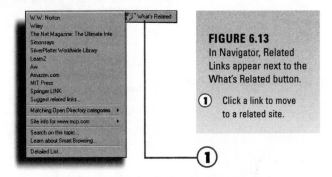

FIGURE 6.13
In Navigator, Related Links appear next to the What's Related button.

(1) Click a link to move to a related site.

Browse Smarter

In the next chapter, you'll learn how to search for special Web sites. Searching successfully means acquiring special skills that may take some practice to perfect. However, if you want to make searching as easy as possible, Internet Explorer and Navigator have a special feature designed for you. Instead of formulating queries, simply enter what you're looking for into the Address bar of either browser. The browser looks through the Web and, in a moment, a list of links to matching sites is returned.

Of course, this type of searching has some limitations. For one thing, your browser will probably miss as many sites, if not more, than it finds. Additionally, you can only search on a few *keywords* and can't exclude any words. For example, if you wanted information about the group "Chicago," you'd probably see links to sites about the location, since you couldn't specify "not city" in your query. Still, even though it can be limited, searching from the browser is a great place to start when you want to find information.

To perform a search from the Address bar, click inside the bar. When the text appears highlighted, type a few words. (If you're just trying this feature out, type `Elvis Presley`.) Try to be as specific as possible and check your typing carefully for errors. When you're sure that the words are correct, press **Enter** to let your browser find matching sites.

Basically the same

Both browsers allow you to type what you're looking for directly into the Address bar; Internet Explorer calls this feature *AutoSearch* while Navigator calls it *Smart Browsing*. No matter which browser you're using, think of searching from the Address bar as a fast way to find Web pages.

Figure 6.14 shows a completed AutoSearch performed in Internet Explorer.

FIGURE 6.14
AutoSearch found links to sites about Elvis.

1 Click a link here to display the page on the right.

2 The message means that a URL for containing "elvis presley" was not found.

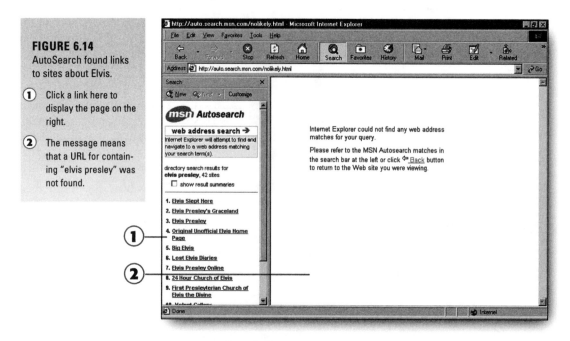

AutoSearch is a good way to find matching words or phrases in Web pages. However, if you're looking for a particular piece of information, such as the name of King Arthur's sword, you'll get better results with one of the Web's many search tools. You'll learn how to use search tools in the next chapter.

Finding What You Want on the Web

- Exploring Internet search tools

- Harnessing the power of many search tools

- Learning effective search techniques

- Using your browser's special search features

Beginning Your Search

The Web gives its users a very special power—the power of knowledge. You can sit at your computer and use the Web to find information about whatever you want to know. Sometimes the information you want might be frivolous, like what comes after "tensies" in the kid's game of jacks. Other times, the information might be important and relevant, such as the latest news and headlines. The wonderful thing about the Web is that it delivers what you want, every time you want it!

With its millions and millions of pages, the World Wide Web is home to every kind of information you might imagine. The combination of existing Web sites, plus all the new pages that appear daily, make the Web a giant library. Whether you're searching for one particular fact, or information on a broad topic, looking through millions of Web pages can be a daunting task.

You can't go to a catalogue and look up references to all the Web sites that match your requirements. For one thing, such an index doesn't exist. Even if a master index could be obtained, the sheer volume of the pages that appear, move, and disappear daily on the Web would render the index obsolete in a very short time.

Before you throw your hands up in frustration, take heart! Indexing or search tools to help you find the pages you want abound on the Web. The tools all work roughly the same way; you form a *search query* made up of a keyword or phrase, and the search tool looks through its database of documents on the Internet. When the search tool has looked through its entire database, it returns a list of documents that match, as shown in Figure 7.1. Each match is called a *hit* and contains a hyperlink to the corresponding Web page.

Document or Web site?

After you conduct a search, some search tools refer to the matching Web pages as documents. Don't get confused; "document" is just another name for a Web site or page.

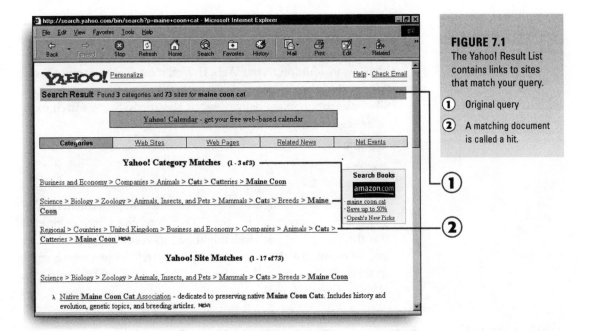

FIGURE 7.1
The Yahoo! Result List contains links to sites that match your query.

(1) Original query

(2) A matching document is called a hit.

Let a Search Tool Do the Hard Part

Search tools have the difficult job of analyzing your request and then finding matching pages. In order to find the right documents, the search tools need to sift through millions of pages—in the span of a few seconds. Think of the search tools on the Web as your virtual research assistants. When you have something to find, you tell your assistants exactly what you're looking for and let them do all of the digging. If you told five human assistants to find something out for you, each would approach the problem in their own personal way. The search tools, like people, each look through the Internet in slightly different ways and, ultimately, might come up with different results.

Take advantage of help

Almost every search tool on the Web has a help system that provides information about how the tool works and the best way to set up your query. Click the **Help** link, and then read and follow the advice when you compose your query. That way you'll be sure you're using the tool to its best advantage.

For the most part, the search tools you use provide more than just the capability to look for documents. Many of the tools enable you to look through Usenet, a collection of discussion groups, or other sources, in addition to the Web. In fact, most search engines now have turned their home pages into portals that offer extra services, like links to shopping, daily news, or classifieds. Some search tools offer regional guides, stock quotes, or chat rooms.

SEE ALSO

➤ *You'll enter the world of Usenet on page 256*

➤ *What's a portal? Read about it on page 139*

Each major search engine on the Web makes improvements and changes to its service all the time. Therefore, the search engine that was the Web's best last week might be superceded by another search engine today. For that reason, run your search on two search engines or services, if you're looking for something important, or using the Web as a research tool.

Different Tools Help You Search

Knowing that search tools exist should help you make the Internet seem a little smaller and easier to manage. Although there are several different types of search tools, you'll use these the most:

- *Site directories.* These sort Web sites into categories. Each category, such as Government, might be further broken down by subcategories like Military, Politics, Law, and Taxes. To move around in a site directory, you generally click the links to each category and subcategory until you find what you're looking for. You can also use a keyword search to find specific sites. Most times, the sites listed in a site directory have been registered by their site designers or Webmasters.

- *Search engines.* These send electronic *crawlers* (called spiders, worms, or robots) through the Web looking for pages to add to their databases of existing Web pages. When the crawler finds a site that hasn't been indexed yet, it adds a new entry to the database with the page title, the URL of the current and any linked pages, and a portion of the text. (Different search engines use different sections of the text.) Even though crawlers work constantly, the fact that there are so many pages to look through means that it might take years to find a new site. Consequently,

Webmasters can provide the URLs of their sites to the search engines and ask the crawler to add the pages to the index.

Other popular search tools are used as well. Meta-search engines, which simultaneously look through the databases of other search tools, are valuable for pinpointing the pages you need. WebRings, one of the latest tools, enable Web sites with similar interests to form "rings" of sites, providing you with a fast and efficient way to find content. Finally, your browser comes with some special tools to help you find what you need.

All search tools work in a very similar way; you enter a search query, and the search tool looks through its index to produce links to matching sites. After you look at the list, you can click the links to move to the matching sites, or you can modify the query and run the search again.

Tips for Setting Up Your Query

When you look for something on the Web, you need to communicate exactly what you want to find. The search tool looks for different documents, based on what you ask for. For example, a query that reads "`restaurants in India`" will produce far different results than the query "`Indian restaurants`". Setting up your search is very important.

Use the following hints to help you find what you want on the Web and other Internet locations.

- *Form your query without articles.* Words like *the* and *an* in your search query could produce skewed results. Unless you're looking for something very specific, such as references to a title or book like *The BookShop: A Novel*, exclude articles from your query.

- *Check your spelling.* Type carefully and re-check your typing. Because your search is based on what you type and not, necessarily, what you mean, correct spelling is essential. For example, typing "Strawberry Fiellds" won't produce the right documents.

- *Be specific.* Take a few moments and think about your query. Are you looking for the Beatles or only references to the song "Strawberry Fields?" Phrase your query based on what you're looking for.

- *Try a few different word combinations.* Getting the hang of Internet searches takes a little getting used to. If your first search doesn't produce the results you expected, change the query and run the search again.

- *Run your search using at least two search tools.* Different search services and search tools index pages on the Web differently. One search service may find the document you're looking for while another may not.

Find It with a Site Directory

Site directories are hierarchically organized indexes of subject categories that allow you to browse through lists of Web sites by subject. The site directories are compiled and maintained by humans and many include a search engine for searching their own database. Subject guide databases tend to be smaller than those of the search engines, which means that result lists tend to be smaller as well.

Site directories arrange their sites by categories. Each category contains a subcategory; most sub-categories have their own subcategories. It's not uncommon to drill down through several layers of hierarchical categories to find exactly what you want. The advantage of using a site directory is that you can find Web sites without having to enter a keyword. Or, to refine your search, you can choose a category and then enter a keyword or phrase.

Because site directories are arranged by category and because they usually return links to the top level of a Web site rather than to individual pages, they lend themselves best to searching for information about a general subject, rather than for a specific piece of information.

You'll find some of the best site directories at:

- **Yahoo!** at www.yahoo.com is the great-grandfather of site directories. You'll find something about everything at Yahoo!. You can read more about Yahoo! later in this chapter.

- **About.com** (formerly known as The Mining Company) at www.about.com adds a human twist to searching. Each category at About.com's extensive categories has an expert human guide, displayed with picture and comments, who's there to give you the benefit of his/her expertise in the subject.

- **LookSmart** at www.looksmart.com is one of the newer search tools on the Web. The site directory is designed for "clean" searches. The LookSmart service provides links to high-quality sites that do not contain pornography. A staff of researchers reviews each site before it can be included in the LookSmart database.

- **Magellan** at magellan.excite.com has recently gotten some new updates that make it easy to use. Magellan doesn't use a lot of flashy graphics and its simple, clean interface is straightforward. Magellan is part of the Excite family of search tools, so the Magellan database is extensive.

In addition, to general site guides, you can turn to a specialized site guide if you want information about a specific area or topic. The Internet Movie Database at us.imdb.com is the place film buffs should start. Professional information is contained at Galaxy (www.galaxy.com). If you're looking for information about the humanities, turn to Voice of the Shuttle at humanitas.ucsb.com. Finally, if you're looking for archives from the dark side of politics, religious fervor, new sciences, and current affairs that you rarely hear on the news, turn to Disinformation at www.disinfo.com. Searching at Disinformation takes a little getting used to, but you'll always come away with a new snippet of information.

Yahoo!

Most people who connect to the Internet have heard of Yahoo! Located at www.yahoo.com, Yahoo!, the most commonly used site index, helps you find just about anything. Yahoo! is organized into top-level categories with layers of subcategories. It generally takes a few clicks to drill down through the subcategory layers and find what you're looking for. Or, you can enter your query in the Search text box and let Yahoo! find the matching sites. As an alternative, you can combine the two search techniques and click down into a subcategory before you type your search criteria.

In addition to its categories, Yahoo! features links to all the hot sites on the Web. You'll find links to people, email, sports, news, weather, and more on Yahoo!'s home page. If you have a few minutes, click the button to **What's New** to find some unusual sites. The **Today's News** button provides links to headlines and full news stories in a wide range of categories.

Checking out your favorite company

1. Type www.yahoo.com in the Address box of your browser and press **Enter** to move to the Yahoo! home page.

2. Click the link to the **Business and Economy** category. When the page of links to the related subcategories appears, click the **Companies** link. (The number of sites grouped under the category appears in parentheses beside the index title. Note how many company sites are contained in the Yahoo! database.) Do one of the following:

   - If you know the name of the company you're looking for, type the company name in the Search text box and click **Search**. After you've viewed the hits on the Result list, click a link to a site that contains interesting information about the company. Read the information, clicking any links on the page.

   - Click a subcategory such as **Cleaning** or **Publishing**. When the next page appears, click a subcategory link to move down further in the index. Or, scroll down past the list of subcategories to the companies shown in the current subcategory. Continue working your way through the sub-categories until you find information about the company you're looking for.

3. After you've viewed the information about the company (and clicked any related links), click the **Back** button on the browser toolbar as many times as necessary to move back to the Yahoo! home page.

4. Click the **Stock Quote** link on the Yahoo! home page. The Yahoo! Finance page appears.

5. Type the stock symbol of the company whose information you've been viewing in the **Get Quotes** text box.

6. Currently the quote search is set to return a basic stock quote. For a more detailed quote, click the down arrow next to **basic** and choose another quote type from the list, as shown in Figure 7.2.

Company not found?

Check the company name you entered for spelling errors. If the search found more than your company, enter the full company name. After you've made adjustments to the query, run the search again.

Find that symbol

If you don't know the company's stock symbol, click the **symbol lookup** link and follow the instructions on the Symbol Ticker page to find out the correct symbol. Click the **Back** button as many times as necessary to return to the Yahoo! **Finance** link.

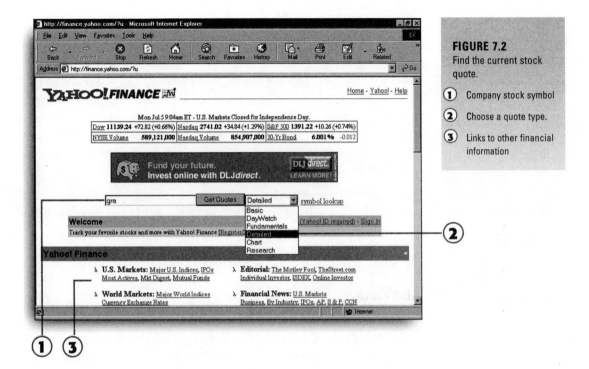

FIGURE 7.2
Find the current stock quote.

(1) Company stock symbol

(2) Choose a quote type.

(3) Links to other financial information

SEE ALSO

➤ *Read about how to set up a personal My Yahoo! page on page 140*

➤ *You'll have the opportunity to set up your portfolio tracker on page 354*

7. Click **Get Quotes**. The current stock quote, generally delayed by 20 minutes, appears onscreen.

Search Engines

Search engines allow you search by entering keywords. Based on your query, the search engine retrieves the documents from its database. Because every search engine works differently, you might notice each search engine gives you different results from the same query.

While all search engines are intended to perform the same task, each goes about this task in a different way, which leads to sometimes amazingly different results. Factors that influence results include the size of the database, how often the database is updated, and the

Search engines aren't live

Your favorite search engine doesn't search the entire Web when you submit a query. Instead, it searches through a fixed database. That's why pages added to the Web today might not appear in your results.

search engine's capabilities. Search engines also differ in their search speed, the design of the search interface, the way results are displayed, and the amount of help they offer.

In the past, search engines had simple pages where it was easy to enter a few keywords and find anything under the sun. Although search engines still perform the same function, many search engines have a carnival look to them, with links to shopping, news services, and more. Some even feature memberships, and free email and other services.

Don't be put off if the search engine page is busy and hard to navigate. Underneath all that glitz is the workhorse, waiting to find documents for you.

Some of the more popular search engines are:

AltaVista

AltaVista, at www.altavista.com, is a search engine that has been a Web fixture for a long time. You can conduct a simple or complex search and limit your results to Web documents, images, or video or audio clips. Additionally, you can phrase your query as a question. For example, asking "What is the distance between Pittsburgh and Miami" finds links that provide an answer to the question.

AltaVista offers lots of ways to define your search. You can use AltaVista's Simple search method. For more complex queries, the Advanced search allows the use of *wildcards*, phrases, and excluded keywords. Click the **Help** link to find out how to formulate your query. In addition to searching, the AltaVista page contains links to the latest headlines and sports scores.

Excite

Excite is a good search engine to begin your search. Find Excite at www.excite.com. Because the Excite spiders index the full text of a Web page, rather than just the title or special pointers called *meta tags*, your query will produce many hits. Additionally, the Excite Result List offers links to "More Like This" sites that match the listed hits. Excite features both a Simple and Advanced Web Search.

In addition to searching, Excite offers channels with links to topics like Business and Investing, People and Chat, and Shopping. New channels are added frequently. Links on the Excite site whisk you to stock quotes, a site that books airline flights, and your daily horoscope. In fact, the Excite page has so much from which to choose that you might forget you came to search!

Similar to My Yahoo!, Excite offers a customized Start page. Excite members get free email, chat, stock tracking, and other features. Additionally, Excite members can participate in a daily Harris poll.

HotBot

HotBot, at www.hotbot.com, (see Figure 7.3) is one of the best search engines on the Web! After you string your query together, you can ask HotBot to include all the words, any of the words, the exact phrase, or use Boolean logic to find matching hits. Within each location, you can add filters that limit your search. Additionally, you can limit your results to documents found in a particular language. (It's always frustrating when your Results list contains links to documents in languages you can't read.)

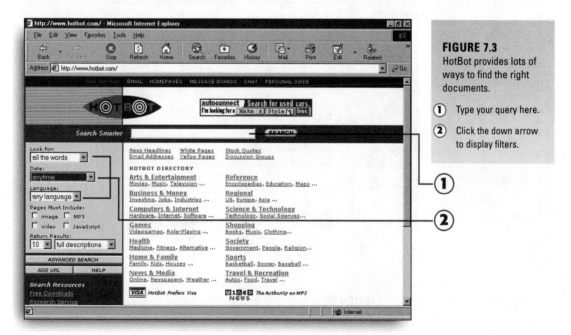

FIGURE 7.3
HotBot provides lots of ways to find the right documents.

① Type your query here.

② Click the down arrow to display filters.

HotBot excels at finding most everything that you're looking for. HotBot ranks your results by percentage, so you can get a feel for how close the found document matches your request. Once HotBot finds a Result list, you can narrow your query by searching through only those results. You can also click to the Advanced Searching page, and structure a sophisticated query that's sure to be effective.

After you've run a search in HotBot, your results are presented in a clear, easy-to-read way, as shown in Figure 7.4. Each hit shows the title, relevancy ranking, a summary, and the date the page was indexed by the HotBot spider (not the date of the page). Also displayed is the page URL and alternate pages, if any are found.

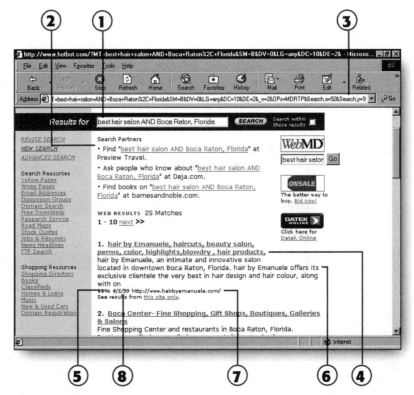

FIGURE 7.4
Results in HotBot are easy to understand.

① What you looked for

② Search Partners show travel books and newsgroups about the query.

③ HotBot translates your query.

④ Page title

⑤ Relevancy ranking

⑥ Brief summary

⑦ The URL

⑧ Date the site was indexed

HotBot uses the services of Direct Hit. The Direct Hit Popularity Engine shows you highly relevant results based only on the search topics that other people have researched. Say you're searching for information on "recipe" and "low carb". In the results page, you'll see a link to the top 10 returns for your search. Direct Hit filters this list so that worthwhile pages stay on top.

HotBot offers some additional destinations. You can click links to HotBot's Directory of links arranged by categories. You can also find quality shops and Web merchants through HotBot's shopping resources. You can also create road maps to and from any point from a link on the HotBot page.

Finding documents with HotBot

1. If it's not already open and visible on the screen, open your browser. When your starting page appears, click inside the Address box, type `www.hotbot.com`, and press **Enter**. The HotBot page appears.

2. Click inside the Search box and type a two or three-word phrase. (If you can't think of anything, type `stock market`.) When you're done typing, click **Search**.

3. HotBot searches its index and displays a page of links to Web sites that match the words you typed. Notice that the URL in the Address box changes to match HotBot's special query language. (Jot down the total number of hits if you want to compare them against other searches.)

4. By default, HotBot is set up to search the Web for all the words you type. Alter the way the search is performed by clicking the down arrow next to the phrase **all the words** and choosing **the exact phrase**. Click **Search**. When the results appear, the number of hits may decrease.

5. Click **Revise Search**. The HotBot search page re-appears, with your phrase in the Search box. Add one or more filters to your search by selecting one of these options:

   - Click the down arrow in the **Date** category. Right now, **anytime** is the default choice. Choose **in the last week** and choose a different date range from the list.

   - Click the down arrow in the **Language** category. Change from the default of **any language** to English.

More or less

Structuring your query to look for **any of the words** generally produces more hits, but might not find the documents that contain the information you want. Using the search filter **the exact phrase** narrows your query and helps find specific documents.

6. When you're done, click **Search** again. When the results appear, notice how the number of hits change as you narrow your search query and filter out potential matches.

Infoseek

Infoseek, at www.infoseek.com, is a part of the GO Network, a group of related services that include free email and chat services and a free Web page for its members. The standard search at Infoseek performs best with simple keyword and phrase searches. The **Advanced Search** (see Figure 7.5) offers some structured fields that narrow down the number of hits and help you find what you want.

FIGURE 7.5
Advanced searching at Infoseek provides lots of ways to find the right documents.

1. Select where you want Infoseek to look.

2. Choose to find a Web **document**, the **title** of a Web page, the **URL**, or a **hyperlink**.

3. Add the filter **should**, **must**, or **should not**.

4. Choose between **phrase, name**, or **word(s)**.

5. Type what you're looking for in the text box.

6. Narrow your query even further by adding additional search criteria.

7. If desired, select a particular domain to look through.

If you're concerned about what your kids might find when they search, you can activate the GO Network's GOgaurdian feature. The guardian actually filters out inappropriate adult content, so you can feel more comfortable about having young people search for sites. The GOguardian is easily turned off or on.

Ask Jeeves

Ask Jeeves at www.askjeeves.com offers a more personal service than many other search engines. You type your query in the form of a question and Jeeves, the online butler, fetches your results, as shown in Figure 7.6.

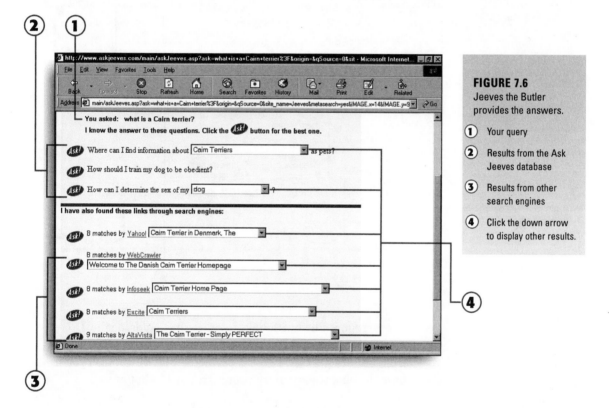

FIGURE 7.6
Jeeves the Butler provides the answers.

(1) Your query

(2) Results from the Ask Jeeves database

(3) Results from other search engines

(4) Click the down arrow to display other results.

Lycos

Lycos (www.lycos.com) was one of the first search engines to gain national prominence. If you're putting together a simple search, Lycos will prove adequate for the task of finding what you need. However, one of Lycos' greatest strengths is its capability to locate some unusual items, like books, sounds, graphics files (pictures), recipes, or information about a particular stock. Figure 7.7 shows the Lycos Advanced Search page.

FIGURE 7.7
Lycos' Advanced Search enables you to find a variety of information.

① Choose how you want to search.

② Type what you're looking for here.

③ Click the category in which you want to search.

④ Choose where you want Lycos to look.

⑤ Click here when you've got the search all set up.

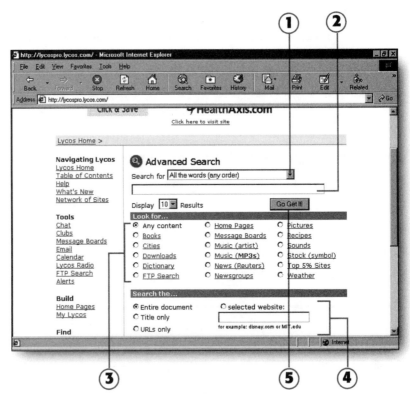

Lycos' page is filled with links to other sites. Additionally, Lycos offers the Lycos SearchGuard, which filters objectionable sites from the Results List. Lycos is partnered with HotBot, so you'll have the opportunity to try your search at HotBot as well.

Northern Light

Northern Light, located at www.northernlight.com, is a new addition to the Web and works as a search engine and a site index. The service, named after a radically new type of clipper ship built in 1851, is committed to bringing the best technology to its customers. You can search the World Wide Web with the search engine portion or use the site index to look through Northern Light's Special Collection of one million documents not on the Web. (Although the article descriptions are free, there is a charge for reading articles from the Special Collection.)

Search results in Northern Light are presented differently than other Web search tools. The results are displayed with Custom Search Folders on the left and the most relevant documents on the right. The Custom Search Folders are unique to each search. To view the documents in each folder, click the folder to open it. The source of each document, such as Personal page or Educational site, is listed with other information about each document.

Meta-Search Engines Harness the Power of the Web

With all these search tools available, choosing the right one can sometimes be intimidating. Instead of using several different search tools in your quest for the right document, you can use a new type of search tool, called a *meta-engine*. Meta-engines work by simultaneously scanning the databases of multiple search tools, and presenting you with the results. Although meta-engines can't utilize all the controls that a single search engine like HotBot offers, they help you look quickly through the indexed databases of many different sources.

Table 7.1 shows some of the Web's best meta-engines and provides a brief description and information about the results.

Keep it short

Don't confuse Jeeves with your questions. Keep them short, simple, and to the point. If you can, make your query specific and avoid the use of adverbs or adjectives. For example, the question, "Where can I find information on police dogs" is likely to bring results based solely in the word police as well as results only about dogs. A query that will produce better results might be "Where can I find information about German shepherds?"

Table 7.1 Popular meta-engines

Engine Name	URL	Description	Results
Meta-Crawler	www.go2net.com	Feeds your search query to six different search tools and collates the results.	Collated into one, easy-to-read sheet.

continues…

Table 7.1 Continued

Engine Name	URL	Description	Results
SavvySearch	www.savvysearch.com	Set up as an experiment at Colorado State University. Your query can be sent to as many as 19 Internet search tools, including search engines and people finders. Offers searching in many foreign languages.	Easy-to-read results listed by search engine. However, because the computer is often busy, search results might take a long time to appear.
All-4-One	www.all4one.com	Searches Alta-Vista, Lycos, Yahoo!, and Web-Crawler at the same time.	Presents the search results in four separate frames.
Dogpile	www.dogpile.com	Lets you choose where to look: for example the Web, Usenet, or Newswires.	Displays the hits beneath each search tool that found them.
Mamma	www.mamma.com	Billing itself as the "Mother of search engines," Mamma queries the top search engines and creates a virtual database of results.	Results are arranged by ranking and show the search tool that found the hit.

Other Notable Search Services

Although most people use only a few search engines, the Web is filled with little-known search engines that await the opportunity to help you.

Here's a sample:

- For a geographically specific search, try **Beaucoup** at `www.beaucoup.com/1geoeng.html`.

- Looking for graphic images? Try **The Amazing Picture Machine** at `www.ncrtec.org/picture.htm`.

- Visit the Combined Health Information Database at `chid.nih.gov` if you want to search on health-related information.

- Find all things related to Europe from **Euroseek** at `www.euroseek.com`.

Form Effective Queries

Designing effective search queries is a skill that takes practice. Don't be discouraged if you don't find what you're looking for on the first try. Rephrase the query and try again. Take a look at the online help provided by most search tools, and then tailor your query to take advantage of each search tool's unique way of looking through the Internet.

Use these general rules to help you find what you're looking for:

- *Keep your query short and use keywords.* Remember, it's a computer, not a person, that will be looking at what you've typed. Long, rambling queries such as `I'd like to find a recipe for lemon chicken` will confuse the search tool and produce poor results. A more effective query would be `lemon chicken recipe`.

- *Enclose each phrase in double quotes.* Some search tools require quotes and some don't. Play it safe by placing double quotes around each phrase. For example, the query `"vegetarian lasagna recipe"` will find sites that show the exact phrase, rather than every site with the words vegetarian or lasagna or recipe.

- *Search with a broad query first, and then narrow it down.* With all of the millions of documents out there, you run the risk of missing some if you zero in on a specific search early in the game. For example, if you're thinking of planting a butterfly garden, try the search `"flowers that attract butterflies"` before you search for `pentas`.

Pay up

The Electric Library at `www.elibrary.com` searches through databases of newspapers, magazines, newswires, classic books, photographs, and major artworks. The results will cost you a few dollars. However, since Electric Library is able to look at so many sources inaccessible to other search tools, the cost can be justified.

- *Use logical operators to string your query together.* Here's how these operators work:

  - *OR.* If your query contains more than one word, the search tool automatically assumes that you're looking for any of the words you typed. Using **OR** is the opposite of using double quotes around words and produces the most hits. For example, the query `"using search tools"` finds documents that contain any of those three words.

  - *AND.* The use of **AND** means that the documents found by the search tool must contain each of the words in the query. However, the words don't need to be together to be counted. **AND**, sometimes represented by the & character, limits the number of documents found in the search.

  - *NOT.* When you want to exclude a specific word, use NOT. For example, the query `"pasta meal" NOT fusili` tells the search tool to eliminate any sites that contain the word fusili, but to display the links to sites that contain the phrase "pasta meal." (Note the double quotes around pasta meal.) The **NOT** character is often represented by a – (minus sign) character.

  - `* (Asterisk).` A wildcard that works as a root expander. Place an * at the end of a word to find all words that begin with the letters you typed. For example, searching for `spider*` produces hits to documents with the word spider or spiders.

WebRings: An Alternative Way to Search

A *WebRing* is a community of related Web pages that are organized into a circular ring. Each page in a ring has links that enable visitors to move to an adjacent site on the ring, access a ring index, or jump to a random site. Web sites are added voluntarily to Web rings. Each ring is managed from one of the sites.

WebRings are fun to visit, but don't contain the volume of information of the other search tools. Still, try a search or two through the WebRings to see if you find something new or exceptional. Currently, there are WebRings on many topics, including acrobatics, quilting, mermaids, the macabre, religion, Spanish hotels, the Chevrolet, Dixieland, medieval studies, Native American sites, and Winnie the Pooh. Most Web rings are devoted to games.

Visit the Web ring home page at www.webring.org. You'll find more information on Web rings and information on how to search. Another site devoted to WebRings is the Ringsurf site, located at www.ringsurf.com.

Getting Search Help from Your Browser

SEE ALSO

➤ *Did you know that you can search directly from the Address bar of your browser? Find out how on page 153*

Both Internet Explorer and Navigator are committed to helping you find the documents you want:

- In Internet Explorer, click the **Search** button to open an Explorer bar on the left side of the browser window that allows you to specify whether you want to find a Web page, a person's address, a business, previous searches, or a map.

- In Navigator, the Search button launches the Netscape Net Page.

Using Internet Explorer's Explorer bar

1. Click the **Search** button on the Standard Buttons toolbar from within Internet Explorer. The Search Explorer bar opens in a separate frame on the left side of the browser window, with a popular Web search tool displayed.

2. Type a keyword or phrase in the empty text box on the Explorer Search bar and click **Search**.

3. The results of your search appear as links on the Search Explorer bar, below your original query. To find out more information about each result link, position the mouse pointer over the link until a screen tip appears that shows both the URL and a description of the linked site. The screen tip might give you a better idea of whether the information on the Web page meets your needs.

Your search results are limited

Although accessing a search tool from the Search Explorer bar is convenient, it does have a drawback. You won't have full use of the custom search features usually provided on each search tool's home page.

4. Click one of the links on the Result list. The Search Explorer bar remains on the left side of the screen and the right side of the frame is filled by the Web page associated with the link, as shown in Figure 7.8.

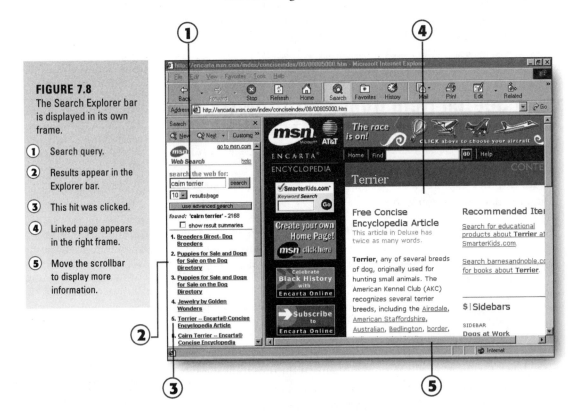

FIGURE 7.8

The Search Explorer bar is displayed in its own frame.

① Search query.

② Results appear in the Explorer bar.

③ This hit was clicked.

④ Linked page appears in the right frame.

⑤ Move the scrollbar to display more information.

5. Close the Search Explorer bar by clicking the **Search** button on the Standard Buttons toolbar. Also, you can click the **Close** (X) button on the Explorer bar.

Using Navigator's Net Search

1. Click the **Search** button on the Navigation toolbar from within Netscape Navigator. The Netscape Net Search page appears, as shown in Figure 7.9.

2. Across the top is a row of links to popular search tools, with one already selected. Click a link to change to that tool.

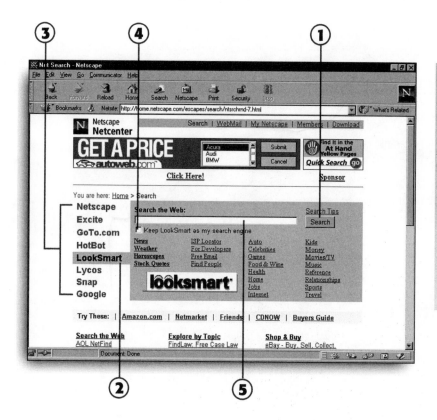

FIGURE 7.9
You can easily choose a search tool from The Netscape Net Search page.

(1) Search button

(2) This tool is selected.

(3) Links to search tools

(4) Check this box to always use the tool that's selected.

(5) Type your search query here.

3. Type your search query in the text box and click the **Search** button to begin the search. In a moment, the Net Search page disappears as the Result list is displayed.

4. When you're done looking at the results, click the **Back** button on the Navigation toolbar as many times as necessary to return to the Net Search page.

SEE ALSO
➤ Review how to use the Navigator Back button on page 118

Resize the Search Explorer bar

You can resize the Search Explorer bar so that you can see more of the Web page. Place the mouse pointer on the border between the Explorer bar and the browser frame. When the mouse pointer shape changes to a double-headed arrow, hold down the left mouse button and drag the border to the left. Release the mouse button when the frames are sized to your liking.

Getting Software and Files Off the Web

Finding sites to obtain software •

Creating a folder to hold
downloaded software •

Preventing computer virus infection •

Downloading programs from the Web •

Saving graphics files •

Files for Your Computer

They mean the same thing

When you download a file from the Web, you're actually saving it to your computer. The terms "download" and "save" mean the same thing.

Your browser is more than just a tool that brings Web pages to your computer. Among its many other uses, your browser can be used to obtain files from the Internet for you to use later on. Some of the files you *download* install programs, like games or programs that help you work with graphics. Some of the other downloadable files extend the capability of your browser. Graphics files can be used in Web pages you design. You can even download music files that can be played whenever you want.

The files you obtain from the Web come from many different sources. You can find files at sites designed for downloading, like Tucows. The Macmillan Computer Publishing site has a page devoted to available downloads of files for books you already own. *MP3 files* (we'll talk more about those files later in Chapter 20, "Hot Tunes and Game Galore") can be obtained from many different sources on the Web. In addition, as long as you have the permission of the Web page's author, you can save graphics from Web pages you visit.

Downloading Is Part of a Process

When you download a file to your computer, you're actually transferring information from a remote computer to yours. After the file is located on your computer, you might need to perform a few steps before you can use it. Files that are *compressed* to make them smaller and quicker to download need to be *decompressed* before you can use them. If the file you downloaded is designed to install a program, you need to run the file to set up the program. Some programs are easy to set up. When you select one of these types of files, the download, decompression, and installation procedure is sometimes handled by your browser and requires little intervention from you.

Different Types of Programs Are Available

Software programs are the tools that enable you to use your computer for a specific purpose. For example, your browser is a program that enables you to look at Web pages. There are thousands of programs you can download from the Web. Both Internet Explorer and Netscape Communicator can be downloaded (for free). You can find simple children's puzzles or elaborate war games with graphics, sound, and movie effects. How about a program that tracks your expenses or sets up a schedule for routine maintenance on your car? Software such as these and other programs are readily available on the Web.

The software you download generally fits into the following four categories.

- *Commercial.* Some well-known programs that you usually purchase from a retail store or catalogue can be obtained from the Web. If a commercial program is available for download, most times you'll find it on the vendor's Web site. Depending on the program, you might need to pay the vendor before you install the program. Sometimes, commercial programs that you download are working demos of the actual program and don't have all the bells and whistles of the full-featured product.

- *Patches, upgrades, and drivers.* Commercial software vendors and hardware manufacturers often offer upgrades or patches to existing files on your computer. For example, Microsoft offered *patches* to the Office 97 suite of programs after the original set of programs was released. Printer manufacturers, like Hewlett-Packard, offer *drivers* for most of their printers. Most patches and upgrades are obtained from the vendor's Web page and need to be installed like regular programs.

- *Shareware.* Most *shareware* is downloaded and installed on an evaluation basis. Many programs allow you to use them for a limited period of time or number of logins. If you like the program after you've worked with it for awhile, you pay a fee and register the program. Registered users often get documentation or technical support that isn't available to unregistered users. Some shareware programs keep track of how many days have elapsed since you installed the program or how often you've used it and don't allow you to open the program when the evaluation period is over.

- *Freeware.* Programs that you can download and use for free. Some *freeware* programs are sophisticated, like Internet Explorer or the Netscape Communicator suite. However, most freeware

Rev up your older printer
If you're working with an older printer, visit the Web page of the printer's manufacturer. Look for links to printer drivers and download the latest driver for your printer. (The driver is the way your computer and your printer communicate.) After you install the driver, you'll probably notice that your printer seems to be working better.

is written by a single author and is not very complex. Many freeware vendors ask you to register your freeware program.

- *Multimedia.* Files that play music, movies, or produce sounds on your computer. Sometimes multimedia files are free. Your computer needs to be equipped with a sound card and speakers and special players to be able to play multimedia files that you've downloaded.

Each time you download a file to your computer, you're using up valuable hard drive space. Additionally, some files can use up a lot of your computer's resources. Some seemingly small files containing programs or sounds take up a surprising amount of hard drive space and memory. Even if you've got a hard drive with lots of free space, before you download a file, find out how much space it requires and what other system requirements are necessary. Uninstall the programs that you don't care for or ones that seem to interfere with your system's performance.

Where Can I Get a New Program?

Programs can be obtained from many places on the Web. Table 8.1 shows the names and locations of some of the best places to find software on the Web.

Table 8.1 Great software sites

Site Name	URL	Description
Tucows	www.tucows.com	Links to some of the most popular shareware on the Web.
Download.com	www.download.com	Reviews of programs, along with the top, popular, and new software titles. Search for the program you want or locate it in a category.
File Mine	www.filemine.com	You prospect File Mine for the files you want. You can select multiple files and download them at the same time or download individual files as you see them.

Site Name	URL	Description
Softseek	`www.softseek.com`	Organized by categories. Additionally, the newest releases, editor's picks, and top downloads are listed.
Jumbo! The Download Network	`www.jumbo.com`	With 250,000 titles, you're sure to find the program you want. In addition to downloading software, visit Jumbo to play games or play Jumbo Lotto.
SquareOne Technology-Shareware Downloads	`www.squareonetech.com/sharware.shtml`	You can download individual programs or purchase a Mega-CD that contains most of the programs for under $40.
Microsoft	`www.microsoft.com/downloads/search.asp`	Free software that can be used with Internet Explorer and other Microsoft products.
Netscape	`home.netscape.com/download/su2.html`	Most of the software obtained here is designed for use in the Netscape Communicator suite. However, Internet Explorer users can download Netscape TuneUp for Internet Explorer.

The Danger of Computer Viruses

One of the biggest obstacles to downloading files from the Web is the threat of computer viruses. Unfortunately, a *computer virus* can wipe out your hard drive or destroy key files on your computer. Viruses are passed unknowingly every day. Sadly, viruses don't generate spontaneously, but are written to perform a malicious function. Because most viruses are invisible, you might not know your computer is infected before it's too late.

Although you can't stamp out the danger of computer viruses altogether, you can take steps to prevent infection. The first step is to download computer files with care. Obtain files from reputable sites that advertise virus-free software. (However, keep in mind that most

Computer viruses pose a real threat

A computer virus is a program designed to affect your computer by altering the way it works without your knowledge or permission. Viruses are transmitted on computer files. After an infected file is introduced inside your computer, the virus can spread from one file to another.

183

software vendors won't absolutely guarantee that their files are virus-free.)

The second rule of prevention is to use common sense. If someone sends you an unsolicited file attached to an email message, delete it without opening it. Be careful about accepting a diskette that contains a file copied from someone else's computer. (My sister's hard drive was wiped out by a virus that invaded her computer when she copied a recipe for chocolate chip cookies from a diskette provided by her neighbor.)

The surest way to prevent infection from computer viruses is to install virus protection on your computer. Many of the best anti-virus programs can be downloaded from the Internet on an evaluation basis, or purchased on CD. New viruses appear daily, so you'll need to update your virus protection program on a regular basis. Virus protection programs are not free; most times you'll pay between $50 and $75 for the full-blown version. Considering the investment of time and money you have in your computer, it's a small price to pay.

Some virus protection programs sit in your computer's memory, scanning all incoming files and watching your system for the symptoms of viruses. Others offer "on demand" file scanning, telling you when and where to check files. If a virus is found in a file, it's removed or disabled so it can't cause any damage. With virus protection enabled, you'll be able to share files with your friends and colleagues without worry.

Table 8.2 shows a few of the best commercial virus protection programs.

Table 8.2 The best virus protection programs

Program Name	URL	Approx. Cost	Description
Norton AntiVirus	`www.symantec.com/nav`	$50	NAV covers all possible sources of infection, including the Internet, floppy disks, email attachments, shared files, and networks. Updates can be downloaded monthly.

Program Name	URL	Approx. Cost	Description
Virus Scan Security Suite	`www.nai.com/ asp.set/products tvd.intro.asp`	$49.95	McAfee's VirusScan antivirus software is one of the strongest defenses you can install on your computer.
Pc-cillin - AntiVirus	`www.antivirus.com`	$39.95	Uses exclusive technology to scan compressed files and email attachments for virus infection. Viruses can be eradicated with the Clean Wizard for step-by-step removal.

Downloading Software from the Web

Visiting a software site on the Web is like going to a candy store. There are so many different varieties and "flavors" of software from which you can pick that it's hard to decide what you want. Understand what you're getting before you download and install new software. Before you download a program, make sure that you can answer the following questions affirmatively:

- Is the program designed to work with your operating system? If the description doesn't say that the program is designed for use in Windows 95 or 98, don't waste your time.

- Will you use the software? Sometimes a program that looks appealing turns out to be a mistake.

- If the program is an evaluation copy and expires after a set period—say two weeks or 30 days—will you have time to work with it? There's no sense installing a program that will expire before you have time to try it out.

- If you're accessing the Internet from work or school, do you have permission to install a new program on the computer you're using? Many network administrators restrict the programs that can be installed on a user's computer. Check before you install a program on a computer that you don't own.

SEE ALSO

➤ *Review information about modem speeds on page 36*

When you find a program that meets your needs, click a link to download it and your browser handles the download. How long the download process takes is dependent on the size of the file, your computer, and the speed of your modem. Fortunately, you can continue browsing the Web or working with other programs installed in your computer while the download progresses. However, don't forget that you're downloading a file and disconnect from the Internet. That will stop your download process.

After the download is completed, you need to install the program. Most programs need many files to run on your computer, which are compressed into one file when you download the program. Sometimes, the decompression steps are built into the installation process and you don't need to do anything to decompress the files. However, many programs require that you manually decompress the file you downloaded before the installation process can proceed.

Hot Downloads

There are literally thousands of files available on the Web. Table 8.3 shows you 10 of the hottest downloads and where you can get them.

Table 8.3 Hot downloads

Name	URL	Cost	Comments
Alexa	www.alexa.com	Free	Used by both Internet Explorer and Navigator to find related pages. If your installation of Internet Explorer has a Related button on the Standard Buttons toolbar, or Navigator has a What's Related button, Alexa is already installed.
Winzip	http://www.winzip.com/WinZip/download.html	Evaluation copy is free, $29 to purchase	WinZip decompresses files in .zip format. You can also "zip" files (compress a group of files into one smaller file) for storage or exchanging with co-workers or friends.

Name	URL	Cost	Comments
ICQ	www.icq.com	Free	Chat client that enables you to engage in text chat conversations over the Internet. Also offers chat rooms, a paging service, and directories of users.
RealPlayer G2	www.real.com	Free	RealPlayer G2 is a media for streaming audio and video. The G2 player enables you to listen to Internet radio or listen to MP3s while you're working on your computer.
Image Explorer Pro	www.cdhnow.com	$50	Use this program to view graphic images in over 50 formats. Also enables you to work with graphics images, using a variety of filters and features such as crop, resize, rotate, print, zoom, flip, or mirror. Advanced users can use Image Finder to animate images or turn them into 3D objects.
Nico's Commander	www.nico2000.com/index.html	$20	Nico's Commander is a Windows file manager that offers a dual directory/folder display and a host of useful options. In addition to performing all the various file-management tasks, it offers optional functions that can be accessed using your mouse or the function keys.
SolSuite 2000	http://www.solsuite.com/downdemo.htm	Free	Over 100 different variations of the Solitaire card game, from one small downloaded file. The games are graphics-rich and range in degrees of difficulty.

continues...

187

Table 8.3 Continued

Name	URL	Cost	Comments
Go!Zilla	www.gozilla.com	Free, with advertising banners, $29 without advertising	Recover from download errors and resume failed downloads, manage and categorize files to download later and get those files from the most responsive site with Go!Zilla. Gather links to files that you want to download by simply dragging them from your favorite Internet browser or with easy click and download integration.
Corkboard	www.pcdynamics. com/corkboard/	Free	Works like a screen saver with note-taking, picture hanging, memo minding, organizing, and calendar keeping functions built in. If you like to keep your notes handy, this program's for you.

Working with Windows Files and Folders

When you download a file, you need to save it to a folder that's located on your computer's hard drive. After the download is complete, it's easy to forget to which folder the program was saved. If the file is misplaced, you can get frustrated very quickly when you try to access the new file.

If you download a lot of files, your hard drive space can get eaten up by all the new files. Compare your hard drive to the drawers of your desk at home or in the office. You wouldn't fill all the drawers with useless paper and supplies, would you? If you did, you'd have to wade through all the junk each time you wanted something from your desk. After awhile, the drawers would become so stuffed that you'd have a hard time opening them at all.

Downloading files calls for some discipline on your part. First, you need to keep track of where the downloaded files are saved. Next, delete the files that aren't being used. For example, if you downloaded a file that was used to set up a program, you can delete the downloaded file after the program is running. Why? Because running the file decompressed it and installed the files necessary to run the new program. The original file you obtained from the Web did its job and is no longer needed. Delete all the downloaded multimedia files that you're not planning to listen to or view again. After all, if you change your mind, you can easily download the multimedia file again.

In the next exercise, you create a file on your Windows desktop to store the files you save from the Web. Although this exercise has more to do with Windows than the Web, following the steps will help you create a folder that will enable you to always keep track of your downloads. If you're a Windows wizard and have another folder you'd like to use, feel free to use your folder instead.

Creating a folder for downloaded files

1. Close or minimize all open programs so that your Windows desktop is visible.

2. Place your mouse pointer on a blank are of the desktop and click the right mouse button. A shortcut menu appears, as shown in Figure 8.1.

> **Minimize all**
>
> If you don't want to close or minimize each open program, accomplish the entire task with a few mouse clicks. Position your mouse pointer on an empty spot on the Windows taskbar and right click one time. Choose **Minimize All Windows** from the resulting shortcut menu.

FIGURE 8.1
Create a new folder for your downloads.

3. From the shortcut menu, choose **New** and then **Folder**.

4. A new folder appears on the desktop, similar to the one shown in Figure 8.2, with the words **New Folder** highlighted. Type **WebSave** to rename the folder. (You needn't delete the highlighted text first; as you type, the new text will replace the old.)

Now you have a folder that will hold all the files you download from the Web. We'll practice saving files to the WebSave folder in this chapter, so you'll have experience before you venture out on the Web for your own downloads.

As you're downloading, mark the name of each file. After you're done working with the file—either installing a program, or watching or listening to a multimedia presentation, delete the file.

Deleting a file from the WebSave folder

1. Close or minimize all open programs so that your Windows desktop is visible.

2. Double-click the **WebSave** folder to open it.

3. Right-click the file you want to erase and choose **Delete** from the shortcut menu.

4. The Confirm File Delete dialog box appears, as shown in Figure 8.3, asking if you want to place the file in the Recycle Bin. Don't be alarmed if the message seems different from time to time; depending on the extension of the file you're deleting, the text of the message may change slightly.

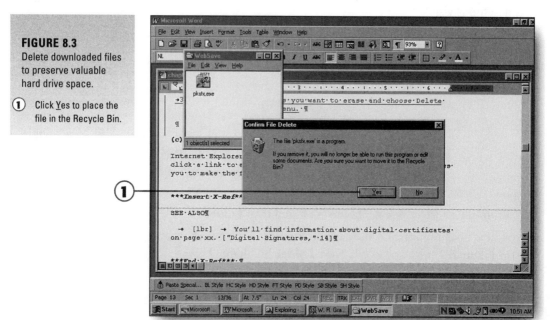

Downloading from Microsoft with Internet Explorer

Internet Explorer makes downloading programs a snap. When you click a link to a downloadable program, Internet Explorer enables you to make the following choices:

- **Run** *or* **Open** *this program from its current location.* When you select this option, Internet Explorer downloads the file and then looks for an application on your computer to run or open the file. For example, if the file is in compressed format, Internet Explorer looks through your installed software for a program that can decompress the file. If the file ends in `.exe`, Internet Explorer tells Windows to install it first and then run it.

  Choosing this option is the fastest way to install programs, although it might not be the safest option for your computer. Additionally, you won't have control over the folder in which the new program is installed.

- **Save** *this file to disk.* Choose this option to save the file to a location that you specify on your computer. After the file is downloaded, you'll need to install it or open it. If you're using a virus checking program, you can check the downloaded file for infection before you proceed.

Security Warning

When you tell Internet Explorer to run or open a file from its current location, a Security Warning dialog box might appear when the file has been downloaded. Usually, the alert is displayed if you've downloaded a program file. The warning lets you know that the program hasn't been digitally signed, another way of saying guaranteed as unchanged, by the software publisher. In fact, most software publishers don't digitally sign their programs. Alternatively, the warning might inform you that the software manufacturer asserts that the software is safe but tells you to install the software only if you trust the assertion. If you're sure that the software comes from a reliable source (such as a vendor like Microsoft), proceed with the procedure.

Empty the trash

When you delete a file, it moves to the Recycle Bin. Periodically, say every two weeks or so, empty the Recycle Bin by right-clicking the Recycle Bin on the Windows desktop and choose **Empty Recycle Bin** from the shortcut menu.

Getting a new font from Microsoft

1. If you're using Internet Explorer, connect to the Internet and open the browser.

2. Type **www.microsoft.com/OpenType** in the Address box and press **Enter**. After a moment, the Microsoft Typography page appears with links to downloadable fonts and information arranged by category.

3. Scroll through the page and click **Free Utilities and True Type Fonts**.

4. When the True Type Core Fonts for the Web page appears, scroll through the page and click the link to the nearest location to download a font that appeals to you, as shown in Figure 8.4. (In our example, we chose Andale Mono.)

FIGURE 8.4
Download the Andale Mono font.

(1) Choose the closest location.

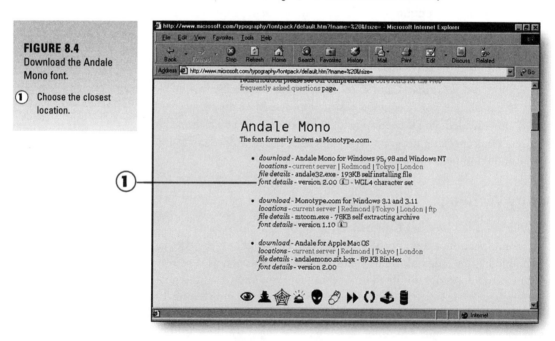

5. The File Download dialog box appears, as shown in Figure 8.5. Because Microsoft is a reliable software publisher, you can click the **Option** button next to **Run this program from its current location** and then click **OK**.

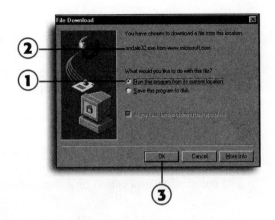

FIGURE 8.5
The File Download dialog box offers options for handling the file.

① Click this option only if you're sure the publisher of the software is reliable.

② The name indicates that the file is a program.

③ Click OK to proceed.

6. The File Download dialog box remains on the screen as the file is copied to your computer. A progress indicator appears on the dialog box that enables you to track the progress of the download.

7. Read the licensing agreement in the next dialog box to appear, pressing **Page Down** to see all of the agreement. When you're ready, click **Yes** to accept the agreement and continue.

8. The download process includes the installation of the font. (You don't need to do anything special to install it.) Briefly, a progress box appears as the Andale font is installed. After the process finishes, a message box appears telling you that the installation is complete. Click **OK**.

9. The next box to appear advises that the new settings will not take effect until you restart your computer. If you want to restart your computer now, disconnect from the Internet, close all open programs, and click **Yes**. Unless you want to see the new font immediately, click **No**. If you choose **No**, the new font will be available the next time you reboot your computer.

Follow the instructions
Depending on the file you choose, you might need to close and then reopen Internet Explorer or disconnect from the Internet and restart your computer. Follow the onscreen prompts when the file has been installed.

Using Netscape SmartUpdate

Clicking a link to a downloadable file begins the process in Navigator. The type of file you've selected determines the action taken by Navigator. If the file belongs to a file type that Navigator recognizes and has seen before, such as a graphics file, Navigator may load a previously installed *helper application* or *plug-in* so you can view the file in the browser. If the file is an executable file (one that launches a program), Navigator displays the Save As dialog box and asks you to specify a folder location so that the file can be copied to your computer. You'll need to run the program later on.

Sometimes Navigator doesn't recognize the type of file you're downloading. In that case, you're presented with an Unknown File Type dialog box and given the option to save the file to disk. After the download is complete, you can work with the file, opening it with a compatible application or decompressing it.

Using Netscape's SmartUpdate

Netscape makes it easy to obtain the latest components or upgrades to existing programs in the Communicator suite. SmartUpdate takes you to the latest and greatest Netscape software.

SEE ALSO

➤ *You'll find information about downloading Netscape Communicator on page 66*

SmartUpdate is a feature used most by users of the Netscape Communicator suite. Downloading software with SmartUpdate is done in four steps—selecting new programs, reviewing your selection, connecting to NetCenter, and then downloading the software. Allow yourself a few minutes to complete all four steps. Be sure to connect to the Internet and open **Navigator** before you begin.

Extending the power of Netscape Communicator

1. Open the **Help** menu and choose **Software Updates** from within Navigator. The SmartUpdate page appears, as shown in Figure 8.6. Notice that page is divided into numbered sections with the Software Components tab selected.

2. In step 1, shown on the page, you select new software. Click the link marked `Click here to select software`. A new page appears, with a list of Communicator software categories, including Premier Software, Netscape Software, 3D & Animation, and Viewers and Presentation. Click a link to the category for which you'd like to obtain a new component. (We've chosen 3D & Animation for our example.)

> **Save it automatically**
>
> If you want to automatically save a file to disk, hold down the **Shift** key as you click the link. Navigator will prompt you to provide a folder location for the file and begin the download process.

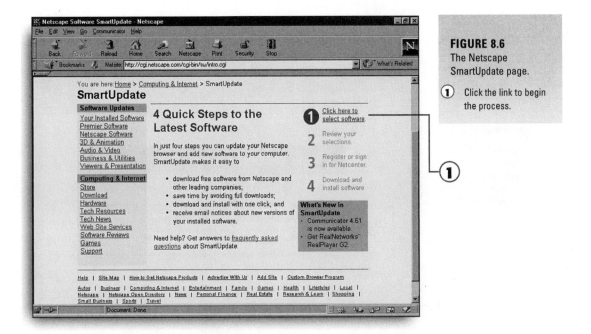

FIGURE 8.6
The Netscape
SmartUpdate page.

① Click the link to begin
the process.

3. A list of software that can be installed appears on the next page. Check the box next to each program you want to install.

4. When you've chosen your new programs, click step 2, **Review**. A list of the programs you've chosen to download appears. Review your selections and then click step 3, **Register or sign in for Netcenter**.

5. To complete the SmartUpdate process, you must be a Netscape Netcenter member. Membership is free and offers a free email account and a customized Start page. As a Netcenter member, you'll get email informing you when updates to your installed software become available.

   If you're not yet a Netcenter member, click the button to Register Now and follow the onscreen instructions to register as a Netcenter member.

   If you're already a Netcenter member, click the link to login. You'll be asked for your Netcenter username and password.

6. When your Netcenter registration information has been verified, the fourth step, Download, is available, as shown in Figure 8.7.

Not too many

You may feel like a kid in a candy store when you see all of the programs you can add to Communicator. Resist the urge to get them all at once. Instead, use SmartUpdate to obtain one or two programs at a time. After they're installed, try to detect any slow-downs or other negative effects in the Navigator browser. When you're sure that Navigator is working correctly, use Smart-Update again to get more programs.

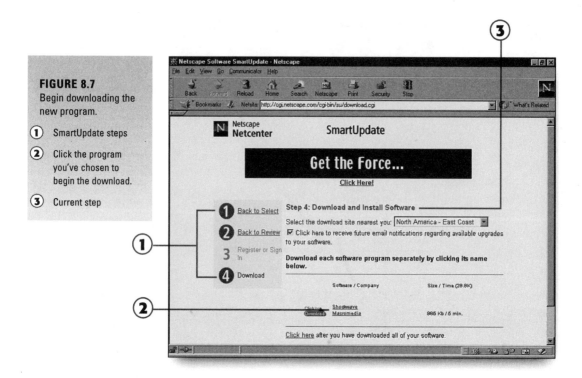

FIGURE 8.7
Begin downloading the new program.

① SmartUpdate steps

② Click the program you've chosen to begin the download.

③ Current step

Every program is different

The download and installation procedure in SmartUpdate can vary from program to program. For example, you might be asked to exit and restart Communicator, or told to restart your computer. To make sure that the program you're downloading will work correctly with Communicator, make sure you follow the instructions exactly as they're shown during the download and installation procedure.

7. The SmartUpdate Download Manager window appears, which contains information about the process and informs you of the progress of the download. When the file has been copied to your computer, another window appears, informing you that Netscape is setting up the files for the installation procedure.

8. (Optional) Depending on the component you've chosen, you might see a Java Security dialog box, advising you that Netscape Communications Company is requesting privileges to install software on your computer. Click **Grant** on this and any Java Security dialog boxes that appear during the installation process.

9. When prompted, click **Install** to install the component you've chosen. Netscape handles the installation process behind the scenes.

10. A message box displaying the name of the component appears when the installation is complete. Follow the instructions in the box to exit and then restart Communicator. When Communicator is restarted, the new component you installed will be available for you to use.

Downloading a New Game

How about a new game for your computer? Taking a game break gives your mind a chance to rest. All types of games are available for your computer. You can download word games, arcade games that are loaded with glitzy graphics and sound, or even computer versions of your favorite television games.

SEE ALSO

➤ *You'll learn all about playing games on the Internet on page 477*

In the next exercise, you'll download a simple game from the Web. Connect to the Internet and open your browser so you can complete the steps.

Downloading a game

1. Type `www.download.com` in the Address box of your browser and press **Enter**. The Download.com page appears in your browser.

2. A list of program categories appears on the page. Click the link to **Games**.

3. A list of Games subcategories appears. Click the type of game you like best. (We've chosen Arcade Games for this exercise.)

4. Scroll down the list of available games, reading each description. If you see a game you like, make sure that the program requirements are a good match for your computer.

5. Click the link to a game you like. A page appears, containing information about the game. Read the information carefully, and print the installation instructions if they seem complicated or confusing. When you're ready to proceed, click the link to download the game.

6. Navigator users see the **Save As** dialog box and can proceed to step 7.

   If you're using Internet Explorer, the File Download dialog box appears. Choose the option to **Save this program to disk** and click **OK** to access the **Save As** dialog box.

7. Click the **Up one Level** button (the button, that looks like a folder with an arrow pointing upwards, located to the right of the **Save in** box) until Desktop is highlighted and the files, folders, and shortcuts on your Windows desktop are displayed

Pages and pages

Download.com generally has more available programs than can fit on one page. Click the link to the next page number located at the bottom of the page to move to the next page.

Best of both worlds

To monitor the progress of the download and still have access to your computer, click the **Minimize** button on the Saving Location dialog box. The box appears as a separate button on your Windows taskbar, displaying the percentage of completeness as the file is copied to your computer.

in the Contents box. Double-click the **WebSave** folder and then click **S̲ave**.

8. As the file is saved, a progress box appears, similar to the one in Figure 8.8, showing you the progress of the download. If you're an Internet Explorer user, you can skip step 9 and click **O̲pen** to launch the file and begin installing the game when the download is complete.

9. To install the game, minimize all open programs so that your desktop is visible. Double-click the **WebSave** folder, then double-click the file you just downloaded. (If the file has a `.ZIP` extension, you'll have to use a program like WinZip to decompress the file manually before you can install the program.) Follow the onscreen prompts to complete the installation of the game.

10. After you've tested the game to make sure that it's working properly, delete the file you downloaded to preserve valuable hard drive space.

Using FTP to Download Files

File Transfer Protocol

FTP, short for File Transfer Protocol, is a way that files are transferred between computers. FTP sites use a hierarchical system of folders and look similar to the view you see in Windows Explorer.

The concept of FTP sites predates the World Wide Web. FTP sites are designed for the downloading of files and don't contain any of the text or graphics you're used to seeing on the Web. The structure of an FTP site is designed as a tree—similar to the files and folders inside your computer.

Although some FTP sites require the use of special FTP software, your browser can handle file transfers from most FTP sites. Both Internet Explorer and Navigator are designed to understand FTPs and work as an FTP client. Your browser displays the information on an FTP site as a column of links, with each link functioning as a file or a directory. You can download text and *binary* files.

The URL of an FTP site begins with `ftp://`, signifying that the site uses the FTP protocol. Your browser makes it simple to visit an FTP site by entering the ftp:// characters for you when you enter the site's address in the Address bar. Files at FTP sites are arranged in a *directory tree*, much like the files and folders on your computer.

SEE ALSO

➤ *Review information about protocols on page 112*

To move to another page in the FTP site, scroll to the top of the page and click the link to the **Up to higher level** directory. When the main page appears, click the link to the new page you'd like to view. When you want to download a file, click its link.

Telnet: An Internet Relic

In the days before the Web, a system called *Telnet* was used to connect one computer to other computers. Telnet works by making your computer a slave or *dumb terminal* of the computer to which you're attaching. The computer to which you're connected is in control during a Telnet session.

Telnet links on Web pages look like normal links. Your browser can access most Telnet links. Telnet is still used in some instances, but for the most part, few people need to use Telnet anymore. However, some government agencies, both local and Federal, maintain Telnet sites. Some colleges and universities also have Telnet capabilities.

As the Web becomes more powerful, Telnet is quickly becoming a relic. Unless you're accessing the Internet from a college campus or computer lab, you might spend your whole life on the Web and never find a link or reference to a Telnet site. You're most likely to find Telnet links on Gopher menus, another Internet antique.

What Is a Plug-In?

Plug-ins are companion programs that work in tandem with your browser. Both Internet Explorer and Netscape Navigator have some

Working with plug-ins

You download and install plug-ins like any other software program. Keep in mind that not all plug-ins are free. You might need to pay a fee or register your new program before you can use it.

basic plug-ins that are included when the browser is installed. As you cruise the Web, your browser lets you know when you visit a page that requires a plug-in that isn't installed. After you install the plug-in, it blends seamlessly with your browser to bring you the special effects called for by the Web page you're visiting.

Table 8.4 displays the name and description of some of the most common plug-ins you might encounter as you visit pages on the Web.

Table 8.4 Commonly used plug-ins

Plug-In Name	Description
Shockwave	Delivers exciting multimedia effects to your browser.
Acrobat Reader	Enables files in **.pdf** format to be viewed. Many U.S. government agencies, such as the IRS, use this format. Additionally, onscreen documentation for programs is often stored in **.pdf** format.
QuickTime	Enables you to view movies and other multimedia effects built into some Web pages.
Live 3D	Turns your browser into a virtual reality program.

Plug-in or helper application?

Programs that work in tandem with your browser can be plug-ins or helper applications. With a plug-in, the integration between the program and the browser is seamless; because the plug-in opens inside or inline in your browser, you aren't aware it's a separate program. Helper applications, on the other hand, are installed programs that your browser launches. For example, your browser might launch Microsoft Word to enable you to read a text file.

Working with Plug-Ins in Navigator

When you visit a page that requires an additional program, Navigator informs you that you need a plug-in and identifies the plug-in needed. If you opt to get the plug-in, Navigator identifies the program you need and provides a list of the sites on the Web from which you can download it. You'll need to click the link to a download site and then follow the download and installation instructions shown to set the program up on your computer. In many cases, after the plug-in is installed, you must close and then restart Navigator and then reload the page you were trying to view.

Instead of downloading plug-ins on an as-needed basis, you can determine the plug-ins that are already installed, and then visit Netscape's Plug-in Finder page to get the ones you want.

Obtaining new Navigator plug-ins

1. When Navigator is open onscreen, click the **Help** menu and choose **About Plug-ins**. The About Plug-ins page appears, showing the plug-ins that are currently installed with Navigator.

   If you're a new Navigator user, you might see only the default plug-in. If you've been using Navigator for awhile, or you're upgrading from a previous version, your list of installed plug-ins might be longer, similar to the ones shown in Figure 8.9.

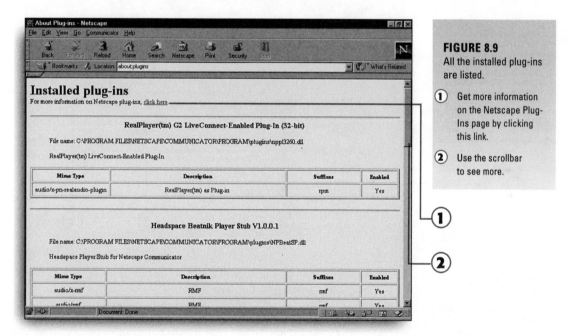

FIGURE 8.9
All the installed plug-ins are listed.

① Get more information on the Netscape Plug-Ins page by clicking this link.

② Use the scrollbar to see more.

2. Click the link to get more information about Netscape Plug-Ins page. The plug-in programs on the next page are arranged by category.

3. Click the link to a category that matches your interests. For example, if you want to view Web pages that contain movies or sound clips, click the **3D & Animation** link (see Figure 8.10).

4. Scroll down the list, reading the descriptions of each of the plug-in programs. To see more information about a particular plug-in, click the link in the plug-in's title. Click the **Back** button on the Navigation toolbar to return to the Netscape Plug-in page when you're through.

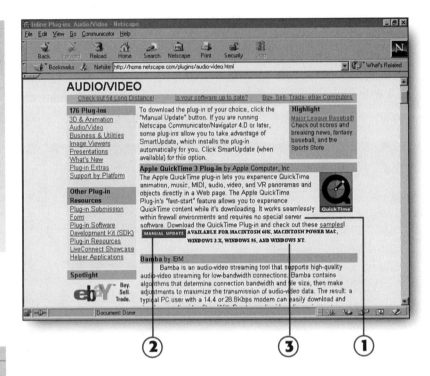

FIGURE 8.10
The 3D & Animation Inline Plug-in page has many programs available for your use.

(1) Read all about the program.

(2) Click the **Manual Update** program to obtain the plug-in.

(3) Make sure that the program will work on your computer.

Plug-ins might not be free

Some plug-ins are available on an evaluation basis. After a trial period, you'll need to pay for the program if you want to keep using it. Other plug-ins are free but might not contain all of the features you could get if you paid for the program. Read the information about the program carefully before you click the link to download the program.

5. If you find a plug-in you'd like to install to work with Navigator, click the **Manual Update** link.

6. The next page contains information about the plug-in, including any applicable charges, and download information. Follow the onscreen prompts to download the plug-in. When the Save As dialog box appears, place the file in your WebSave folder and then click **Save**.

(You can get to the Windows desktop by clicking the down arrow next to the **Save in** box and scrolling to the Windows desktop at the very top of the list. Click **Desktop** to display the folders and files on your Windows desktop in the Contents box, as shown in Figure 8.11, and then double-click the **WebSave** folder.)

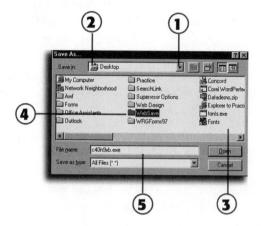

FIGURE 8.11
Navigate to your WebSave folder.

① Click this arrow to open the list of the drives and folders on your computer.

② Desktop is at the top of the list.

③ The shortcuts, files, and folders on your Windows desktop are displayed here.

④ Double-click the WebSave folder.

⑤ File you're downloading

7. When the download is complete, close all the open programs on your computer, including **Navigator**. Double-click the file to begin the installation procedure.

8. Open the **WebSave** folder and delete the file you downloaded, after you determine that Navigator is working properly following the installation.

SEE ALSO

➤ *Review the steps to delete a file from the WebSave folder on page 190*

9. (Optional) Repeat steps 3 through 7 to download and install additional plug-ins to work with Navigator.

Plug-Ins, ActiveX, and Internet Explorer

Internet Explorer utilizes plug-ins to extend its capabilities. Like Navigator, Internet Explorer informs you that a plug-in is required when you click a link to a Web site that needs one. Some plug-ins, like Shockwave at www.macromedia.com/shockwave/download/ have an AutoInstall feature that automates the download and installation procedure for you. Other times, you need to download plug-ins and install them.

ActiveX Controls also extend Internet Explorer's capabilities. ActiveX is a powerful technology, developed by Microsoft, that brings special effects to Web pages viewed in Internet Explorer. ActiveX Controls might include live audio and video, banners, or windows within your Internet Explorer window.

When you encounter a page that uses an ActiveX Control, you don't need to download or install anything to view the effects. Because ActiveX Controls are so easy to use, many Web designers now add them to pages instead of using plug-ins. In many cases, ActiveX Controls take the place of many plug-ins in Internet Explorer. In the future, even more ActiveX Controls will be available.

Saving Graphics Files from Web Pages

Internet Explorer and Navigator make it easy to download images from Web pages. You can include the graphic in another document. You can also open the image with a graphics program and modify it.

SEE ALSO

➤ *You'll learn about graphics images on Web pages on page 507*

Free clip art is available

If you want thousands of images that are free for the taking, search for "clip art" in Yahoo! You'll find a long list of links to sites who offer images for your use.

Before you grab a graphic from a Web page, make sure that you have the permission of the owner of the page or the Webmaster. Copying a graphic without permission amounts to Internet theft. Be very cautious when you're taking someone else's work; don't save the image if you're not sure that it's free and available.

Saving a graphics image

1. When you're connected to the Internet, and the image you want to save is onscreen in your browser, position the mouse pointer in the image and right-click.

2. A shortcut menu appears. Internet Explorer users choose **Save Picture As**. If you're using Navigator, choose **Save Image As**.

3. The Save As dialog box appears with the name of the image displayed in the **File name** box. Navigate to the folder in which you want to save the image file and click **Save**.

That's it! The image is saved to your computer.

part

III

CONTACTING THE WORLD

Starting Out with Email

An Overview of Email

Mail is often the highlight of your day. Even if you're dreading what the mailbox holds, you probably go through the letters, bills, and magazines before you get started with anything else. You toss out the junk mail, read the important letters, and set the other, less pressing mail aside to look at later. Mail plays an important role in the way people communicate.

Email is the Internet version of regular, or "snail," mail. You might already be familiar with email at your office or school. Most office and school mail systems work as an interoffice communication tool; you can send and receive messages from others connected with your organization. Internet email broadens this range. You can send or receive a message from an Internet mailbox, whether the person with whom you're corresponding is located across the street or across the world.

You don't need to be connected to the Internet for messages to be delivered to your electronic mailbox. Just as the letter carrier leaves your mail in your mailbox for you to pick up at your convenience, your electronic messages are waiting for you when it's convenient for you to retrieve them. They can be picked up whenever you're connected to the Internet. If you're like me, you can check for new email every hour. You can wait and check it once a day, or whenever it's convenient for you.

Using email has many advantages over making a telephone call or sending a fax. Email is fast and inexpensive. You don't have to pay long-distance or connection fees. You never have to play "telephone tag" with someone because your message can be delivered and answered in a matter of minutes. Files like letters, memos, and invoices, can be attached to email messages. If you're sending the same message to a more than one person, you can send the message to a group name once instead of sending it over and over to each person individually.

> **Check it out first**
>
> If you're connecting to the Internet from the office or school, check with your network administrator before you set up your own mail program or make any changes to the one you're using. Many companies use a particular mail package and don't allow individual users to use another one.

Understanding Email Addresses

Before you can send an email message, you need to know the email address of the recipient. Anyone who's connected to the Internet through an ISP or through a commercial online service like America Online or CompuServe has an email address. You or your co-workers might even have an Internet email address at your company or business. (Check with the network administrator if you're not sure.)

The following example is a standard email address:

`guinivere@knightsoftheroundtable.com`

The first part of the address is the person's username and is already set up with the ISP. A username can be made up of any combination of letters and numbers. In the example, `Guinivere` is the username. The `@` sign is used as a separator between the name and second part of the address, which denotes the location. The third portion of the address, the part after the @ sign, shows the location of the mail server or domain name, which is `knightsoftheroundtable.com` in our example.

Dealing with Spam

Spam is the Internet's version of junk mail. The subject of spam mail, the part of the message you see in your Inbox, is usually eye-catching. "Make $50,000 extra a year," offered one spam headline. Another asked, "Lonely? Call me now." If unsolicited advertising for goods and services shows up in your mailbox, you've been spammed. Usually you're invited to call a toll-free number to take advantage of the spammer's too-good-to-be true offer. Just like "snail" junk mail, the unsolicited offers and advertising are a nuisance. Valuable time and dollars are lost as the offending emails are sent, read, and deleted.

Spammers get your email address from several different sources. Some unscrupulous ISP's sell lists of their subscriber's addresses, although, fortunately, this practice is not common. More likely, your address was lifted from an email that you sent, probably to obtain information or request a free brochure. Another method spammers use to get email addresses is by the use of Web-Bots, electronic spiders that roam the Internet looking for email addresses on personal Web pages. Many spammers share their lists so your address might be passed around several times. Or, your address might be obtained from postings you make to newsgroups.

To send the junk mail, spammers use sophisticated software that can send up to 250,000 emails at one time. Most spammers use a fake return address, so it is difficult to determine where the mail originated. Don't waste your time composing an angry reply to a spam message; it will probably be bounced back to you because the address is incorrect.

Spam mail is illegal. Spam mail is distracting. If you get spammed, forward the offending message to your ISP or network administrator. Fortunately, spam mail is starting to get the attention that it deserves. Recently, Juno Mail, a provider of free Internet email, took legal action against spammers that were falsifying return addresses to look like the messages had been sent from Juno accounts. New lawsuits against spammers are filed everyday.

SEE ALSO

➤ You'll find all about Juno Mail on page 230

For the most part, spam mail is annoying, but harmless. However, spam mail may cost you money if you respond. One recent spam offer contained a toll-free number that was set to switch to a phone number overseas. The unsuspecting people that called were forced to pay thousands of dollars in long distance charges. If you're tempted to respond to a spam offer, think carefully. After all, spam might be another word for scam.

Different Email Protocols

When you send a letter or package through the regular postal service, your mail is routed to different locations and handled by several postal agents before it's delivered to the addressee. Electronic postal agents called *mail servers* handle email. The mail servers send, sort, and deliver email messages using special mail protocols.

Internet mail goes through Simple Mail Transfer Protocol (SMTP) gateways. Consider SMTP the official email language of the Internet because it processes messages sent from one email server to another. For example, your outgoing message is translated from Outlook Express or Messenger to SMTP, and sent over the Internet to your recipient's mail server. When it's received at the second SMTP gateway, the recipient's server, the message is translated again into the correct format, and then delivered to your recipient's mailbox.

POP3 and *IMAP* are protocols that also are used only during the processing of incoming messages. A new message is first received at the incoming mail server and held there until you retrieve it. If your company or ISP uses Post Office Protocol 3 (POP3), your messages are generally deleted from the mail server as soon as you retrieve them. IMAP, short for Internet Message Access Protocol, is the latest standard protocol for receiving email messages from the mail server. IMAP does everything that POP3 does, and more. If an IMAP server handles your incoming messages, you might have other options, such as viewing just the headings and the senders of mail messages before you decide to retrieve them.

Another recent development is the use of *LDAP*, short for Lightweight Directory Access Protocol. LDAP is a protocol that stores directories of email addresses in a standard format. Public LDAP directories are available all over the Internet. An LDAP directory on your company's server can contain the email addresses of all employees.

Comparing Outlook Express and Netscape Messenger Email Programs

Both Internet Explorer and Netscape Communicator come with full-featured email programs. Outlook Express and Netscape Messenger enable you to send and receive email messages. Both offer the ability to customize your mail to suit your personal needs.

Table 9.1 compares both Outlook Express and Messenger's use of some common mail features.

Table 9.1 Comparison of Outlook Express and Netscape Messenger

Features	Outlook Express	Messenger
Send and receive messages	Yes	Yes
Store messages in folders	Yes	Yes
Create custom folders	Yes	Yes
Search through folders	Yes	Yes

continues...

Table 9.1 Continued

Features	Outlook Express	Messenger
Allow multiple mail accounts within one username or profile	Yes	Yes
Enable return receipts	No	Yes
Set up custom filters for incoming messages	Yes	Yes
Additional security features	Yes	Yes
HTML formatting in messages	Yes	Yes
Allow use of Address Book	Yes	Yes
Support for LDAP (Internet directories)	Yes	Yes
Spell checker	Yes	Yes
Insert personalized signature	Yes	Yes
Send business card with outgoing message	Yes	Yes
Read newsgroups	Yes	Yes

Looking at Outlook Express

Outlook Express gives you almost everything you could desire in an Internet email client program. In addition to the capability to send and receive messages, you get support for multiple accounts, security features, the option to filter incoming mail filters, and the capability to handle Internet newsgroup messages in addition to your personal email. Using *LDAP*, Outlook Express also lets you quickly search Internet directory services right from within its address book.

Outlook Express is simple to use. When you first open Outlook Express, you see the Outlook Express window, as shown in Figure 9.1. The Outlook Express window is your starting point for mail and contains icons to other mail functions. If you want to bypass this window and go directly to your Inbox the next time you open Outlook Express, uncheck the box next to **When starting, go directly to my Inbox folder.**

FIGURE 9.1
The Outlook Express
window contains links to
many different options.

① Click an icon to start its
function.

② Type a query to search
the Web with MSN.

The Outlook Express window provides all the tools you need for
online communication. The page is arranged in frames (see Figure
9.2), each containing a separate aspect of the mail program. Across
the top of the page is a toolbar with buttons for the most commonly
used functions of the program. The frame to the left of the screen
contains a list of the folders you use to store your messages. The top
frame on the right contains a list of the message headers contained in
the folder that's currently selected. The bottom frame contains the
text of the message that's highlighted. If the message text is hard to
read, you can double-click it to open the message in a separate, layered window.

SEE ALSO

➤ *Detailed information about using frames is contained on page 130*

FIGURE 9.2
The Outlook Express window contains all the tools you need.

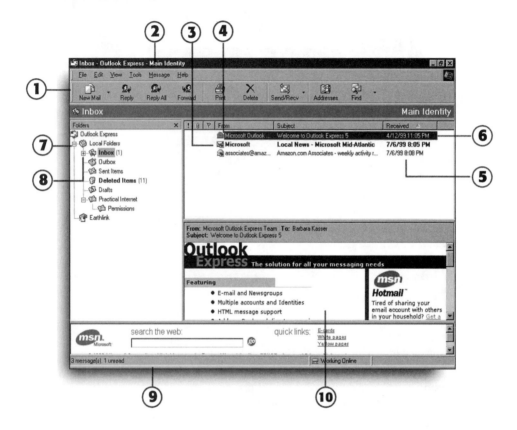

(1) Toolbar

(2) Identity is displayed

(3) Closed envelope means message is unread

(4) Open envelope means message has been read

(5) Highlight bar means message is selected

(6) List of mail folders

(7) – sign indicates subfolders are expanded

(8) + sign indicates subfolders are collapsed

(9) Status bar shows information about current folder

(10) Contents of selected message appears in the Preview pane

The Inbox is where most of Outlook Express' action takes place. New messages are deposited in your Inbox when you click the **Send and Receive** button. When you click the **New Message** button, a New Message window appears, ready for you to type the new message. If you're sure that the mail recipient can receive mail with graphics formatting, click the **Format** menu and choose **Apply Stationery** to select a message style from the list of stationery, as shown in Figure 9.3.

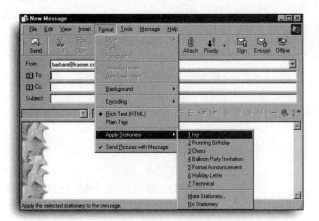

FIGURE 9.3
Creating a customized message style is a snap.

Setting Your Email Preferences

Before you use Outlook Express, you've got to tell it a few things about you and your email preferences. After your preferences are set up, the program will refer to them each time it sends and receives mail. The first time you open Outlook Express, the Connection Wizard asks your email address, POP account name and password, names of the incoming and outgoing mail servers, and whether the incoming mail server uses POP3 or IMAP protocol. Unless you switch to another ISP or something else about your Internet account changes, you'll only have to work through these steps once. If you're not sure about any of the information, call your ISP before you configure your mail. However, you can always run the Connection Wizard again to change any of the information you've entered.

The Connection Wizard sets up Outlook Express Mail

1. If it's not already open, open Outlook Express by clicking the **Start** button, choosing **Programs**, and then select **Internet**

Explorer and **Outlook Express**. Alternatively, click the Launch Outlook Express icon on the Quick Launch toolbar.

2. When Outlook Express appears on the screen for the first time, the Internet Connection Wizard appears to walk you through the setup process. Type your name in the **Display Name** text box and click **Next>**.

3. In the next dialog box, if you already have an email address, click the option box next to **I already have an e-mail address that I'd like to use** and type your email address in the **Email Address** text box (something like arthur@camelot.com).

   If you don't have an email address, click the option box next to **I'd like to sign up for a new account from**: and select Hotmail, the only choice available.

   SEE ALSO
   ➤ To learn more about Hotmail, check out page 230

4. The third dialog box (see Figure 9.4) deals with email server names. Verify that the type of server listed in the box next to the words **My Incoming Mail Server Is A** is correct. If it's not, click the down arrow and choose the correct server type from the list.

   Type the exact name provided by your ISP in both the **Incoming Mail** and **Outgoing Mail** text boxes. When you're ready to move along, click **Next>**.

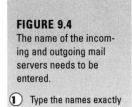

FIGURE 9.4
The name of the incoming and outgoing mail servers needs to be entered.

① Type the names exactly as your ISP provided them.

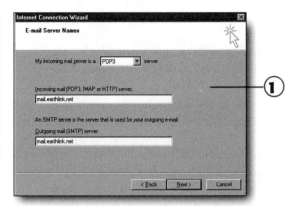

5. In the next dialog box that appears, type your mail account name and password. Check the box next to **Remember pass_word** if you don't want to type your password each time you open Outlook Express.

Click the **Log on using _S_ecure Password Authentication** option box if your ISP requires SPA to log on and fill in the subsequent screen with the specific information provided by your ISP. Click **_N_ext>** to continue.

6. The final dialog box reads **"Congratulations"** and tells you that you have successfully entered all of the information required to set up your account. Click **Finish**.

Since Outlook Express shares Internet Explorer's connection settings, you needn't fill in specific connection options. However, you can select some connection options that affect Outlook Express.

Changing connection options in Outlook Express

1. From within Outlook Express, click **_T_ools** and select **_O_ptions**.

2. Click the Connection tab to display the options shown in Figure 9.5.

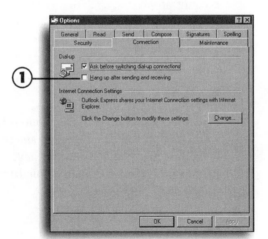

■ If you have more than one ISP or mail account, be sure that **Ask _b_efore switching dial-up connections** is checked.

> **Convenience versus privacy**
>
> If other people have access to your computer, think twice before you tell Outlook Express to remember your password. Even though it's sometimes a nuisance to have to key in your password, no one can read your email or send messages in your name.

> **FIGURE 9.5**
> Select the Connection option that matches your work style.
>
> ① Checking this box will break your Internet connection after sending and receiving mail.

- If your telephone and modem share the same phone line, you might want to select the option to **Hang up after sending and receiving**.

3. (Optional) Click the **Change** button to change the way you connect to the Internet. Remember that any changes you make to the way you connect here will affect Internet Explorer, as well as Outlook Express.

4. Click **OK** to close the Options dialog box and return to Outlook Express.

Changing Account Properties

The name of the incoming mail server appears as the account name when you set up a mail account. Sometimes, this account name is not very helpful. You can change the account name to a more friendly name, like "Mom's Mail" or the name of your ISP. My friend Dave's twin daughters each labeled their own account with their names.

You can change other information as well. For example, you can change your username, organization or even erase your email address so that it won't be displayed on your outgoing mail. To change mail account properties, click the **Tools** menu and choose **Accounts.** When the Internet Accounts dialog box appears, click the Mail tab and then click the account you want to change. (The account appears highlighted.) Click the **Properties** button.

Change any information shown in the General tab, as shown in Figure 9.6.

The information in the General tab is for display purposes only and will not affect the actual sending and receiving of email. However, make sure that you don't change anything in the Servers or Connection tabs, unless you get updated account or connection information from your ISP.

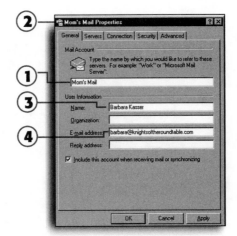

FIGURE 9.6
Select the Connection option that matches your work style.

① Type a more descriptive name for the account.

② Account name is reflected on the title bar.

③ Type the username that you want to appear on your outgoing messages.

④ If you want a reply address on messages you send, type one here.

Identities Give Outlook Express Multiple Personalities

Although Outlook Express always contained support for more than one mail account, Outlook Express 5 is more suited to multiple users. Each user can configure a separate *identity* on the program. When the identity is accessed, the user sees only the messages associated with that identity. (This feature is especially handy at my house, because my son and I share one computer, but each have our own email addresses.)

The main advantage to setting up identities is the privacy granted to each user. Since each user's messages are kept separately, no one can read someone else's mail by accident. Although it is not required, each identity can be set up with a password to make the mailbox even more secure.

Even if you're the only one using your copy of Outlook Express, you might have a good reason to set up more than one identity. If you've signed up for a free mail account with Hotmail, or one of the other free services on the Web, you can access your messages from this account at a different time than your regular mail. If you participate in chat sessions or discussion groups, you can receive any related mail in your alter-ego identity (the second one you set up) and keep your regular mailbox private.

The process of creating a new identity takes only a few minutes. You, or the user who sets up the identity, will need to know his/her email address and the name of the Incoming and Outgoing mail servers.

Creating a new identity

1. From within Outlook Express, click **File**, **Identities** and then choose **Add New Identity**. The New Identify dialog box appears, as shown in Figure 9.7.

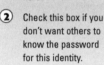

FIGURE 9.7
Create an identity for each email user.

① Type the username here.

② Check this box if you don't want others to know the password for this identity.

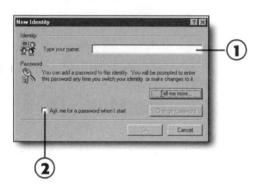

2. Type a name for this identity. Click **Tell me more** if you want to add a password to the identity. For extra privacy, check the box next to **Ask me for a password when I start** and click **OK**.

3. The Manage Identities dialog box appears, with the new identity shown on the list of mail accounts. Layered over the box is a smaller box, asking if you'd like to switch to the identity you just added. Click **Yes**.

4. The Internet Connection Wizard appears. If you are setting up the account for the first time, click the option next to **Create a new Internet mail account**. You'll then repeat the procedure to set up a new account for the identity you're creating.

   If the new identity will use the same account that you set up originally, choose the option next to **Use an existing Internet mail account**. In the next dialog boxes to appear, you'll be asked to import the account into the new identity and to choose to import **Messages and Address Book**, **Messages only** or **Address Book only**. You'll also be asked which mail folders you want to import into the new identity.

5. When the setup process is complete, Outlook Express displays mail for the new identity.

Switching Identities

Switching identities is a snap with Outlook Express! Anytime you're working in Outlook Express, open the **File** menu and choose **Switch Identity**. The Switch Identities dialog box, as shown in Figure 9.8, appears. Choose the Identity to which you want to switch and click **OK**. If the identity requires a different Internet connection, you'll be asked whether you want to switch connection. Of course, if the identity was set up with a password, you'll need to type the password correctly to open the mailbox.

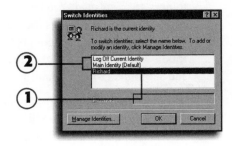

FIGURE 9.8
Switch to a different identity in Outlook Express.

① Current identity is highlighted

② Choose another identity from the list.

Making One Identity the Default

Outlook Express remembers the identity of the user who was using the program when it was closed. The next time Outlook Express is opened, it automatically loads the folders and Address Book of the last identity. However, if you log off the current identity before you close Outlook Express, the program will use the default identity the next time it starts.

Setting a default identity

1. From within Outlook Express, click **File**, **Identities** and then choose **Manage Identities**. The Manage Identities dialog box appears with the current identity in parenthesis.

2. Click the identity you want and then click **Make Default**.

3. In the **Start up using** box, choose the identity that should be accessed whenever Outlook Express is opened.

4. Click **Close**.

Looking at Netscape Messenger

Multiple accounts for one user

If you have more than one mail account and you'd like to see messages from all of them in your Outlook Express mailbox, there's no reason to create a new identity. Instead, click the **Tools** menu from within Outlook Express and choose **Accounts**. The Internet Accounts dialog box appears. Click the **Mail** tab and then click the **Add** button and choose **Mail** from the submenu. Complete each dialog box in the Connection Wizard, just as you did when you set up your first account. When you're done, the new account is added to the list.

You must set one of the multiple accounts as the default account; click the mail account name that corresponds with the ISP to which you're connected and then click **Set as Default**. (If you connect to another ISP later, select the mail account and click the **Set as Default** button.)

Netscape Messenger is a full-featured email client program that handles all your messaging needs. Messenger stores both your mail and newsgroup folders in a set of hierarchical folders. Because Messenger is tightly integrated with Netscape Navigator, you can switch between the browser and mail program with ease. Messenger offers enhanced mail security and a Return Receipt option that lets you know when your outgoing message has been received. Because Messenger supports all mail protocols, your messages are sure to reach their recipients without becoming garbled.

Messenger is very intuitive and easy to use. Messenger opens to the Netscape Communications Services, an area where your message folders are displayed. You're able to see the total number of messages stored in each folder, plus the number of read and unread messages (see Figure 9.9). Messenger creates six default folders, including Inbox, Unsent Messages, Drafts, Samples, Sent, and Trash. You can add subfolders to the default folders or add them to your Local Mail.

The first time you use Messenger, you'll need to provide some personal information. In the following step-by-step exercise, you set up Messenger mail for the first time.

Call your ISP if you don't know any of the information you're asked for during the setup procedure. If you fill in the wrong information, you'll get errors instead of mail!

Setting up Netscape Messenger

1. If it's not already open, launch Messenger by clicking the Windows **Start** button and sliding the mouse pointer to **Programs** and then **Netscape Communicator** and **Netscape Messenger**.

2. When Messenger appears on the screen, click the **Edit** menu and chose **Preferences**. The Preferences dialog box appears.

3. Click the **Mail and Newsgroups** category.

4. Click the **Identity** subcategory. The Identity dialog box appears on the right side of the screen, as shown in Figure 9.10. Type your name and email address in the appropriate boxes. If you want to, fill in your reply-to email address (if it's different from your regular address), organization, and location of your signature file.

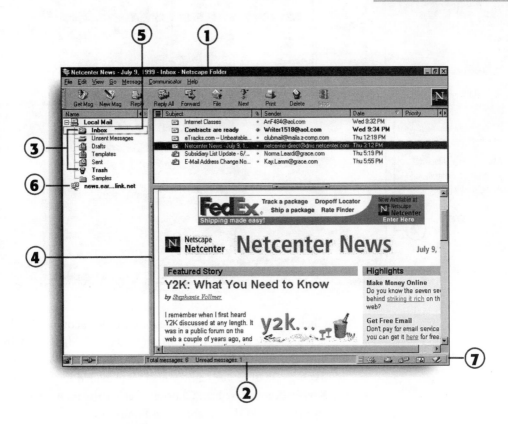

1. Header of message that's displayed appears in the title bar

2. Total number of unread messages in the folder appears in this column

3. Default folders created by Messenger

4. Drag the border to resize the pane.

5. Folder names are in boldface if they hold unread messages

6. This folder holds newsgroup postings.

7. Docked Component bar

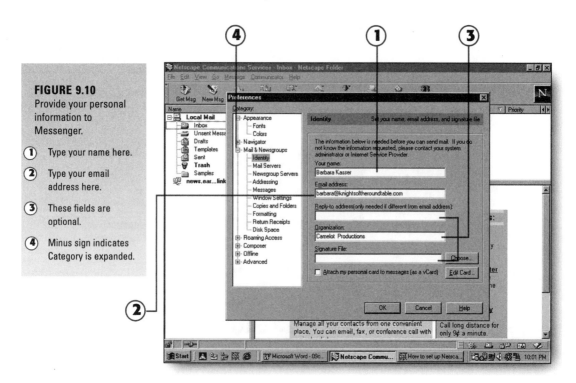

FIGURE 9.10
Provide your personal information to Messenger.

① Type your name here.

② Type your email address here.

③ These fields are optional.

④ Minus sign indicates Category is expanded.

5. Click the Mail Servers subcategory. In the Incoming Mail Servers section at the top portion of the box, click the **Add** button to display the General tab of the Mail Servers dialog box. Type the mail server name your ISP provided to you in the **Server Name** text box. Choose whether the incoming server is an IMAP or POP3, as shown in Figure 9.11.

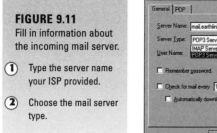

FIGURE 9.11
Fill in information about the incoming mail server.

① Type the server name your ISP provided.

② Choose the mail server type.

Type your user name in the **User Name** text box. If you don't want to have to type your password each time you open Messenger, check the box next to **Remember password**. Click the box next to **Check for mail every 15 minutes**, changing the interval if desired. Check the **Automatically download messages** box to have want Messenger to check for new messages when the program starts. When all the information in the General tab has been filled in, click **OK**.

6. In the Outgoing Mail (SMTP) Server text box, type the name of the mail server your ISP provided. Most people don't have a special user name for outgoing mail, but if your ISP gave you one, type it in the appropriate box. (Leave it blank if you're not sure.) If your ISP protects your connection to the outgoing mail server with a security protocol, check the appropriate option button.

Although there's lot of other information that you can provide to Messenger, you're ready to start sending and receiving mail.

Other Messenger Setup Options

Since Messenger is a very flexible mail program, many different options are available for you to set up. For example, you can change the appearance of your messages, indicate how quoted messages will be displayed, and even specify where Messenger should look for email addresses. To access your Messenger mail preferences, click **Edit**, **Preferences** and then click the subcategory you want to change.

The following section provides information about the other setup options in the Preferences of the Mail and Newsgroup category in Messenger.

Newsgroup Servers

In this category, you set up the servers your ISP uses for access to Usenet newsgroups in the Newsgroup Servers subcategory. The news server name is similar to the name of your mail server. You'll also need to know whether the server requires you to log in with a user name and password. Check with your ISP if you're not sure about any of the information about news servers. If you're using Messenger from your office and school, don't make any changes or additions to this category until you've checked with your network

---

Other ways to open Messenger

If Navigator is open, you can access Messenger (or the other programs installed in the Communicator suite) by clicking the **Communicator** menu and choosing **Messenger**. Alternatively, click the **Inbox** icon on the **Component** toolbar to make a fast switch to your mail.

Where are the choices?

The Mail and Newsgroups selection has a number of subcategories. If a plus sign appears to the right of the Mail and Newsgroups category, you won't be able to see any of the subcategories. Click the minus sign to expand the Mail and Newsgroups category and display the subcategories beneath it.

administrator. Some companies have a corporate news server that only employees can reach.

SEE ALSO

➤ *You enter the world of newsgroups on page 256*

Addressing

The Addressing category deals with addresses on outgoing email messages. The email address of each message that you send must be correct for the message to reach its destination. Email messages with incorrect addresses can go to the wrong recipient (bad news if the message is personal or contains confidential information.) More often, email messages that are addressed badly get lost out in cyberspace—without letting you know that the message was lost.

If you're lucky, you have a list of all of the names and email addresses you need. They might be organized into an address book, or tucked into corners on scraps of paper. Using a feature called *pinpoint addressing*, if you don't know the email address of a recipient, Messenger will try to find it in an online directory or address book.

Messages

The Messages subcategory (see Figure 9.12) is divided into four sections. The first, Forwarding and Replying to Messages, lets you set how a forwarded message will appear. The most commonly used selection is Quoted, which means that the original message will appear in the message you forward, along with any comments you add. This option makes the most sense, since it enables the person who receives your message to follow the message completely. (If the original message was not shown, your reply might be meaningless.) The other option available in this section deals with where the quoted message will appear. Most people are used to see seeing the quoted message below the reply. Accordingly, check the box next to **<u>A</u>utomatically quote the original message when replying** and then choose **start my reply above the quoted text** from the drop-down list.

In the second section, check the box next to **<u>S</u>pell check messages before sending**. Nothing trivializes an important message as much as typographical error or spelling mistake.

> **Moved, left no forwarding address**
>
> Called pinpoint addressing, Messenger can search through online directories for an email address you don't know. Even if an email address is found, however, there's a good chance that the address may be out of date or wrong. Play it safe. If you've got an important message to send, call the recipient to verify the address beforehand.

FIGURE 9.12
The Messages
subcategory affects
the messages you send.

① Set reply and
forwarding options
here.

② Unless you're a
spelling champion,
check this box.

③ Leave the system
defaults unless
you've got a good
reason to change
them.

The third and fourth sections deal with message wrapping and sending messages that use 8-bit characters. Unless you have a good reason
to change these options from the default settings, leave them alone.

Window Settings

Messenger has two settings for its main window, as shown in
Figure 9.13. There's no right or wrong way to set up your window,
so experiment with each one. You can also choose whether a folder,
newsgroup, or message will appear in a new window when you
double-click it. Your third selection covers whether clicking the
Newsgroup button on the Messenger toolbar opens newsgroups in
a Messenger window or opens the Message center.

Copies and Folders

In this section, you can choose where to send copies of sent messages
and newsgroup postings. Although you can send a "blind" carbon to
yourself or another recipient, most mail users chose to insert a copy
of outgoing messages and postings in the Sent folder.

SEE ALSO
➤ *You'll work with mail folders in Messenger on page 253*

227

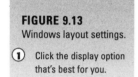

FIGURE 9.13
Windows layout settings.

① Click the display option that's best for you.

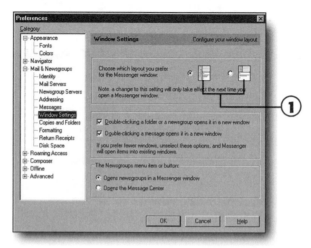

Formatting

Messenger enables you to select the formatting options of outgoing messages. This option may be important if you're sending messages to someone who's using an older mail program that does not support HTML formatting. Older mail programs can't read HTML formatting and might not be able to display the message. (Newer mail packages, like Messenger and Outlook Express, have no problem with HTML code.)

SEE ALSO

➤ You'll get a better understanding of HTML on page 488

Unless you're absolutely sure that your recipients are using newer mail programs like Messenger, Outlook Express, or Outlook, send messages in plain text.

Return Receipts

Return Receipts give you the option of following your email message to its destination. There are two types of return receipts: *Message Delivery Notifications*, or MDNs for short, and *Delivery Status Notifications* (DSNs). MDNs are generated from the recipient's mail program, while DNSs come from the mail host.

You can specify which notification you want to receive. Generally, the MSN is the most important and the one you'll want to see. However, keep in mind that some mail hosts and mail programs cannot generate return receipts. If you're sending an important email, consider asking the recipients to reply to your message as a confirmation that they received your messages.

Disk Space

Just like the mail you receive at home, email has a way of building up and eventually taking over your computer. Although you can control the amount of disk space that mail can occupy in this subcategory, only expert users should make changes here.

Learn good mail habits. Delete unwanted or unimportant mail after it's read. Since not all mail programs automatically delete messages you place in the Deleted or Trash folder, make sure you delete any messages that remain in the folder.

Return receipt alphabet soup

The terms MDN and DSN can be confusing when you're trying to determine if any important message was delivered. Think of them in alphabetical order—the DSN tells you if the message was delivered to the recipient's post office while the MSN tells you if the message was placed in the recipient's Inbox.

Using Third-Party Email Programs

In addition to the mail packages that come with the popular browsers, you can choose to use a mail program from a third-party company. Why would you do that? Well, there are a few reasons:

- For one thing, if you had your email already set up before you upgraded to the latest version of your browser, you probably don't want to switch now.

- Or, maybe you don't want to have to go through a transition period, each time a new revision of the browser and companion programs is released.

- If you're using email at work, the computer professionals might have chosen a mail program package that's independent from a specific browser and will work with all of the computers in the office or network.

Many people use third-party email programs. Although it's hard to get a handle on the actual number, many third-party software developers claim that users of their programs actually outnumber those using Outlook Express or Messenger. Table 9.2 provides a listing of some of the most popular email programs used by Internet users.

Table 9.2 Popular email programs on the Internet

Program Name	Description	Web Address
Eudora Pro	Powerful, full version mail program with support for IMAP, LDAP, and integrated address books and directories. Has superior capability to filter incoming messages. Easy to set up for multiple users. Eudora Pro has over 15,000,000 users world-wide.	www.eudora.com
Eudora Light	Freeware version of Eudora Pro.	www.eudora.com
Email Connection	Simple to use and configure. Graphic interface is easy to understand.	email-connection.com
Pegasus	Needs minimal installation, contains a glossary of common words to speed up typing, provides enhanced support for Return Receipt and Delivery notices.	www.pegasus.usa.com
Postman	Full-featured email program with enhanced support for users who have more than one email account.	www.netsoftdesigns.com/postman

Keep in mind that most of these programs are not freeware. You'll have to pay a small fee and register them to use the programs legally. Visit the home page of each program for more complete information.

Free Mail on the Internet

Free email is offered all over the Internet. You're probably thinking, "I already have an email account. Why do I need another one?" Well, there are several reasons why having another email account makes sense.

The most obvious reason to have two email accounts is that you have a private email address and make the other one public. Your private email address is the Internet equivalent of an unlisted telephone number—you provide it to only the people you want. When you visit a chat room or discussion group, your public email address is the one people see. If you start to get unwanted mail at your public address, you can get another email address somewhere else.

Families who share one computer or business travelers who want to be able to check their mail anywhere, anytime are also good candidates for free email. Some people who want a special email address, instead of the standard username@isp.com, get free email. If you have a child or teen who uses the Internet, an email address that protects their real identities should be used.

SEE ALSO

➤ *More information about protecting kids online can be found on page 412*

Unfortunately, the old saying about not getting something for nothing applies to free email. Even though you don't pay for the service, most likely you'll be subjected to advertising banners whenever you're using the mail account. Although it's rare, some unscupulous vendors sell lists of their free email subscribers to other Web advertisers.

Different Classes of Free Email

Free email comes in three different "flavors." If you're planning to get a free email account, choose the type that best suits your needs.

- Web-based email can be accessed anytime you're on the Internet. Think of Web-based email as mail that needs to be handled while you're at the post office. You can't turn away from the window, or in this case, leave the site, until you're through sending and receiving messages.

- POP3 email is handled by its own mail server. Free POP3 mail usually offers the widest range or services.

- Email forwarding is done by many free mail services. Forwarding services are often used by businesses. The forwarding service gives you an email address, but forwards the messages to your private address. You can update or change the address the mail is forwarded to at any time. The main advantage of using a forwarding service is that even if you change ISPs and,

Get it while it's hot(mail)

Outlook Express users can sign up for Hotmail in a jiffy. Click **Tools**, **New Account Signup** and then **Hotmail** to access the Setting Up Hotmail Connection Wizard.

consequently your email address changes, your email address (the address given to you by the forwarding service) remains the same.

You can find free Web-based mail at many sites, including many popular search engines and site directories like Yahoo! Check out your favorite start page for free email. Table 9.3 shows you a few places where you can get free Web-based email.

Table 9.3 Free Web-based email

Name	Get It At	Sample Address	Type	Comments
Netscape Webmail	`webmail.netscape.com`	user@netscape.com	Web-based	Great mail package, provided by Netscape. Webmail users get the advantage of Netscape Netcenter membership. Additionally, you can customize your messages, forward messages, and consolidate other email accounts.
Hotmail	`www.hotmail.com`	user@hotmail.com	Web-based	Owned by Microsoft. Many spam e-mails are sent (sometimes falsely) with a Hotmail address.
N2Mail	`www.n2mail.com`	user@many	Web-based	Pronounced N2 (Into). Many domain names to choose from, such as n2acting or n2bikes.com.
PostMark	`www.postmark.net`	user@postmark.net	Web-based	A good mail package with spell checking.
Headbone Zone	`www.headbone.com/hbzmail/`	user@headbone.com	Web-based	Mail for kids.
Telebot	`www.telebot.net`	user@telebot.net	POP3	Get your voicemail, fax, and email all in one location. Access all your messages through the Web or the telephone.

Name	Get It At	Sample Address	Type	Comments
Friendly E-mail	`www.mypad.com`	user@many	POP3 and Web-based	Has dozens of domain names to choose from. One of the better POP3 accounts you can find.
NewMail	`www.newmail.net`	user@newmail.net	POP3	Bills itself as the first international email, with services in English, Arabic, and German.
iName	`www.iname.com/member/login.page`	user@many	Forwarding	The king of email forwarding. Dozens of domains to choose from. iName also services dozens of other free email sites on the Internet.
EasyTo	`easy.to/REMEMBER`	custom name, such as hello.to/barbara	Forwarding	Choose from 12 domain names. Also offers URL forwarding service.

Free Mail Without Internet Access

If you're not in a position to set up an account with an ISP, and you don't have access to email from your workplace or school, you can send and receive electronic mail across the Internet. A service called Juno provides free email accounts. To use Juno, all you need is a computer running Windows and a modem (14.4kps minimum).

Juno is easy to use and displays a point and click screen that makes it easy for beginners and experienced email users to move around. The program offers many customizable features, including the following:

- A spell checker
- A personal Address Book

- The capability to create mailing lists
- The capability to set your own colors and fonts
- Mail folders for storing your mail messages

In addition, you can set up Juno accounts for multiple users if several people use the same computer. One of Juno's best features is that you can select your user name. Instead of a generic mail account name that has no meaning, you can use a name that makes sense. (For example: `kingarthur@juno.com`.)

All this for free? If you sign up with Juno, you don't pay anything for their email service. Juno is able to provide the service at no cost to its subscribers by running advertisements on the screen while the service is active. The advertisers actually support the cost of the email service. Ads, called banners, appear on the screen in the top right corner as you compose and read your email messages. While the Juno mail servers are contacted and mail is sent and received, showcase ads, which appear in separate window, are visible. If one of the ads interests you, click it to view the advertiser's Web page. To use Juno, you need to set up the Juno software on your computer.

After the software is installed, you connect to Juno through one of their many local access numbers. You can't "surf" the World Wide Web with Juno's free service, because it's only designed as an email program (although you can click through to an advertiser's Web page.). However, you can correspond with anyone who has an Internet email address. The service doesn't limit you to sending and receiving email with only other Juno members.

In addition to their free email service, Juno offers Juno Gold, an upgraded mail package, and Juno Web. You can now use Juno as your ISP and get Internet access for a small fee. Contact the folks at Juno at 800-654-JUNO for more information.

Email Without a Computer

Although almost everyone has heard of email, some people still don't have an email account. To date, email has been limited to those individuals who have access to a computer with a modem, the appropriate software applications and an account with an ISP. Some people see email as too complex, while others can't afford the costs.

Fortunately, a new product called the MailBug can provide email access to anyone with a telephone line. The MailBug is an email terminal device, which looks more like a telephone answering machine than a computer. MailBug users can exchange email with each other or anyone else with an email account.

MailBug users are primarily home or small office/home office users who are relatively new to email. You might consider a MailBug for a senior citizen or someone who has no interest in learning to use a computer but who wants to communicate by email. (My grandfather loves his MailBug.) The MailBug costs around $170. Email service costs an additional $10 per month. The MailBug home page at www.mailbug.com, is shown in Figure 9.14. Visit the site for more information about this unique service.

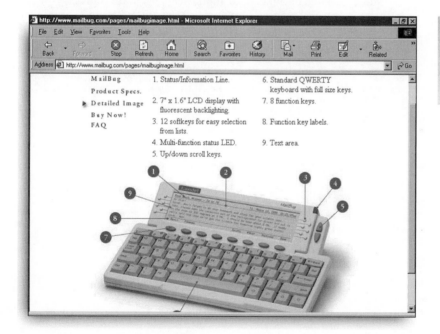

FIGURE 9.14
Visit the Mailbug site to see more about the service.

PocketMail: a Cool Tool

Another solution to email without a computer is a nifty gadget called PocketMail. The service is remarkably easy to use. Once the account is set up, PocketMail customers compose a message on the Pocket-Mail device, dial the nationwide toll-free access number and push one button while holding the PocketMail device against the telephone handset to send and receive messages. No cables or special connectors are required.

Outgoing messages are routed to the central PocketMail server and transmitted over the Internet to their ultimate electronic mailbox or fax destination. Incoming messages are received at the same time. A beep and LED display informs the user when the transmission has been completed successfully.

PocketMail can be used as a user's only email account or as a companion with an existing email account. When acting as an email companion, PocketMail retrieves copies of email messages from the user's primary Internet mailbox.

PocketMail is optimized for high speed, accurate transfer of messages. Before you can use the service, you'll need to buy a compatible device for around $150. After that, the combination of inexpensive service (around $10 per month) and the portability of the device make PocketMail a winner for travelers and business people. You can find out more about PocketMail at www.pocketmail.com.

chapter

10

Sending, Receiving, and Managing Email

Sending and receiving email messages •

Handling files attached to email messages •

Setting up a personal address book •

Creating a distribution list •

Organizing your mail in folders •

Creating and Sending a Message

In the last chapter, you did most of the hard work with email—getting your mail program set up properly. Now it's time to enjoy the fruits of your labor and begin using email. We'll start by creating a message.

To complete the steps in this exercise, Outlook Express or Messenger needs to be open and active on the screen. If you're not connected to the Internet, you won't be able to send the message you create.

Composing and sending a message

1. Click the **New Mail** (Outlook Express) or **New Msg** (Messenger) button on the toolbar. A new window appears for the new message.

2. Click in the **To:** text box and type the recipient's email address. If you'd like to enter multiple addresses, press Enter after you type each address. (If you want to fine-tune your mail skills before you send email to others, use your own address.)

3. Click in the **Subject:** text box and type the subject of the message. Condense the subject into a few words or a phrase. Mail users who receive loads of email judge the importance of a message by its subject. Messages with the Subject field left blank often get deleted without ever being read.

4. Click in the message area and type your message. The message area functions like a standard word processor, so only press Enter when you want to create a new paragraph. A finished message in Outlook Express is displayed in Figure 10.1.

5. When you're done typing, read the text carefully. To make sure you haven't included an embarrassing typographical error, click the **Tools** menu and select the option to check your spelling.

6. If you want to send the message later, click the **File** menu and choose **Send Later**. The message is placed in the Outbox and will be sent later on. When you're ready to send the messages in your Outbox, make sure you're connected to the Internet:

   - In Outlook Express, click the **Send and Receive** button on the toolbar.

- If you're using Messenger, click the **File** menu and choose **Send Unsent Messages**.

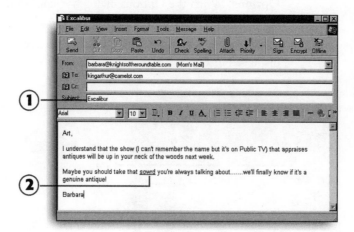

FIGURE 10.1
A finished message
in Outlook Express.

① Subject is brief and
to the point

② Spelling error trivial-
izes the message and
should be corrected

7. To send the message now, click the **Send** button on the toolbar. The message is placed in the Outbox while the outgoing mail server is contacted to pick up the message and send it out. Delivery might take anywhere from a minute or so to a few hours.

Creating a Personal Signature File

A *signature file* is a great way to personalize outgoing email messages. Your "sig" might reflect your name, address, and email address, or it can contain a funny or philosophical message. (My favorite sig states "I'm hoping to be the person my dog thinks I am" and is used by a fellow member of one of my favorite newsgroups.)

Both Outlook Express and Messenger support the use of signature files, although each program uses a different method to create them. I'll explain how to create a signature file in both of the following email programs.

Actually, signature files are an art form for many users, so expect funny and provocative sig files on many of the messages you receive. Some people take signature files to the extreme and include vulgarity or a crude message. Let good taste be your guide when you create your own sig.

Did you get an error message?

If you typed a recipient's email address incorrectly (with even a letter out of place or a misplaced @ character), you'll receive a notice that the message couldn't be delivered.

Setting up a signature file in Outlook Express

1. From within Outlook Express, click the **Tools** menu and choose **Options**. When the Options dialog box appears, be sure that the Signature tab is selected.

2. Click the **New** button to display the Signature dialog box, as displayed in Figure 10.2.

FIGURE 10.2

Create your own personal signature in the Signature dialog box.

(**1**) Check this box to make your signature appear every time.

(**2**) Click the Text option and type your signature here.

(**3**) Click the File option to choose a file from your computer if you've got a signature already set up.

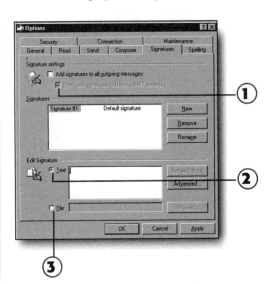

3. Click the option button next to **Text** and type your distinctive signature. Press **Enter** to advance to a new line.

4. If you've already created a file that contains the text you want to use, click the **File** option button and type the folder path and filename in the File text box. (You can use the **Browse** button to locate the file on your disk.)

5. Click the box next to **Add signatures to all outgoing messages** if you want the signature file to be included by default.

6. (Optional) If you have more than one account set up, click the **Advanced** button and check the box next to each account for which you'd like to use the signature. When you're done, click **OK**.

7. Click **OK** when you've finished creating the signature file and setting options for its use. Click **OK** to close the Options dialog box.

8. If you checked the option to attach your signature to all outgoing messages, your sig will automatically appear each time you send a message. If you didn't check the box, click **Insert** and choose **Signature** whenever you want the signature to display.

Setting up your messenger sig

1. From within Messenger, click the Windows Start button, choose **Programs** and then Accessories. Select Notepad from the list of Accessories. The Windows Notepad program opens with the cursor flashing in the top-left corner of the screen.

2. Type your signature file, using no more than 72 characters per line. If you want more than a one line sig, press Enter after each line. When you're done typing, click the **File** menu and choose **Save As**. The Save As dialog box appears.

3. Move to the folder in which you want to save the file. In the **File name** text box, type a name for the file and click **Save**. (If you can't think of a name, use **my signature**.)

4. The Save As dialog box closes and you're returned to Notepad. Close Notepad by clicking the **File** menu and choosing **Exit**.

5. Return to Messenger. If necessary, click the **Inbox** button on the Windows taskbar to make Messenger the active window.

6. From within Messenger, click the **Edit** menu and choose **Preferences**. When the Preferences dialog box appears, click the **Mail and Groups** category on the left side of the screen.

7. Click the **Identity** subcategory. Type the folder path and filename of the file you created in the **Signature File** text box, as demonstrated in Figure 10.3. You can also click **Choose** and navigate to the folder and filename.

8. Click **OK** to close the Preferences dialog box and return to the Messenger screen. Your signature file will now be added to all your outgoing messages.

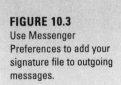

FIGURE 10.3
Use Messenger
Preferences to add your
signature file to outgoing
messages.

① Identity subcategory is
selected

② Type the folder path
and filename here.

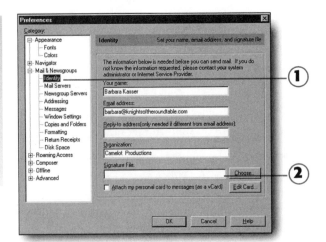

Reading a New Message

Whoever said something like, "It's better to give than receive,"
must have never used email! Sure, sending messages is fun. Receiving
messages is twice the fun without any of the work. Of course, email
messages in your Inbox can hold bad news or requests for you to
provide information. But no matter what the new messages hold,
most everyone loves to see them in the Inbox.

To receive your mail in Outlook Express and Messenger, you need
to be connected to the Internet. Click the appropriate button on
the toolbar (In Outlook Express, click **Send and Receive** and in
Messenger click **Get Msg**. The mail program contacts your mail
server and your new messages are delivered from the mail server
to you. Depending on how your mail is set up, you may see a dialog
box, like the one shown in Figure 10.4, that asks for your mail password. If so, type very carefully. Passwords are case-sensitive. Even if
you type the password characters correctly, you won't get your mail if
the case is wrong. Because the characters you type appear as asterisks
on the screen for security reasons, you won't know if you've made an
error.

When your mail is delivered, you'll see one line for each new message that includes the header (subject line of the message), the name
of the sender, and the date and time the message was sent. Closed
envelope icons located at the left side of the message line denote new

messages. Although both Outlook Express and Messenger provide preview areas below the list of messages, it's hard to read a long or important message when only a portion of the message is visible.

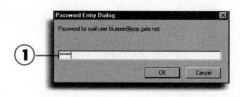

FIGURE 10.4
You may need to enter your mail password.

① The password appears as asterisks.

Double-click a message to open it in a separate window. You can drag the message window around the screen or maximize it, because the window is like any other in your Windows program. (If you look at the Windows taskbar, you'll see a button for the message window, as well as the mail program.) When you're done reading the message, close it by clicking the **Close (X)** button on the message window title bar.

Answering a Message

Some messages are self-contained and don't require any further action from you. Other times, you need to answer the message or forward it on to someone else for further handing. In Outlook Express and Messenger, replying to a message takes a few mouse clicks.

Replying to a message

1. Reply to a message by opening the message or selecting it in the Inbox.

2. In Outlook Express, click the **Reply** button on the toolbar if you want to reply to the person who sent the message or **Reply to All** if you want everyone who received the message to see your response.

   In Messenger, click the Reply button and then choose either **Reply to Sender** or **Reply to Sender and All Recipients**.

   The message opens with the recipient's name filled in the **To:** box and the subject of the original message preceded by **Re:**

3. Type your reply and click **Send**. Your reply will be displayed above the text of the original message. Figure 10.5 demonstrates an example of a Reply in Outlook Express.

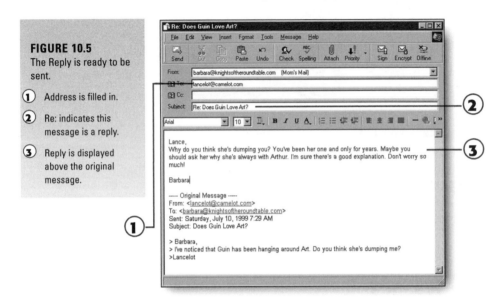

FIGURE 10.5
The Reply is ready to be sent.

(1) Address is filled in.

(2) Re: indicates this message is a reply.

(3) Reply is displayed above the original message.

4. To forward a message, open or select the message first and then click the **Forward** button. The message opens with the subject of the original message preceded by Fw: (Outlook Express) or Fwd: (Messenger).

5. Type the email address of the person to whom you're forwarding the message in the **To:** text box. If desired, type a brief message and click **Send**.

Print it fast

Want a hard copy of the message you're reading? Click the **Print** button while the message is open. The message will print at your default printer.

How Private Is Email?

Where you send and receive email has a lot to do with how private your messages are. Most employers consider email to be the property of the company, not the property of the person who sends or receives it. Many companies routinely look through the mail messages of their employees to make sure that confidential information isn't being disclosed. If you're using the company email for surreptitious, illegal or even personal reasons, you could lose your job.

If you are connecting to the Internet from home, check with your ISP if you have any questions about the privacy of your email communications. A search warrant is required to read messages while they are in transit. However, most ISP's keep backup tapes of mail which are not protected by Federal law.

A little caution when sending email goes a long way. Incorrectly addressed messages can be delivered to the wrong mailbox. Someone could sit down at your computer and read your saved messages while you were at the coffee machine or at lunch. A confidential message can be printed by the recipient and passed around or displayed without breaking any laws. Play it safe. Don't use mean, foul, or sexually explicit language in messages you send. Your email Inbox isn't a permanent storage area, delete or file messages after you read them. Make sure that your Wastebasket or Trash folder (or whatever folder holds the messages you delete) is emptied at the end of each business day. Close your mail program when you leave your desk.

> **Ask if you don't know**
>
> Check with your boss or Human Resources representative about the company's email policy if you have any questions. Getting fired because you unintentionally abused the mail policy just isn't worth the risk.

Dealing with File Attachments

Files can be attached to email messages that you send and receive. Any file that resides on your computer can be attached to an Outlook Express or Messenger email message. In addition to standard text files such as memos, letters, and other business documents, you can use mail to send and receive graphics images and even sound or movie clips.

- If you want to attach a file to an outgoing message in Outlook Express, click the **Attach** button on the New Message toolbar. When the Insert Attachment dialog box appears, type the folder path and filename in the **File Name:** text box. Alternatively, navigate to the folder that holds the file and click the file you'd like to attach. When the file name and folder path are displayed correctly, click **Attach** to close the Insert Attachment dialog box and return to the message. The attachment appears in a new box in the header portion of the message.

- In Messenger, as you're preparing your message, click the **Attach button,** and then click **File** from the submenu. type the folder location and file name in the **File name** text box on the Enter file to attach dialog box and click **Open**.

Problems with Attaching Files

If the recipient doesn't have the same program on her computer that you used to create the file, the attachment might not be able to be opened. If the recipient has a similar program, the translation process might produce formatting or other serious errors.

Another problem occurs if the recipient's mail program doesn't have an automatic decoder to translate incoming file attachments. If this is the case, the attachment hasn't been translated properly; instead of the correct file, the recipient opens a file filled with strange, unreadable characters.

If you're sending a file attachment to a company or business, you need to find out in advance if file attachments are permitted. Some companies routinely strip attachments because they feel that attachments create an unnecessary security risk. Other companies permit attachments, but limit the file size. If you're attaching an important file, like a business presentation, test it out before you actually send the real file. A few minutes of your time could save you a big headache later on.

Save yourself time and grief by checking with the recipient before you send an attachment. Find out if his mail program can accept attachments.

Files You Get Can Create Headaches

Files can also be attached to messages you receive. Alarm bells need to go off in your head when you see a file attachment. With the vast number of computer viruses floating out in cyberspace, you don't want to do anything to infect your computer. Be very careful; if the file attachment was unsolicited and you don't know the sender, don't open the file.

SEE ALSO

➤ Read an in-depth explanation of computer viruses on page 183

In both Outlook Express and Messenger, file attachments are shown apart from the text of the message. Each attachment is listed separately, with the name of the file displayed. Double-clicking a file attachment will open it if your computer recognizes its *file type*. The file type is based on the three-letter suffix of the file name, such as .DOC, .XLS or .GIF. If the file attachment contains a virus, the dirty work will be started as soon as you open it. (An unopened file attachment, even if it contains a deadly virus, can't harm your computer.)

The best way to deal with computer viruses is to run a program designed to find and eradicate them. If you're not running such a program, resist the temptation to open an attachment. My sister's computer was infected with a virus that came from a disk containing a recipe for chocolate chip cookies she'd gotten from her unsuspecting neighbor. The virus wiped out both my sister's and the neighbor's hard drives.

Hoax Viruses

A virus hoax is a false warning about a computer virus. The message typically warns about opening a message with a specific title, like "Penpal Greetings" or "Good Times." Hoax virus messages always contain frightening language that warns you not to open the message because it will delete your hard drive, or something to that effect.

Hoax viruses always ask you to forward the message to everyone you know. Because most people are good citizens, they follow the instructions and send the message to everyone at work or in their circle of friends. The same hoax message can be sent thousands of times, tying up bandwidth and clogging mail gateways. No one knows how these messages originate, but they take the email community by storm.

Even though hoax viruses seem legitimate, resist the temptation to panic. Remember that you can't infect your computer with a virus by opening an email message. Delete the hoax message; don't forward it to anyone else. The best defense against hoax viruses is education. You can read about hoax viruses at the IBM Hype Alert Page at `www.av.ibm.com/BreakingNews/HypeAlert` and at Symantec's Virus Alert page at `www.symantec.com/avcenter/hoax.html`. Consider sending links to these pages to the individual who sent you the virus hoax message.

Play it safe!

Play it safe with files attached to mail messages. Never assume that because you know the sender, the file is not infected. Computer viruses happen on the computers of some of the nicest, most trusting individuals (as well as on computers of the malicious rats who design them in the first place). Take the extra time necessary to make sure you're not opening a damaged file.

Other Hoax Emails

Although not quite as common as hoax virus messages, a new type of hoax email has appeared on the Internet. This type of hoax promises that you will receive a premium or gift for forwarding the message to everyone you know. The messages are false.

My favorite bogus message is one in which you're assured that Microsoft will pay you $5.00 each time you forward the message to someone else. Another one promises that a popular theme park will send you coupons for free admission if you forward the message to 50 people. Yet another message warns that the United States Congress wants to tax each email message you send and asks you to take appropriate action.

The tip-off that these, and similar messages, are a hoax is that they ask you to send the message to everyone you know. If you receive a message that seems incredulous, it probably is! (Obviously, Microsoft can't track every email message that's sent through the Internet.) Before you waste your time and the time of the people to whom you're planning to send the message, do a little research. Search for the topic of the message using your favorite search engine. Chances are you'll find that it's a hoax.

SEE ALSO

➤ *Review how to use a search engine on page 158*

Creating Entries in Your Address Book

It's mighty hard to remember everyone's email address. Even if you've got the name and mail server right, you might forget the exact syntax of the address, like the placement of the @ (at) or . (dot) characters. Make it easy on yourself and create an entry in your Address Book for each person with whom you correspond. After you've created some individual entries, you can combine the names into a group. You use the group like a master distribution list; for example, if you're sending the same email message to many recipients, why not send the message one time to all the names in the group.

Using the Outlook Express Address Book

1. Click the **Address** button on the Outlook Express toolbar.

2. When the Address Book window opens, click the **New** button and choose **New Contact** from the list to display the Properties dialog box (see Figure 10.6).

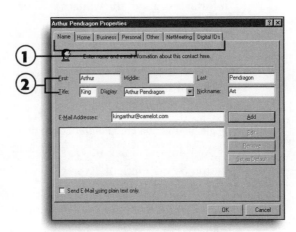

FIGURE 10.6
Create an entry in the Outlook Express Address Book.

(**1**) Tabs for contact information

(**2**) Applicable boxes have been filled in

3. Enter the information for your new contact in the appropriate panel by selecting one of the six tabs shown at the top of the Properties dialog box. Table 10.1 shows the Tab name and what type of information about the contact you might want to include under each tab. You needn't fill in every field on each of the tabs. Enter only the data you need.

Table 10.1 New contact information

Tab Name	Data
Personal	Full name, nickname, and email address
Home	Home address and telephone number, URL of Web page, if any
Business	Business address and telephone numbers, job title, department name
Other	Personal notes about the contact
NetMeeting	Server name and other information used in Internet conferencing with Microsoft NetMeeting
Digital IDs	Digital IDs and associated email address for advanced security

4. Click the **Personal** tab and type the name and email address of the contact in the appropriate fields.

5. (Optional) Click any of the other tabs and enter applicable information about the contact.

6. Click **OK** to close the Properties dialog box when all the information about the contact is entered.

7. Repeat steps 1 through 5 to add additional contacts to your Windows Address Book.

Instead of sending out the same message to multiple recipients, why not create a distribution group? That way, you don't need to waste time sending the same message again.

Creating a distribution group in Outlook Express

1. If the Address Book is not already open, click the **Address Book** button on the Outlook Express toolbar.

2. Click the **New** button on the Address Book toolbar and choose **New Group** from the list. When the Properties dialog box appears, type a descriptive name for the group in the **Group Name** text box.

3. Click **Select Members** to display the Select Group Members dialog box. A list of all of the contacts in your Address Book appears in a box on the left.

4. Select the name of the first person you want to add to the group and click the **Select** button. The name you chose now appears in the **Members** list on the right.

5. Repeat step 4 to add each additional person to the distribution group. Alternatively, hold down the Ctrl key and click each name that you want to add to the group. When all of the desired names appear highlighted, click **Select**.

6. When you're done adding names to the group, click **OK** to return to the Group Properties dialog box. Click **OK** to close the Group Properties dialog box and display the Windows Address Book. The name of the Distribution Group appears in bold type on the list of contact. The icon to the left of the group name displays several people, letting you know the entry is a group.

Create an automatic entry in your address book

From within Outlook Express, click **Tools** and choose **Options**. When the Options dialog box appears, select the General tab and check the box next to **Automatically put people I reply to in my Address Book**. Click **OK** to close the dialog box and return to Outlook Express.

To send a message to the group, type the Group name in the To: box when you're composing a message. Outlook Express will send the message to each member of the group.

Using the Messenger Address Book

Messenger's Address Book makes it easy to keep track of all your mail contacts. Right-click a message on the Message List and choose **Add to Address Book** to place the sender's information in your Address Book. Select **Sender** if you want to add an entry for the person who sent you the message or **All** to add all the recipients if the message was sent to multiple addressees. You can also create a manual entry.

Creating an entry in the Messenger Address Book

1. Click the **Communicator** menu and select **Address Book** from within any open Communicator program. The Address Book opens in its own window.

2. Click the **New Card** button. The New Card dialog box appears.

3. The New Card dialog box is divided into three tabs: Name, Contact, and Notes. The first tab, Name, is open. Fill in any of the fields in the Name tab, pressing the Tab key to advance from field to field. An example of a completed Name tab is shown in Figure 10.7.

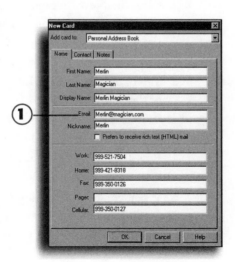

FIGURE 10.7
Fill in the fields you want.

(1) The Email address field must be filled in.

4. If you want to store additional information, click the Contact tab and fill in any of the fields shown, including Address, Home and Work Telephone, and Fax number.

5. If you have any additional information you'd like to add, click the Notes tab and type it there.

6. When all of the information has been added to the card, click **OK**.

7. Repeat steps 2 through 5 to create additional Address Book cards.

8. Close the Address Book by opening the **File** and choose **Close** or click the **Close** button on the Address Book toolbar.

9. To use an Address Book entry when you're creating an email message, position your mouse pointer in the To: box and click the **Address** button on the toolbar. When the Address Book opens, double-click the name you want on the list. The list closes and the name is added to your message.

Make a distribution list to send one message to multiple recipients.

Creating a distribution list in Messenger

1. If the Address Book's not already open, click the **Communicator** menu and select **Address Book** from within any open Communicator program.

2. Click the **New List** button on the Address Book toolbar. When the Mailing List dialog box appears, type a descriptive name for the list in the List Name text box. If you want, type a nickname for the list and a brief description in the appropriate text boxes.

3. Tab to or click in the **Members Names** area and type the name of the first list member exactly as you entered it in the Address Book. As you type, Messenger completes the entry for you. Press **Enter** when the first name has been entered.

4. Repeat step 3 for each additional member you want to add to the list.

5. When you're done adding names to the list, click **OK**. The Mailing List dialog box disappears and you're returned to the Address Book. In addition to the entries for individuals, an entry for the list is displayed. (Individual entries display email addresses; list entries do not.)

6. When you want to send an email message to the members of a Distribution List, position your mouse pointer in the To: box of the message you're composing and click the **Address** button on the toolbar. When the Address Book opens, double-click the **List** name you want. The Address Book closes, and the Distribution List name is added to your message.

Managing Your Mail Messages

When you first start using email, you probably won't get too many mail messages at one time. However, after you've established your cyber-identity and made a few online friends, your Inbox overflows with mail. With loads of messages stacked in your Inbox, you can't manage your mail efficiently. Stop the problem before it starts by devising a filing system for your mail messages.

The first rule to follow for your mail is to get rid of all messages that you don't need to keep. Unless you need to refer to a message later, delete it after you read it. Deleting a message is a snap. After you've double-clicked a message to open it, click the Delete button on the message toolbar when you've read the text. In both Outlook Express and Messenger, clicking the **Delete** button provides the added benefit of opening the next message on the message list.

Undoubtedly, some messages need to be retained. Rather than piling up in the Inbox, set up folders for the messages you plan to keep. Use your email Inbox like the Inbox at your office or your mailbox at home—deal with each new piece of mail as it comes in. Think of the Inbox as a starting place for the mail you receive.

How many folders should you create? Your filing system can be as elaborate or as simple as you choose. You can create folders and subfolders. If you're not sure, start with a few folders and see how it goes. You can create new folders, or delete existing ones, any time you're using mail.

Creating Mail Folders

Designing the structure of the filing system is the hard part, creating the folders is easy!

To begin, Outlook Express users should click **Outlook Express**, the first entry in the list of folders shown on the left side of the Outlook Express screen. If you're using Messenger, click the **Communicator** menu and choose **Messenger**.

Highlight the Local Folder in Outlook Express or the Local Mail in Messenger and click the right mouse button and choose **New Folder** from the resulting submenu. Type a name for the new folder and click **OK**. The new folder you created appears in the list of folders.

Repeat the procedure to create as many folders as you'd like. Remember, you can create a new mail folder any time. If you need to delete a mail folder, select it and then click the right mouse button. Choose **Delete** to remove the mail folder from the list (only after you've first moved the messages you want to keep that were saved in the folder).

Placing Messages in Mail Folders

Now that you've gone to the trouble to design a filing system, how about moving some of your messages into the folders you just created? Do it now. Mail has a way of building up.

Filing mail in Outlook Express and Messenger

1. Click a message to select it. (The message appears highlighted.)

2. Without releasing the mouse button, drag the mouse pointer so that the tip of the arrow is positioned over the folder in which you want to place the message.

3. Release the mouse button and the message is transferred to the new folder.

4. To open a folder and display its contents, double-click the folder name.

chapter 11

Joining Newsgroups and Mailing Lists

Joining a newsgroup •

Learning newsgroup slang •

Using Microsoft Outlook Express and •
Netscape Messenger for accessing
newsgroups

Subscribing to a mailing list •

Discussion Groups

Two different types

Internet discussion groups can be moderated, in which submissions are automatically directed to a moderator, who edits or filters them and then posts the results. Most discussion groups are unmoderated; anyone can post anything. Discussions in unmoderated groups can become heated or raunchy.

Can you imagine thousands upon thousands of people gathering every day to discuss everything under the sun? Such gatherings take place every day on the Internet. The discussions happen in discussion groups called *newsgroups* and *mailing lists*. From the Internet's earliest days, discussion groups have been popular venues.

Most individual discussion groups talk about a particular topic, from a character's development in a soap opera, reported Elvis sightings, the meaning of life, or the latest news and information about popular software programs. There's a good chance that, whatever your interest, people are discussing it right now.

Discussion groups are handled in two distinct ways: newsgroups and mailing lists.

Newsgroups

More than news

The term "newsgroup" sounds as if the discussions within each group are about news. In fact, the discussions are about every topic you can think of, including very non-newsworthy subjects. Discussion topics range from philosophy to soap operas. There are even some newsgroups that discuss actual news events.

To find newsgroups and participate in discussions that interest you, you need a program called a *newsreader*. Microsoft Outlook Express, part of the Internet Explorer suite, works like a newsreader, as does Netscape Communicator's Messenger. You can also use an independent newsreader that is available for free such as Free Agent, distributed by Forte Software.

Newsgroups are threaded, which means you can follow the flow of a conversation, from the original question or comment, to its reply, to the reply's reply, and so on. Newsgroup messages, called *postings*, can be long and eloquent, or short one word replies. Sometimes one thread can go on for a long time.

You can jump into your newsgroups anytime with your newsreader. When you find groups that look especially interesting, you *subscribe* to have the newest postings automatically downloaded to your computer. Unlike when you subscribe to a news service, a magazine or Internet mailing list, your name isn't put on a master list when you subscribe to a newsgroup. Subscribing to a newsgroup tells your newsreader to get the latest postings for you. Depending on your newsreader, you can look for newsgroups and read and reply to the postings without becoming a member of the discussion group. Either way, it's best to hang back and read the postings of any new group for while, called *lurking*, before you become an active participant.

Most of the Internet groups are part of a system called *Usenet*, short for user's network. Usenet has been around for more than 15 years. Usenet discussion groups talk about everything from soup to nuts—general topics, like current events or history, or very specific topics, like the exchange of low fat recipes can also be found in Usenet discussion groups.

SEE ALSO

➤ *Read about Internet history on page 14*

Also, your Internet service provider might sponsor some newsgroups that are limited to use by subscribers and talk about technical-support issues or connectivity issues. And, if your company or school has an intranet, newsgroups might exist that deal with inside topics or issues. Only the people who have access to a corporate or school intranet can read and reply to its newsgroups.

Newsgroups at the office

Many companies have strict rules against viewing newsgroup postings from your office computer. Check with the folks that provide Internet access before you get started. Find out if your company has any special or industry-related newsgroups you can join.

Mailing Lists

Before you can participate in a discussion that's handled by a mailing list, you to need to join the list. (You'll learn how to find and join a mailing list later in this chapter.) Joining the list requires a simple email to the list manager. Sometimes, real people manage mailing lists; many times the management is automated and handled completely by computer.

Once the list manager (humanoid or computer) knows you're a list member, generally no longer than a day or two, you'll begin receiving the list postings in your email. When you respond to a mailing-list posting, your comments are sent to the list manager who then forwards your response via email to everyone on the list. Some lists generate only a few messages a day but others can swamp your mailbox.

One at a time

Because one mailing list can generate hundreds of messages a day, join one list at a time. View the messages for a few days and decide whether you can handle the volume of email. Only when you're comfortable with the group should you consider joining another mailing list.

Like your daily newspaper or snail mail, it's best to let the list manager know if you're not going to be around to read your email. Otherwise, even a weekend trip can result in an overflowing email box. Of course, if you decide to leave the list, you'll have to tell the list manager to stop sending you the list's messages.

The difference between newsgroups and mailing lists can get blurry, especially because some mailing lists also post their messages to a Web page and form a threaded discussion. Now that both Outlook Express and Messenger handle both email and newsgroup duties, you don't need to have a separate program for each one. There are two distinct differences between newsgroups and mailing lists. The first is that you have to physically join a particular mailing list to read its postings. The other difference is that, although some mailing lists have a newsgroup or Web interface, most times the postings are handled by email.

Practicing Basic Netiquette

A system of rules and manners, called *netiquette*, governs everyone's conduct in a discussion group. Visit the Netiquette Home Page at `http://home.netscape.com/menu/netet/news2.html#netiquette` for more information on the ins and outs of discussion group behavior. (See Figure 11.1.)

FIGURE 11.1
The Netiquette page provides good advice for new discussion group users.

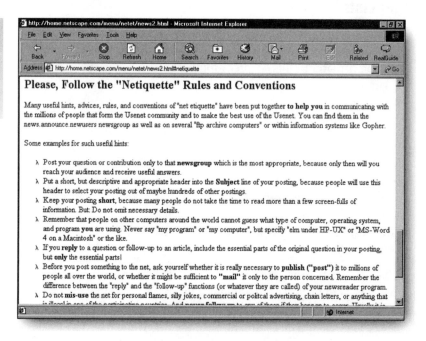

If you don't have time to learn all of the rules of Netiquette, you won't get into trouble if you follow my top 10:

1. Always remember that the other members of the group are people, just like you. Be courteous and polite.

2. Don't expect your readers to figure out when you're being serious and when you're trying to write something that's funny or sarcastic. Your feeble attempt at humor could hurt someone's feelings.

3. Have a thick skin when you read through the postings. Newsgroup and mailing list participants are a tough bunch. Even though you're courteous and polite (see Rule 1), they may not be.

4. If you're answering someone else's posting, don't type something like "I agree" or "I second the motion" without referencing the original statement. Most people don't remember what they had for breakfast yesterday, and they certainly won't remember what comment you're answering.

5. Post appropriate messages to discussion groups. For example, don't post a message about a tofu recipe to a current events newsgroup. (I accidentally did this and got very nasty responses.)

6. Resist the temptation to post a comment like "Mordred is an idiot" or some other slight to Mordred's intelligence. Other people in the group may like what Mordred writes—even if he is an idiot. Insulting posts just cause *flame wars* and get everyone off topic.

7. Don't jump into someone else's flame war, even if you agree with one side and disagree with the other. Ignore flaming posts or you'll end up in the crossfire.

8. Don't present yourself as expert to a new group, even if you know more than the group participants do. If you have good information, ease into the group slowly. After all, what's your gut reaction to a know-it-all?

9. Unless you mean to make a point, NEVER SEND A POST-ING IN ALL UPPERCASE LETTERS. All caps indicate anger or shouting and are considered VERY BAD FORM.

10. When you get caught up in a discussion, remember that no one is forcing you to join in the discussion. If you don't like the people in the group or the conversation isn't going in a direction you like, unsubscribe to the group and join another.

Discussion group etiquette isn't very different from the way that you expect to be treated by your colleagues and associates. If you treat your fellow discussion group members with courtesy and common sense, you won't step on any toes.

Getting Started with Newsgroups

You need to set up your newsreader program before you can become active in newsgroups. You might have already filled in this information when you installed your browser suite. If not, you'll need to know the following information to be able to create and respond to newsgroup postings:

- The name of the *Network News Transfer Protocol* (NNTP) server your ISP uses for news
- Your email address
- The logon name, authentication code, and password you need to access the news server

You'll need the information for the third item only if your ISP requires it. If you're not sure about your ISP's logon procedure to the news server, or any other piece of required information, call your ISP and confirm what you need to know before you start setting up your newsreader.

Setting Up Outlook Express to Read News

If you're an Internet Explorer user, you're already familiar with using Outlook Express as your email client program. Outlook Express doubles as a newsreader as well as a great way to send and receive email. When you first set up Outlook Express, you used the Internet Connection Wizard to set up mail, and you might have already entered all of the information needed to use Outlook Express as a newsreader. If not, the Internet Connection Wizard will walk you through the steps you need to enter the world of newsgroups. Unless you switch to another ISP, or something else about your Internet account changes, you'll only have to enter the information once.

SEE ALSO
➤ *For information on using the Internet Connection Wizard, re-read page 215*

To access the Internet Connection Wizard, open the Outlook Express **Tools** menu and choose **Accounts**. When the Internet Accounts dialog box appears, click the News tab and then the **Add** button. Fill in the information requested in each dialog box, clicking **Next>** to advance to each box. (An example of the Internet News Server Name dialog box of the Connection Wizard is displayed in Figure 11.2.) The final dialog box reads "Congratulations" and tells you that you have successfully entered all of the information required to set up your account. Click **Finish**.

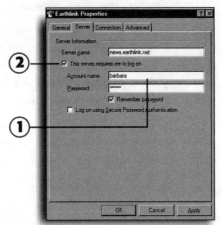

FIGURE 11.2
The name of the mail server needs to be entered to access the newsgroups.

① Type the name exactly as your ISP provided it.

② Check this box if your ISP requires a separate log on.

The first time you set up a news account, Outlook Express asks if you'd like to download the newsgroups from the news server you added. Click **Yes**. The Downloading Newsgroups dialog box appears and records the progress of the total number of groups downloaded. When the download is completed, the Downloading Newsgroups dialog box closes and the list of newsgroups from your news server appears in the Newsgroups dialog box.

Setting up multiple news accounts

As with mail, you can have multiple news accounts if you have more than one service provider. If you need to set up additional news accounts, bring up the Internet Connection Wizard and type the applicable information about the other account in the dialog boxes. You'll need to run the Internet Connection Wizard for each separate account.

If you ever need to change any information about your news account, open the Outlook Express **Tools** menu and select **Accounts**. After the Internet Accounts dialog box appears, click the **News** tab and select the account for which you want to make the changes. When the account name appears highlighted, click **Properties** and make the necessary corrections.

Setting Up Messenger for Newsgroups

Netscape Communicator users are already familiar with Messenger, the program that handles newsgroups for the Netscape suite. You read and reply to newsgroup postings the same way you handle your mail messages. If you'd like, you can store newsgroup postings in the same folders as you store your mail.

SEE ALSO

➤ *For information on using Netscape Messenger as your mail program, review page 222*

Configuring Messenger for news

1. If Navigator is already open, click the **Newsgroups** button on the Component bar, as shown in Figure 11.3. Notice that when Messenger opens, the news folder is highlighted. (This folder is simply a placeholder for your news folders and won't actually retrieve any newsgroups).

   Alternatively, click the Windows **Start** button, choose **Programs, Netscape Communicator**, and then **Netscape Messenger**.

FIGURE 11.3
Read Newsgroups appears on the Communicator Component bar.

① If the bar is docked, only the icon will be displayed on the button.

2. Open the **Edit** menu and select **Preferences**. The Preferences dialog box appears, with a list of categories displayed on the left side. If a + sign appears next to the Mail and Groups category, open the subcategory list by clicking the +. (The + sign changes to a - and all of the Mail and Groups subcategories appear.)

3. Click the **Newsgroups Servers** subcategory on the left to display the corresponding sheet.

4. Click the **Add** button to display the Newsgroup Server Properties dialog box, illustrated in Figure 11.4. Type the news server name and any other information that has been provided by your ISP.

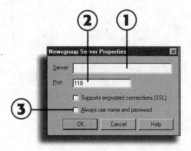

FIGURE 11.4
Fill in the newsgroup server information that your ISP provided to you.

① Server name goes here.

② Don't change the port unless you've been given other information.

③ Check this box if your ISP requires you to log into the newsserver.

5. When you're done, click **OK** to close the Newsgroup Server Properties dialog box. Click **OK** to close the Preferences dialog box and return to the Messenger. The news server you entered is displayed.

6. Right-click the new folder and choose **Subscribe to Discussion Groups** from the submenu. The **Communicator: Subscribe to Discussion Groups** dialog box appears on your screen.

7. The first time you click the **Subscribe to Discussions** button after you've set up a news account, Messenger contacts your news server to download the listing of available newsgroups groups to your computer. The status indicator located at the bottom of the dialog box tracks the percentage of completeness as the list of groups is being downloaded, as displayed in Figure 11.5. When the list is complete, group names appear in the box and the status indicator displays **Document:Done**.

Be patient

With thousands and thousands of discussion groups, it might take a few minutes for the group list to appear on your computer. If you're not sure if anything is happening, watch the status indicator at the bottom of the dialog box.

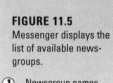

FIGURE 11.5
Messenger displays the list of available newsgroups.

(1) Newsgroup names appear here.

(2) + indicates group category is collapsed.

(3) Total number of groups that are included in the category.

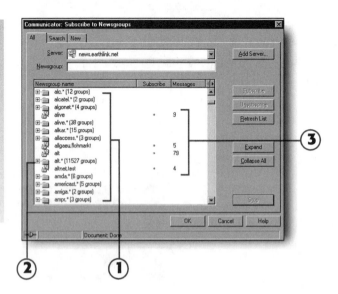

Deciphering Newsgroup Names

Newsgroup names are structured, and might seem like a secret code when you first see them. After you crack the code, the names are easy to understand. Like a URL, the names are hierarchical and each portion of a newsgroup name is separated by periods. The first portion of the name reflects the category of the newsgroup. The second portion shows the topic. Subsequent words break down the topic into subtopics. So, the newsgroup name alt.music.byrds translates into an alternative group that discusses music by the old sixties group, The Byrds.

SEE ALSO
➤ *You'll find everything you need to know about the structure of URLs on page 112*

Table 11.1 shows the most common Usenet groups and provides a brief description and a group name example.

Table 11.1 Common Usenet groups

Name	Description	Example
alt	Alternative subjects, ranging from the serious (computers and psychology) to the bizarre and unconventional (occult and alternative lifestyles)	alt.fan.actors

Name	Description	Example
bit	Conferences that start as mailing lists	`bit.listserve.big.lanlistserve`
biz	Business subjects, including advertisements and solicitations	`biz.books.technical`
comp	Computer-related subjects	`comp.infosystems.www.misc`
k12	Educational topics relating to elementary and secondary education	`k12.ed.math`
misc	Miscellaneous topics such as jobs, items for sale, and so on	`misc.forsale.comcomputer`
news	Information about newsgroups themselves	`news.announce.newusers`
rec	Recreational topics such as hobbies, sports, the arts, movies, and television	`rec.arts.tv`
sci	A vast variety of scientific topics, including comets and cloning	`sci.bio.evolution`
soc	Discussions center around topics containing a social nature	`soc.history.what-if`
talk	Controversial topics that lead to debate and heated discussions	`talk.religion.course-miracles`

In addition to the names shown in the table, you might find several other group names. Groups that begin with **de** are discussions held in German, while Japanese discussion groups start with **fj**. Corporations also maintain newsgroups. UPI offers a fee-based set of current events newsgroups that begin with **clari** (paid for by your ISP). As you look through the groups on the Internet, you'll find even more names.

Locating and Subscribing to the Right Group

Unless you're already aware of a specific newsgroup to which you want to subscribe, you probably want to peruse the list of group names and search for a group that best matches your interests. When you've picked out one or more groups that talk about topics that interest you, you're ready to become a member of the group. Don't worry; subscribing to a newsgroup doesn't represent a major commitment on your part. You can drop out or find a new group any time.

Subscribe to the newsgroups that contain discussions in which you regularly want to participate. Subscribing to a newsgroup is a lot like joining a discussion group at your local public library or community center. As part of the group, you can comment on the discussions and even receive recognition or accolades from the other members of the group.

Because the discussion takes place over the Internet, you don't need to attend special meetings or pay dues to be a group member. In fact, because your subscriptions are tracked only by your ISP, the other members of the group won't know you've joined unless you tell them. Because your interests, tastes, and available time change, you can subscribe and *unsubscribe* to as many newsgroups as you want.

Visiting Newsgroups with Outlook Express

Outlook Express makes it easy to work with all of the newsgroups. You can read the postings of a group, or you can subscribe and become a member of the group. In the following step-by-step exercise, you find a group that's right for you and subscribe. Be sure you're connected to the Internet with Outlook Express open and visible on the screen.

After you subscribe to a newsgroup, Outlook Express displays a subfolder for the group in your news server folder in the Outlook Express Folder list pane. When you're connected to the Internet and using Outlook Express, click the news server folder and then click the specific newsgroup subfolder to read that newsgroup's postings.

Subscribing with Outlook Express

1. From within Outlook Express, right-click the news server folder in the Folder bar to display the Newsgroup Subscriptions dialog box.

2. Drag the vertical scrollbar down the list of newsgroup names and descriptions.

It's not up to you

Your ISP makes the decision about which newsgroups are available to you. Depending on the newsgroups to which your ISP subscribes, you might not be able to see all of the groups on the Internet. If you can't find a group, check out the NewsSearch Public Server Web page at newssearch.pilum. net.

Your first newsgroup experience

If you haven't subscribed to any newsgroups, you'll see a box advising that you are not currently subscribed to any newsgroups and asking if you'd like to see the list of available newsgroups when you click the newsgroup folder. Click **Yes** to display the list and find the first group you'd like to join.

3. When you see a newsgroup that interests you, click the group name to select it.

4. If you want to find groups that discuss a specific topic, click inside the text box beneath **Display newsgroups, which contain** and type the word or phrase you're looking for. Notice that, as you begin typing, the list of newsgroup names changes to match the letters you've typed. Check the box next to **Also search descriptions** to broaden your search.

When you're done typing, the list is shortened and displays only the groups that match the words you typed. The title of the first group on the list appears highlighted. If you see an interesting group, click the group name to select it, as shown in Figure 11.6.

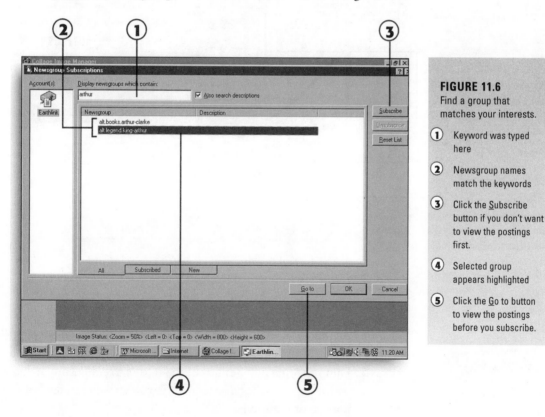

FIGURE 11.6
Find a group that matches your interests.

① Keyword was typed here

② Newsgroup names match the keywords

③ Click the Subscribe button if you don't want to view the postings first.

④ Selected group appears highlighted

⑤ Click the Go to button to view the postings before you subscribe.

5. To find different groups, click inside the text box again and type new keywords. To display the entire list, clear the contents of the box.

6. If you haven't already selected a newsgroup name, click a name from the list that appears on the screen. If you're sure you want to subscribe to the group, click the **Subscribe** button and skip step 7. If you'd like to look over the postings before you subscribe, click the **Go** to button, as shown in Figure 11.6. In Figure 11.7 the Newsgroups dialog box closes and the postings of the group you selected are displayed in Outlook Express, very similarly to the way that your email messages appear.

FIGURE 11.7
Postings appear on the screen.

① Posting headers

② Posting of selected header is displayed here

③ Folder bar

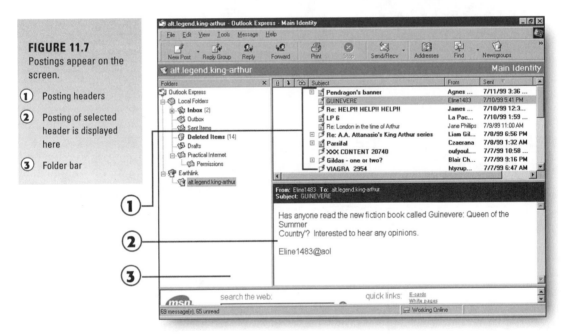

No postings appear

If you don't see any postings, the group isn't active and doesn't have any messages. Repeat the steps to select another group.

If the newsgroup you selected is active, with lots of postings, it might take a few minutes for the messages to download. However, the next time you view that newsgroup, the postings will appear much faster because Outlook Express will download only the messages not previously downloaded.

7. Up to the first 300 headers of the most current postings appear on the screen. Click a header to view the posting in the bottom portion of the window.

8. Subscribe to a group whose postings appear on the screen by right-clicking the newsgroup name that's displayed beneath the

newsserver folder and choosing **Subscribe.** The next time you open the News portion of Outlook Express, the newest messages will automatically be downloaded and displayed on your screen.

Subscribing to Newsgroups with Messenger

Messenger arranges the list of available discussion groups in a logical order. The master list of group names is organized in a hierarchical structure with the group categories arranged in alphabetical order. If a category contains subcategories, the number of subcategory groups is displayed next to the category name. Along with the number, a + sign next to a category name lets you know that the category is collapsed. (A – sign indicates that the subcategories are expanded; you'll see the subcategory names on the screen.) Click the + sign to display the subcategories.

In some categories, the subcategories drill down through several layers. For example, to view the discussion group name `alt.animals.feline.snowleopards`, you'd need to first open the alt category and then the animals and feline subcategories.

In the next step-by-step exercise, you use Messenger to find and subscribe to a newsgroup. For Messenger to find the master list of newsgroups, you must be connected to the Internet with Messenger open.

Finding and subscribing to newsgroups with Messenger

1. If the Communicator: Subscribe to Discussion Groups dialog box is not displayed on your screen, open the **File** menu and choose **Subscribe to Discussion Groups**. When the Communicator: Subscribe to Discussion Groups dialog box is visible, note the three tabs at the top: **All**, **Search**, and **New**.

2. Click the **All** tab to display the master list. Scroll down through the list. If you want to expand a category to see the subgroups underneath it, click the **+** sign.

3. When you find an interesting group name, click it to select it.

4. If you don't want to look through categories and subcategories, click the **Search for a Group** tab and type a keyword in the **Search for** text box. Click the **Search Now** button to begin the search.

Missing Folder bar?

Can't find the Folder bar or view any mail or news folders on the Outlook Express screen? No problem. Click the **View** menu, choose **Layout** and check the elements you want to see.

5. In a moment, the search results are displayed. If you're not interested in any of the displayed groups, or no groups are found, type a new keyword and click **Search** again. If a group looks promising, select it.

6. When you've found a group to which you want to subscribe, click the **Subscribe** button. As displayed in Figure 11.8, a check mark appears in the **Subscribed** column. Click OK to close the Communicator: Subscribe to Discussion Groups dialog box. You're returned to the main Messenger screen.

FIGURE 11.8
You've found the perfect group.

① Check indicates you've subscribed to the group

7. In the area next to the name of your news server, the group name to which you subscribed is shown. Double-click the group name to view the postings. If the group has more than 500 postings, the dialog box shown in Figure 11.9 appears. Choose whether to **Download all headers** or **Download 500 headers** and then click the **Download** button. In a few moments, the message headers are displayed.

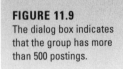

FIGURE 11.9
The dialog box indicates that the group has more than 500 postings.

Learn the Lingo

People who post regularly to newsgroups have a language all their own. The language can seem insurmountable to inexperienced posters. Here are a few phrases to get you going.

- *Newbies* are individuals who are new to the Internet or one of its aspects. In a posting, you might say something like "I'm a newbie around here" to let the other group members know that you haven't followed the previous discussions.

- *FAQs* is short for Frequently Asked Questions. Most discussion groups can direct you to the appropriate FAQs (often a Web page) that answers most of the basic questions about the group. Established group members often get upset when newbies ask questions covered by the FAQs. You might try asking where you can find the FAQs ("Can you direct this newbie to the FAQs?") to prevent getting nasty responses.

- *Spam* refers to unsolicited postings, usually touting a pyramid scheme or snake oil remedy, that are sent to newsgroups. Spammers often *crosspost* or send their messages to a number of discussion groups at the same time. (The term "spam" is derived from the meat product and a famous English comedy troupe's classic movie.)

- *Flames* are online versions of hate mail. Flaming postings often contain verbally abusive language and "yelling" (typing in all caps) and frequently target one hapless individual, although some flames target certain groups of individuals. A `flame war` is a succession of personal attacks under the same message heading.

Message Madness

In addition to the use of distinct phrases, discussion group postings often look like alphabet soup to a newbie. (There, see how fast you're getting it!) Table 11.2 shows some of the common phrases you'll see in discussion group postings.

> **How much time do you have?**
>
> Downloading 500 headers is Messenger's default setting. Although Messenger will download more than 500 headers at a time, you probably won't be happy with the results. Depending on the speed of your Internet connection, it may take a while to download all the headers. More importantly, any more than 500 postings at one time can seem overwhelming to a new newsgroup subscriber. Downloading less than 500 headers at one time will go faster, but means that you'll have to take additional time to download more postings.

Chat talk

The same abbreviations are commonly used in Chat conversations. You'll learn more about chatting on the Internet in Chapter 12.

Table 11.2 Commonly used abbreviations

Phrase	Stands for	Context
BTW	By the way	You want to include some relatively unimportant piece of information or to introduce a new topic
LOL	Laughing Out Loud	Comment was moderately funny
FOCL	Falling Out of a Chair, Laughing	What someone said was really funny
ROFL	Rolling On the Floor, Laughing	Similar to FOCL, denotes great mirth
HOGFA	Hunched Over, Gasping for Air	Used in situations of extreme humor
IMHO	In My Humble Opinion	Preface to an earnest or serious statement
IMNSHO	In My Not So Humble Opinion	Preface to a sarcastic or nasty comment
SGAL	Sheesh, get a Life	A comeback to a sarcastic or nasty comment
YMMV	Your Mileage May Vary	What worked for one person may not work for another

Don't worry if you aren't quite ready to use the phrases here right away. You'll see how quickly they become second nature to your postings!

Reading and Replying to Newsgroup Postings

Like mail, the headers of newsgroup postings appear in Outlook Express and Messenger. Headers contain the subject, sender, date and time, and size of the posting. When you click a header, the actual message is displayed in the Preview pane below.

Reading and replying to newsgroup postings

1. Click a message header with a closed envelope icon next to it. The text of the message is displayed in the Preview pane and the closed envelope icon changes to a letter icon to signify that the message has been read.

2. Double-click a header to display it in its own message window. (If a posting is very long, opening it in a separate window makes it easier to read.)

3. Click the **Close** button at the top-right corner of the message window to close the posting.

4. A + sign to the left of a header signifies that the message header is the most current posting in a thread, or series of messages about the same topic and based on the same original posting. Click the + sign to expand the thread and display the other messages below the one that's showing now.

   When a thread is expanded, the + sign changes to a – sign. Click the – sign to collapse the thread.

5. If there are postings that don't interest you or that you don't have time to read, you can mark them as having been read. In Outlook Express, right-click the header and choose **Mark as Read** on the pop-up menu, as shown in Figure 11.10. If the posting is one of a thread that you don't choose to read, choose **Mark Thread as Read** on the pop-up menu.

FIGURE 11.10
Mark a posting as read from the Outlook Express pop-up menu.

① Click Mark as Read to mark the selected message.

② Click Mark Conversation as Read to mark all the postings in the thread.

Messenger users should select the message they don't want to read and then click **Message**, **Mark** and then **as Read**. Alternatively, if the posting is one of a thread that you don't choose to read, choose **Thread as Read** from the sub-menu.

6. If you're using Outlook Express and you want to send a response to the newsgroup, click the **Reply to Group** button on the toolbar. Messenger users need only click the Reply button.

When the message window opens with the text of the original posting displayed, type your response and click the **Send** button. Shortly, your posting will appear as part of the thread.

You have the option of replying personally to the author of a posting without having the reply appear on the newsgroup's postings. If you're using Outlook Express, click the **Reply** button, type your response, and click **Send**.

Messenger users have several options regarding who will receive a reply. If you're using Messenger, right click the message to which you want to reply and choose one of the options shown on the menu, as illustrated in Figure 11.11.

SEE ALSO

➤ *For instructions on composing new mail messages, refer to page 238*

FIGURE 11.11
Reply to a posting in Messenger.

① Click Reply to Sender Only to send a private message.

② Click Reply to Sender and All Recipients to send a response to the sender and anyone else that the sender sent the posting to.

③ Click Reply to Newsgroup to send a response that will appear in the group postings in a short while.

④ Click Reply to Sender and Newsgroup to post your response publicly and privately to the sender.

⑤ Click Forward Quoted to send the original posting and your response as a mail message.

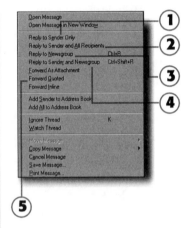

7. Because both Outlook Express and Messenger are configured to handle both mail and news, you can forward a posting from a newsgroup to an individual. While you're viewing a newsgroup posting, click the **Forward** button. The message window opens with both the text and the header information of the original posting displayed in the message body. The subject of the original message appears preceded by FW: and the sub.

8. Create a new posting by clicking the **New Post** button in Outlook Express or the **New Msg** button in Messenger. A new

message window appears, very similar to the one you see when you're creating an email message. Notice that the name of the newsgroup is already filled in the To: portion of the message. When you're done typing your message, click the **Send** button to send it to the group.

9. You can view the latest messages that have been posted to the newsgroup anytime you'd like. Outlook Express users should open the **Tools** menu and select **Get Next 300 Headers.** Messenger users should click **File**, and choose either **Get New Messages** or **Get Next 500 Messages**. In a few moments, the latest headers will be downloaded to the postings already shown on your screen.

10. To return to the list of newsgroups, click the **Newsgroups** button if you're using Outlook Express. If you're a Messenger user, click **Communicator** and then **Newsgroups**.

Unsubscribing to Discussion Groups

Let's face it—things change. The newsgroup that seemed so exciting last week seems to be rehashing the same old stuff with every posting. Or, you just don't have time to keep up with all the postings of a newsgroup because of your work or school schedule. Relax. You're never locked into a newsgroup. You can unsubscribe any time you decide you no longer want to read the postings of the group. If you change your mind down the road, you can always subscribe again without any penalty or fear of reprisals.

In Outlook Express, click the news server folder in the Folder list pane. The folder opens and the names of all the newsgroups to which you're subscribed appear. Right-click the group from which you want to unsubscribe. Choose **Unsubscribe** from the resulting pop-up menu.

If you use Messenger as your newsreader, it's a breeze to unsubscribe from a newsgroup. Right-click the group from which you want to unsubscribe and choose **Remove Newsgroup** from the pop-up menu. The group disappears from your list.

Open it first

Before you can unsubscribe to a newsgroup in Outlook Express or Messenger, the program must be open and on the screen.

Using Other Newsreaders

Although both Microsoft and Netscape have worked hard to make Outlook Express and Messenger good newsreader programs, there are several other newsreader programs you can use. If you really get involved with posting and subscribing to newsgroups, you might find that a dedicated program works best. Table 11.3 provides more information about some of these newsreaders.

Table 11.3 Dedicated newsreader programs

Program Name	Company	Find More Information At	Cost	Comments
Agent	Forte	`http://www.forteinc.com`	$29	Considered the best newsreader by many users. Features include full email integration, the ability to set up special folders, and enhanced search for special postings.
Free Agent	Forte	`http://www.forteinc.com/forte`	Free-ware	Not quite as many features as Agent, but an excellent, full-featured program. Contains an easy to use interface.
News Ferret	FerretSoft	`http://www.ferretsoft.com`	$26.95	Enables users to search and retrieve Usenet news articles for a topic of interest, without having to access each newsgroup separately.
News-Monger	Tech Smith Corporation	`http://www.techsmith.com`	$39.95	Supports multiple searches, search scheduling, and email notification when new articles matching your criteria are discovered.

SEE ALSO

➤ *For more information on downloading software, see page 185*

Tracking Postings with Deja.com

With so many available newsgroups and so many postings, there's no way you can keep track of everything that's discussed. Fortunately, you can obtain postings on just about anything by using Deja.com on the World Wide Web. The Deja.com site, shown in Figure 11.12, at www.deja.com contains archives of most postings on the Internet.

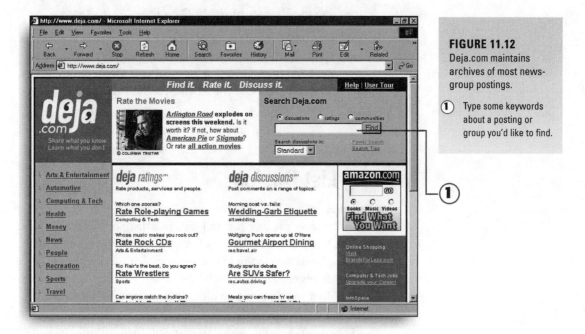

FIGURE 11.12
Deja.com maintains archives of most news-group postings.

① Type some keywords about a posting or group you'd like to find.

Deja News offers several search tools for finding the postings you want to see:

- *Quick Search*. Offers a simple search. Type your keywords into the Find text box and click the **Find** button. Don't worry about capitalizing words as the search isn't case-sensitive.

- *Power Search*. Provides more complex search capabilities. Structure your query with Boolean logic, using the terms AND, NOT, or NEAR, for example. Additionally, specify which archive is to be searched and how the keywords should be matched. For further control, specify how many and in what format the results should appear.

- *Search Filter.* Enables you to refine your searches by filtering on any message field. You can tell Deja.com to look through the Group, Author, and Subject dates and specify a date range for the posting.

- *Post Messages.* Enables you to post noncommercial messages to any newsgroup. If this is your first time using the Deja.com News posting service, take a moment and register (for free) by clicking the **Register for My Deja** link.

In addition to these options, Deja.com also features arrangements of newsgroups by categories and a technical support section for computer-related questions. You can also visit Deja.com to access online resources, Deja classifieds, and Yellow Pages search.

SEE ALSO

➤ *Bone up on search techniques on page 159*

Mailing List Basics

Thousands of mailing lists are out in cyberspace, just waiting for you to join. Internet mailing lists fall into two distinct categories: *closed* or *open*. Closed lists are set up by a list owner to keep you informed about the latest developments in a specific area. For example, a software development company might send out postings about its latest release. Or, a weather service might send hurricane tracking bulletins, whenever a hurricane threatens land. No matter what the subject, closed lists are one-way tickets of communication. You can receive postings but you can't reply.

Open lists are more like newsgroups because the communication is open to all list members. Some open lists generate hundreds of postings that are all delivered to your mailbox. No matter who wrote the posting, your response goes to the list owner, who sends the response to other list members.

Basic Training

Before you get busy hunting for and joining Internet mailing lists, you should know a bit more about how they work. Most lists are unmoderated, meaning that anyone can post anything to the list. Other lists are moderated and only on-topic or relevant messages are passed on. List moderators are usually volunteers and can take an incredible amount of abuse from individuals whose messages were squelched.

Unlike newsgroups, the list owner knows who you are. You must provide a real email address so that you can receive the messages. When you post to the list, other people might see your email address. If you're concerned about your privacy, or want to keep your personal email box from overflowing, consider signing up for a free Internet mail account and using the second address for your list mail.

SEE ALSO

➤ *Read about obtaining a second email account on page 230*

Each mailing list has two email addresses—the one used to contact the administrator to set up or cancel a membership and the one used to post messages to the list. When you find a list you like, write each address down and mark it carefully. Otherwise, you're likely to mix up the two and post a message saying that you want to unsubscribe to the actual list instead of the administrator. (I've switched the address and embarrassed myself more than my share of times.)

Even small lists generate loads of email. If you'd rather have the mail sent in batches, check to see if you can get mail sent in *digest* form. If a digest is available, it might be sent weekly or even daily.

Most mailing lists are free. You can even create your own mailing list if you can't find one you like. There are several list managers on the Internet. Listserv and Majordomo are two of the best-known automated list managers.

Finding a Mailing List

Many mailing lists are mirrored in newsgroup format. Before you join a mailing list, find out if the same postings are available in newsgroup form. If so, you might be better off subscribing to the newsgroup. In fact, you can find many Listserv mailing groups in the bit.listserv hierarchy, as shown in Figure 11.13.

SEE ALSO

➤ *Read about finding a newsgroup on page 256*

Mailing lists at work

Some companies take a dim view of employees receiving mailing-list messages through the company's email system. Check it out with the folks who handle the email before you find yourself in hot water.

Who's looking?

Remember that the postings on a mailing list go to every member of the list. You probably ought to be careful what you say since you don't know the identities of everyone who's reading what you wrote.

FIGURE 11.13
Many Listserv groups are mirrored in the bit.listserv newsgroups.

(1) Scroll through the list to find a group you like.

You'll need to be connected to the Internet with your browser open to complete the next step by step exercise. Although there are other places to find a collection of mailing lists, the easiest is the Web site of Liszt, the mailing list directory. (Although they share the same name, the site has nothing to do with the famous composer, Franz Lizst.)

Finding and subscribing to an Internet mailing list

1. Type **www.liszt.com** in the Address box of your browser and press **Enter**. In a moment, the Liszt home page appears. The mailing lists are arranged by categories and there's also a search box where you can type some keywords about the list you want.

2. The links are arranged by topic in hierarchical order. If you were looking for a mailing list about digital cameras, for example, you'd click the link to **Arts**, and then to **Photography**, to display all of the related lists.

3. Search for a list by typing a few keywords in the Search box. Liszt will look through both the titles and descriptions of its groups to find matching groups.

4. When you find a list that looks interesting, click the link labeled **Learn more about the list here**. If there is no information about the list, click the link labeled **Send Commands** to find the proper command needed to subscribe to list. Click the link that displays to the list administrator's name and email address, as displayed in Figure 11.14.

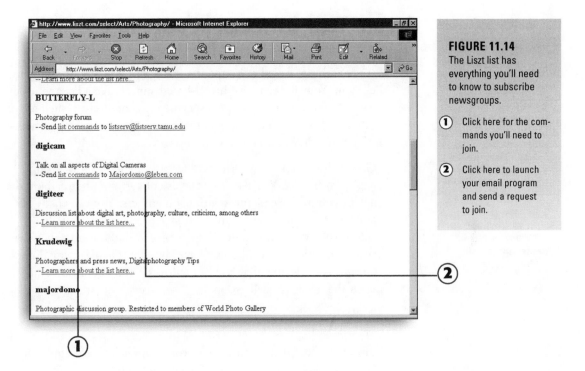

FIGURE 11.14
The Liszt list has
everything you'll need
to know to subscribe
newsgroups.

① Click here for the com-
mands you'll need to
join.

② Click here to launch
your email program
and send a request
to join.

5. Follow the instructions and send an email to the list administrator.
   You'll receive further information and a confirmation, letting you
   know that you're now a list member.

That's it! You'll receive the list messages in a day or two.

Unsubscribing to a List

There are a lot of reasons to unsubscribe from a mailing list. For
one, the volume of the messages can be overwhelming. Or, the group
seems hung up on a point that doesn't interest you. (Although I love
needlepoint, I found the discussion about different stitches to be
incredibly boring after a while.) For whatever the reason, you can
unsubscribe to a group with the same ease you joined.

Simply send a message to the group administrator, taking care to follow the instructions that you printed when you subscribed. If you've
misplaced the instructions and can't figure out the correct syntax, you
can always post a message to the group, asking how to unsubscribe.

It's not a done deal

After you send a subscribe
message to a mailing list,
you'll receive a confirmation. You'll need to send
the confirmation back
before the list messages
will appear in your mailbox.
The confirmation is for your
protection as well as the
mailing list—someone may
have tried to play a prank
or, worse, typed their own
email address incorrectly.

Create Your Own List at eGroup

Different strokes

Different lists have different commands for subscribing and unsubscribing. If the list is managed by Listserv, the standard way to unsubscribe is to send an email message to the list administrator with the words "**SIGNOFF**" followed by the name of the list in the Subject portion of the message. If the list is managed by Majordomo, use "**unsubscribe listname your email address**" in the subject line.

If you have an interest or specialty, why not create your own mailing list? A Web site called eGroups at www.egroups.com will be happy to help you. Your list can have broad-based appeal, like a list about puppies or kittens, or it can address specific areas of interest, such as Arthurian England. How about creating a list for your family members or friends. With eGroups, it's up to you.

eGroups lists offer a lot of exciting features in addition to group email distribution. You also have the use of a group photo album that enables you to share pictures with list members. You can chat with your group members in real time. A group calendar is available. Additionally, you can poll group members to find out how they feel about a specific issue or if they're available for Thanksgiving dinner. eGroups is so flexible that you can tailor the available features to match the needs of each group.

SEE ALSO

➤ *Learn about chatting on the Internet on page 285*

Before you can create your own eGroup, you'll need to register at eGroups. Click the link on the eGroups home page to get your account set up. The registration process (shown in Figure 11.15) asks a few questions and is completely free.

Free and not free

There's no charge to create a group at eGroups. However, you'll see advertisements for various goods and services included in the email postings and other eGroup features. For $4.95 per month, you can select a special no-ads option.

After you've filled out your email address, a validation email is sent back to you. Click **Continue** and fill in the information on the next eGroups registration screen. (This form asks for your validation number, full name and a password.) Click **Done** when the form is filled out correctly.

Click the link to start an eGroup. As the group moderator, you have complete control of the group. You can specify whether messages can be seen by everyone or just members and whether messages can be posted directly to the group or if you'll monitor them first. When the form is complete, click **Create It**.

If yours is a personal group, send an email to each person whom you want as a member. If you're hoping for a general discussion group, sit back and wait for people to find you.

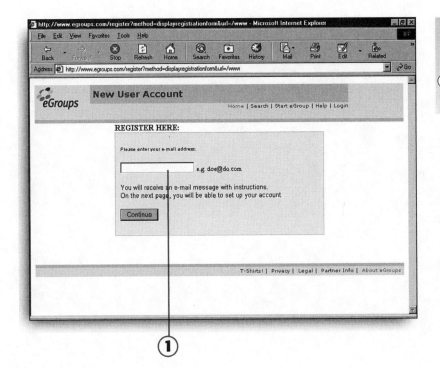

FIGURE 11.15
Sign up at eGroups.

① Type your email
address in the box.

12

Chatting on the Internet

What Is Chatting?

Chatting on the Internet is similar to attending a large family gathering. Many different conversations occur at the same time in the same room. On the Internet, the conversation appears as text in a window on your screen instead of bantered about at the dining room table. Even though chat conversations are written, they still progress at a very rapid pace! Don't be surprised if you actually forget you're typing your conversation on your computer and not having a "real" discussion.

Chat rooms have a bad reputation. Many people think that a chat room is an area to avoid. Because chatting allows people to hide behind "nicks," slang for *nicknames*, participants can often be either rude or risqué. Don't let these boors discourage you. If you feel uncomfortable with the group in a particular chat room, just leave it and go to another room. As you chat on the Internet, you're sure to meet many great people who you'll wind up chatting with regularly!

If you're not interested in meeting new people, chatting can still be of great value to you. Many Internet users use chat as a free, convenient way to stay in touch with friends and family. For example, I chat with my friend Noel in Sweden several times a week. In addition, many businesses are turning to chat programs for communicating both inside and outside of their organizations. Some companies use chat to stay in touch with clients, others as a means of providing technical support, and still others use it for in-house communications.

Chatting on the Web

Historically, a special standalone program had to be installed on your computer to enable you to chat. More recently, chat applications have been developed that enable you to enter a chat session from a Web page. Because you're already Web-savvy, we'll begin by exploring Web-based chatting. Table 12.1 shows a few popular Web-based chat sites where you can have some great conversations.

Table 12.1 Web-based chat sites

Name of Site	URL	Comments
Ultimate TV's TV Chat	`tvchat.ultimatetv.com`	Conversations about popular television programs.
Spiritual Web Chat	`www.spiritweb.org/ Spirit/chat.html`	Conversations about spiritual or religious matters.
Yahoo! Chat	`chat.yahoo.com/`	General chat with loads of "guest stars" and celebrity events.
Sports Chat	`www.chatsports.com`	Chat Sports is your one stop chat house for anything relating to sports.
Ceramics Chat	`www.wiseowlceramics. com/chat/`	Conversations for ceramists and potters.
Free Trade Chat	`www.tradingsystems. net/ocs/`	Talk about stocks, bonds, mutual funds, and other market-related topics.

Visiting Talk City

Talk City is one of the most comprehensive Web chat sites on the Internet. Talk City has hundreds of different chat rooms available for you to enter. Some rooms are "hosted," which means that there are people available all the time to help with any problems or to enforce the rules (known as City Ordinances). Enforcement of the Ordinances ensures that the site is a fun and safe place for all visitors. In addition to special events and conferences, Talk City helps users to form "communities" for the continued sharing of information.

Because Talk City uses a Java-based program, you don't need to download any plug-ins or any extra software to chat. You simply go to Talk City, choose a chat room, and wait for the program to load.

SEE ALSO

➤ *Flip over to page 512 for an explanation of Java.*

Chatting at Talk City

1. Type `www.talkcity.com`, in the Address box of your browser and press **Enter**. The Talk City home page appears, as shown in Figure 12.1.

FIGURE 12.1
The Talk City Home Page is filled with interesting information.

① Links to Talk City venues

② Coming attractions

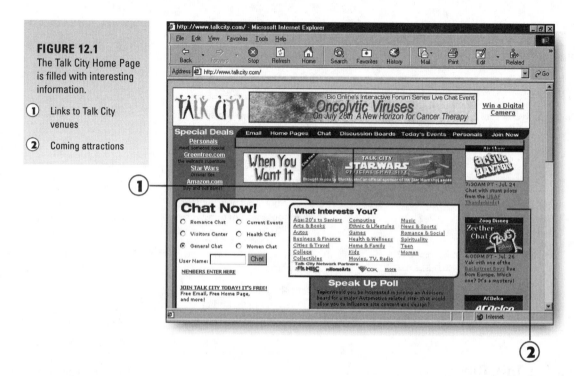

Be patient

The first time you visit a Talk City chat room, it might take a few minutes before you can enter a chat room. After you've visited Talk City, your connections will be faster because the information you entered in step 5 is already registered.

2. Click the **Chat** link on the top of the page.

3. A new page appears, displaying a list of links to Talk City Chats. Scroll down the list and click the link to a chat topic that interests you. (For this exercise, we chose **Computing**.)

4. A panel on the right side of the screen shows all of the available chat rooms that are talking about your topic. The rooms are grouped by category. The number of chatters in each room is shown, as displayed in Figure 12.2. Click the room name in which you'd like to chat. (We chose **New2TalkCity**.)

5. On the next page, you're asked to enter a username. Since you haven't registered at Talk City, click inside the **User Name** box and type a nickname that you'd like to be known as. The nickname you type is the name that other Talk City participants will see. When you're done typing, click **Go Chat**.

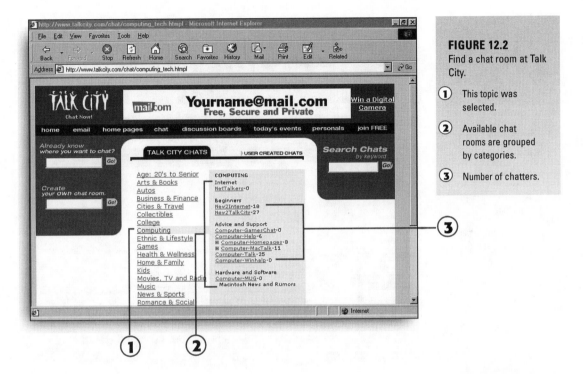

FIGURE 12.2
Find a chat room at Talk City.

(1) This topic was selected.

(2) Available chat rooms are grouped by categories.

(3) Number of chatters.

6. A window appears in the center frame, as shown in Figure 12.3. A list of the participants displays on the left side and the conversation appears on the right. Your nickname appears with a guest designation. A text box also appears on the bottom in which you can type what you want to say.

   Before entering into the ongoing discussion, watch the conversation for awhile. This practice is known as "lurking."

7. Type a comment in the **Talk to Everyone** text box and press **Enter**. Your comment appears in the conversation next to your nickname (in brackets).

8. Continue chatting as long as you want. Notice how quickly the conversation moves.

9. Click the **Change Rooms** link on the bottom of the page. A new window opens in your browser displaying the list of Talk City Chats. As you did in steps 3 and 4, choose a topic and then select a room.

Make your own

As you become more experienced with Talk City, you can create your own chat rooms. Create a room by typing its name in the **Other Room** box and clicking the **Enter Room** button.

Cat got your tongue?

Many verbal, articulate people get tongue-tied when they first start chatting on the Internet. If you're feeling shy or awkward, let the participants in the room know that you're new.

289

FIGURE 12.3
The Chat window shows the current discussion.

(1) Room name

(2) Participants

(3) Conversation

(4) Type your comment in the box.

(5) EZTalk button on the Windows taskbar

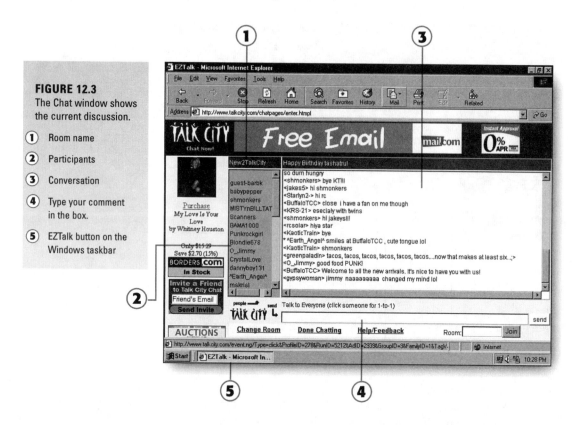

10. (Optional) If you want to chat privately with someone else in the room, click the person's nickname on the **Who's Here?** list. The line above the text box changes from "Talk to Everyone" to "1-to-1 with [the person you chose]." Whatever you type shows up only on the chosen person's screen. Click the blank slot at the top of the list to continue chatting with everyone in the room.

11. When you've finished chatting, click the **Done Chatting** link at the bottom of the window. The Talk City home page reappears.

Talk City has conferences and events to please everyone! Make sure you check out the Events Calendar link.

Become a Talk City Citizen

If you enjoyed chatting at Talk City as a guest, why not become a full-fledged Talk City Citizen? Citizenship is free; all that's required is some information such as your name and email address. In addition to chatting, you can use Talk City's Discussion Boards to share your opinions with others. Joining Talk City also entitles you to a free email account and homepage and the opportunity to post personal ads.

SEE ALSO

➤ *Talk City Discussion Boards are similar to newsgroups. Refresh your knowledge about newsgroups on page 256*

Spiffing Up Your Conversation

Chatters have developed a language of terms that are used in most typed conversations. Many of these terms are leftover phrases from the old days of CB radio. For example, the term "10-4" means "I'm signing off." Most chat terms are used interchangeably with the ones you use in newsgroups.

SEE ALSO

➤ *For the special terms used in newsgroups, see page 271*

Emoticons, often called "smileys," are used in most chat conversations. Table 12.2 shows the most common emoticons and what they mean. Show that you're a chatting pro and use them in your own conversations.

Table 12.2 Common chat emoticons

Emoticon	What It Means
:)	Smile
;)	Winking smile
:(	Sad face
:P	Sticking out your tongue
:X	My lips are sealed or I'm tongue-tied
:D	Laughing out loud
:O	Yelling or astonished
:-{}	Blowing a kiss
\-o	Bored
:-c	Bummed out
(((((name)))))	Hug (cyber hug)

Instant messaging is one of the Internet's greatest tools. Netscape, Microsoft (MSN), and Yahoo! are among the many providers of instant messaging services. What is instant messaging? Primarily, it's a form of chatting that allows people to communicate in "real-time" over the Internet. *Instant messages* are spontaneous and fun. You can see an example of an instant message conversation in Figure 12.4.

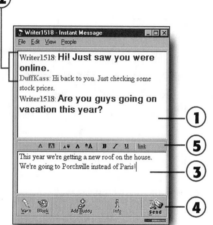

FIGURE 12.4
A conversation between buddies in Netscape Instant Messenger.

① Conversation appears in top pane

② Screen names of participants

③ Type your message here.

④ Click the Send button to send your comments.

⑤ Use the Formatting toolbar to change the appearance of the text you send.

Instant messaging basically works on a *client/server* model. When you run the client, (the instant messaging software) it connects to a central computer (the server) that verifies your identity and registers you as being online. Other users, once they register and connect, can see that you're logged in because the server knows that you're online. Depending on which instant messaging package is used, instant messages take place either through the server or directly from client to client.

Messaging wars

Both Netscape and Microsoft offer their own instant messaging programs. Netscape's program, called Netscape AOL Instant Messenger, has a tie-in with users of America Online. Microsoft's program, called MSN Messenger Service, is a newer entry into the market.

One advantage instant messengers have over chat rooms is the flexibility they give users to decide whom they want to speak to and when. Most programs have privacy features that enable users to block unwanted messages, or to hide their online presence from others. Most programs have a Block or Status feature, which can shield their online status. Some programs can even block messages from seeing your name and prevent them from sending you instant messages. As shown in Figure 12.5, users of the MSN Messenger service can change how their online status is displayed with a few mouse clicks.

FIGURE 12.5
Choose how to display your online status in MSN Messenger.

① Click the Status button to change how your name will appear on the Contact Lists of users who have added you.

② Choose an option from the drop-down list.

Instant messaging software is becoming more sophisticated all the time. In addition to enabling you to communicate through short text messages, some messaging programs also let you exchange computer files. Other programs provide the capability to create a "Buddy Chat Room" for communication with more than two people. Yahoo! Messenger even has built-in Stock, News, and Scoreboard tabs built into its messaging program.

Table 12.3 shows some of the most popular programs used for instant messaging and includes a few comments about each program.

> **IM is a word**
>
> Most people use the term "im" (pronounced as eye-em) to describe instant messages. You can use the term as a noun, as in "I love **im**'s" or as a verb, such as "Please **im** me."

Table 12.3 Instant messaging software

Name	Where to Get It	Comments
Netscape AOL Instant Messenger	`www.newaol.com/aim/ netscape/adb00.html`	Included with Netscape Communicator but can be downloaded for free. Can be used by anyone with an Internet connection. AIM has links to the AOL subscriber list, so it's a snap to add AOL users to your Buddy List.
MSN Messenger Service	`messenger.msn.com`	Setup requires a free Hotmail email account. (You can set one up at the same time you set up the MSN Messenger.)

continues...

Table 12.3 Continued

Name	Where to Get It	Comments
Yahoo! Messenger	messenger.yahoo.com	In addition to the standard contact list of friends and colleagues, Messenger offers voice chat if your computer is equipped with a microphone and speakers.
ICQ	www.icq.com	Used internationally, ICQ (short for "I Seek You") offers an entire communication network in addition to instant messages. You can send an offline message to an ICQ user (similar to email), make yourself available to anyone on the ICQ network, or post a message to an ICQ message board.
Tribal Voice PowWow	www.powwow.com	Originally set up for use by Native Americans, PowWow is one of the oldest instant messaging programs on the Internet. It offers group chat, real-time point-to-multi-point communications, voice chat, Buddy Lists, text to voice, Web tours, White Pages, bulletin boards, whiteboarding, games, and more.

Both you and your buddy need to be using the same instant messaging software to communicate. If your friend has MSN Messenger and you're using Yahoo! Messenger, you won't be able to communicate. However, most of the popular instant messaging programs contain an invitation feature, like the one from ICQ shown in Figure 12.6. You enter the email address of someone with whom you'd like to exchange instant messages, and an invitation to join the service is sent to your friend.

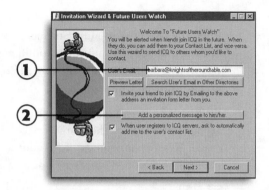

FIGURE 12.6
Invite your pals to join ICQ.

① Type the email address of the person you're inviting.

② Add your personal comments to the invitation.

The current crop of instant messaging programs work somewhat differently "under the hood." However, Microsoft has called for open standards that would enable all instant messaging programs to be built on the same platform. Such a standard would be good for all users, since messaging could take place between users, no matter which software was in use. Hopefully, such a standard will be agreed to by all the parties involved and put in place sometime very soon.

All instant messaging software works basically in the same way. You set up a buddy or contact on a list, using their screen name or email address. As your buddies come online, their screen names appear active on the list (depending on any blocking options they've set). You can send an instant message to anyone on your list when they're online.

The Dark Side of Instant Messaging

Although instant messaging is a fast and fun way to stay in touch with your friends and colleagues, there are a couple of negatives to consider. Many companies consider instant messages inappropriate for business use. If you're planning to use instant messaging while you're connected to the Internet at work, find out in advance if your company allows it.

Instant messaging on the Internet can represent an invasion to your privacy, without you even knowing it. Users of instant message programs can enter your screen name or email address on their Buddy or Contact Lists and then know when you're online. If you have an account with America Online, or you sign up with one of the other,

Teens do it

Many instant message users carry on simultaneous conversations with different buddies. My son often participates in three or four conversations at one time. Each conversation appears in its own, separate window.

messaging programs, make sure that you keep your screen name private. You wouldn't mount your name and contact information on a billboard outside a major metropolitan area, right? In the same vein, tell your screen name to only those people with whom you want to exchange instant messages.

Additionally, if you haven't done so yet, sign up for a secondary email account with one of the many services on the Web that offers free email. Keep your primary email address private, and use the secondary, free address whenever you're asked to provide it.

SEE ALSO

➤ *Find out more about obtaining a free email account on page 230*

If your kids use the Internet, they probably know all about instant messaging. Before kids of any age get too involved, set some limits on the use of instant messages. Quite frankly, my son finds my rules restrictive. Since I know that teens pass around screen names, I won't let him exchange instant messages with a sender whose identity he doesn't know. I also don't allow instant messages on school nights, because it can be a big waste of time. I won't let my son set up a profile in any of the messenger programs, because I don't want his information available to anyone trolling the profiles.

The rules you make will depend on the age of your children and the level of Internet usage of both your kids and their friends. It's important to set up those rules in advance. If your children are younger, sit with them if they use instant messaging. Talk over your concerns with other parents and teachers. Instant messaging is a great way for kids to stay in touch and can be used safely with a little advanced planning.

SEE ALSO

➤ *You'll read about keeping kids safe on the Internet on page 412*

Chatting for Internet Explorer Users at MSN Web Communities

If you're using Internet Explorer, why not pop over to the MSN Web Communities and share your thoughts. Similar to Talk City, the MSN Communities are made up of a collection of subject-oriented communities that host related chat rooms and discussion groups.

Before you can chat at the MSN Communities site, you'll need to download a program called MSN Chat. The program is relatively new and differs from the standalone Microsoft Chat (often called Comic Chat). After it's set up, the MSN Chat program is embedded into your Internet Explorer browser. In fact, your conversations will appear in Internet Explorer.

Within each MSN community, you can visit an MSN-hosted room or discussion group, or you can create your own. The MSN Communities contain both public and private chat areas that are arranged by categories (see Figure 12.7). Public chats are shown in the MSN-created and user-created lists. Private chats are user-created chats that don't appear in any list. You can join a private chat only if you know its exact name.

What about Navigator users?

You must be running Internet Explorer to chat at the MSN Community through your browser. However, if you prefer the Navigator browser, you can connect using standalone Microsoft Chat or another chat program. We'll talk more about Microsoft Chat later in this chapter.

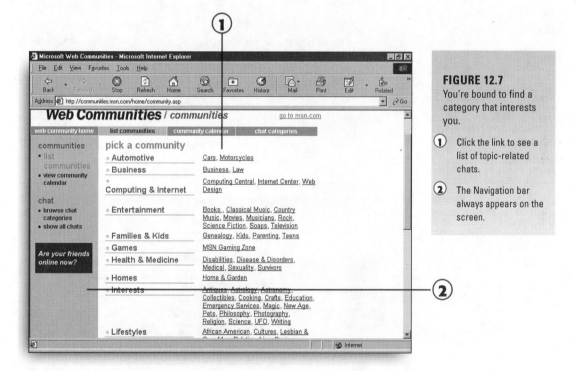

FIGURE 12.7
You're bound to find a category that interests you.

① Click the link to see a list of topic-related chats.

② The Navigation bar always appears on the screen.

Starting Out with MSN Chat

The first time you chat at the MSN Communities site, you need to download the MSN Chat program and select a nickname.

The download process takes only a few minutes. As part of the down-load, the MSN Chat software plugs directly into Internet Explorer, so you don't have to follow complicated instructions to get it up and running.

There is one caveat you need to know for the installation process to be successful. You must have Internet Explorer set to accept cookies. When Internet Explorer is set to refuse cookies, MSN Chat can't complete the setup.

Click **Yes** if you're asked to accept a cookie during the download process.

Chatting at the MSN Web Communities site for the first time

1. When you're connected to the Internet with Internet Explorer open and visible on the screen, type `communities.msn.com/chat` and press **Enter**. The MSN Web Communities page appears, as shown in Figure 12.8, displaying a list of Web communities, a community calendar, and Chat categories.

FIGURE 12.8
The MSN Chat home page.

(1) The Navigation bar helps you move around.

(2) Pick a chat topic that interests you.

(3) Chat highlights

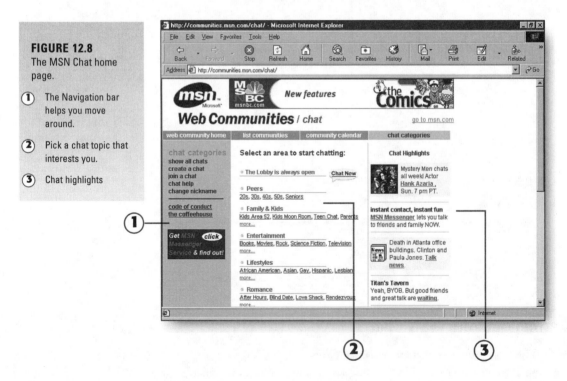

2. Click the link inside the yellow balloon labeled **Chat Now**. The Prepare to Chat page appears, displaying information about the MSN Chat program you'll need to chat at the MSN Communities. The program is small and takes only a short while to download.

3. Click the **Download** button. As the download takes place, the word Downloading appears in place of the button. (See Figure 12.9.)

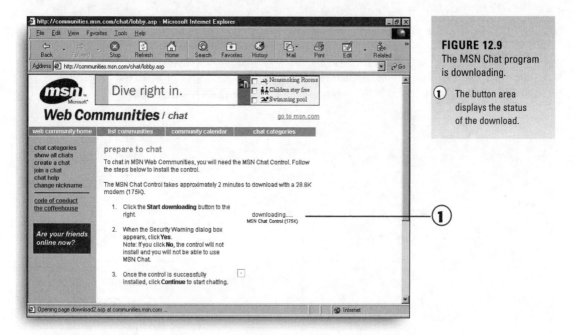

FIGURE 12.9
The MSN Chat program is downloading.

(1) The button area displays the status of the download.

4. As part of the download and installation procedure, the Security Warning dialog box appears, asking if you want to run and install the Microsoft Chat Protocol Control. Click **Yes**. (If you click **No**, the control will not install and you won't be able to use MSN Chat.)

5. The status area informs you that Control was installed successfully. Click **Continue** to start chatting.

6. In the next screen to appear, you're asked to choose a nickname. Type your nickname in the **enter a nickname** text box and click **Go**.

7. In a moment, you're taken to a chat room in the MSN Lobby. The Lobby rooms are moderated at all times so you're assured help if you need it. The Lobby, pictured in Figure 12.10, is a great place to begin your MSN Community experience.

FIGURE 12.10

Get started by talking in the Lobby.

(1) Conversation pane

(2) Nicknames of chatters appear in member list pane

(3) Gavel indicates the chatter is a host of the chat

(4) Type your comment in the Compose box.

(5) Send button

(6) Whisper button

(7) Action button

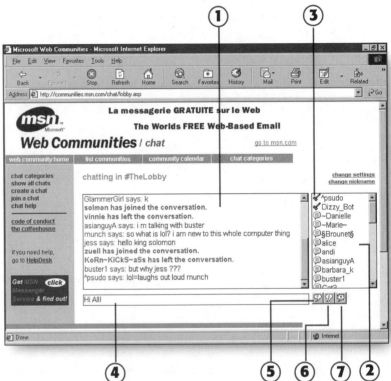

8. Type a comment in the **Compose** box, as shown in Figure 12.10, and click the **Send** button. That's it—you're now an official MSN Community chatter!

9. The comments you type appear in the conversation pane and can be seen by anyone. If you want to direct a comment to only one person in the chat, click that person's name, type your comment, and then click **Whisper**. Your comment appears in the conversation pane on your screen, but only you and the person to whom you whispered see it.

Your MSN Chat nickname

A valid nickname must begin with a letter, can contain numbers, but cannot contain the following symbols:

? : ; , .' " ! @
$ % / & + = *)
(< >

10. Continue chatting a while longer. You don't need to do anything special to cancel the chat. You'll be automatically disconnected from a chat session whenever you navigate to any other part of Web Communities (except Chat Help or HelpDesk), click the **Back** button, go to another Web site, or, simply close your Internet Explorer.

The software you downloaded will remain on your computer. The next time you visit the MSN Web Communities, you can click the **Chat Now** button and start chatting.

Adding Action to Your Conversation

Action is an important part of conversation. The next time someone talks to you, observe the speaker's body language. Those little gestures enhance the spoken conversation.

Chat conversations are sometimes flat, because action doesn't accompany the conversation. If you want to let everyone in the room "see" your actions, you can include them in your conversation.

Type your action in the **Compose** box and then click the **Action** button. Your action appears next to your name in the conversation pane, as shown in Figure 12.11.

Let Your Fingers Fly with Keyboard Shortcuts

Instead of clicking buttons to portray thinking, whispering, performing actions, or playing sounds, you can use keyboard shortcuts. Table 12.4 lists the keyboard shortcuts for each type of communication.

Ignore a boor

If someone in a chat is directing unwanted messages at you or keeps whispering to you, all you have to do is right-click his or her nickname in the member list and select **Ignore**. You won't see anymore whispers from that person in your Conversation pane.

Table 12.4   Keyboard shortcuts in MSN Chat

Effect	Keyboard Shortcut
Say	**Ctrl+S**
Whisper	**Ctrl+W**
Action	**Ctrl+A**

FIGURE 12.11

Action spices up a conversation.

① Your action appears in italics in the conversation pane.

② Type a new action in the Compose box.

③ Click the Action button to display it in the conversation pane.

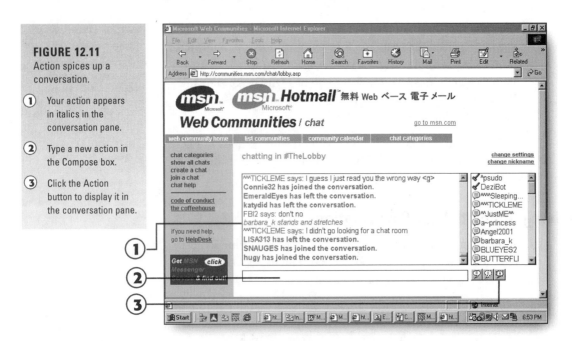

Moving Through Chat Rooms

Make it a Favorite

When you've found a group that you really like, you can add it to the Internet Explorer Favorites list for a fast way to return to it later on. (If you need help with Favorites, see Chapter 5, "Let the Browsing Begin.")

Even the most sparkling conversations lose their punch after a while. If the conversation in your current chat gets dull or offensive, MSN Chat makes it easy to move to chat in another conversation. If you're good at carrying on two conversations at one time, you can load Internet Explorer a second time and enter another chat while remaining in your current chat.

If you're already in a conversation or you're just opening the program, there are several ways to find a new chat.

Finding a new chat

1. Click **show all chats** to see alphabetized lists of all chats on the Find a Chat page. Each time you go to the Find a Chat page, the first list that displays is the MSN-created chats. To see user-created chats, click the link to **show me user-created chats**. Scroll the list of whichever list you use. When you find a chat that interests you, click the chat name one time to immediately join it.

2. Click the link to **chat categories** to see the list of categories. Click a category to see a list of all the MSN-created chats in

that category. If you want to see the user-created chats for that category, click **show me user-created** chats. Scroll through the list to find a chat that interests you. Click a chat to immediately join it.

3. If you know the exact name of the chat you wish to join, click **join a chat**, type the chat name and your nickname in the boxes provided, and then click **Go.**

Creating Your Own Chat

If none of the available rooms looks appealing or you'd like to create your own conversation, why not set up your own chat?

Click the link to **create a chat** in the left navigation bar. Type your nickname, select the category that best fits your chat from the category drop-down list, and then give your chat a name. Think carefully about the description that you enter for your chat, since it will be used as your chat topic. Figure 12.12 illustrates a chat being created.

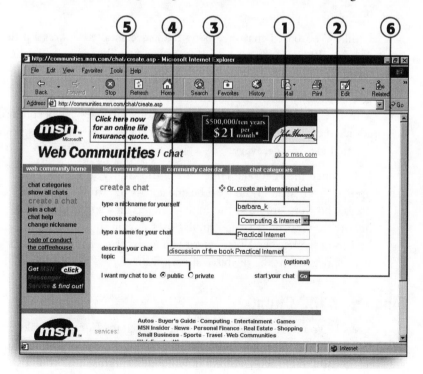

FIGURE 12.12
Create your own chat.

1. Your nickname is displayed

2. Click the drop-down arrow to display the list of choices.

3. The chat name you type should be descriptive.

4. The description will be displayed as the chat topic.

5. Click Private to keep the chat off the Public list.

6. Click Go to move to the chat.

If you want your chat to be available to anyone, select **public** so that your chat appears in the list of user-created chats. If you want only selected individuals to use your chat, choose the **private** option. Only those people who know the exact name of the chat will be able to join it. Click **Go** to start your newly created chat.

Internet Relay Chat

Everyone's gone

Occasionally, through no fault of yours, one or a group of servers on an *IRC network* disconnects from that network and loses contact with one another. This disappearing act is called a *Net split*. If a group of chatters appear to leave a chat room all at once during an animated discussion, you can bet a Net split occurred. Wait a few moments and see if the servers reconnect before disconnecting from the program and starting again.

Although chatting on the Web is relatively new, special *IRC* programs, short for Internet Relay Chat, have been around for many years. These programs use the same client/server model that much of the rest of the Internet uses.

The *IRC servers* are computers connected to the Internet that host Internet Relay Chat connections. Users (chatters) connect to these servers by using special client software on their local computers. Like other Internet servers, IRC servers enable multiple users to be connected at once. However, IRC servers enable users to talk to each other.

Unlike Web-based chatting, using IRC successfully requires a little training. Beside your Internet connection, you'll need a special IRC program.

IRC is used by hard-core chatters! Once users get up and running with IRC, many people love it. In fact, some people have become so addicted to chatting on the Internet that there's a Usenet newsgroup entitled `alt.irc.recovery`.

IRC gained international fame during the Gulf War in 1991, where updates from around the world came across the wire, and most IRC users who were online at the time gathered on a single channel to hear these reports. IRC had similar uses during the *coup* against Boris Yeltsin in September 1993, where IRC users from Moscow passed live reports about the unstable situation there.

Finding an IRC Client

Just like you need a Web browser like Navigator Internet Explorer to browse the Web, you need an IRC client program to connect to an IRC server. Once you have downloaded and installed your IRC program, you'll be ready to log on to an IRC server and talk away.

For an easy introduction to IRC, Microsoft Chat is one of the most exciting *standalone chat programs* that can be used on the Internet. Microsoft Chat has some great features that set it apart from other standalone chat programs. Microsoft Chat works differently from most chat programs; in addition to viewing plain-text conversations, you can also view your conversations in comic strip form. In fact, many users use the term "Comic Chat" (the original name of the program) when they refer to Microsoft Chat.

If you're an Internet Explorer user, you might already have Microsoft Chat already installed. Click the **Start** button, point to **Programs** and then **Internet Explorer**. If you don't see Microsoft Chat on the list of programs in the Internet Explorer Start Menu folder, you'll need to download and install the program. When you're connected to the Internet with the Internet Explorer browser open and on the screen, click **Tools** and then **Windows Update** to find and download the latest version of Microsoft Chat.

If you're a Netscape Communicator user, you can download the latest version of Microsoft Chat from Download.com (www.download.com) or Tucows (www.tucows.com). The software is free. However, you'll need to register your version with Microsoft when the program is set up.

SEE ALSO
➤ *For complete information on downloading files from the Web, see page 185*

If you're becoming a "chat-o-holic," you might find that programs like Microsoft Chat don't supply the advanced features you'd like. Other IRC programs are not for beginners, but they have a legion of loyal fans. Table 12.5 shows you some of the most popular IRC programs that are available.

> **Microsoft Chat versus MSN Chat**
>
> The MSN Chat program that you worked with earlier in this chapter is different than Microsoft Chat. Microsoft Chat is a full-bodied standalone IRC program. You don't need to have your browser open to use Microsoft Chat (although you must be connected to the Internet). MSN Chat enables you to chat at the MSN Communities through the Internet Explorer browser.

Table 12.5 Popular IRC programs

Name	URL
mIRC	www.mirc.com
PIRCH	www.pirchat.com
EZ-IRC	www.surfingsquirrel.com

Using IRC

The first thing you'll need to do is choose a nickname; everyone on IRC uses one. People will soon recognize you by your nick, or even search for your nickname on IRC. Choose your nick with care; since it's the identity by which you'll be known. Unless you want to be the butt of jokes or harassment, try to choose something non-controversial.

Your IRC client will point you to some IRC servers. From there, you need to find an *IRC channel* (similar to chat rooms). Many IRC servers have dozens, hundreds, or even thousands of chat channels open at the same time. Some channels are permanent and others come and go. A channel's name usually reflects the general nature of the conversation within, each channel can also have a specific topic. Channel names tend to remain constant, while topics change continuously. For example, in a channel called "PC Users" the topic might be "Windows 2000 Bug Fixes" one day and "How to Choose a Cable Modem" the next day.

All channel names begin with the number character (#). One popular and longstanding channel, for instance, is #hottub. If you decide to wade in, just type: '/JOIN #hottub' and you're in the group. The rest is easy. Type your comments. In a moment, your comments will appear with the rest of the conversation.

If you want more information about using IRC, you'll find a wealth of information on the IRC Help Web site. The site, located at www.irchelp.org, contains links to over 800 helpful files, including FAQs, primers, guides, downloadable clients and scripts, server lists, and more.

PUTTING THE INTERNET TO WORK FOR YOU

chapter
13

Getting News and Information on the Web

Finding people on the Web •

Read the latest headlines •

Listen to a radio broadcast •

Keep up with sports •

Politics, Internet style •

Track the weather •

Searching for People

Have you ever wakened from a sound sleep wondering where your third grade chum lives now? Or, have you tried, unsuccessfully, to locate the address and phone number of someone you need to contact? Unless you've received advanced training as a Private Investigator, tracking down people can be incredibly difficult.

Searching for a phone number, or a snail mail, or email address can be a chore. Instead of fruitlessly calling Directory Assistance or looking through the small print of a telephone directory, turn to the Web. Several sophisticated sites help you locate information about the person you're looking for.

Most of the people-finding services on the Web work best if you're looking for a person in the United States. As a rule, non-published numbers will not appear in public directories. You can find information about a person by entering only a name. However, the more information you can provide, such as a city or state, helps to narrow down the list. People move all the time; the databases used by most of the services on the Web don't always reflect up-to-the-minute information, so you might find an old address or phone number instead of the newest one.

Table 13.1 lists some of the best sites on the Web used to find information about a person.

Table 13.1   People-finding services on the Web

Name	URL	Description
Switchboard	`www.switchboard.com`	Contains listings for million sonal and business phone numbers, as well as mailing addresses. You can also find Web sites and email addresses.
Yahoo! People Search	`people.yahoo.com`	This service features separate listings for email addresses. Also found here are telephone numbers for individuals, Yellow Page listings, and AT&T toll-free numbers. You can also find links to email and mailing addresses for various celebrities.

Name	URL	Description
Big Foot	`www.bigfoot.com`	Featuring an Advanced Directory Search, free personal email, and other "feetures," Big Foot is more like a community than a directory.
Internet Address	`www.iaf.net`	Contains almost a million email addresses. Users add their listings to the database. The service is available in five languages other than English.
Who Where	`www.whowhere.com`	Use this site to find not only people, but apartments, cars, and jobs. Choose whether you want to find an email address or a phone number and address.
Infospace	`www.infospace.com`	Infospace finds phone numbers, addresses, and email addresses. The best part of the service is Reverse Lookup; type in an area code and phone number or address to find the owner. Infospace also features a Yellow Pages directory and some links to Canadian listings.

Hire a Web Detective

Most of the people-finders on the Web can deliver phone numbers or email addresses. However, fee-based services conduct more exhaustive searches to provide a complete picture. The information that is obtained by fee-based services comes from two sources:

- *Public record information* is information about an individual that is obtained from the records of a governmental entity and is available to the public. Examples of public records include state and federal court decisions, state and federal statutes and regulations, corporation records maintained by a state office of the secretary of state, and real-estate filings maintained by a county recorder or register of deeds.

311

> ■ *Publicly available information* is information about an individual that is available to the general public from non-governmental sources. Publicly available information often includes data obtained from newspapers, magazines and other periodicals, telephone and business directories, and professional and scholarly journals.

If you need to find information about someone, such as a prospective business partner or an employee, you might consider using a fee-based service. You'll be able to discover if the person has any liens, for example. The most well-known service is Lexis-Nexis, located at www.lexisnexis.com. Lexis-Nexis, used by the law profession for years, is a recent addition to the Web. Previously, Lexis-Nexis was a dial-in service whose users needed proprietary software to access the information. Another fee-based service can be found at www.1800ussearch.com.

Extra! Extra!—Get the Latest News

If you're like me, you can go through an entire day without knowing the latest news. Today's families are always on the go; sometimes the morning newspaper never makes it out of its plastic wrapper. All too often, the television or radio news is a backdrop to your activity—on your way to the kitchen or while you're falling asleep in the evening you might catch a few words.

Even if you read the newspaper or watch the news, your knowledge might not be current. Things happen fast; a criminal who was on the FBI Most Wanted List at breakfast time may be in custody when you eat lunch. Bombings, wars, and good news too, all happen at various times during the day.

The Internet brings you the latest breaking news. When you're connected to the Internet, your computer can function as a modern newsroom, complete with scrolling tickers, live news feeds, and

PART IV

Extra! Extra!—Get the Latest News **CHAPTER 13**

videos of the latest stories. You can view the news on pages provided by television networks and national newspapers.

Table 13.2 shows a few of the Web's best sources for headlines.

Table 13.2   Great sources for news on the Web

Site Name	URL	Description
ABC News	abcnews.go.com	Updated headlines, news, and weather. Local news and audio clips are available.
CBS	www.cbs.com	Enter your zip code to get news, sports scores, and weather presented from your local CBS television affiliate's perspective.
MSNBC	www.msnbc.com	Microsoft and NBC team up to provide you with the latest news. Click the link to Quick News if you're in a hurry.
CNN Interactive	www.cnn.com	The news is broken into categories—such as World, U.S., Local, Showbiz, and Books— making it easy to find what you want to know. You can also view the site in Spanish.
BBC Online	news.bbc.co.uk	Find out what's happening on the other side of the Atlantic. The headlines are up-to-the minute.

If you use the MSN or the My Netscape home page as your start page (the first page you see when you open your browser), you can see the latest news. (See Figure 13.1.) Both Microsoft and Netscape feature links to the latest news headlines. Additionally, many popular search engines, including AltaVista, Excite, and HotBot, feature the latest headlines. News is available in so many places on the Web that there's no reason to remain uninformed.

How about a scrolling news ticker?

How about a scrolling news ticker that delivers timely information on stocks, news, sports scores, and weather. You can set the scrolling bar on your desktop, windows taskbar, or in your favorite screen saver. The bar is completely free and available from MyYahoo! at my.yahoo.com/ ticker.html. The only prerequisite is that you have to be a MyYahoo! member.

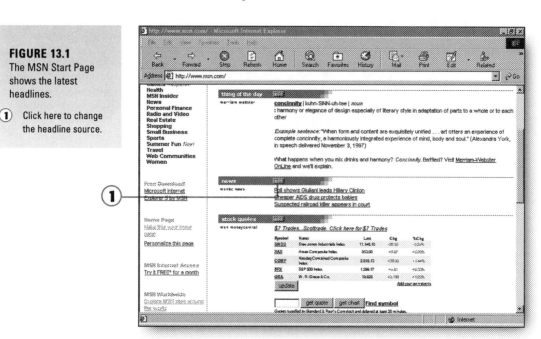

FIGURE 13.1
The MSN Start Page shows the latest headlines.

(1) Click here to change the headline source.

Reading the Newspaper

If you have a few minutes, reading the newspaper is the best way to keep up with all the news. In addition to the headlines, newspapers hold editorials, local stories, classifieds, and entertainment listings. When you're connected to the Internet, your computer becomes a virtual newsstand.

Thousands of newspapers can be found on the Web. You can read the newspaper on your computer screen, or you can print out the stories you want and read them in hard copy.

Table 13.3 shows you where to find some of the most famous newspapers.

Table 13.3 Great sources for news on the Web

Site Name	URL	Description
OnLineUSA Today	www.usatoday.com	The online version of this popular newspaper is easy to read and move through. Click a headline to read the full story.

Site Name	URL	Description
Wall Street Journal Interactive	www.wsj.com	The Wall Street Journal online packs as much financial clout as its print version. Subscriptions cost around $49 per year, but you can preview the site for free for two weeks before you decide to subscribe.
The New York Times	www.thenewyorktimes.com	The New York Times online is free, but you'll need to register first. The online version retains the look of the print version.
Washington Post	www.washingtonpost.com	For what's happening in Washington, the Washington Post can't be beat. Political stories and the paper's Style section are its strong points.
The Times	www.the-times.co.uk	How about the news from a British perspective? You'll find international news at the site, along with the latest cricket scores and standings.

Finding Your Hometown Newspaper

Your hometown paper is probably out on the Web, even if you don't come from a big city. It's fun sometimes to browse through local news or find a familiar face in print.

Finding newspapers is as easy as clicking a few links. Over 5,300 newspapers are linked at Yahoo!. Type **www.yahoo.com** in the Address box of your browser and press **Enter** to get to the main Yahoo! page. Click the link to the **News & Media** category and then click **Newspapers.** When the Newspapers page appears, choose **By Region** and then choose **Counties, Regions,** or **U.S. States,** as shown in Figure 13.2. Choose the appropriate category and continue

New at Yahoo!

As you look through the categories at Yahoo!, many display an icon that shows the word **New**. The New icon doesn't indicate that the category is new; instead it indicates that new links have been added to the category.

clicking through the category links until you find your paper. Of course, if you know the name of the newspaper you're looking for, you can type it in the Search box and click **Search**. However, you'll miss the opportunity to see all of the links to newspapers that Yahoo! has assembled for you.

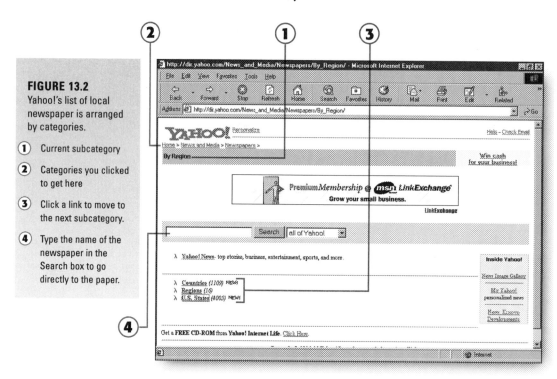

FIGURE 13.2
Yahoo!'s list of local newspaper is arranged by categories.

1. Current subcategory

2. Categories you clicked to get here

3. Click a link to move to the next subcategory.

4. Type the name of the newspaper in the Search box to go directly to the paper.

About Editor and Publisher

Editor and Publisher is a 115-year-old, privately held company that publishes both print and electronic periodicals, as well as a line of annual newspaper industry reference books and market data reports in both print and CD-ROM formats.

Yahoo! has tons of links to newspapers but most of them are in the United States. If you're looking for a paper outside the U.S., or the newspaper you want is not listed, there's a good chance you'll find it at the Editor and Publisher Interactive site.

Finding a newspaper with Editor and Publisher Interactive

1. Connect to the Internet and open your browser.

2. Type www.mediainfo.com in the Address box of your browser and press **Enter**. In a moment, the Editor and Publisher Interactive home page appears. Read the information on the page to find out about the site.

3. Click the menu link to **Media Links**.

4. The Online Media Directory appears. Choose one of the following options:

   - **Browse newspaper sites by regional map.** Choose from between the USA/Canada, Africa, Asia, Oceania (Australia), Europe, Latin and South America, and Asia.

   - **Browse by media category and region.** Select a media category, including choices such as newspaper, association, or cityguide. Choose a region or U.S. city and state and then click **Browse**.

   - **Media Quick Links** to all U.S. newspapers, all Canadian newspapers, U.S. daily newspapers, Canadian daily newspapers, newspapers worldwide, or daily papers worldwide.

5. Continue following the links to the paper you're looking for. When you have the newspaper displayed in the screen of your browser, consider marking it so that you'll have no trouble returning to the site later on.

   If you're using Internet Explorer, click the **Favorites** menu and then choose **Add to Favorites**.

   Netscape Navigator users can set a bookmark with a quick keyboard shortcut by pressing **Ctrl+D**. Or, use the mouse by clicking the **Communicator** menu and selecting **Bookmarks**. When the **Bookmarks** menu appears, choose **Add Bookmark**.

Radio News on Your Computer

Imagine listening to a radio broadcast of the news while you're connected to the Internet. Sound intriguing? Well, there's a good chance that you're only minutes away from hearing the news and other radio broadcasts, too.

There are thousands of radio stations worldwide, and most of them broadcast locally. You probably have a favorite station or two that you can't listen to unless you're in range of the city in which the station originates. The Internet brings radio stations online and helps them reach a global audience.

How's the sound quality?

The sound quality of Web broadcasts is largely based on your computer hardware and the speed of your Internet connection. If your computer is a few years old, or has an inexpensive sound card, you might think about upgrading the sound equipment. Even a set of better speakers can make a world of difference. Additionally, if you're going to make a practice of listening to radio broadcasts, get a fast modem or connect using a cable modem or DSL connection.

TV too

The RealPlayer also brings streaming video to your computer, turning your computer into a television set. Pretty nifty, especially when you realize that the cost of the software and the broadcast are free!

Get your audio player here

The Windows Media Player is available from Microsoft at www.microsoft.com/ windows/ mediaplayer/ default.asp. RealPlayer is available at www.real.com.

The technology that makes this all possible is called *audio streaming*. "Streaming" means that you don't have to download the complete audio file before the show starts. Since a 30-minute broadcast could take forever to download and use up loads of hard drive space, audio streaming is a technological marvel.

SEE ALSO

➤ *See page 36 for information about cable modems and page 44 to review information about DSL connections.*

To listen to radio online, your computer must be equipped with a sound card and speakers. You'll also need a separate program, called a plug-in, to listen to a broadcast. Although streaming audio can work on any speed Internet connection, faster connections are definitely more effective.

SEE ALSO

➤ *Review information about plug-ins on page 199*

Although many different *media players* are available, your best bets are the Windows Media Player and RealPlayer. Depending on the version of Windows that's installed on your computer and your browser, you may already have one or the other, or both.

Most times, when you click a link to a site that requires the Media Player or another streaming audio player, one of two things happens. If the appropriate software is installed, you'll see the media player open in a separate window and shortly after, hear the sound you requested after a few moments. If the software isn't installed, or it's not set up properly, you'll be directed to a site where you can download the appropriate player, as shown in Figure 13.3.

You can find directories of radio stations all over the Web. Since new stations appear all the time, the best way to find a current listing is to search for "Internet radio stations" or "Internet radio broadcasts" using your favorite search engine.

Here are a few other places you can find listings:

- The MIT List of Radio Stations on the Internet at wmbr.mit.edu/stations/list.html has links to over 8,000 radio broadcasts.

- Broadcast.com at www.broadcast.com has loads of listings to many Internet broadcasts. You'll find links to live and pre-recorded radio shows, arranged by category.

- NetRadio.com at www.netradio.com can turn you on to over 150 streaming audio broadcasts covering a wide range of topics.
- The World's Radio Station Web page at web.engr.uark.edu/~kaw has links to radio stations in such far-flung locations as Drugi, Croatia, and Thessaloniki, Greece. You'll also find links to live radio broadcasts in the United States and Canada. Soon to come are listings for broadcasts in Africa and Australia.

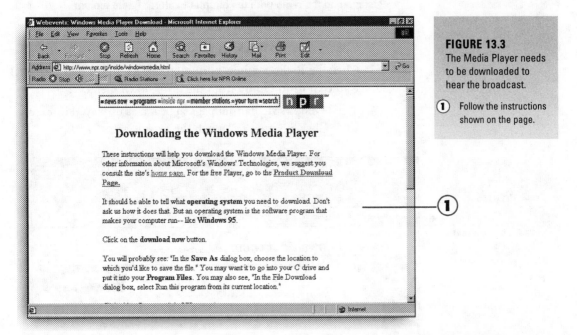

FIGURE 13.3
The Media Player needs to be downloaded to hear the broadcast.

(1) Follow the instructions shown on the page.

If you're interested in listening to your favorite radio personalities while you're online, contact the station from which they broadcast. There's a good chance that the station already has an Internet presence or is planning on establishing one soon.

Listening to a Broadcast

Can you believe that listening to a radio broadcast is as simple as clicking a link? It is—if you've got everything set up correctly.

Internet Explorer 5 users can use a new feature called the Windows Radio toolbar to tune into a radio broadcast. The toolbar can even be customized with your own favorite radio station.

Microsoft can tell you more

For more information from Microsoft about the Radio toolbar, visit the Windows Radio toolbar page at www.microsoft.com/ windows/Ie/ Features/Radio/ default.asp.

Look around

When you open a radio broadcast Web page, it's often hard to determine what you need to click to start the transmission. Look around for a speaker icon (usually a good visual clue) or hold your mouse over the graphics and links on the page to see what's displayed in the status bar. When you find the one you're looking for, click it to launch the broadcast.

Windows Radio works in conjunction with Windows Web Events: your gateway to more than 300 radio stations around the world. You can find stations from around the world. The list of stations is even searchable, so you can search by Format, such as country music, talk radio or news, state or country. After you find the station you're looking for, Windows Web Events sends you straight to the radio station's home page with one quick click.

Listening to the radio with the Internet Explorer Radio toolbar

1. Connect to the Internet and open Internet Explorer
2. Click **View**, **Toolbars** and choose **Radio**.
3. Click the Radio Stations button on the Radio bar and then click **Radio Station Guide** from the drop-down menu.
4. The WindowsMedia.com page appears, as displayed in Figure 13.4. Click a button to launch the broadcast.

FIGURE 13.4
Display the Radio toolbar.

(1) Click a button to hear a broadcast.

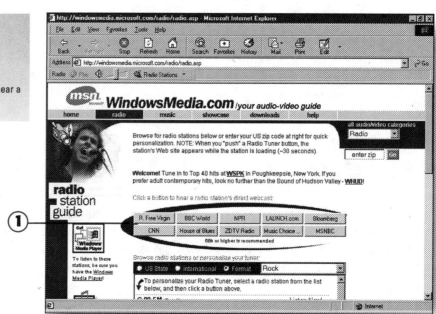

5. A button for the station you clicked appears on the Radio toolbar. Additionally, the Web page that corresponds to the button you clicked appears in Internet Explorer, as shown in Figure 13.5.

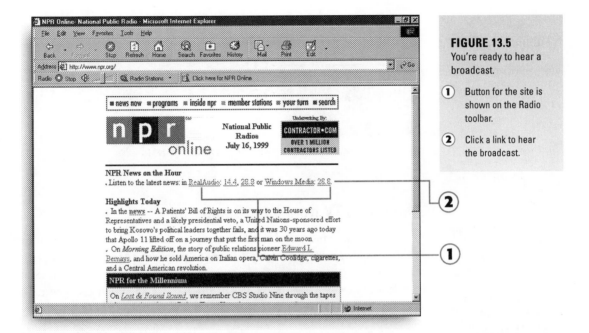

FIGURE 13.5
You're ready to hear a broadcast.

(1) Button for the site is shown on the Radio toolbar.

(2) Click a link to hear the broadcast.

6. Click the **Play** button on the Radio toolbar. The Play button toggles to a **Stop** button. As the radio broadcast is downloaded to your computer, the Radio toolbar displays various messages letting you know of the download's progress. When the broadcast is ready, the button on the Radio toolbar reads "Playing" and your computer comes alive with sound. Additionally, the Windows Media Player, shown in Figure 13.6, RealPlayer, or other media player appears on the screen.

7. To stop playing the broadcast, click the **Stop** button.

If you're using Navigator or simply want to get your broadcast choices from the Web, instead of the Radio toolbar, visit a Web page that has links to radio broadcasts and click the link you want. You might want to start out at SoundAvenue.com, www.soundave.com, or one of the other choices shown previously in this chapter.

Listen to the cops

If you have hankerings to know what goes on police radio, visit the Police Scanner site at www.policescanner. com. You'll be able to listen in on live police and fire scanner broadcasts from several U.S. cities.

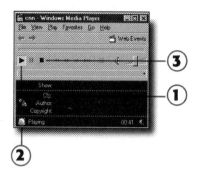

FIGURE 13.6
The Windows Media player appears on the screen.

(1) Play button is depressed

(2) Status

(3) Click the Stop button to stop the broadcast.

Watching TV from Your Computer

TV listing

Go to Broadcast.com at
`www.broadcast.com/`
`television` for a list
of television shows on
the Web.

The same media player that enables you to listen to radio broadcasts can also bring television directly to your computer. For example, one of the local television stations in my town broadcasts the local evening in a *Webcast*, as well as the regular television broadcast.

Unfortunately, unless you've got a super-powered computer, and a very fast Internet connection, streaming video broadcasts might be a disappointment. The movements can appear jerky and disconnected and the sound isn't always true. Worse, because your computer must utilize so much memory to bring you Webcasts, your computer might hang or crash.

Reading an Online Magazine

If you count on magazines to keep you posted on the latest and greatest news, trends, and gossip, turn to the Web. You can choose between two distinct types of publications. You can look through an *e-zine* for an original, often bizarre or opinionated viewpoint. Or, you can turn to the online version of many popular magazines, called *Webzines*, found at newsstands.

In the early days of the Internet, many independent publications flourished. E-zines, as they're called, are not generally considered to be mainstream publications because they generally cater to small groups. E-zines contain their own flair and style and feature original articles. Many e-zines deal with topics and subject material that could be considered objectionable or downright crude. Other e-zines deal with "hot" topics, like politics and religion. Advertising and endorsements (unless they're for another e-zine) are rare.

E-zines are still an important part of Web culture. One of the best e-zines is Salon, at www.salonmag.com. Salon contains irreverent, sophisticated articles guaranteed to make you think. Suck, at www.suck.com is worth a look. Don't be put off by the crudeness of the name; the e-zine contains articles and great satire. HotWired, at www.hotwired.com is considered by many to be the voice of the Net.

With the explosion of the Web, Webzines burst onto the scene. Webzines are the online versions of many of the same magazines that you find at the newsstand. Webzines contain advertising. Most Webzines retain the look and feel of their printed counterparts. Webzines are commercial publications—most e-zines are not.

Whatever your tastes or preferences, you'll find an electronic publication that meets your needs. If you'd like a list of links to many of the best e-zines on the Web, visit John Labovitz's page at www.meer.net./~johnl/e-zine-list. The page contains links to 1,770 e-zines. If your tastes are more mainstream, you'll probably be able to find the online version of your favorite newsstand magazine. Table 13.4 shows several popular Webzines and where to find them.

Table 13.4   Popular online Webzines

Name	URL
Ebony Online	www.ebony.com
Newsweek	www.newsweek.com
Gourmet	www.gourmet.com
Harper's Magazine	www.harpers.org
Car and Driver Magazine Online	www.caranddriver.com
Elle International	www.elle.com
Reader's Digest World	www.readersdigest.com
Soap Opera Digest	www.soapdigest.com
The National Enquirer	www.nationalenquirer.com

Keep Up with Sports

The Web has a lot to offer sports buffs. You can read the latest gossip about your favorite player, look at a schedule of events in your town or somewhere else and keep up with the latest scores. If you're the gambling type, you can even get the latest odds from Las Vegas.

Most big league teams in major sports have their own home pages. Additionally, most teams also have their own pages. You can find pages for American teams, Canadian teams (Figure 13.7 shows the home page of the Hamilton Tiger-Cats, my favorite team), and teams from all over the world.

FIGURE 13.7
The Hamilton Tiger-Cats have a home on the Web.

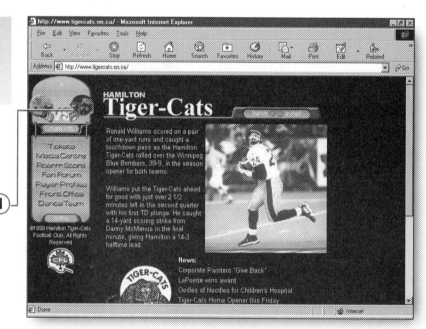

Just for fun, try looking at few unusual sites devoted to sports, like the ones shown here.

- For all things related to cricket, visit the CricInfo page at `www.cricket.org`.

- People who spend their leisure time in pursuit of extreme sports will have a ball at the Charged: Extreme Leisure at `www.charged.com`.

- Surfer dudes can catch a curl at the World Sufing site, located at
www.goan.com/surflink.html.

If you're serious about sports, you can search for links to your
favorite team or league. Unless you set up your query to look for a
phrase, you might get some seemingly unrelated results. Check your
start page to see if there's a customizable area where you can list all
of the sports information you wish to see when you open your
browser.

Yahoo! has a comprehensive sports category that covers almost every
aspect of sports. The Yahoo! sports category, shown in Figure 13.8,
can provide links to more sports than you can imagine. If you go
looking there, be prepared to spend a lot longer looking around than
you'd planned originally.

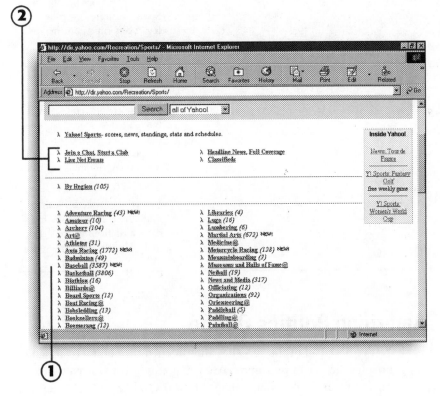

FIGURE 13.8
The Yahoo! Sports
Category to many differ-
ent sports sites on the
Web.

① Links to sites

② Click here to chat with
other sports fans.

Table 13.5 shows some of the best general sites to get the latest
scores and news about your favorite sports.

Table 13.5 Best sport sites on the Web

Name	URL	Comments
CBS Sportsline	www.sportsline.com	News, scores, photos, gossip, and more at this mega-sports site. Fast Facts section gives you access to standings, schedules, stats, teams, and players.
ESPN SportZone	espn.go.com	ESPN does here what it does best—talk about sports. Scores, news, and more can be found at this site.
CNN/SI	cnnsi.com	What do get if you cross CNN and Sports Illustrated? The answer is the best of two worlds. CNN's reputation for getting the latest, scoops matches with Sport Illustrated's excellent writing. Everything done here is first-class sports.
Major League Baseball	www.majorleague baseball.com	Everything you can imagine is here at this stunning site. In addition to the regular team links, stats, and scores, you'll find daily box scores. Even listen to a live game or see what happened this day in baseball. Team merchandise is available, too.
NBA.com	www.NBA.com	Everything basketball can be found here. Movie clips and a news feed give the site a slick look. There's even links to the WNBA, among others.

American Politics Online

You've heard all of the speeches and watched the commercials, and now it's the day of reckoning. Are you going to vote for your favorite candidate and make your feelings known? Or, like most people, are you going to leave the decision-making to someone else?

Getting involved in politics has never been easier. The growth of the Internet has brought politics out of the hands of a few politicians and into the hands of the people. Sitting right at your computer, you can begin the process to get registered to vote, find out how your current representatives voted on important legislation, and join others in a political rally. If you want to hook up with like-minded people, why not join a news group or mailing list. You can also create your own group and make a political statement. You can even send an email message to your legislative representatives to tell them how you feel about the issues.

The Internet can bring you political empowerment. Don't be a couch potato who lets other people lead. Get involved in the issues that matter to you.

Voter Registration

The right to vote is a privilege that many Americans take for granted. Voting gives you a voice in important decisions that directly affect you. From local to presidential elections, make sure that you don't squander your right to vote.

In the Presidential election of 1996, over 88 million people who were eligible to vote stayed away from the polls. Were you one of these individuals? If you're already a registered voter, take the time to go to the polls on Election Day. If you're not registered, use the Web to find out how you can register.

- The Voter Registration site at register2vote.org, shown in Figure 13.9, has links to every state in the Union. Click the link to your state to find out how you can register.

- Project Vote-Smart at www.vote-smart.org/state/Topics/register.html is another site that provides state-by-state information on where to register. Click the link to your state to find out more information about how and where to register. The site also lists the election dates in each state.

FIGURE 13.9
Register2Vote helps you get registered.

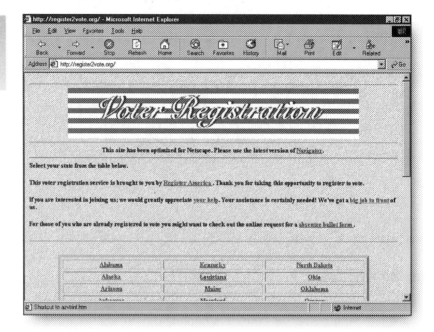

Meet Your Legislators

Do you know the names of your U.S. Senators and Congressmen? Do you know who represents you in the State Legislature? You should know who is going to bat for you in the government.

Several sites on the Internet can provide the names of the elected officials who represent you. Scroll down to the bottom of the page at the Project Vote Smart page at www.vote-smart.org and enter your zip code for a complete listing of your Federal and State representatives.

Up close and personal

The sites of both the House of Representatives at www.house.gov, and the Senate at www.senate.gov hold links to the home pages of individual legislators. You'll find email addresses and contact information at these sites.

Identify the Issues

The Democrats (www.democrats.org) and the Republicans (www.rnc.org) maintain Web sites with information about their respective parties and related issues. Reform Party supporters can find their page at www.reformparty.org. If you have leanings toward the Libertarian Party, visit them at www.lp.org. If you want to find out about the issues of other political parties, search for the party in your favorite search engine.

For further information about the issues, The Political Insider at www.politicalinsider.com, provides a great way for you to learn about federal issues. If you really like the site, you can sign up to receive a free daily email briefing about the sites. Policy.com at www.policy.com is another good site for identifying current issues.

The Web's many search services can help you identify the issues. Yahoo! has some excellent links to current political issues as well. From the Yahoo! main page, click the links to **Government, Countries, United States, Politics, Political Issues,** and then browse through the issues for information that interests you. Or, run a search, similar to the one pictured in Figure 13.10 at HotBot and read through the Results List for issues that interest you.

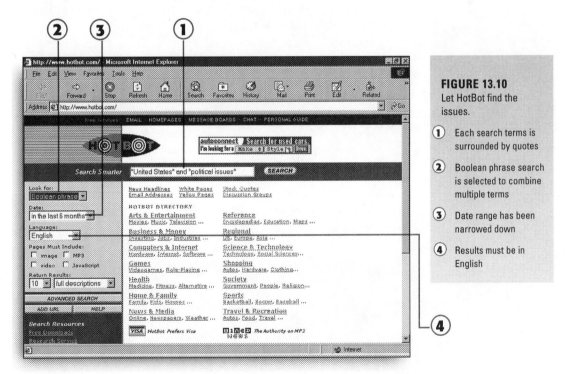

Slanted

Many of the Web sites that present the issues are owned by groups or individuals with a particular slant. Take everything you read with a grain of salt; sometimes the manner in which issues are presented can show bias towards one side or the other.

FIGURE 13.10
Let HotBot find the issues.

(1) Each search terms is surrounded by quotes

(2) Boolean phrase search is selected to combine multiple terms

(3) Date range has been narrowed down

(4) Results must be in English

SEE ALSO
➤ *For information about searching at HotBot, review page 165*

Get Involved

A light touch

The subject of politics doesn't always need to be serious. Visit the Humorspace page of Politically Correct Taglines at www.humorspace.com/humor/taglines/upc.htm for a quick smile.

Knowledge is power! Now that you understand the issues, get involved. Newsgroups like `alt.activism` and `alt.activism.community` will put you in touch with people who want to make a difference. Visit the Web site of 20/20 Vision for Peace and The Environment at `www.2020vision.org` or Greenpeace at `www.greenpeace.org` to find out what you can do to save the earth. See how other activists are faring at the ProActivist.org site at `www.proactivist.org`.

Consider starting your own group. You can set up a group at E-groups at `www.egroups.com` that will only cost you an investment of your time.

You can make a difference to the world in which you live. You can make a big splash or a small ripple. It's totally up to you. Get active. Get involved.

Type it right!

Some URLs are quite lengthy and can seem hard to type. Make sure that you type a URL, like the ones shown here, correctly. Uppercase letters must be typed in uppercase. Don't add extra spaces or slashes. Check your typing before you press the **Enter** key.

Gain an International Perspective on Politics

Most Americans have enough trouble keeping up with their own political scene and don't know much about what's going on in the rest of the world.

Table 13.6 lists some sites that will inform you about international politics.

Table 13.6 Political sites from around the world

Region	URL	Comments
Australia	www.pcug.org.au/~bpalmer/	Find out what's happening in the "land down under."
China	www.insidechina.com/	Gain an understanding of the tangled web of Chinese politics at this site.
France	www.adetocqueville.com	Read all about French news and analysis here. A scrolling ticker updates the latest French news.

Region	URL	Comments
Great Britain	www.ukpol.co.uk	The site is sponsored by Politco's, a London bookstore and coffeehouse. You can click a link to find related sites, or send an email to an MP (Member of Parliament). You can also use their search engine to look for other related information.
India	indiafocus.indiainfo.com/ politics/	You'll find an in-depth focus of Indian politics at this site.
Ireland	www.solaseireann.com/temp/ SolasNews.html	Links to many different resources and news publications are grouped under the categories of Peace and News.
Middle East	magellan.excite.com/ reference/politics_and_ government/foreign_ governments/middle_east	Links to both Arab and Israeli sites can be found here. There's also a list of subtopic categories for most of the countries in the region.
Russia	www.agora.stm.it/politic/ russia3.htm	Learn about Russian politics, parties, government, and legislation at this site.

Tracking the Weather

Everyone is affected by the weather. Rain, cold, and stormy days will keep most of us indoors (and connected to the Internet) while warm, sunny days beckon us outdoors. Travelers need to know the weather at their destination to help them determine what to pack.

The Web holds hundreds of sites that deal with the weather. The Start pages at My Netscape and MSN both contain customizeable weather information. Here are my favorites weather sites.

1. The National Weather Service home page, pictured in Figure 13.11, at www.nws.noaa.gov receives so many hits each day that you might have trouble connecting. It's worth the trouble though, since the site has everything you can imagine about weather. Look at storm predictions, radar charts, and forecasts at the site.

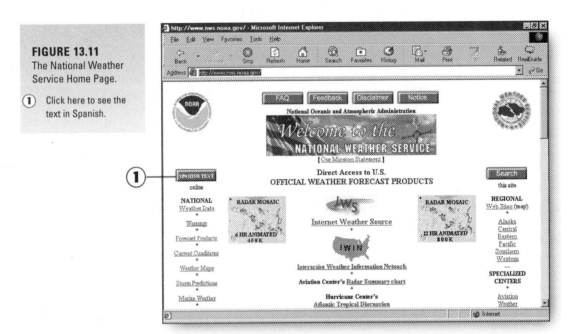

FIGURE 13.11
The National Weather Service Home Page.

① Click here to see the text in Spanish.

2. The home page of The Weather Channel, at www.weather.com has links to Breaking Weather and Weather News. Type in a city or zip code to find weather information about the location. You can even create a custom weather page with interactive maps and up to 10 city forecasts.

3. Intellicast.com at www.intellicast.com bills itself as "Weather for Active Lives." The site can provide your local weather or weather conditions anywhere else. Take a weather class at Dr. Dewpoint's page.

4. The Weather Underground at www.wunderground.com lets you click a map to get weather conditions at any U.S. location. You can also find the Heat Index, Wind Chill, or Dewpoint of places in the United States.

chapter 14

Managing Your Money Online

Banking online •

Maximize your savings •

Buying stocks and bonds online •

Examining day trading •

Banking Online

A trip to the bank used to be a regular weekly routine for most people. In today's busy world, few people have time to go to the bank. Most folks are at work themselves when the bank is open. Check-cashing cards and Automatic Teller Machines have replaced the lines at the teller's window.

Many banks have cut way back on tellers and other customer personnel. Some banks actually charge for every transaction handled by a teller. Cashing a check inside the bank might result in a service charge while using the ATM machine outside is free.

Online banking is the newest way to bank. Using your browser and special access codes from the bank, you can check your balance, transfer funds between accounts, or even pay your bills or loans online. Many banks offer different levels of online service. For example, my bank enables customers to view balances and account transactions for free, but charges for other online services.

The convenience of online banking is unsurpassed. While you're connected to the Internet, you can handle banking chores any time of the day or night. If you have a simple interest loan on which interest accrues on a daily basis, you can control the exact day that your loan payment is made. The bank handles all of the details if you pay your bills online, so you don't need to worry about rummaging through your drawer for stamps or remembering to drop your payments in the mailbox. Parking problems, long lines, and harried tellers, are all things of the past.

Most of the bigger banks in urban areas now offer some level of online banking. Check with your bank to find what online features are available. Even if your bank doesn't offer online banking right now, chances are that they will sometime soon.

National banks like Wells Fargo (wellsfargo.com/home), Bank of America (www.bankamerica.com), and Citibank (www.citibank.com) have online branches to supplement their regular service. Some *"virtual" banks*, like the ones shown in Table 14.1, have no physical branches, and only do business over the Internet.

Quicken or Microsoft Money

Many banks can output your banking and credit information directly into money management software such as Microsoft Money or Quicken. Some banks work with Microsoft Money, and others interface only with Quicken, so check with your bank before you sign up for online services.

Online banking from American Express

Check out the online banking services offered by American Express. Called Membership B@nking, the service, at www.americanexpress.com/banking, offers high interest rates on deposits, low rates on credit lines, rebates on ATM surcharges, and free unlimited electronic bill payments, in addition to money market and checking accounts and certificates of deposits.

Table 14.1   Internet banks

Name	URL
Security First Network Bank	www.sfnb.com
NetB@nk	www.netbank.com
CompuBank	www.compubank.com
Wingspan Bank (division of FCC National Bank)	home.wingspanbank.com

Is My Bank for Real?

Choosing an Internet bank requires the same care as choosing an Internet merchant. A slick Web site that piques your interest doesn't necessarily mean that a bank is reputable. If a bank offers unbelievable low interest rates on credit cards or high rates on savings accounts, there's a good chance that the bank is fraudulent.

In the United States, a reputable bank must have a charter and should be a member of the Federal Deposit Insurance Corporation (FDIC). Visit the FDIC Web site at www.fdic.gov/consumer/suspicious to determine if a bank is properly authorized to conduct business. The site also contains helpful hints about choosing an Internet bank.

SEE ALSO

➤ You'll learn how to guard against fraudulent Internet merchants on page 438

Obtaining a Secure Browser

If you're located in the United States or Canada, some online banks prefer that your browser use *128-bit encryption*. The standard version of the Netscape Communicator suite provides 56-bit encryption, while Internet Explorer offers 40-bit encryption.

The number of encryption bits, like "128," "56," or "40" refers to the size of the key used to encrypt the information that's passed to and from your browser when you're connected to the Internet. As a point of reference, 128-bit encryption is 309,485,009,821,345,068,724,781,056 times stronger than 40-bit encryption.

International encryption

Individuals outside the United States and Canada cannot download the 128-bit browser. However, the standard version of both browsers includes *Server Gated Cryptography* (SGC) technology that enables international customers to conduct 128-bit transactions with banks and financial institutions around the world.

The rules might change

At the time this book was written, only U.S. and Canadian users were authorized to download and install the 128-bit version of Netscape Navigator and Internet Explorer. That rule, and the way to obtain the browser, many change. Check with your bank if you need further assistance.

The U.S. government restricts the export of 128-bit encryption outside the United States and Canada. To download the 128-bit version of your browser, you must agree to an export notice and your Internet connection, your ISP or company, for example, must be verifiable as being provided by a U.S. or Canadian carrier.

Your online bank will let you know if you need to use the 128-bit version of your browser and, most likely, provide a link to the site where you can obtain it. Alternatively, Internet Explorer uses can go to www.microsoft.com/windows/ie/download/128bit/intro.htm for information about downloading and installing the 128-bit encryption. Netscape Navigator users will need to download and install a secure version of the Communicator suite. Visit home.netscape.com/download/index.html to obtain the installation file.

SEE ALSO
➤ *Review how to download files on page 185*

Work with a Financial Planner

Hiring a good financial planner might just be one of the smartest decisions you'll ever make. A financial planner has a broad knowledge of areas such as tax planning, investments, and estate law. Your financial planner will help you produce a personal financial plan for your household. This plan will cover the household's financial goals, budget, insurance and risk review, asset allocation, retirement plan, and, quite possibly, a review of an estate plan.

Finding the right financial planner can be tricky. Get a few recommendations from your friends and colleagues. The Web can help match you with a planner who will help you set and reach your goals.

The Institute of Certified Financial Planners is a good place to find a professional who can plan your financial future. Visit the site at www.icfp.org/plannersearch and click the link to **Search Now**. Follow the onscreen instructions to search for a certified planner in your area. The form, shown in Figure 14.1, enables you to search for a professional in your city, or a nearby town with a population of over 100,000 people.

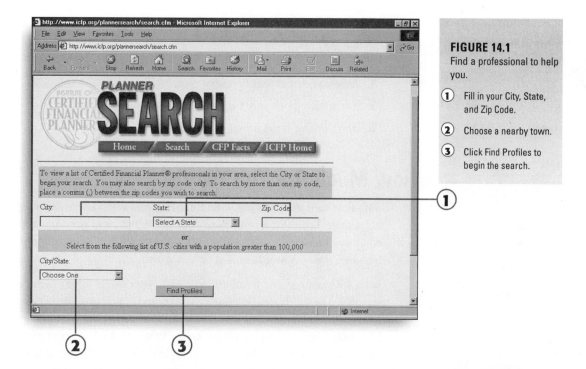

FIGURE 14.1
Find a professional to help you.

(1) Fill in your City, State, and Zip Code.

(2) Choose a nearby town.

(3) Click Find Profiles to begin the search.

When you've filled in the requested information, click the **Find Profiles** button. In a few moments, a list of planners appears that includes names, addresses, and phone numbers. Your financial planner is going to be a key player in your future, so make sure you have a good rapport with the one you select.

Control Your Own Destiny

If you're not quite ready to enlist the aid of a professional, try managing your money yourself. Begin by paying attention to how much money you spend casually—on newspapers and magazines, lunches, or even your morning coffee. You'll be amazed at how much money flies out of your wallet without your notice. After you're aware of how much you're spending on incidentals, widen your focus. Do you purchase impulse items at the grocery or discount store? How much are you spending on fast food? Get a handle on how and where you spend your money.

Find a certified financial planner by phone

In addition to the online form, you can contact The Institute of Certified Financial Planners by a few other methods. Send them an email message at search@ifcp.org for help in finding a planner in your area. You can also call the toll-free hotline at 800-282-PLAN.

Once you become more aware of your spending habits, you're ready to take control. Although there are thousands of strategies to managing your money, a simple three-step plan may be all you need.

1. Assess your current financial picture.

2. Set goals—both short and long term.

3. Start saving right now.

How Much Are You Worth?

The first step to achieving your financial goal is to determine your net worth. Basically, to compute your net worth, you need to add up what you own and subtract from this what you owe. The difference between the two numbers is your net worth.

Start with your assets. In addition to cash, your assets might include securities, property, and even jewelry. Try to be as thorough as possible when you figure out your assets; after you've made your preliminary list, walk through your house to see if you've overlooked anything of value, like an original painting or an antique vase. It's important to be objective about the actual value of some of your possessions. For example, a car or computer that you've had for several years is probably worth less now than when you bought it.

Next figure out your liabilities. Credit card balances, mortgage and car payments, and insurance charges should be included. If you've got a big home repair planned, like a new roof, include that too. Also be sure to include items like your tax liability. How about school loans or even current tuition?

When you're done, subtract your liabilities from your assets. Now you have an idea of your actual net worth. Try to be honest and not fudge any of the numbers. Even if you're not in the greatest financial position right now, no one is looking over your shoulder or judging you.

If you need help figuring your net worth, you can use a great online net worth calculator. Visit the Altamira Financial Services home page at www.altamira.com and click the link to the **Toolkit** and then the **Net Worth Calculator**. Fill in each applicable field as you scroll down the page. When you're done entering the numbers, click the button to **Calculate Net Worth**. The calculator, shown in Figure 14.2, does the math for you and presents you with a result.

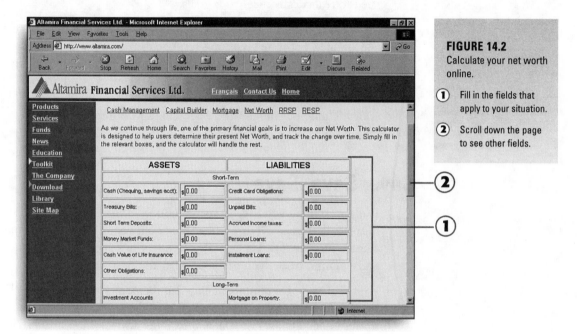

FIGURE 14.2
Calculate your net worth online.

① Fill in the fields that apply to your situation.

② Scroll down the page to see other fields.

Once you've figured your net worth, take a look at your income and expenses. Look over your pay stubs, receipts, and credit card statements to get a handle on your income and expenses for a month or a quarter. Add in income and expenses that didn't occur during this period, such as an insurance payment, but that you know will during the next three months, six months, or year. Include the money that you spend on incidental items. The difference between your total estimated income and expenses is what you're saving (or not saving).

Set Financial Goals

Once you know what you've got, you can begin to think about what you'd like to have. Instead of setting an unattainable goal for yourself—such as saying you want to have 20 million dollars at the end of five years—make some reasonable goals for yourself.

Consider your personal circumstances. Maybe you want to save for your toddler's college education, or a vacation on the Orient Express. What about your retirement? Determine how much money you'll need to realistically meet your goals.

To a certain extent, your goals dictate how you're going to manage your money. Separate your long-term goals from your short ones. If you're planning a big wedding next year, you don't want to tie up your funds in a long-term investment. On the other hand, if your goal is to achieve a comfortable retirement in 20 years, you can afford to put your money into a growth fund and forget about it for awhile.

Save, Save, Save

With everything you have to spend money on, it's sometimes hard to remember to pay yourself first. However, saving needs to become a habit. Deposit a percentage of your salary in a special account every month, before you pay your bills. You're worth it!

For a little positive reinforcement, visit the Armchair Millionaire Web site at www.armchairmillionaire.com. You can follow the success stories of people just like you, and read the advice of top financial wizards. Attend a chat session, complete with guest speakers, for some conversation in real-time. The chats are generally structured around a particular theme or subject and can be enormously informative. A typical week's chat schedule is shown in Figure 14.3.

SEE ALSO

➤ *Chatting on the Internet is a great way to meet new friends. Read more about it on page 286*

Savings Accounts and CDs

Cookie jars or shoeboxes under your bed are not the best places to stash the money you've saved. For one thing, it's awfully tempting to raid your cash stash when you're a little short of funds. If you're like most of us, your promises to repay the money will be forgotten by the next day. For another thing, money that's hidden in the house isn't secure. Most importantly, money that's tucked away at home isn't earning interest for you.

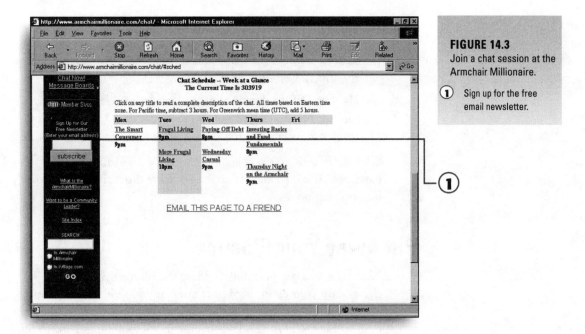

Instead of keeping your savings at home, you might want to put your money in the bank. Most banks offer interest-bearing savings accounts. You might consider purchasing a Certificate of Deposit, commonly known as a CD. Whichever you choose, make sure that you're getting the highest interest rate on your savings.

Savings rates fluctuate from bank to bank and even account to account. Use these sites to help you determine where you'll get the best return on your money.

- **BanxQuote** at www.banx.com provides daily market quotes and rates on Banking, Auto, Home and Consumer Finance, Money & Investments, and Global Commerce. You can search for CD rates by geographical region. Although BanxQuote doesn't have a comprehensive list of banks, you'll get an idea of the typical rates in your area.

- **Bank Rate Monitor** at www.bankrate.com offers news and advice on banking, as well as a search of some of the best CD rates in the nation. The rates of over 2,500 institutions covering all 50 states is updated daily.

- **Rate.Net** at www.rate.net serves up recent banking news and CD interest rates, including market movement, current and historical rate trends, for banks nationwide. You can search for the top 10 best rates at this site.

- **Bank-CD Rate Scanner** at www.bankcd.com claims to find the highest FDIC-insured rates in the USA on CDs and money market accounts. Search results are sent via an email message.

Save as much as you can, even if it's only a small amount each paycheck. You'll be amazed at how quickly those tiny sums grow into one big one.

Put Away Your Plastic

Next time you pay your bills, add up the interest you've been charged on your credit card purchases. If you're like most people, using plastic is the easiest way to buy what you want. Because shopping with a credit card is so convenient, it's sometimes hard to think about how very much the convenience costs you.

Paying off your credit card debt should be an attainable goal. Stop by the Debt Reduction Planner (www.quicken.com/saving/debt) at Quicken.com. You can use the planner to add up all of your debts. Use the planner to help you create a strategy to help pay off what you owe.

Try not to use a credit card for your purchases, unless you can pay off the balance when you receive the bill. Switch to a credit card like the American Express standard green card at www.americanexpress.com, where you're required to pay off the bill each month. You can apply for the card online.

The first month of shopping without a wallet full of plastic will be the hardest. You'll probably find that you can get away with fewer new possessions than you thought previously. As a side benefit, you'll probably become a better shopper, looking for better value at a lower price.

Save your credit cards for when you really need them. Credit cards can help you obtain big items, like appliances or computers. If you do charge a big purchase, make sure you send your payments in on time and maintain a good credit standing.

That's a lot of debt

If you think you're carrying a lot of debt, check out The Public Debt Online Web site at www.publicdebt.treas.gov/opd/opdpenny.htm. You'll find the latest figures for the National Debt.

Even if you stop using your credit cards for the most part, you will still want to maintain a card or two for emergencies and big purchases. The interest rate and payment schedule can vary from card to card. Are your present credit cards giving you the best deal? It's worth a little research to find out. You might find a card with a much lower interest rate, or easier payment terms.

Use the sites shown in Table 14.2 to learn more about the best credit cards deals.

Check the APR

APR stands for the annual percentage rate that's charged on the outstanding balance on your credit card. The lower the number, the less interest you pay. Check out the APR rate on a credit card before you sign up.

Table 14.2   Credit card information on the Web

Site	URL	Comments
Credit Card Advisor	`www.creditcardmenu.com`	Credit card listing with descriptions and a search tool to select the card that matches your requirement.
Credit Card Network	`www.creditnet.com`	A mega-site of credit card products, services, and information.
Credit Card Rates Guide	`www.abcguides.com/creditcards`	Comparative shopping service for credit cards.
The Payment Card Planet of Cyberspace	`ramresearch.com`	Find a universe of low-rate, no annual fee, secured rebate credit cards.
Using Secured Credit Cards	`www.bbb.org/library/securecard.html`	Information about credit cards for individuals who have no credit or a bad credithistory.

In addition to these sites, visit the Visa International page at `www.visa.com` and the MasterCard home page at `www.mastercard.com` for information about their cards. You'll find tips to maximize your cards at both sites.

Next time you reach for your credit card, dig for cash instead. Use your credit cards wisely. Recognize how much they may have been costing you.

Check Your Credit History

Your credit report is a kind of report card of how you pay your debts. A bad credit report can stand in the way of a home or car purchase. Disputed payments or erroneous items can make you look like a poor risk or worse, an individual who doesn't pay what's owed.

Check out your own credit report at iCreditReport.com (www.icreditreport.com). The site, pictured in Figure 14.4, is easy to navigate. After filling out a brief form, you can view your credit report online for around $8. For approximately $30, you can merge your report from three of the leading credit reporting services.

FIGURE 14.4
Take a look at your own credit report.

① The https portion of the address indicates the site is secure.

② A drop-down list of choices is displayed when you click this arrow.

③ Click the locked padlock to view additional security information about the site.

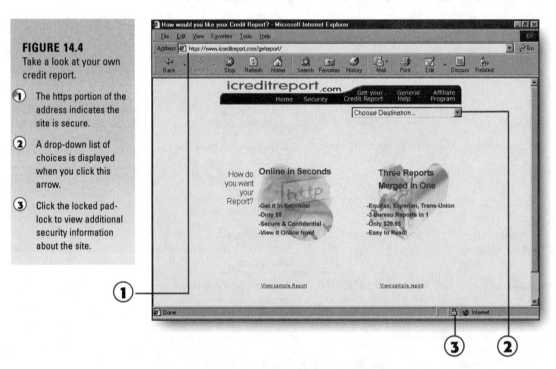

Making Online Investments

Online investing has everyone's attention. With an Internet connection and an account with a firm that allows *e-trading*, you can become your own broker. Stories of people who have made a pile by trading stocks on the Internet can be heard everywhere. Are you the next e-millionaire?

Investing can be risky if you don't know what you're doing. Picking a stock or mutual fund that's on the way up can be impossible without all of the facts. Even if your stock or fund goes up, how can you predict the ups and downs of the daily market? Your carefully planned investments could lose money, fast, instead of making you rich.

My broker says that good investments are the result of business acumen, market knowledge and sometimes, a dash of luck. Online investing adds another dimension of risk to the mixture. If you want to give online investing a try, consider starting slowly. Pay attention to what you're doing and carefully track the results.

The Pros and Cons of Online Investing

Weigh the positives and the negatives of online investing before you get involved. The are several good reasons why online investing might work great for you. Consider these points:

- *Immediate access to your account.* You can check the value of your portfolio anytime. When you buy or sell a stock, the transactions are posted to your account at the end of the day, and you can access account information 24 hours a day.

- *Save brokerage and transaction fees.* You'll save money by doing it yourself. The fees for online trading costs generally cost less than what you'd pay a traditional broker.

- *Trade anytime.* Just log on and enter your transaction. If you live in a different time zone than New York, you won't need to adjust your schedule to adjust for New York business hours. Your broker or someone on the brokerage staff doesn't need to be there for you to buy or sell. (Of course, the trade won't be posted until the market is open.)

On the flip side, there are some reasons why you might invest exclusively through a trained, professional stockbroker. Online investing has its down side—especially if you're inexperienced. Mull these points over.

- *You're totally on your own.* Although some online brokerages can set you up with an advisor, most of the time you'll never deal with another human being. Are you prepared to handle all your own research and make big decisions all by yourself?

- *Timing can be an issue.* With most online brokerage firms, the time your transaction is handled is not necessarily the time you post the trade. The price of a stock can fluctuate by a few percentage points. If your Internet connection is slow or your broker is inundated with trades, the stock you want can move very quickly against you, leaving you with a larger loss if you're selling or a higher purchase price.

- *Your trades are computer-dependent.* Even the most reliable computer can crash through no fault of your own. The electricity or phone lines can go out in your area, making your computer useless. A non-working computer can stand in the way of a major trade.

If you decide to trade online, start slowly. Learn as much as you can about the stock market and the stocks you want to buy before you spend any money. Choose a broker that has backup phone service and post the phone numbers where you'll find them if you need to use the backup phone service. Make sure your computer is in good working order.

Factor in Some Risk

All the buzzwords

Investing has its own words and phrases. You can find most all of the terms you'll need at the Investorwords Web site, located at www. investorwords.com.

As an investor, you spend your money with the anticipation of receiving a return. The possibility that an investment will return less than expected is known as "investment risk." Remember that risk and reward go hand in hand. The greater the risk you are willing to assume, the greater the potential reward. However, unless you can afford to gamble, balance your risky investments with some safer choices.

Many different types of online investments are available. Each type has its own advantages and disadvantages. Tax consequences are always an issue when you invest, so do some research to determine which investment makes the most sense for you.

What Can You Buy?

There are many different investments that can be handled online. Let's look at the three most common types.

Stocks, generally sold in units called shares, purchase a portion of a company. In essence, you are a part owner of every company whose stock you purchase. If the company does well and profits go up, the value of the company and your stock rises. If the company struggles, the value of your stock goes down.

Most companies listed on the stock exchange have thousands or millions of part owners. As a stockholder, you won't be asked for your opinion on company policy or business decisions. However, you will have a chance to vote on major issues during the company's annual meeting. If you can't make the meeting, you can cast your vote by proxy or absentee ballot.

Some company's issue two types of stock—preferred and common. Preferred stock is more expensive. However, preferred stock owners receive a fixed dividend before the owners of common stock receive anything. If the company dissolves, preferred stock owners collect assets ahead of common stock owners.

Bonds offer a reasonably safe way to invest your money. You might buy government bonds, treasury bonds, or even corporate bonds. A bond is basically an IOU. By purchasing a bond, you're actually lending money to the bondholder. In return, you get a note stating that you will be paid back the amount you lent plus interest by a certain date.

More money is invested in bonds than stocks each year. Yet, many people don't know very much about bonds. Visit the InvestinginBonds.com site (www.investinginbonds.com), pictured in Figure 14.5, to learn more about investing in bonds.

Mutual funds are investments that combine the money of many investors. The fund's manager uses the pooled funds to purchase securities such as stocks and bonds. The securities purchased are referred to as the fund's portfolio.

When you give your money to a mutual fund, you receive shares of the fund in return. Each share represents an interest in the fund's portfolio. The value of your mutual fund shares rise or fall, based on the performance of the stocks and bonds in the portfolio. Similar to a shareholder in a corporation, you receive a proportional share of income and interest generated by the portfolio. You can receive these distributions either in cash or as additional shares of the fund.

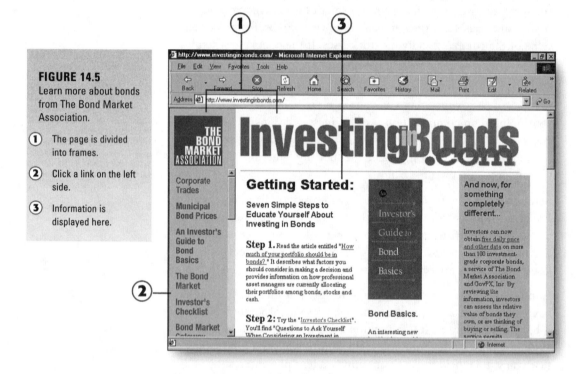

FIGURE 14.5
Learn more about bonds from The Bond Market Association.

① The page is divided into frames.

② Click a link on the left side.

③ Information is displayed here.

Visit the Stock Exchange

Stocks are bought and sold at a stock exchange. You can think of a stock exchange as a superstore for stocks. Only traders can buy and sell stocks at a stock exchange. The action on the floor of a stock exchange can get pretty crazy at times.

The best known stock exchange is located on Wall Street in New York City. Spend a little time at The New York Stock Exchange Web site, located at www.nyse.com. The site, pictured in Figure 14.6, can help you gain some insight into the volume of shares traded at the New York Stock Exchange each day.

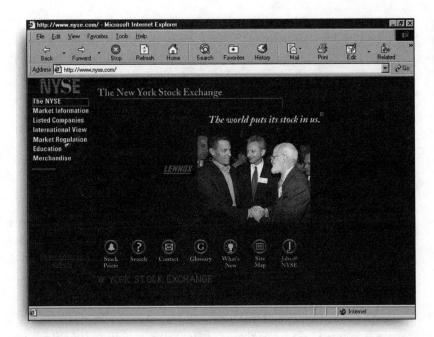

FIGURE 14.6
Follow the action at the
New York Stock Exchange.

In addition to the NYSE, stocks are traded at the American Stock
Exchange and the NASDAQ. Visit their combined Web site at
www.nasdaq.com. Additionally, many regional stock exchanges can
be found in cities like Boston, Chicago, and Philadelphia. London,
Tokyo, and other international cities have their own stock exchanges.
Some small companies might be listed only on a regional exchange.
In the reverse, some companies that are listed on the NYSE or
NASDAQ exchanges also appear on regional stock exchanges.

Choosing Your Online Broker

A brokerage firm is a dealer of stocks and other securities that works
as your agent when you buy and sell stock. Online brokers offer a
wide range of services and fees. With a little investigation you can
find one that meshes well with your investing plans. Most online
brokers require a deposit to open your account.

Choose your online broker carefully. The group that your neighbor
uses might not work well for you. Consider how much service you
need and how much you're willing to pay when you consider various
online brokers.

If you're a market whiz and can handle all of your own research and analysis, an inexpensive broker like SURETRADE.com (www.suretrade.com) might be the best for you. Generally, brokers in this range charge under $10 per trade. For the price, you'll be granted online access to your account and, possibly, some general information and research. Remember, though, that the cheaper services rarely have brokers available to speak with you. If something goes wrong, you can spend hours trying to track someone down.

Mid-range brokers like E*Trade (www.etrade.com) charge around $25 per trade. The Web sites of most mid-range brokers feature real-time quotes. Additionally, you'll find helpful articles and information at the broker's site. Most mid-range brokers offer the option of trading by phone (although there may be a surcharge). Choose a mid-range broker if you're past the newbie stage of online investing, but still require some hand-holding or guidance.

The most expensive online brokers, like Schwab (www.schwab.com), provide the highest level of service. For around $30 per trade, you'll get a wide range of services, generally available from the broker's Web site, as shown in Figure 14.7. In addition to 24-hour access to your account, you'll have the benefit of the brokerage's extensive market research and analysis. You'll also have telephone service available whenever you need it.

Take your time and perform some research before you choose your online broker. The online brokerage business is a growing source of revenue and many brokers are jumping on the Internet bandwagon. For this reason, many brokers change their services and fees to stay competitive with the other firms on the Internet.

Use the sites shown in Table 14.3 to help you find the broker that's right for you.

Table 14.3 Internet broker advisors

Name	URL	Comments
Gomez Advisors	www.gomez.com	You'll find rankings and comments about brokers and their services. Sort brokers according to ease of use, customer confidence, onsite resources, relationship services, and overall costs.

Name	URL	Comments
CyberInvest.com	www.cyberinvest.com/ guides/brokers.html	CyberInvest.com offers seven different ways to view the online brokers compared (1) alphabetically, (2) in order of lowest commissions, (3) deep discounters only, (4) by lowest initial investment required, (5) investing tools, (6) the market leaders, and (7) those brokers who have been rated #1 in one or more media surveys.
SmartMoney.com	www.smartmoney.com/ si/brokers/	SmartMoney.com offers rankings divided by online brokers, discount brokers, and full-service brokers. Check out the Online Investor's Survival Kit for practical, savvy advice.
Broker BROKER	broker-tip.com	Links to many different brokers put you in touch with the broker who's right for you.

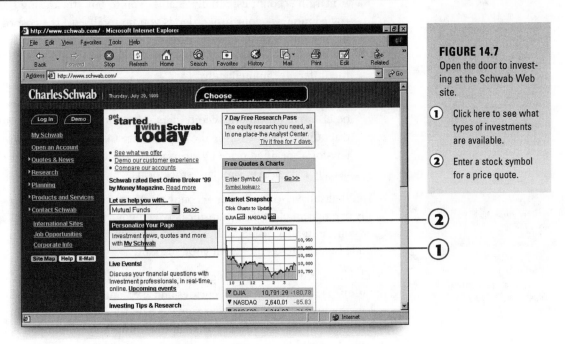

FIGURE 14.7
Open the door to investing at the Schwab Web site.

① Click here to see what types of investments are available.

② Enter a stock symbol for a price quote.

Setting Up Your Account

After you've chosen your online broker, you're probably ready to jump into the world of investments. Not so fast! You need to set up your account before you can proceed.

You can fill out the forms online to get started. You'll probably set up a standard brokerage account enabling you to buy and sell stock. You can set up a standard account in your name, the name of a corporation or investment club or a trust. You'll have to provide tax information, such as a social security number or corporate tax identification number.

Based on the broker, you might need to select what type of account you'll use.

- A cash account is the most basic type. A cash account is like a checking account. You deposit money into the account and the broker withdraws the funds needed to cover your purchases. Profits from dividends and sales are deposited to the account.

- A margin account essentially enables you to buy stock using borrowed money—your broker lends you up to 50% of the cost of buying the stocks you want. Buying on margin is very risky. If the value of the stock goes down, you'll have to come up with the difference immediately.

- An option account is less common than the other two, but can be effective for experienced traders. An option works like a contract that gives the buyer the opportunity to buy or sell a security for a specified price by a certain deadline. Option deals are usually riskier than standard stock deals.

You'll also have to fund your account to get started. You can generally arrange an electronic transfer between your bank and the broker, or you can mail a cashier's check. Most brokers won't allow you to trade before there's money in your account.

The broker will need your signature on a printed copy of the application, as required by the Securities and Exchange Commission. By law, the broker must have your signature on file, verifying that you have opened the account and that all the information about you is true. To speed the process, most times you can fax a copy of the application and use snail mail for the real signature. Make sure you

T plus 3

Although you generally need to put money in the account before you can buy any stocks, some brokerages will let you enter orders if you have good credit. You're required to make sure that the funds are available by the settlement date, or three days after you make the trade. The settlement date is often referred to as "T plus 3."

Check out the SEC

The Web site of the Securities and Exchange Commission is packed with some great information for investors. You'll find the site at www.sec.gov.

mail the application; if the broker doesn't receive your signed application within a specified period of time (usually between 15 and 30 days), your account will be closed.

When all the paperwork is in place, you'll receive a Personal Identification Number (PIN) from the broker. You'll probably receive your number through regular mail or by express delivery, rather than email. When you've got your PIN, you're ready to log in and start trading.

Research, Research, Research

Now that your account is set up, you're ready to start investing! The Web has thousands of sites that can help you research the best investments. Use your favorite search tool, like Yahoo! or HotBot, to find information about the companies in which you want to invest.

Table 14.4 shows some of the best general stock sites on the Web. Use these sites to learn about the latest trends, obtain quotes, and even meet other investors.

Table 14.4 Stock sites on the Web

Name	URL	Comments
Motley Fool	www.fool.com	Make the Fool your first stop for stock information. The site contains links to information, trends, articles, and message boards. You'll find companies with excellent management, a large profit margin, and a tendency to generate large amounts of cash. Learn about the Fool Ratio, an easy mathematical formula that enables you to calculate whether a company's stock is over or under priced.
Quote.com	www.quote.com	Read the latest financial news, get quotes, charts, and research at this massive site. You can even create a custom Quote.com personal page, and get a free email account.

continues…

Table 14.4 Continued		
Name	URL	Comments
Reuters Moneynet	www.moneynet.com	You'll find all the information you need, packed into a tight, easy to follow format. The site contains links to all of the latest financial news and market briefs.
MSN Money Central Investor	investor.msn.com	Run by Microsoft, the site bills itself as the best place on the Web to track your investments, get new investment ideas, and do the research to make smart investment decisions. You'll have to join (for free) to take advantage of the wealth of information you'll find here.

Hone Your Skills with a Portfolio

Before you invest real money, you might want to work on your investing skills. Cyber-investing for profit takes patience, knowledge, and skill. One of the best ways to practice, before you play for keeps, is to track a portfolio of pretend investments.

Start with a set investment amount, close to the amount you're actually planning to invest. Pick several stocks and watch their performance over time. "Buy" and "sell" your shares based on your hunches and information you've gained from your research. If you've got friends who are interested in investing, have them set up portfolios and then compare your results against theirs.

You can build a portfolio at Stockmaster at www.stockmaster.com. The Stockmaster site, pictured in Figure 14.8, contains plentiful information and is a great place to visit to polish your investing sills. After you sign up, you can build an unlimited number of free portfolios. You can log in anytime and record your own buy/sell transactions to track your portfolio value. You can also view your portfolio in six different views, including quotes, earnings, historical performance, and total valuation.

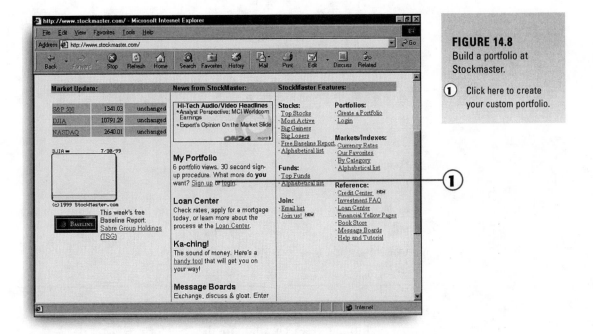

FIGURE 14.8
Build a portfolio at Stockmaster.

① Click here to create your custom portfolio.

Yahoo! at `yahoo.finance.com` is another great place to build a free portfolio. Yahoo! uses a Java-based portfolio manager and displays real-time prices and quotes. CBS.MarketWatch at `cbs.marketwatch.com` and StockSmart Pro at `www.stocksmart.com` also offer great free portfolios.

Treat your pretend investments seriously. After all, the knowledge you gain playing with pretend dollars can be transferred to your real investments.

Read an Investing 'Zine

There are many online versions of popular investing magazines. The e-zines are available to you, anytime you're connected to the Internet. The advantage to reading the Web versions is that you're not inundated with print material that needs to go out to the trash. Of course, you can print any article you want.

SEE ALSO
➤ *Review information on printing Web pages on page 132*

Sometimes the online version of the financial magazine is stripped down from its printed counterpart. Use Table 14.5 to find some of the best free investment e-zines on the Web.

Table 14.5 Investment e-zines

Name	URL
Business Week	www.businessweek.com
Fortune	www.fortune.com
Forbes	www.forbes.com
Kiplinger Online	www.kiplinger.com
Money.com	www.money.com
Mutual Fund Magazine	www.mfmag.com
Worth Online	www.worth.com

Read everything you can before you invest. The time you spend performing research will more than pay for itself later on.

Looking at Day Trading

Day traders conduct business on a single day. Every morning a day trader starts with a clean slate. A day trader starts the day with a buy and, no matter what transpires in between, ends the day by selling off all of the day's unsold acquisitions.

Day traders often use a technique called scalping, which is used to profit on very small movements of stocks, over and over throughout the day. For example, a day trader might buy a stock at $100 per share and sell it 25 seconds later at 100 1/4. Getting 1/4 of a point may not seem like much, but trading 500 or 1,000 shares at a time, and making a dozen or more similar trades during a typical day, can lead to a good income and return on investment.

Some people liken day trading to playing fantasy football. Day traders are like armchair quarterbacks, matching their skills against investment professionals. However, unlike fantasy sports leagues, there's real money involved. In the course of one day, a day trader can accumulate enormous gains, or lose hundreds of thousands of dollars.

There are no accurate estimates for how many people are full-time day traders. Using trading patterns from active customers, online brokerages believe that the total is easily in the tens of thousands.

Day trading has been around for approximately 10 years. However, day trading became popular in the last year or so. In 1998, day trading really grew as Internet stocks soared and Web brokerage firms rushed to take advantage of surging demand. In the volatile tech stock market, the shares of some companies rose at a phenomenal rate. Using a small amount of capital, some day traders made millions.

Day traders use special software that can be installed on most computers. With the software and an Internet connection, a day trader can do business anywhere. Many day traders lease a phone, computer, and Internet access from special day trading brokerage houses. It's not uncommon for 10 or 15 day traders, each at their own desk, to be crammed inside a single room.

Day trading is not for the casual investor. You can lose everything you own, and more, during the course of a single day. Only a handful of day traders make a profit.

There's lots of information on the Web about day trading. Recent publicity about day trading has made it a popular search topic. Use your favorite search tool to find the latest information. Be sure to check out the Day Traders Online site at www.daytraders.com. If you want to become a full-time day trader, visit the Careerdaytrader.com site at www.careerdaytrader.com for more information.

Using the Internet As an Educational Resource

The World's Biggest Library

Imagine standing at the doorway of the world's biggest library. Floors of books, videos and reference materials await you. To your left is a staff of people, many famous, who want to assist you with whatever research you need to conduct. To your right are records of scientific experiments, laboratories, and other scientific equipment that can help you accomplish any task you've been assigned. Sounds pretty good, doesn't it?

Actually, the World Wide Web is that library. A collection of information about just any topic is available to you. Unlike most libraries, your Web library is open all the time. You never have to pay overdue fines. There's no dress code and you can make as much noise as you want when you're there.

The only down side of the Web library is that, because of the volume of information it contains, you might need to search through lots of material to find what you want. As you're searching, you might find something even better than what you were looking for originally! Using the Web as an educational resource makes good sense.

The Library of Congress

More than books

In addition to housing a wondrous collection of books, the Library of Congress is also a legislative agency of the United States government. The Library of Congress is entrusted with maintaining the documents that hold the nation's laws.

The granddaddy of U.S. libraries, the Library of Congress is home to over 110 million items in a variety of formats and languages. Visit the Library of Congress at lcweb.loc.gov. You can tour an exhibition in the Library's online gallery, visit the Copyright Office for forms and information and search through the Library's catalogs and collections. You can even use the Library of Congress' research services. There's just one catch—the huge online catalog undergoes nightly maintenance and may not always be available between the hours of 11 p.m. and 6 a.m.

Infomine

INFOMINE at infomine.ucr.edu is the product of 30 California university and college libraries, and bills itself as the home libraries base for Scholarly Internet Resource Collections. The Infomine site isn't very glitzy and, at times, may seem a bit slow. However, what the site lacks in glamour, it makes up in research power.

You can find links to a wide variety of topics at Infomine, from acronyms and abbreviations to writing styles and grammar aids. The Infomine home page has so much information that it may seem overwhelming. If you can't find what you're looking for from the home page, click the link to General Reference. The Infomine General Reference page, pictured in Figure 15.1, contains links to many valuable resources on the Web.

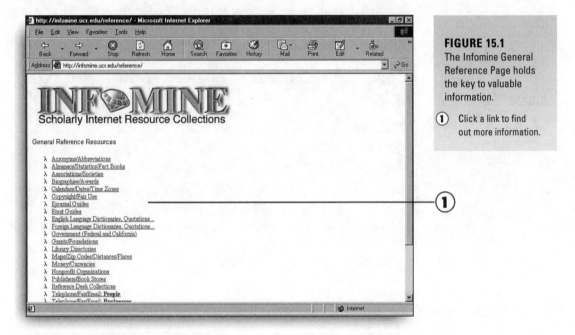

FIGURE 15.1
The Infomine General Reference Page holds the key to valuable information.

① Click a link to find out more information.

The Internet Public Library

The Internet Public Library at www.ipl.org includes tons of reference material, information on youth services, and an education division. Look through magazines and serial publications, online texts, and newspapers. There's even a section for librarians.

Setting Up a Virtual Reference Desk

If you've ever written a term paper or thesis, you know how difficult it is to get everything right. When you've got everything together, the facts, direct quotations, and the correct wordings blend to elevate your work from average to excellent.

Check your favorite search engine

Reference desks are everywhere. Many popular search engines, including HotBot and Excite, feature links to reference sites on their home pages.

Reference sites abound on the Web. Although they might not be the most exciting sites to visit, reference sites provide you with the tools you need to do a great job. Dictionaries, thesauruses, encyclopedias, and even Bartlett's quotations exist online.

Yahoo! has links to an entire section of some of the best reference sources on the Web. If you're not sure exactly what you're looking for, take advantage of all the legwork done by the researchers and indexers at Yahoo! to provide you with a variety of sites. Just go to the Yahoo! Web site at www.yahoo.com and click the Reference link (see Figure 15.2).

FIGURE 15.2
Yahoo! has a section of links devoted to online reference.

① Category links

② Type your query in the box.

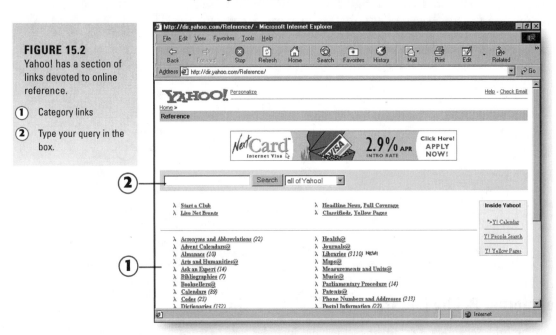

Click one of the category links to move down through the index. Or, if you know what you're looking for, type your search query in the text box and click **Search**.

Search an Encyclopedia

An encyclopedia is usually the first place you turn for information. Online encyclopedias are usually packed with up-to-date facts. In addition to text, many encyclopedias contain sound, or movie clips. Some Internet encyclopedias, like Encyclopedia Britannica, at www.eb.com, are subscription-based. Although you can try Britannica free for 30 days, you'll need to subscribe to use the service on a permanent basis.

Table 15.1 shows you some of the Web's best encyclopedias and provides a brief description about each one.

Table 15.1 The Web's best encyclopedias

Name	URL	Cost	Comments
Microsoft Encarta	encarta.msn.com	Free for first 7 days, $49.95 annually	Site contains over 40,000 articles containing text, photos, and audio and video clips.
Encycberpedia	www.encyberpedia.com	Free	Known as the "Living Encyclopedia of Cyberspace"— Encycberpedia features both links to categories and a search engine.
Compton's Encyclopedia Online	www.comptons.com	Free 7 day trial, then unlimited use for $29.95 per year	Compton's Online contains up-do-date information about a range of topics.
Information Please Encyclopedia	www.infoplease. com/encyclopdict. html	Free	Encyclopedia Search gives you access to more than 57,000 articles from the Columbia Encyclopedia, Fifth Edition.
Freeality Online Encyclopedias	www.freeality.com/ encyclopt.htm	Free	Search through several online encyclopedias. Site also contains links to other online encyclopedias.

Meet the gopher

Long before the World Wide Web, a system called *Gopher* connected universities, colleges, and government facilities all over the world. Even now, many online documents and books exist on Gopher servers across the Internet. The Gopher system is easy to use; because it's based on a sets of related menus, you can make a series of menu choices until you find the information you want. Each time you make a menu selection, a *Gopher Server* is contacted to fulfill your request. Gopher sites are accessed by URLs that begin with **gopher://**, instead of the **http://** that you're used to. The Gopher system generally contains documents that are text-based, although you might find sound or graphics files.

A Reference Sampler

If you're the impatient type who can't stand to click links, or you just want to find some great reference sites fast, visit some of the sites listed here:

- One Look Dictionary at www.onelook.com contains an index of over 208 dictionaries with more than 1 million words. Additionally, you can match words under different categories, including spelling and pronunciation.

- Roget's Internet Thesaurus at www.thesaurus.com enables you to find words that might be more suitable than the word you've chosen. As shown in Figure 15.3, type a word or phrase in the Find text box and click the **OK** button. In a few moments, a list of entries that match your text appears as links. Click an entry link for a detailed look at its definition and usage.

FIGURE 15.3
Type the word or phrase you want to match in the Find text box.

① Click the OK button to find matches.

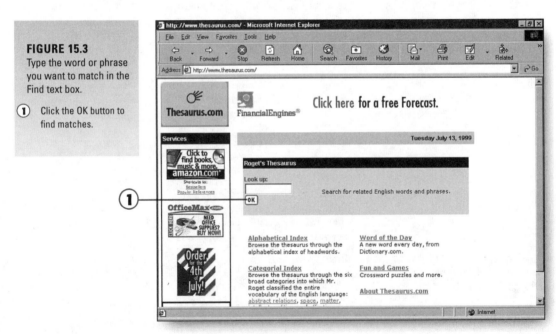

- Refdesk.com at www.refdesk.com may be the only place you ever need to go to get information. You can search for anything on the Search section of the page. Farther down, you'll find links to news, research tools, weights and measures, history, genealogy and lots more. (Everyone at my house loves the Refdesk!)

- Bartlett's Quotations at `www.cc.columbia.edu/acis/bartleby/bartlett/` is maintained by Columbia University. Click a link to one of the authors listed on the page or type the phrase you're looking for in the text box and click Search. Either way, you'll find thousands of famous quotes.

Getting Help with Homework

If you quake every time your child needs help with homework, you can breathe a little easier now. Instead of rolling up your sleeves and trying to figure out a rough homework problem, turn to the Internet.

When you're looking for some homework assistance, start with your favorite search engine or navigational guide. Most of what you're looking for can be found with a simple search or two. If you want to harness the power of many search engines, use Metacrawler at `www.metacrawler.com` or Mamma at `www.mamma.com`.

SEE ALSO

➤ *To learn more about queries, read "Form Effective Queries" on page 173*

If you're more comfortable clicking links, return to Yahooligans!, the navigational guide for kids. You're already familiar with the Yahooligans! navigational guide and its parent site, Yahoo!. The Yahooligans! database holds thousands of documents, so there's a good chance you'll find exactly what you're looking for. Use the index to find a related site, and then keep working your way down through the links. You can also enter a query in the Search text box and click the **Search** button.

SEE ALSO

➤ *For more about Yahooligans!, check out page 406*

If you're looking for a very specific answer, visit Homework Help at `www.startribune.com/stonline/html/special/homework/`. The site is staffed by volunteer teachers and functions like a newsgroup. You post your question to a discussion group, and the answer is posted to the same group. Before you post your question, look through the

Set up your query

Remember to set up your search query so that you can find the most documents first. For example, if you're child needs information on how clouds affect weather, first use only the search term **clouds**. After you've viewed the resulting hits, narrow your query and search again, using a query such as **clouds + weather**. That way, you'll be sure you're getting the right documents.

questions that have already been answered. (There's a good chance some other student had the same question first!) If you can't find the answer you're looking for, add your question to the discussion group. Make sure your question is clear and concise. In approximately one day, an answer to your question will appear in the discussion folder you selected.

Another great place for general homework help is a Web site called StudyWEB. Like Yahooligans, the StudyWEB site contains categories. However, each category is sorted according to its approximate appropriate grade level, making the categories valuable tools for teachers looking for lesson plan and curriculum ideas. The information for each topic also advises if there are downloadable or printable images that might be used for visual aids in school reports or projects. The variety and depth of topics makes StudyWEB a great ally in tackling homework problems.

A study session with StudyWEB

1. Connect to the Internet and open your browser.

2. Type `www.studyweb.com` in the Address box of your browser and press Enter. In a moment, the StudyWEB home page appears. Scroll down the page to familiarize yourself with StudyWEB's page, including the Table of Contents, Search box, and Links.

3. Click the link to a topic in which you're interested. We've chosen Animals and Pets in our example.

4. Scroll down the resulting page and click the link that further defines the topic you want (in our example, we chose Pets— Companion Animals, which opens a new page containing links to pages about many different animals.

5. Click a link that interests you. If you click the link to Cats, the resulting page, shown in Figure 15.4, provides both links and detailed information about the information contained within the links.

6. Click a link on the page to go to a site about cats. View the site, clicking any other links that seem interesting.

7. When you're done viewing the link to a site about cats, click the StudyWEB link in the top left corner of the page to return to the StudyWEB home page.

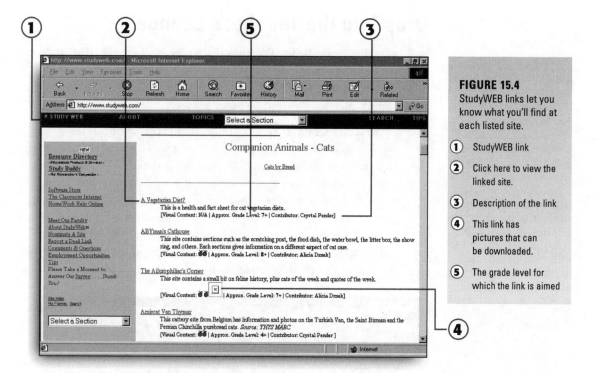

FIGURE 15.4
StudyWEB links let you know what you'll find at each listed site.

(1) StudyWEB link

(2) Click here to view the linked site.

(3) Description of the link

(4) This link has pictures that can be downloaded.

(5) The grade level for which the link is aimed

8. (Optional) If you think you might want to return to StudyWEB in the future, add it to your list of personal sites, following the instructions shown here:

- If you're using Internet Explorer, click the **Favorites** menu and then choose **Add to Favorites**. If you've organized your Favorites into folders, select the folder you want to add StudyWEB to when the Add to Favorites dialog box appears. Otherwise, simply click **OK** to add the Favorite to the list.

- Netscape Navigator users can set a bookmark with a quick keyboard shortcut by pressing **Ctrl+D**. Or, use the mouse by clicking the **Communicator** menu andselecting **Bookmarks**. When the **Bookmarks** menu appears, choose **Add Bookmark**.

SEE ALSO

➤ *For detailed information about returning to your favorite sites, see page 144*

Drop Into the Teacher's Lounge

Teachers, take heart! Pop into the Internet whenever your students push you to the limit. You can find lesson plans, classroom-ready materials, ideas for field trips and special projects, and even some funny anecdotes shared by other teachers.

The CEARCH Virtual Classroom at `metalab.unc.edu/cisco/schoolhouse` (shown in Figure 15.5) provides a comprehensive guide for teachers of all grades. (Students can go, too.) The site offers a free service to educators, parents, and administrators (anyone involved in kindergarten through twelfth grade education)and includes everything from listings of schools with Web sites to lesson plans and a step-by-step guide to getting a school online. The site contains no advertising. CEARCH is one of the most popular resources for educators on the Web; approximately 150,000 people visit each month.

FIGURE 15.5
The Virtual Schoolhouse can be a teacher's best friend.

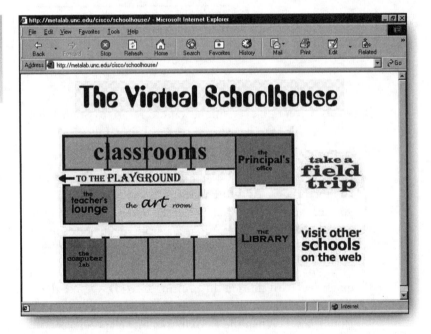

Call On Teacher Resources

Table 15.2 lists some great Web sites for teachers. Use them as an aid to getting great classroom materials and ideas, or simply as a way to take a break from the rigors of the day. One word of warning—because many of the sites shown contain links to other great sites, you'll probably spend longer than you intended!

Table 15.2   Starting point for teachers

Site Name	URL	Description
National Education Association	www.nea.org	Sponsored by America's oldest organization to public education, the site features articles on timely topics, such as how schools are faring with budget cuts, and tips and tools for better schools.
ENC Online	www.enc.org	The Eisenhower National Clearing House (sponsored by the U.S. Department of Education) holds class materials, grant opportunities, and loads of curriculum resources.
K-12 Sources	www.execpc.com/~dboals/ k-12.html	More than 500 links for teachers are offered here. Links to lesson plans, a wide variety of training materials, and health and safety issues.
Classroom Compass	www.sedl.org/ scimathcompass/ cchp.html	This site contains a collection of ideas, activities, and resources for teachers interested in improving their instruction of science and mathematics. Interactive science or mathematics classrooms provide activities that illustrate abstract concepts.

continues...

Table 15.2 Continued		
Site Name	URL	Description
AskERIC	http://ericir.syr.edu/	This site is a pilot project of the Educational Resources Information Center and the Department of Education. Its main purpose is as an Internet-based request service for teachers. Answers to questions about any topic in K-12 education are sent back within 48 hours.
TeleEducation New Brunswick	teleeducation.nb. ca/lotw/	This Canadian site contains a structured tutorial to help teachers create an online learning resource. A French version of the site also exists.

Take a Crash Course in Science

Assignments for science class can reduce anyone to tears. There's a right way and wrong way to complete the work. If you choose the wrong method, or make a mistake tabulating the results, your project is doomed to failure.

Of course, you need to have a rudimentary understanding of the material before you look to the Internet. If you're really stumped, ask your instructor or the class whiz for a hand. Then, jump on the Web.

The best way to find answers is to type a query into the search box of your favorite search tool. If you want to phrase the query as a question, such as "Why is the sky blue?" turn to Ask Jeeves at www.askjeeves.com or AltaVista at www.altavista.com.

SEE ALSO

➤ Review page *169* for information from Ask Jeeves. AltaVista is covered on page *164*

Use the sites listed here as the basis of your scientific research. Bookmark the most helpful sites so you can find your way back later.

Physics

Make Physlink.com at `www.physlink.com/reference.cfm` your first stop for information about physics (see Figure 15.6). The site has links to information about the Periodic table, equations and fundamental physical constants. If you can't find what you're looking for, use Physlink's search tool to look through the Physlink.com site In the near future, Anton Skorucak, the creator of Physlink, plans to make Physlink even better. In the works is a state-of-the-art online forum where topics such as student's homework, school physics projects, cool physics experiments, and topics like understanding the world around us, will be discussed in real time with the guidance of professional physicists and engineers.

> **Saved by Physlink**
> Physlink.com helped my son bridge the gap between confusion (and a bad grade) and success during the last school year. Even his teacher started using the site to make the class more understandable to most of the students.

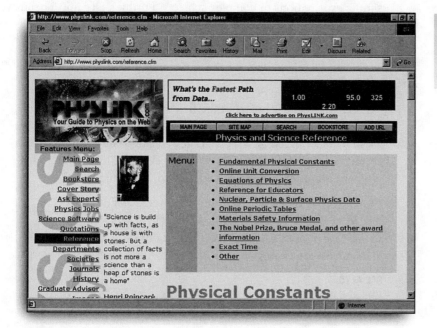

FIGURE 15.6
Demystify Physics at Physlink.com.

The Nist Reference on Constants, Units, and Uncertainty at `physics.nist.gov/cuu/Constants/index.html` and the Physics Help Room at the University of Michigan at `www.physics.lsa.umich.edu/helproom/Contents/welcome.htm` can ease you over the hump. If you want to talk with some experts in physics, check out the Usenet sci.physics.

SEE ALSO

➤ *Learn how to configure your newsreader and join a Usenet group on page 276*

Chemistry

The brains at MIT put together a fantastic Chemistry Review page at esg-www.mit.edu:8001/bio/chem/chemdir.html. The pages aren't very graphics-intensive, making them easy to print out and study.

SEE ALSO

➤ *Need help printing a Web page? Review page 132*

Another good site for Chemistry help is The Internet Chemistry Page at naio.kcc.hawaii.edu/chemistry/default.html. The site was a joint project of several Hawaii colleges and universities and provides simple explanations of complex subjects. Purdue's Organic Chemistry Help Homepage at chemed.chem.purdue.edu/~organic can be your lifeline if you're really stuck.

Biology

Top scientists and scholars in the field of biology answer all your one-on-one biology questions for free at the AllExperts Biology site, located at www.allexperts.com/edu/bio.shtml. While you might not receive an answer for a few days, where else could you find such an eminent group of experts, just waiting for your questions?

Other great biology help sites are the Biocrawler at www.biocrawler.com and the Bio-Med page at members.tripod.de/biomedpage/biomedpage_eng.html. Check out the BioScience Webring at www.geocities.com/CapeCanaveral/2435/ring.html.

SEE ALSO

➤ *A WebRing is a community of related Web pages that are organized into a circular ring. You can read all about WebRings on page 174*

Online Learning

Long-distance learning has been around for a long time. A huge range of courses has always been available. From schools that advertised in the back of publications for mechanics to Ivy League colleges, many institutions offered lessons by mail.

The Internet has made online learning much more of an accepted way of getting information. Using all of the Internet's tools, including the Web, email, and chatting, students who are physically located thousands of miles apart can feel like they're sitting in the same room as the instructor.

Learning with Macmillan

Macmillan Publishing, the folks who bring you this book and other exemplary publications about computer hardware and software, also provide an online learning center. From Internet topics to advanced programming, MCP's Distance Learning facilities help you enrich your computer knowledge. The Distance Learning Center, shown in Figure 15.7, offers a great way to learn about the newest technologies. Macmillan's *eZone* offers courses, with college credit, on such topics as C++, HTML, Java and JavaScript, PERL, Photoshop, VBScript, and Visual Basic.

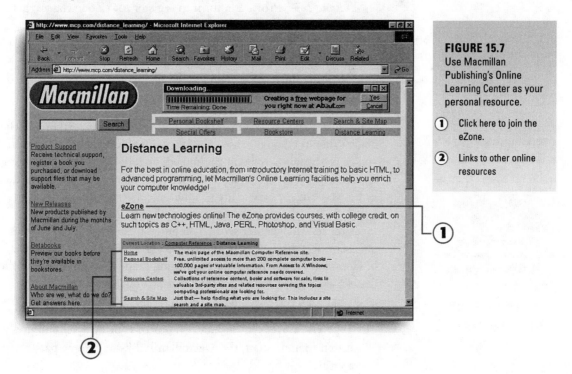

FIGURE 15.7
Use Macmillan Publishing's Online Learning Center as your personal resource.

① Click here to join the eZone.

② Links to other online resources

Start Out As a Guest

Before you sign up as a member of the eZone, you're free to look around. The eZone is set up so that you can review the first chapter of each course. Evaluate the quality of the entire course and look through the pages of the virtual class textbook. Additionally, you're welcome to take the quizzes for the first chapter. (However, your test scores won't be saved in the student database if you're not registered.) You're free to visit the Initiation pages to ask support questions and find out late-breaking news.

The eZone has several different zones to visit:

- *Learn Zone.* Shows a list of all of the available courses and certificates, as well as how the interactive achievement programs work.
- *Mentor Zone.* Answers your questions.
- *Chill Zone.* Includes tools and resources that relate to your course.
- *Initiate Zone.* Provides a form to register for eZone classes, get support, or find out what's new.
- *Catalog and Pricing.* Displays a description of the textbook used in the class, as well as the cost of the book and the class. (Most classes cost around $49.00, although a few are priced slightly higher.)

You register and pay for the course, and receive your textbook in the mail. When the book arrives, read through each chapter and, when you're ready, take a quiz on the subject material in the chapter. Your quiz results are stored in the Lesson grid. When you enter the Learn Zone, you can see how many chapters you have started, passed, or failed. As you pass the quizzes for each lesson, the chapter LED turns on and the chapter score, computed by averaging the lesson's quiz scores, is displayed. To receive access to download a Certificate of Completion, you must score a passing grade for each lesson in the course, as well as passing the midterm and final exam.

Visiting Macmillan's eZone

1. Type www.mcp.com in the Address box of your browser and press Enter. In a moment, the Macmillan Publishing home page appears.

Guest privileges are limited

Some eZone features, such as the ability to ask a question in the Mentor Zone, are available to registered users only. You'll find some links and menu features are dimmed out as you tour the eZone as a guest.

2. Click the link to **Distance Learning**. When the Distance Learning page appears on the screen, read through the text to find out what's available. When you're done reading, click the **eZone** link.

3. The eZone page, shown in Figure 15.8 is divided into frames. When you click a link in the navigation frame, the content in the instruction frame changes. If you're uncomfortable working with frames, the page also contains a horizontal menu bar. Click the **Learn Zone** icon in the left navigation frame, or click the **Learn** link on the horizontal menu bar.

SEE ALSO

➤ *To find out how to navigate through frames, review the information in "Dealing with Frames" on page 130*

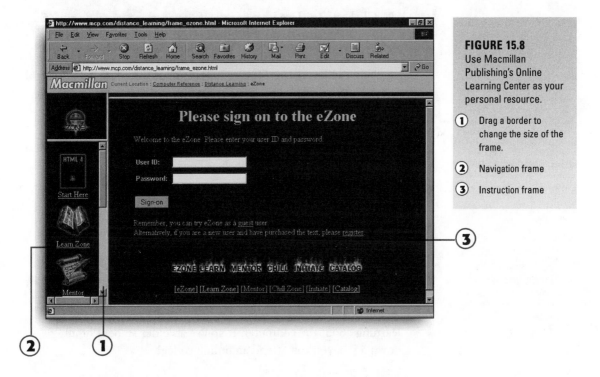

FIGURE 15.8
Use Macmillan Publishing's Online Learning Center as your personal resource.

① Drag a border to change the size of the frame.

② Navigation frame

③ Instruction frame

4. Text boxes for your User ID and password appear in the instruction frame. Because you're visiting as a guest user, scroll down the page and click the word **guest** to continue.

No grades now

When you take an online course, the grid on this page keeps track of your performance and the completion status for each lesson. At present, because you're a guest, all the LED status lights are grayed out and the *Scores* are all marked N/A, for Not Available.

5. A page appears which shows the **Courses and Certificate** programs. Click a course subject you want to review.

6. The Chapter grid for the course you selected appears. Click the link to Chapter 1. (Because you're a guest, you can only view the contents of the first chapter.)

7. To read a lesson, click on the **Read** link for that lesson. To take a quiz, click on the **Quiz** link for that lesson. Normally, you should read through the lesson before taking the quiz. However, if you feel you know the subject material, take a quiz without further reading.

8. (Optional) Click the **Mentor** icon in the navigation frame or the **Mentor** link in the horizontal menu bar to read through the FAQs list about the course.

9. Click the **Initiate** icon in the left navigation frame, or click the word **Initiate** in the horizontal menu bar.

   Unlike the other areas in the eZone, the Register, Support, and What's New options in the Initiate Zone are universally available to both registered students and guests. To register for a course, click the **Register** icon and fill in the resulting onscreen form. Click the **Support** icon to get help with shipping, media, and billing problems. Click **What's New** to find out about the latest additions and deletions at the eZone, as well as previews of new courses.

Getting Ready for College

College is a big step in the lives of many people. The Internet is waiting to assist college students of all ages and backgrounds. How? For one thing, you can do some serious test preparation for those infamous college entry exams. Or, you can get college credit for learning about the computer. If you're an older student holding down a job, you can attend an online college.

Online Counselors Help You Get Prepared

Say the words "College Boards" to a group of high school students and watch them turn green. The test scores seem to swing more weight than grade point averages or activity records for admittance to most colleges. Use the sites listed in Table 15.3 to get prepared for the tests and maybe even raise your scores a notch or two.

Table 15.3   TestPrep made easy

Site Name	URL	Description
College Board Online	www.collegeboard.org	Provides test questions, online registration, a calendar of test dates and places, and features links to financial aid information and a college search.
The Princeton Review	www.review.com	Offers information on college admissions, courses, and test prep skills.
TESTPREP.COM	www.testprep.com	Designed by Stanford Testing Systems, Inc., the site contains a free SAT preparation course.
Syndicate.com	www.syndicate.com	Students from middle school and up can visit this site for quizzes that help prepare students for PSAT(R), SAT(R), SSAT, GRE, or LSAT tests.
Kaplan Educational Center	www.kaplan.com	A comprehensive site that covers everything from online sample tests to financial aid and counseling.

Earn a Cyber-Degree

One of the latest ways to obtain a college degree is over the Internet. Over one million students now attend *cybercolleges*. Many four-year colleges and universities offer virtual college classrooms, in addition to their regular onsite classes. The number of cyberstudents grows with each school term.

Cybercolleges offer many advantages over their more traditional counterparts. Many cyberstudents hold down full time jobs; taking online classes usually means that the students don't need to interrupt their careers to pursue higher education. Online education makes it possible for students to transcend their geographic locations. Students from all over the world can participate in degree programs at prestigious schools without leaving home.

The Internet plays a huge role in cyber-education. Assignments are transmitted via email. Students put together study groups that meet in Internet conferences, using software like Microsoft NetMeeting or Netscape Conference. Coursework and other classroom materials can be downloaded from the college's Web page (see Figure 15.9).

College degrees are earned

Don't confuse genuine cybercolleges with phony correspondence schools that offer to "sell" a degree to a student in exchange for money. A cybercollege degree needs to be earned, rather than bought.

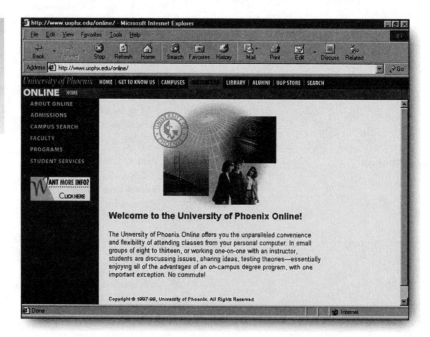

FIGURE 15.9
The University of Phoenix Online Campus home page has links to information about its many programs.

Tuition costs at cybercolleges vary. Generally, a premium for online participation is added to the per-credit cost. However, because you won't need to pay dormitory or athletic fees, you'll probably end up spending less on your cyberdegree.

Table 15.4 lists a dozen top Cyber-U's. If you don't see your favorite college on the list, call and ask if they're offering online classes. Many of the programs are new, so not all degrees are available in all disciplines.

Table 15.4 Top cyber universities

School Name	Physical Location	Phone	URL	Comments
California State University, Dominguez Hills	Carson, CA	1-310-243-2288	`www.csudh.edu/dominguez online`	B.A., B.S.N, M.B.A., M.A., and M.S. via computer, video-conferencing
Bellevue University	Bellevue, NE	1-402-291-8100	`www.bellevue.edu`	A.S., B.A., eM.B.A., M.P.A., and M.E. via computer
Michigan State University	East Lansing, MI	1-517-353-1771	`www.msu.edu`	M.S. via computer, video-conferencing
Rochester Institute of Technology	Rochester, NY	1-716-475-2411	`www.rit.edu`	B.S., M.S., and M.B.A. via tele-conferencing, Internet
Old Dominion University	Norfolk, VA	1-800-968-2638	`web.odu.edu`	B.S., M.S., and M.B.A. via tele-conferencing
University of Alaska Southeast at Sitka	Sitka, AK	1-907-465-6457	`www.jun.alaska.edu`	A.S., B.S., and M.P.A. via computer, tele-conferencing
University of Phoenix University Online Campus	Phoenix, AZ	1-800-742-4742	`www.uophx.edu/online`	B.A., B.S., M.S., and M.B.A. via computer
Washington State University	Pullman, WA	1-800-222-4978	`www.wsu.edu`	B.A. via computer

Finding a New Career on the Internet

Designing the résumés you
need in today's job market ●

Posting your résumé to an Internet
résumé bank ●

Looking through job listings
on the Web ●

Networking with newsgroups ●

Begin with a Résumé

Years ago, you landed a job with a company and planned to stay there forever. Things are much different today. The U.S.Department of Labor projects that you will change professions at least three times in your work life, by your own choice or because modern t echnology has made your job obsolete.

Switching careers is a thrilling challenge if you make the decision to do something more rewarding. Changing your career, or at least your job, is exciting if you're not happy with your present work situation. It's tougher to find a new position when you've been "downsized" or you're in a shrinking or dying profession.

A good résumé is the first thing you need to find a new job. Your résumé is your calling card. It sells you to your potential employer. So, it behooves you to take extreme care in preparing a résumé that will be a professional presentation of your qualifications.

A standard résumé lists things like your name, address, experience, and education. You probably have a résumé and think it's effective. If you set your résumé up like most people, it's designed to be folded into an envelope and sent through the mail. When it gets where it's going there's a good chance that your résumé will never be viewed by the person who's doing the hiring.

Why? Because many companies now rely on electronic résumés, or *e-résumés* for short. An e-résumé is one that can be stored on a computer. Most companies bundle all of the e-résumés into one giant database, so they can search for a particular keyword or qualifier. For example, if a company's looking for someone with experience in Environmental Health and Safety, they can extract the names of the qualified candidates from the hundreds of résumés they receive.

There are a few different ways your résumé can become electronic:

- You send a paper copy of your résumé, and it's scanned into the computer system with the use of OCR software.
- You email your résumé.
- You post your résumé to the Internet.

Keywords Pave the Way to Success

Part of the challenge of creating a great paper copy résumé is designing an artistic masterpiece. Finding the exact shade and thickness of the paper (with a matching envelope, of course), using the right fonts, and balancing the margins is almost as important as what the résumé says. After all, a paper résumé needs some visual excitement to make it stand out from all the others. Getting noticed is half the battle.

E-résumés, on the other hand, depend on content more than form. Because no one is going to judge the appearance of your e-résumé, you don't need to worry about the color or quality of the paper. Fonts and margins are also irrelevant.

Keywords are the most important part of your e-résumé. These special words describe your special talents, skills, and experience. Keywords are almost always nouns. If you've been taught to use action words, or verbs, on your résumé, you need to adjust your thinking.

Use keywords to describe:

- *Skills*. Skills include problem-solving, network administration, or word processing.
- *Education*. Phrase your education like the following: Bachelor of Arts, Philosophy, or High School Graduate.
- *Job titles*. Some good examples are Help Desk Specialist, Webmaster, or Sales Representative.

After a keyword search is performed on electronic résumés, the ones that contain the best matches or hits are sorted into job categories. If your résumé comes up with multiple hits, it can be placed in more than one job category. The more categories in which your résumé is placed, the better your chances are for finding the perfect job.

A Résumé for Every Circumstance

Consider maintaining your résumé four different ways. Because the job market is so competitive, why not have the capability of submitting your information in whatever format is required? Set up your résumé in the following formats:

- traditional
- scannable
- ASCII
- Web-ready (HTML)

The Traditional Version

Your traditional, hard copy résumé is the first form you should keep on hand. If you've been looking for a new job for a while, you might have one ready. Your hard copy résumé needs to list your name and contact information, experience, education, and skills. It's up to you whether you want to include a section discussing your objectives. Check your word processing program for built-in résumé templates if you need some help.

Unless you're applying for a job as an artist or graphic designer, make sure the résumé looks elegant and businesslike. Fancy fonts, brightly colored text, and graphic images make you seem unprofessional. Limit yourself to one or two fonts, and don't use wildly colored paper or ink. Draw attention to the headings with text attributes, like boldface and underlines.

If you're using networking strategies to find a new position, distribute your traditional résumé to as many people as you can. If you send it, use a matching envelope and a cover letter.

The Scannable Version

Look at the job listings in the paper or online Classified sections of most large town newspapers and you'll note that the word "*scannable*" appears. By using the scan method, a company can quickly enter and evaluate hundreds of applicants.

Scanning a résumé is similar to making a copy on a copy machine. After it's received, an operator feeds your résumé into a scanner that copies the image from the paper. Next, special *OCR* (Optical Character Recognition) software is used to turn the résumé image into text data.

OCR software can't work miracles

Depending on the sophistication of the OCR software used, the accuracy of the resulting scanned document can range from very accurate to imprecise. Because you don't know which OCR program will be used to translate your résumé, make sure it's as crisp and simple as possible.

To be effective, the scannable version of your résumé needs to be different from your traditional one. The old rules don't apply with this version. When you design your scannable résumé, think keywords, keywords, keywords. A résumé that's set up to be scanned needs to contain as many keywords as possible. Remember to use nouns, the more the better. List your job titles and areas of expertise. Try to look over your résumé and pick out the keywords. For example, if your résumé says something like "Supervised staff of three clerks," consider changing the phrase to "Clerical supervisor."

Because your scannable résumé is going to be fed into an electronic device, send it in a 9×12-inch envelope to avoid creases. Folds can pull the paper off track and make it difficult for the OCR software to read your text. If the paper is too heavy, like extra-thick bond, or too light, like onionskin, the scanner might have problems pulling it through. Use regular weight paper to ensure a good scan.

A clear, crisp font like Arial or Helvetica will enable the OCR software to read the text. A font in the 10 to 14 point size works best; don't use tiny fonts. Never use a script font or one that's ornate or heavy. Borders or shading don't work on a scannable résumé, because the OCR software will (unsuccessfully) try to convert the border characters to words.

The ASCII Version

Many job listings ask for you to email your résumé. Email speeds your résumé to its destination in a matter of minutes. To make sure that the receiving computer can read it, send your résumé in *ASCII* text format.

SEE ALSO

➤ *For more information on sending email, see Chapter 10, "Sending, Receiving, and Managing Email," on page 237*

ASCII is computerese for plain-text format. Although ASCII documents aren't visually exciting, their great advantage is that any computer can read them. To ensure this compatibility, a document saved in ASCII doesn't contain any special fonts or attributes like boldface, italics, or underlines. In fact, an ASCII document has no tabs or indents.

Creating the ASCII version

You can create an ASCII version of your résumé in most word processing programs, making sure that you haven't used fonts, attributes, or tabs. Save the file as a text file; your word processing program will assign it a .TXT file extension.

Like its scannable cousin, your ASCII résumé should contain noun keywords because it will probably be placed in a searchable database. Make sure you proofread and spell-check your ASCII résumé carefully. Just because it's ASCII doesn't mean that typos won't stick out! Obviously, the color and grade of the paper doesn't matter, because your ASCII résumé is totally electronic.

The Web-Ready Version

If you really want to make a splash with your résumé, post it on the World Wide Web! Think of the impact your résumé might have on the computer screen of a prospective employer or recruiter. If you're looking for a computer-related position, your Web résumé proclaims that you're on the cutting edge of technology.

The World Wide Web is a multimedia paradise. In addition to links to relevant sites, you can add graphic images, like your photo, or sound or movie clips to your résumé. Use different background colors or font faces to create a visual feast for your viewers.

What's HTML, anyway?

Web pages are written in a special language called HTML, short for Hypertext Markup Language. HTML documents contain the formatting instructions for properly displaying the text and graphics on a Web page. When you view a Web page in your browser, the underlying HTML code is responsible for the page you see on the screen.

You can create your own Web résumé. If you're unsure about how to set up an HTML document, contract with a *page designer*. Many Web design companies create résumés in HTML, the language in which Web pages are written. If you decide to pay someone, ask to see some of their previous designs and get references. Because the service can get expensive, find out in advance what you'll have to pay. Try to choose a designer who will place your page on the Web and maintain it as part of the service.

SEE ALSO
➤ *You'll learn all about HTML documents on page 512*

When you're ready to publish your résumé, contact your ISP or network administrator for instructions on the best way to proceed. If you're placing your résumé in a Web community like Yahoo! GeoCities at www.geocities.com or Tripod, A Lycos Community at www.tripod.com, go to the community on the Web and make sure your page conforms to the community's standards. When your page is published to the Web, open your browser and visit the page. Have your family and associates visit the page, too. When you're sure that your Web résumé is ready for the scrutiny of a prospective employer, distribute your URL.

Creating a Web Résumé with Netscape Templates

If you're using Netscape Communicator, you can create a Web résumé in a few minutes, even if you don't know a bit of HTML. Netscape understands that you want to jump into Web design right away. Accordingly, their design team has done all of the preparation work for you by setting up page templates for many types of Web pages. Use the Netscape résumé template as a springboard for your own creative Web résumé.

Using Netscape's résumé template

1. Connect to the Internet and open the Netscape browser.

2. Click **File** and choose **New**. When the submenu appears, select **Page from Template**.

3. When the New Page from Template dialog box appears, click **Netscape Templates**. A page on the Netscape site appears that displays instructions and information about the templates at the top and links to the templates as you scroll down the page, as shown in Figure 16.1.

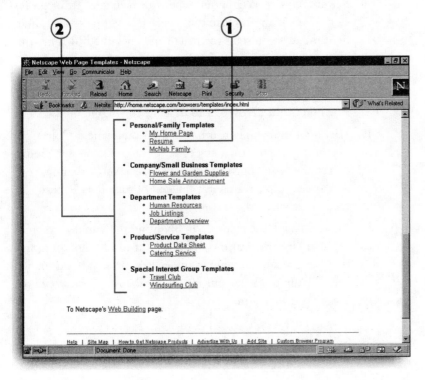

FIGURE 16.1
The Netscape Templates page contains links to templates in many categories.

① Résumé template

② Template categories

Using Composer

Netscape Composer is the program in the Communicator suite that enables you to create great-looking Web pages. You'll continue working with Composer in Chapter 21, "Creating Your Own Web Site."

Adding your photo

If you have a scanner that can handle photos, you can scan your picture and add it to the résumé. Although there are many brands of scanners, Hewlett-Packard's ScanJet line is top notch and easy to use. You'll learn more about adding pictures to HTML documents in Chapter 21, "Creating Your Own Web Site."

4. Scroll down the page until the categories appear and click the **Resume** link. A sample résumé appears, along with instructions on the use of the template at the top of the page.

5. Click **File**, **Edit Page** to copy the template to your computer so that you can make changes to it. (When you first open the page, you're looking at the original version maintained by Netscape.) The page now appears in Netscape Composer.

6. If you haven't worked with Composer before, take a moment to familiarize yourself with the screen. Pass your mouse pointer over the buttons on the Composition and Formatting toolbars and read each tooltip. Notice the title bar reads Composer, and that buttons for Navigator and Composer are displayed on your Windows taskbar.

7. Select the sample name of "Clea Barnett" and type your name. Your name now appears at the top of the page.

8. Click the sample photo so that it appears framed and press **Delete**. The picture is removed from the résumé.

9. Select the word **Writer** and type your own job title or profession. If you want to make the typeface larger or smaller, highlight the text you want to change and click the **down arrow** next to the current point size button on the Formatting toolbar. Choose another size from the list, as illustrated in Figure 16.2. The list closes and the text appears in the size you selected. Press the **right arrow** key to deselect the highlighted text.

10. Highlight the sample text under the Employment Objective section and type your own objective. Because Composer handles text similarly to your favorite word processing program, you don't need to press Enter at the end of each line. Instead, Composer wraps the text for you.

11. Move through the résumé, highlighting the sample text and replacing it with your own. If you want to add more information, such as additional lines under Educational Background, press **Enter** and type your information, just as you would on a word processing program.

FIGURE 16.2
It's a snap to change the formatting of text.

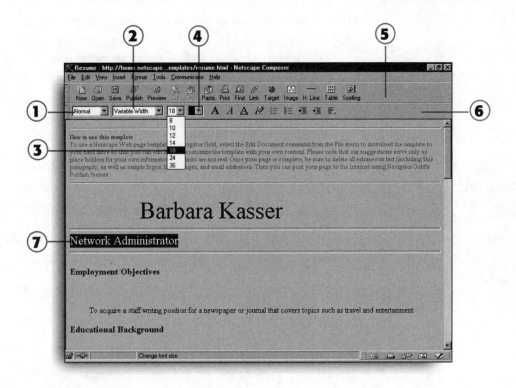

1. Font style
2. Font name
3. Font point size
4. Font color
5. Composition toolbar
6. Formatting toolbar
7. Selected text

12. Change the color of text by highlighting it first and then clicking the **down arrow** next to the Font Color button on the Formatting toolbar. Choose the desired color from the palette. Press the **right arrow** key to deselect the text.

13. Change the alignment of text by selecting it first, and then click the **Alignment** button on the Formatting toolbar, as shown in Figure 16.3. Click the **Left**, **Center**, or **Right** button to move the highlighted text. Deselect the text by pressing the **right arrow** key.

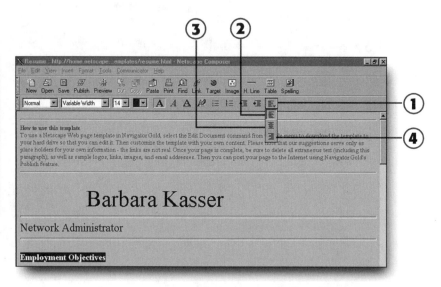

FIGURE 16.3

Change the alignment of the selected text.

(1) Alignment button

(2) Left alignment

(3) Center alignment

(4) Right alignment

14. Give your résumé some added pizzazz by changing the background color. Click **Format**, **Page Colors and Properties**. When the Page Properties dialog box appears, click the **Colors and Background** tab.

15. Click the **Background** button to open the color palette, as shown in Figure 16.4, and click a new background color. The palette closes and the color you selected appears in the sample. Uncheck the box next to **Use Image**. (The current gray, pebbly background on the résumé page is actually a graphic image, which overrides the color selection.) Click **OK** to close the Page Properties dialog box and return to the résumé in Composer.

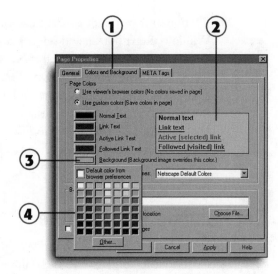

FIGURE 16.4
Use the Page Properties
dialog box to change
your résumés colors.

① Colors and Background
   tab is selected

② Changes are reflected
   in the sample page

③ Background button

④ Color palette

16. Click the **Tools** menu and choose **Check Spelling**. Even if you can't see any apparent spelling mistakes, double-check for them now. If Composer encounters an unfamiliar word, like your name or a real typing error, your options include replacing the selected word, ignoring it, or adding it to the Composer dictionary. When the spell check is completed, read the résumé for grammar mistakes.

17. Press **Ctrl+Home** to move to the top of the page. Highlight the instructions about how to use the template and press **Delete** to remove them from the page.

18. Save the résumé by clicking **File**, **Save As**. When the Save As dialog box appears, type a name for your résumé in the **File name**: text box. Make the name descriptive (something like My Web Résumé or HTML Résumé) so you'll have no problem identifying it later. Also, don't change the file extension; Composer assigns an .html file extension to indicate the document type. If you want to change the location of the file from the folder that's displayed, navigate to the new folder or drive. Click **Save**. The Save As dialog box closes and the file name you typed appears in the Composer title bar.

19. Close Composer by clicking the **Close (X)** button on the Composer toolbar to return to Navigator.

391

20. (Optional) If you want to make additional changes later, click the Windows **Start** button and select **Programs, Netscape Communicator**, and then select **Netscape Composer**. When Composer opens, click **File, Open Page** to open the Open File dialog box. Type the drive letter, folder location, and filename (for example, `C:\My Documents\MyRésumé.html`) in the location text box. You can also click **Choose File** and navigate to the correct folder location. Either way, when the correct file name appears in the box, click the **Open** button.

Get Résumé Help Online

There are a number of sites on the Web that provide help with e-résumés. Table 16.1 lists the Web addresses and some information about some of these sites.

There's help online

E-résumé help exists all over the Web. Use your favorite search tool, like Yahoo! or HotBot to find additional sites.

Table 16.1   E-résumé sites on the Web

Page Title	URL	Comments
Rebecca Smith's eRésumés and Resources	`www.eresumes.com`	An online guide to preparing effective electronic résumés for a variety of online situations.
Résumé Tutor	`www.umn.edu/ohr/ ecep/resume/`	A site put together by the University of Minnesota to help you design an effective résumé by using tutorial-type exercises.
Proven Résumé Career Center	`www.provenresumes. com`	Site offers 40 free online résumé and job search workshops.
Résumé Help	`www.trooper.net/ res-help.html`	A no-nonsense one page guide on writing an effective résumé that will get you noticed.

Posting Your Résumé to a Résumé Bank

If you're serious about using the Internet as a resource in finding a job, post your e-résumé to several of the résumé banks that are out on the Web. A *résumé bank* holds thousands of individual résumés that can be looked at anytime.

Posting your résumé to a Web résumé bank offers some definite advantages. For one, all prospective employers have access to your résumé. For another, because most résumé banks are free or charge a small fee, you won't need to make a substantial investment to get worldwide exposure. If you decide to post your résumé to a Web bank, consider letting your present employer know you're looking for a new job. Think what might happen if your boss comes across your résumé in a résumé bank, and plan accordingly. After all, you don't want to do something that will cause you embarrassment, not to mention possible repercussions.

SEE ALSO

➤ *Review how to search for information on the Web on page 156*

Do some research to determine which résumé banks meet your needs. Search for the term "résumé bank" on some of the major search engines and services, like Infoseek, HotBot, and Yahoo!. Although there are many large résumé banks, you might have better results if you post your résumé on a bank that offers specialized jobs, such as positions in the automotive field. To find a résumé bank that limits résumés to a particular field, narrow your search criteria. For example, the query `résumé +"automotive job"` finds links to Web sites that specialize in automotive positions. Table 16.2 shows a listing of résumé banks.

SEE ALSO

➤ *Review more information on choosing the best wording for queries on page 159*

> **Find the right employer**
>
> See Appendix B, Employers A to Z, for a list of employers who regularly use the Web to fill vacant positions. You'll find the employer name, a brief description of the company, and the applicable URL.

> **Everybody's doing it**
>
> Over 80% of new college graduates turn to the Web for help in looking for a job.

Table 16.2 Major résumé banks on the Web

Résumé Bank Name	URL	Fee	Résumé Format Comments
Job Options	www.joboptions.com	Free	Complete online form or cut and paste ASCII text. You can submit up to three different résumés; claims that the site has over 9,000 companies using its services.

continues...

Table 16.2 Continued

Résumé Bank Name	URL	Fee	Résumé Format Comments
Monster.com	www.monster.com	Free	Online form or cut and past ASCII text. Sign up for free email at the site. Monster.com also features extensive assistance to job seekers. Take an online workshop or chat with prospective employers and other job seekers.
The Job Force Network	www.jobforce.net	Free	Résumé is created based on personal information you fill in online. Employers can contact applicants directly.
Pro Hire	www.prohire.com	Free	Type in or cut and paste ASCII text. National service posts links to "hot jobs" on the main page.
SkillSearch	www.skillsearch.com	Approx $99	Custom résumé is designed for you. Works more like an employment agency than a résumé database. SkillSearch claims that they actively match employers with prospective employees.

Submitting Your Résumé

Submitting your résumé to a résumé bank is simple. Even if you're sure of the finished product, check and then recheck your handiwork before anyone else sees it. (My good friend Kathy used the phrase "detial-oriented" on her e-résumé and was mortified when she received an email message from a national recruiter, advising her of the misspelled word.) Each résumé bank has different submission requirements; read them over carefully before you begin.

In addition to submission requirements, most résumé banks post detailed instructions about how to submit your résumé. Since résumé banks really want your résumé, most of the time the instructions are clear and easy to follow. Take a few minutes and make sure you understand what you need to do.

Some résumé banks ask you to email your résumé. If you're familiar with sending email, you might be tempted to attach the computer file containing your résumé to the email message. Don't! Instead of sending a file attachment, paste your résumé into the body of the email message.

SEE ALSO

➤ *For details on sending email, see Chapter 10, "Sending, Receiving, and Managing Email," on page 237*

If you're unsure how to manage cutting and pasting your résumé, let a little bit of Windows magic help you accomplish the task in short order. Make sure that the email message in which you'll send your résumé is open before you start the steps.

Copying your ASCII résumé into an email message

1. Open the file that contains your résumé and, if necessary, re-save it in ASCII format. Remember not to use any fonts, attributes, or tabs.

2. Highlight all of the text and click **Edit**, **Copy** or press **Ctrl+C**.

3. Press and hold the **Alt** key and press **Tab**. An icon bar appears, displaying the icons of open application on your computer. Without releasing the **Alt** key, cycle through the open applications on your computer by repeatedly pressing Tab. Each press of the **Tab** key selects the next application on the bar. When you see the email message displayed on the bar, release both the Alt and Tab keys. The email message is now displayed on your screen.

4. Position the insertion point at the top of the message body area and press **Ctrl+V**. Like magic, your résumé is pasted into the email message.

5. Look over the message to make sure that your résumé appears correctly. (If not, delete the text that you pasted by highlighting it and pressing **Delete**. Next, switch back to the open résumé file and repeat steps 2, 3, and 4.) Click the **Send** button when you're ready to post your résumé.

Fill-in forms are another way many résumé banks request your information. Because a fill-in-the-blank résumé format uses pre-defined fields, each résumé in the bank conforms to a common standard. Résumés submitted via a form are easy for an employer to look through and search.

Figure 16.5 demonstrates a fill-in online résumé form. Type the information in each field, pressing **Tab** to move from one field to another. If you want, you can copy and paste text from your ASCII résumé into the online form, or you can retype it in the appropriate boxes.

FIGURE 16.5
An online résumé form is easy to complete.

① Fill in each field with accurate information.

② Required fields are marked with an arrow.

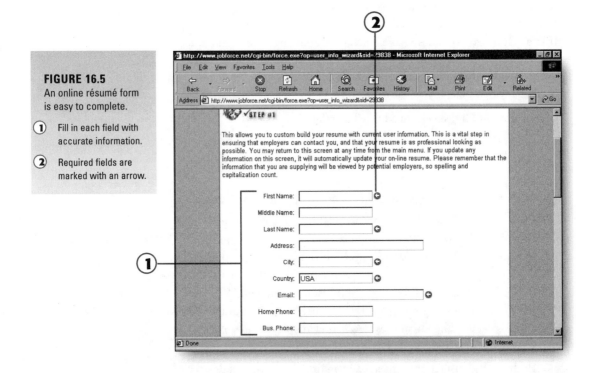

When all of the fields are completed, take a second to review the information you filled in and make any necessary corrections. After all, employers can view your online résumé worldwide so you need to make sure the information has been entered correctly. Click the **Submit** or **Send** button to transmit the information to the résumé bank.

Some résumé banks accept your résumé in HTML format. If you've created an HTML version of your résumé or had one designed by a professional Web designer, follow the résumé bank's instructions on the proper way to submit the HTML file. You may be asked to send it as an email attachment or on a disk, via snail mail.

Searching for a Job Online

Online job listings exist in many different places on the Web. Many local newspapers now post their classified sections on the Web. Some newspapers even combine their classified ads with other nearby towns, or offer links to other help wanted sections. If you don't know if your local newspaper has an online presence, call and ask.

Résumé banks are another great source for finding job listings. The same résumé banks to which you posted your résumé often offer job listings. Some job banks, like E.span, perform the search for you and email you the listings that match your qualifications.

Looking at Online Listings

Many Web employment resource sites offer some great job listings. In addition to job listings, you might find online job fairs and links to employer home pages. The listings are updated frequently, so don't be discouraged if you don't find the perfect job the first time you search. Successful job-hunting is a matter of being in the right place at the right time, so plan to check back several times a week.

To find the right job listings, you need to enter keywords that match your qualifications and the type of job you hope to find (see Figure 16.6). Choose your keywords carefully. As a general rule, use specific

words to describe the job you're looking for. The database holds
hundreds of job listings and the more exacting your search, the more
accurate your results.

FIGURE 16.6
Keywords make the
search go faster.

① Enter job-specific
keywords.

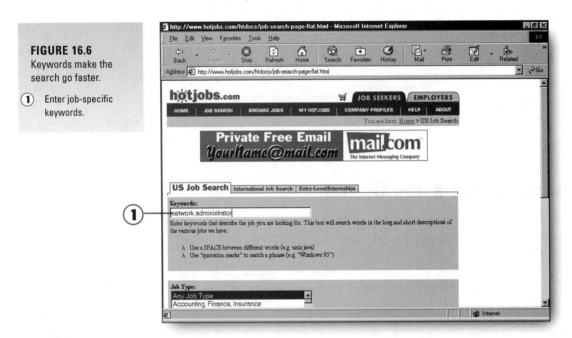

Generally, the search results appear in a list, similar to the result list
from a search engine or search service (see Figure 16.7). If one of
the listings interests you, click the link to find out more about the
position.

Read the job description and information. If the job looks good,
follow the instructions shown to submit your e-résumé. If your first
search doesn't produce the job listings you hoped for, use additional
keywords and search again.

**Start with a broad
search**

Make sure you're looking
at all of the jobs that match
your interests and
qualifications. Enter
some general keywords
first, like network
administrator.
After you view the results,
narrow the field by adding
a word or phrase to your
keyword search, such as
Novell or Microsoft.

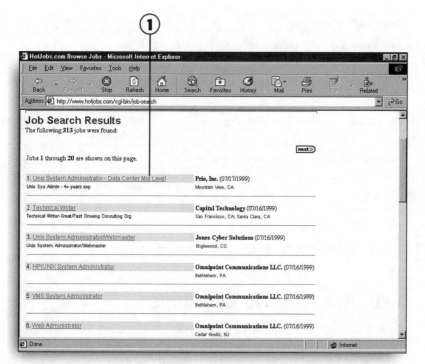

Table 16.2 lists Web sites that you can visit to see job listings. Use
the sites shown here in addition to the résumé banks listed in Table
16.3 to find your dream job.

Table 16.3 Popular Web job banks

Job Bank Name	URL	Comments
Monster Board	www.monster.com	Site offers listings for over 50,000 jobs worldwide.
Hot Jobs	www.hotjobs.com	Technical jobs worldwide, easy to search.
Job Web	www.jobweb.com	Offers regional listings in the U.S. and Canada.

continues…

Work for the Feds

Want to work for the U.S. Government? If you're considering becoming a civil servant, visit the site at `www.usajobs.opm.gov/`. The site shows available Federal positions and enables you to apply online. (The U.S. Government's official site for jobs and employment information is provided by the United States Office of Personnel Management.)

Table 16.3 Continued

Job Bank Name	URL	Comments
Eagleview	`www.eagleview.com`	Find a position with a Fortune 500 company.
America's Employers	`www.americasemployers.com`	Listings contain over 120,000 positions and 60,000 company profiles.
Career Path	`www.careerpath.com`	Contains links to want ads listed in major US newspapers; also offers résumé posting.
Wall Street Journal Interactive	`careers.wsj.com`	Offers job listings, career news, and articles as well as additional job resources.

Network with Newsgroups

Looking for a job can be a lonely proposition. It's hard to sit and wait for the phone to ring, or for an email to land in your Inbox. Newsgroups are great ways to meet and greet both employers and other job seekers on the Internet.

SEE ALSO

➤ *Learn all about newsgroups on page 256*

Newsgroups are Internet discussion forums. Think of a newsgroup as a virtual bulletin board. Instead of sending a letter to individual members, messages are posted to the group, as shown in Figure 16.8. In turn, responses are posted to the group.

Newsgroups can be organizational in nature. For example, the group `misc.job.résumé` contains postings of résumés. Groups can also be regional. The group `houston.jobs.offered` holds postings about jobs offered in the Houston, Texas area. Although there are more than 30,000 newsgroups, many ISPs don't carry all of them. If you hear of a group that isn't available to you, contact your ISP.

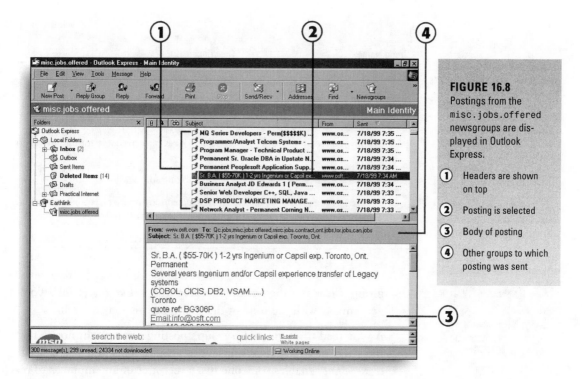

FIGURE 16.8
Postings from the `misc.jobs.offered` newsgroups are displayed in Outlook Express.

(1) Headers are shown on top

(2) Posting is selected

(3) Body of posting

(4) Other groups to which posting was sent

Table 16.4 lists some of the miscellaneous job-related newsgroups.

Table 16.4 Job-related newsgroups

Group Name	Description
`alt.jobs`	Primarily technical jobs offered
`alt.jobs.offered`	Variety of available positions offered outside the U.S.
`alt.building.jobs`	Constructions jobs offered
`can.jobs`	Canadian positions
`can.jobs.gov`	Canadian governmental jobs
`fl.jobs.computers.misc`	Computer-related positions in Florida
`la.jobs.offered`	Los Angeles, California positions
`misc gov.us.topic.gov.jobs.`	Miscellaneous U.S. Government positions

continues...

Table 16.4 Continued

Group Name	Description
misc.jobs.contract	Contract jobs located in the U.S.
misc.jobs.offered	Global positions
misc.jobs.offered.entry	Entry level positions throughout the U.S.
misc.jobs.résumés	Postings of résumés available for employers to view
pnet.jobs.wanted	People looking for jobs
vmsnet.employment	Workplace employment-related issues discussed, jobs looked for and offered
za.ads.jobs	Jobs sought and offered

Keep it light

Resist the temptation to slam your present or former employer in a newsgroup posting. Because you have no idea who might be reading your posting, you don't want to come across as nasty or vitriolic.

Check out these and other newsgroups. Before you post to a newsgroup, check out the postings for a few days. *Lurking* enables you to get familiar with the tone of the group before you chime in.

As you read through a newsgroup's postings, you might notice that the same message appears in several groups. This practice, called *cross-posting*, enables someone like a recruiter or an employer to reach as many people as possible with one message. Keep track of the postings to which you respond. You'd hate to accidentally send two résumés for the same open position that appeared in two different newsgroups.

Use newsgroups as a valuable resource in your quest for the perfect position. You'll find a wealth of information. You might also find a group of great people, willing to help you find your dream job.

part

V

LET THE FUN BEGIN

chapter

17

The Internet for Kids

Finding Web sites designed
just for kids •

Keeping children "net-safe" •

Taking a break with some games •

What's on the Internet for Kids?

It's hard to keep kids off of the Internet! Even the littlest tots enjoy visiting Web pages designed just for them. The Internet makes it easy for children to reach out to other kids, play games, and learn new facts. Global boundaries don't exist on the Internet; online, your children have the whole world at their fingertips. With the help and guidance of parents and teachers, the Internet can be a safe and entertaining place for kids to visit.

Kids can choose from sites that offer a range of activities from playing games to sharing original poetry and compositions. Many sites offer help with schoolwork. Children can chat with one another in real-time conversations, post messages to bulletin boards, and exchange email with cyber-pals.

Of course, one of the Internet's greatest strengths, its tremendous size, can make it a scary place to send our children. The sheer volume of information and content on the Internet enables a child to accidentally (or intentionally) visit a site that contains objectionable words or content. Parents and teachers need to supervise their children's Internet experiences and make sure that the kids are practicing "safe-surf" techniques.

Yahooligans! Is a Great Place to Start

Yahooligans! is a wonderful Web navigational guide for kids. The service contains a searchable index of Web sites designed for children ages 7 through 12. Like its adult counterpart, Yahoo!, the Yahooligans! home page (see Figure 17.1) contains both a search area and a launch pad to several different categories, like Entertainment, Arts, and Recreation. From the home page, you can click links to New and Cool sites for kids, or join Club Yahooligans!.

SEE ALSO

➤ *For detailed information on how to search in Yahoo!, see page 161*

Using Yahooligans! as a homebase for kids offers some great advantages. Lots of time and resources have been invested by the folks at Yahooligans! to research the Web sites listed in the index. Because the sites are listed hierarchically, under defined categories, it's easy

Yahooligans! Is a Great Place to Start **CHAPTER 17**

for children to click through the sub-categories to find the sites they want. For example, locating Web pages devoted to a child's favorite television show can be accomplished with a few mouse clicks.

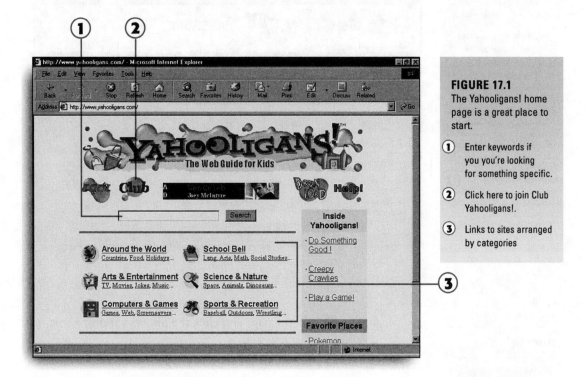

FIGURE 17.1
The Yahooligans! home page is a great place to start.

① Enter keywords if you you're looking for something specific.

② Click here to join Club Yahooligans!.

③ Links to sites arranged by categories

Finding information with Yahooligans!

1. If you're not already connected to the Internet, connect now and open your browser. When the start page appears, type **www.yahooligans.com** in the Address box and press **Enter**. In a moment the Yahooligans! home page appears.

2. Click the link to **Arts & Entertainment**. An index of entertainment-related categories appears.

3. Click the **Television** link. A new index page appears, displaying links to several television categories, such as TV show listings, actors and actresses, and networks. The categories followed by an "@" sign let you know that the category is listed in multiple places within the Yahooligans! directory, as shown in Figure 17.2.

Join the club

Club Yahooligans! is a special kids-only Internet club. Members receive a monthly email of cool sites, get early notification of contests and other offers, receive a Web newsletter, and get discounts on Yahooligans! merchandise. Best of all, it doesn't cost anything to join.

FIGURE 17.2
The Television index makes it easy to find a site about a TV-related topic.

① The @ sign indicates the heading can be found in other Yahooligans! Categories.

② Links to sub-categories pinpoint what you're looking for.

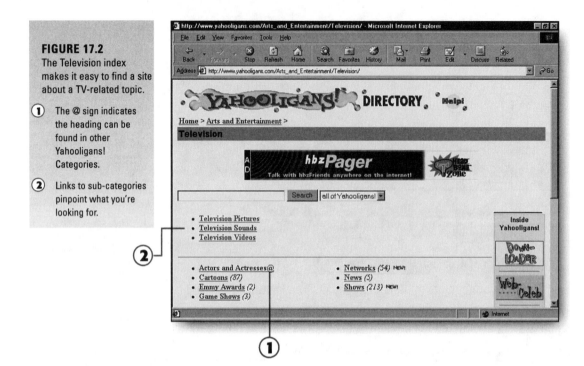

Learn the lingo

The numbers that appear next to each Yahooligans! category tell how many Web sites are listed in those categories. The word "New" next to a category title indicates that new sites within the category have been added recently.

4. Scroll down the page and click the **Shows category** link.

5. When the index of sites about television shows appears, click a link to a site about a show you enjoy.

6. "Surf" the new page that appears by clicking a link to a related site on the Web.

7. Click your browser's **Back** button as many times as necessary to move back to the Television page or to the Yahooligan's! home page.

SEE ALSO

➤ *For ways to cycle back through pages you've already viewed, Navigator users see page 127 and Internet Explorer users see page 123*

In addition to maintaining an index of sites kids like, Yahooligans! provides links to the latest and greatest sites, news, and sports information. Table 17.1 shows the name of the link and where it takes you.

Table 17.1 Links for kids on Yahooligans! home page

Link	What You'll See
Cool	Links to sites that might be entertaining, funny, wild, educational, or useful.
Club	The link to Club Yahooligans! takes kids to Awesome Areas on Yahooligans! Different exciting links appear here, including the current Web Celeb, a collection of pictures of live video feeds from all over world, called Web-Cam and the Yahooligans! Sports Page and News Beat.
Download	Snag a picture sound or video from Yahooligan!'s collection.
Help	The Yahooligans! Information Booth features links to information about Yahooligans! and tips for using it. Parents will also find important links to an exciting site selected by Yahoo!. The hypersite changes weekly.
News	Current events aimed at kids. Click a headline to display the full story.
Sports	An index of major sports, with links to teams, scores, statistics, and other related information.

Touring Cyberkids

Cyberkids at www.cyberkids.com emphasizes creativity and participation for children on the Internet. The Cyberkids site has been an Internet fixture for a long time. Started in November 1994, the site published original work from Mountain Lake Software Inc.'s First Annual Kids' International Writing and Art Contest. From there, the site mushroomed to include many other facets.

Cyberkids features thought-provoking pages and displays. The site changes often to stay current; for example, you might see a link to a review of a new movie or interviews with noteworthy celebrities. Cyberkids also encourages children to submit original artwork and music compositions to the site. Click the links to **Art Gallery** or **Young Composer** to see and hear what other kids are doing.

Cyberkids works best for the under-12 set. If you're child is older than 12, the related Cyberteens site at www.cyberteens.com has links to sites and Web attractions that are age-appropriate for teenagers.

Figure 17.3 shows the Cyberteens home page. Cyberteens encourages creativity and provides feedback from other teens.

FIGURE 17.3
The Cyberteens site is for teenagers.

Cyberteens publishes an *e-zine* called Zeen that changes every few months. The magazine welcomes submissions from teenagers around the world. Featured in Zeen are original poetry, editorials, and original art work, as well as links to sites set up by major teen advertisers.

Cyberteens Connection is a Cyberteens attraction that enables teens from all over the world to get together. You can access the Cyberteens Connection as a guest, but unless you register, you can't post to the site's messages boards or participate in a real-time chat conversation at the Cosmic Café. In the following step-by-step exercise, you get connected at the Cyberteens Connection.

Connecting with other cyberteens

1. Type `www.cyberteens.com` in the Address box of your browser and press **Enter**. In a moment, the Cyberteens home page appears.

2. Click the link to **Connection**. If you've registered previously, type your name and password and click the **Login** button.

If you're new, you can click **Guest Access** to read the messages on Cyberteens Connection.

To register, click the **Register** button; when the New User Registration page appears, enter a name, password, and your email address. Follow the onscreen instructions to complete the registration process

3. The Cyberteens Connection Welcome Page is the starting page for both the real-time chat and the message boards. Click the link to **Cyberteens Chat**. Read the instructions on the page that appears and click the link to move to the **Cosmic Café**. (You need to have a Java-enabled browser, like Internet Explorer or Netscape.)

SEE ALSO

➤ *Java is explained on page 489*
➤ *You learn all about real-time chatting on page 286*

4. When the program is downloaded, a real-time chat conversation appears on the Message Display area, as shown in Figure 17.4. The participant's names are listed on the right side of the screen (your name appears in color). Type your comments in the message box and press **Enter**. Your messages appear in the Message Display area, along with other chatter's responses.

Don't get impatient

The Cosmic Café is powered by different software than your browser program and opens in its own window. Depending on your computer hardware, it might take a few minutes for the Cosmic Café to appear on your computer screen.

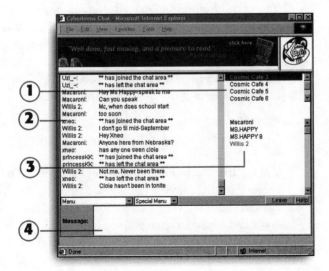

FIGURE 17.4
Real-time conversation in the Cosmic Café.

(1) More Cyberteen chat rooms

(2) Conversation takes place in Message Display area

(3) Participant's screen names

(4) Type your message here.

5. When you're done chatting, close the chat window by clicking **File** and then **Close**. Click the link to **Cyberteens Connection** to view the other Cyberteen Connection options.

6. From the available discussion topics, click one that interests you. Each discussion group is organized in folders, which might have related sub-folders. When you open a folder, the subject lines of the messages that have been posted are displayed.

Keeping Kids Net-Safe

Keeping children *net-safe* is a prime concern for parents and educators. Web sites can contain violent, lewd, or lascivious language and pictures that are not suitable for viewing by children or young adults. News stories of unsuspecting children engaged in chat conversations or email with adults pretending to be children pop up with some regularity. Because of these problems, many adults are afraid to let children use the Internet.

Dangers for children on the Internet are similar to the dangers they face in everyday life. The same basic safety rules—not to speak to strangers or give out personal information—apply to the Internet as well as the mall or playground.

Young children should never be left alone while they're online. If your children are older, use your judgment. Make it a point to check what your children are looking at when they're online. My son understands that I will periodically look over his shoulder when he's using the Internet. If I don't approve of what's on the screen, his Internet session is over—with no further discussion.

SEE ALSO
➤ *Review how to use your browser's History feature to track viewed Web sites on pages 122 and 123*

You control the Internet access in your home. The simplest way to prevent your children from logging on when you're around is to change your connection password. Contact your ISP for help if you don't know how to change the password. If you're worried about sites that your children might be viewing on the Web when you're not supervising, let them know that you can and will track the sites they visit.

Log-in logs

Many ISP's, such as EarthLink, will furnish a list of your log-in dates and times. If you think your child is connecting when you're not home, ask for a printout of your connect time.

The following list of five rules should be discussed with kids before they use the Internet. Make sure that your kids understand that they can lose their Internet privileges if they don't stick to the rules.

Internet commandments for kids

1. If you click a link or type a URL to a Web site that looks like it's for adults only, or contains pictures or material that's offensive, leave immediately! There are plenty of good "kid sites" on the Web.

2. If you receive email from someone you don't know, don't respond without checking with an adult.

3. Never give out personal information like your real last name, address, telephone number, or login password to anyone on the Internet. If someone asks for information you know you're not supposed to give out, log off immediately and tell an adult.

4. If anyone uses nasty language or mentions things that make you uncomfortable, don't answer and log off immediately.

5. Never agree to meet with someone you met in a chat room or with whom you exchanged messages without asking permission from your parents first.

Lay the basic ground rules for Internet safety before your kids go online. Spend a little preparation time explaining the rules. Sit with older children during their online sessions for a while. Of course, if you're really worried, you can limit your child's access to sites by using a few different methods.

Everyone needs to be involved

If your children access the Internet from school or the public library, contact their teachers and the librarians. Protecting children on the Internet needs to be a joint project by all concerned adults.

Screening Web Content

Several programs designed to filter undesirable Web pages from children's eyes are available on the Internet. The programs work in different ways. Some block Web sites based on a master list that's been downloaded to your computer. Other blocking software works by scanning the text on a page and looking for objectionable words. Other programs maintain a history of visited sites that can viewed later by parents. However, you can't depend solely on blocking software to prevent your children from seeing sites that have not been designed for them. Even the most stringent blocking software can't keep up with the volume of new sites that appear on the Web every single day.

The following list shows some of the most effective blocking software you can buy.

- **CYBERsitter** at www.solidoak.com is a popular blocking program. CYBERsitter will block or alert you to access of adult-oriented Web sites. Additionally, the program can be set up to filter offensive terms and phrases from incoming and outgoing email, newsgroup articles, and WWW pages. Parents can also set up CYBER-sitter to keep their children from giving out their name, address, and phone number while online. CYBERSITTER costs approximately $40 for a one-year subscription. You can contact CYBERSITTER by phone at 1-800-388-2761.

- **Net Nanny** at www.netnanny.com is another screening program. Net Nanny's screening lists are completely customizable and editable. Web sites lists are supplied and viewable, but you can also set up your own user lists. You can screen and block any words, phrases, Web sites (including HTML code), IRC chat rooms, newsgroups, and personal information according to your particular values. Net Nanny can be reached by phone at 1-604-662-8522.

- **CyberSnoop** at www.pearlsw.com (see Figure 17.5) shows you which Internet sites have been visited by your children by monitoring their online activity. If monitoring components are disabled without a password that you've set up, the computer will shut down and reinstate the missing monitoring modules. Full Internet blocking is optional. CyberSnoop believes that education and responsibility go hand-in-hand with Internet usage. You can reach the folks who produce CyberSnoop at 1-877-732-7579.

- **Cyber Patrol** at www.cyberpatrol.com works from two lists. The CyberYES list contains sites that are acceptable for viewing by kids. The CyberNOT list holds he sites that kids shouldn't visit. Staff, committees, teachers, and parents carefully maintain both lists. Call 1-800-828-8608 for more information about the Cyber Patrol software.

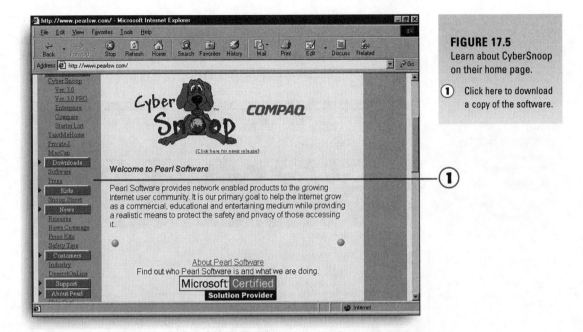

- **SurfWatch** at www.surfwatch.com offers filtering in five core categories—Drugs/Alcohol/Tobacco, Gambling, Hate Speech, Sexually Explicit, and Violence. SurfWatch Productivity Categories offer filtering in an additional 15 categories. Contact SurfWatch at 1-800-458-6600.

All of the programs on the list are designed for non-technical users and are relatively easy to install and set up. Each of the programs screen most types of Internet-related material, such as Web pages, Chat sites, and FTP archives. Additionally, each of the programs offers free, downloadable demo versions so you can try them out before you buy.

Using RSACi Ratings

RSAC, short for the Recreational Software Advisory Council, is an independent, non-profit organization based in Washington, D.C., that helps parents and educators make informed decisions about Internet sites and software games. The section of RSAC that deals with rating Internet sites is called *RSACi* (for Internet). Their mission is twofold: to empower parents and educators to make appropriate choices as to what their children see and experience on the Web, while protecting the rights of free speech of Internet participants. The RSACi Home Page and related pages such as the About RSACi page, shown in Figure 17.6, are great places to visit for information about the service.

FIGURE 17.6
The About RSACi Web page provides in-depth information about the rating service.

① Links to additional information

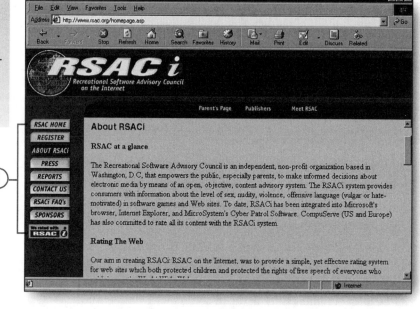

Netscape Communicator version 4.6 or higher

Currently, only the newest versions of the Netscape browser contain the NetWatcher. You can always download the latest version from home.netscape.com.

The system provides consumers with information about the level of sex, nudity, violence, and offensive language (vulgar or hate-motivated) that might be found at a Web site. Using a ratings system designed by the Platform for Internet Content Selection, or *PICS*, RSACi encourages Web designers to take a self-administered test to rate their sites, based on the information found in Table 17.2. After a score is determined, a rating is assigned to the site and added to the list.

Table 17.2   The RSACi rating system

	Violence Rating Description	Nudity Rating Description	Sex Rating Description	Language Rating Description
Level 4	Rape or wanton, gratuitous violence	Frontal nudity (qualifying as provocative display)	Explicit sexual acts or sex crimes speech	Crude, vulgar language or extreme hate
Level 3	Aggressive violence or death to humans	Frontal nudity	Non-explicit sexual acts	Strong language or hate speech
Level 2	Destruction of realistic objects	Partial nudity	Clothed sexual touching	Moderate expletives or profanity
Level 1	Injury to human being	Revealing attire	Passionate kissing	Mild expletives
Level 0	None of the above or sports related	None of the above innocent	None of the above or kissing; romance	None of the above

* Table used with permission of RSACi

SafeSurf

Both Navigator and Internet Explorer users can also take advantage of filtering options based on standards set by a group called Safe-Surf. Ratings by SafeSurf is completely mandatory. Sites that wish to be added to the SafeSurf listing fill out an online form that asks questions about the site's content and then hit a "Generate Rating" button. After the content has been given a rating, the Web site can display the SafeSurf logo on its pages.

Setting Viewing Options in Your Browser

Both Navigator and Internet Explorer users can set viewing options. Parents or educators set the acceptable levels allowed for viewing in Internet Explorer by configuring a feature called the *Content Advisor*.

Also customizable are the options to allow access to unrated sites and to enable a supervisor to enter a password to access blocked sites. Netscape Communicator users who are using version 4.6 or higher can set filtering options with NetWatcher. The RSACi service can be enabled or disabled at any time by the parent or teacher who set the supervisory password.

Setting Up Internet Explorer Content Advisor

Configuring the Internet Explorer Content Advisor

1. From within the Internet Explorer browser, click the **View** menu and choose **Internet Options**. The Internet Options dialog box appears.

2. Click the **Content** tab located near the top of the dialog box. The **Content** tab is divided into three sections, **Content Advisor**, **Certificates**, and **Personal Information**.

3. Click the **Enable** button in the **Content Advisor** section. The Content Advisor dialog box appears, with four tabs across the top: **Ratings**, **Approved Sites**, **General**, and **Advanced**.

4. Click the **Ratings** tab in the Content Advisor dialog box. In the **Category** section, click the first key item, **Language**, and drag the **Rating** slider to the level you find acceptable. As you drag, the text in the **Description** section changes to match the selected level, as shown in Figure 17.7.

5. Repeat step 5 for the other Categories shown on the list.

6. When you've set Rating levels for Language, Nudity, Sex, and Violence, click the **General** tab. In the User Options section, check the box next to **Users can see sites that have no ratings** or **Supervisor can type a password to allow users to view restricted content**. You can check both boxes if you want.

Think before you act

Because only a percentage of Web pages are RSACi-rated, you'll severely limit what sites can be accessed if you leave the box next to the Users Can View Unrated Sites option unchecked.

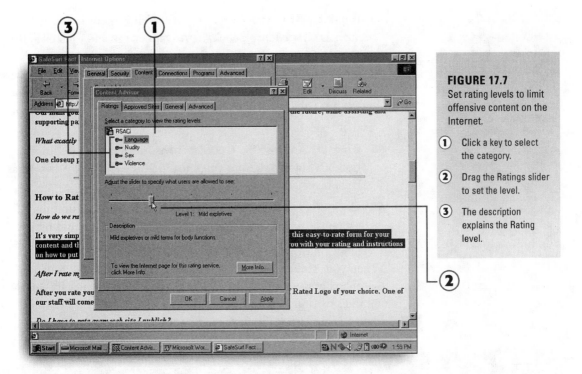

FIGURE 17.7
Set rating levels to limit offensive content on the Internet.

① Click a key to select the category.

② Drag the Ratings slider to set the level.

③ The description explains the Rating level.

7. In the center section of the dialog box, entitled Supervisor Password, click **Change Password**. As displayed in Figure 17.8, the Create Supervisor Password dialog box appears.

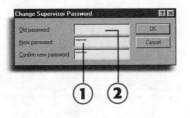

FIGURE 17.8
A password is required to prevent children from turning off or changing the Content Advisor.

① Password appears as asterisks.

② The Old Password text box is empty if you haven't enabled the Content Advisor previously.

8. Click in the **New Password** text box and type a password. Tab to the **Confirm new password** text box and retype the password. Click **OK** to continue. A box appears telling you that the password has been changed successfully.

9. (Optional) If you've subscribed to a Web-content rating system, such as Cyber Patrol, click the **Advanced** tab and then click the **Rating Systems** button to choose the file provided by the system. (The Rating System generally provides detailed instructions on how to proceed.) If you want to use the SafeSurf system, click **Find Rating Systems** and choose **SafeSurf** from the Web page that appears.

10. Click **OK** to close the Content Advisor dialog box. An information box appears, letting you know that the Content Advisor has been installed.

11. Click **OK** to close the information box. When the Internet Options dialog box re-appears, click **OK** to close it and return to the Web page you were viewing previously.

When your child attempts to go to a rated site that contains material that matches the rating level you selected, a warning appears, advising the site cannot be accessed. A box similar to the one shown in Figure 17.9 appears if you've opted not to let unrated pages appear.

FIGURE 17.9
The page cannot be accessed.

① If the page is acceptable, type the secret password and click OK.

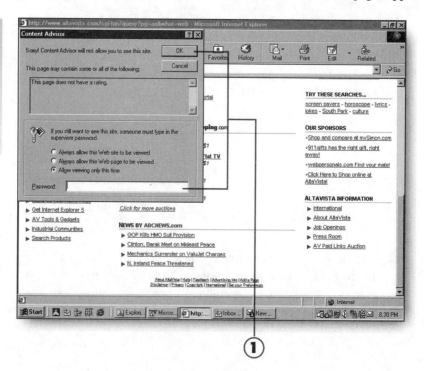

Experiment with the levels and categories in the Content Advisor until you find the combination that works best for your child. Keep in mind that if a site does not contain a RSACi rating, you won't be able to block it. However, if you choose to block all unrated sites, you'll severely limit the sites that appear on your computer.

You can change the levels you selected or disable the Content Advisor completely at any time. Click the **View** menu from within Internet Explorer and then choose **Internet Options**. Click the **Content** tab and then click the **Settings** button under the Content Advisor section. Make any changes to the categories or levels and click **OK**. You can also click **Disable** to remove the Content Advisor. Click **OK** to close the Internet Options dialog box.

> **Lasting changes**
> If you change a level within the Content Advisor, or disable it completely, the changes will be in effect the next time you access the Internet. You need to select new changes to overwrite the ones you effected.

Working with Netscape Netwatch

NetWatch allows you to select the types of sites that can be viewed on your computer and filters out those that you do not want. You control the settings with a secret password. The settings you select won't be seen by any of the Web sites that you visit with the Navigator browser.

Netwatch uses the RSACi and SafeSurf ratings systems. Each system uses a different method to describe the levels of potentially offensive content, and you can choose to use one or both of these ratings systems in NetWatch. Web publishers voluntarily rate their pages for these systems.

Setting up Netwatch

1. From within Navigator, click **Help** and then **Netwatch**.
2. In a moment, the NetWatch page appears in Navigator. Read through the content on the page and then click the the button labeled **Click to set up NetWatch**.
3. The Netwatch setup page appears. Under the First Time User section, click **New User**.
4. The next page to appear is divided into three sections. Scroll down through Section 1, **Set Acceptable Viewing Levels**, and choose the system you think is best for yourself, either the RSACi Rating System, the SafeSurf Rating System, or both.

> **Grant Java privileges**
> To use NetWatch on your computer, you'll need to click the **Grant permission** button in the Java security alert window. This window will open automatically when you click the **New User** button. If you don't grant permission, you won't be able to use NetWatch.

5. Click the **down arrow** next to each rating category, such as Language, Violence, Nudity and Sex (RSACi) and choose the acceptable level from the list (see Figure 17.10).

FIGURE 17.10
Set an acceptable level for each category.

(1) Click the down arrow to display the available categories.

(2) Choose the one you want from the list.

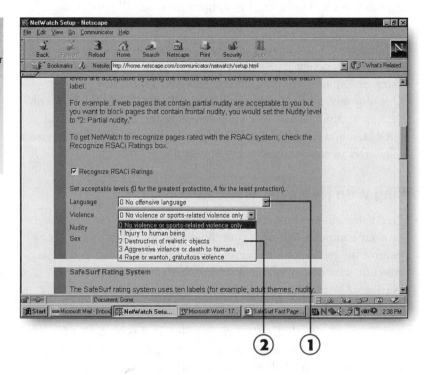

6. Scroll to the center of the page and type a password in the **Enter your NetWatch password** text box. Confirm your password by retyping it in the appropriate text box.

7. Move down to the third section of the page, **Turn NetWatch On or Off** and click the option next to **Turn NetWatch On**. When you access Web sites with Navigator, NetWatch will compare the pages with the ratings that you chose. If a page is requested that has higher levels than what you set, NetWatch will not display it.

8. (Optional) For greater control, uncheck the box next to **Allow users to see unrated sites**. By not allowing any unrated pages to appear in Navigator, you'll have greater control over what types of Web sites can be accessed. However, because the

Your NetWatch password is top secret

Make sure that you keep a record of your NetWatch password. The password is encrypted and can't be recovered. If you forget your NetWatch password, no one can help you change your NetWatch settings, including Netscape.

PART V

Have a Blast **CHAPTER 17**

majority of sites are unrated, you'll severely limit the pages that
can be viewed.

9. Click **Save Changes** at the bottom of the page to save the
settings. You'll be informed when the settings have been saved
successfully. Your NetWatch settings will be in effect the next
time you open Navigator. If you or someone who's using your
computer tries to access a page with unacceptable ratings, you'll
see a Protection Alert, like the one shown in Figure 17.11,
instead of the page you were expecting.

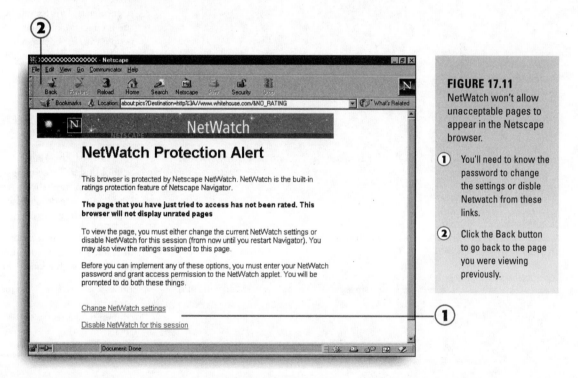

FIGURE 17.11
NetWatch won't allow
unacceptable pages to
appear in the Netscape
browser.

① You'll need to know the
password to change
the settings or disble
Netwatch from these
links.

② Click the Back button
to go back to the page
you were viewing
previously.

Have a Blast

The World Wide Web can be your child's playground. Special sites
designed just for kids offer safe, exciting places where kids can take a
break. Kids of all ages can find sites designed just for them.

Table 17.3 shows some great sites for kids and teens that offer some
unusual and exciting features. Use the listed sites as a gateway for fun.

Table 17.3 Unusual sites for kids

Kid's Site	URL	Description
Berit's Best Sites for Kids	db.cochran.com/li_toc:theoPage.db	This site features links to rated sites with excellent descriptions. Many of the links point to unusual links that you won't see anywhere else.
Yuckiest Site on the Internet	www.yucky.com	Although this site is actually designed as a resource for science facts, kids forget the site is educational! Meet people who eat cockroaches or who grow worms for fun.
Crayola	www.crayola.com	Visit a virtual museum or color an interactive card. The site changes often to match the season so check back often.
Just for Kids	scholastic.com/kids/	Kids can visit the Magic School Bus, a Goosebumps page, or join the Baby Sitters Club at this site designed by Scholastic Magazine.
Sports Illustrated for Kids	www.sikids.com	Similar to the magazine of the same name, this site features sports with a kids slant.
Teens (sites.com)	www.sites.com/Teens/	Links to a variety of sites just for teens, including sites that contain movie reviews, advice on dating, and even a page for new teen drivers.

Just for girls

Visit Amber's Place at www.davelash.com/amber/girlpage.html for a special place on the Web for girls under age 12. The links lead to several non-commercial sites designed just for girls.

Game Sites for Kids

Visit the Off Ramp for a collection of activities that are kid-friendly. The Off Ramp Web site at www.theofframp.com/kids/, shown in Figure 17.12, contains links to hundreds of sites from which you can download games and links to games that can be played online.

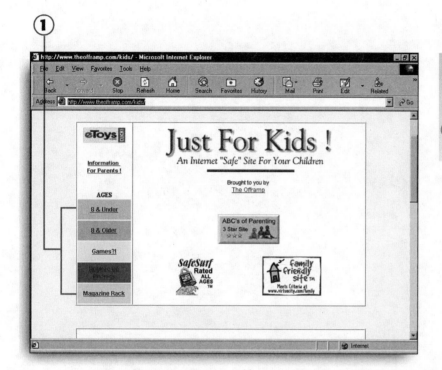

FIGURE 17.12
The fun begins on the Off Ramp.

① Links to age-appropriate sites

Internet games for kids (and adults) come in many different varieties. The following list shows two of the most common types of games you'll encounter on the Web.

- *Single Player Games.* Designed to be downloaded to your computer or played online. The Official Lego Site at www.lego.com contains virtual Lego's with which your kids can build. (Best of all, you'll never need to pick up the pieces!)

- *Interactive Web Games.* Played together by kids across the Internet. Some interactive games are violent or sexual in nature and not suitable for kids. Susie's Place at www.primenet.com/~hodges/susplace.html features some thought-provoking word games that older children will enjoy.

SEE ALSO

➤ *For details on downloading software, review page 180*

Every game is different
Pay careful attention to the instructions and hardware requirements on each game site. Some can be played directly from your browser, but others require you to download and install the game to your computer. Some games need extra hardware, like a joystick or an accelerated graphics card. In a few cases, you'll need to register or pay a small fee. Make sure you know what you need before you try to play.

chapter 18

Shop 'Til You Drop

Finding your favorite CyberMall ●

Letting Bots do your comparison
shopping ●

Looking at online consumer resources ●

Paying for your purchases ●

Bidding at online auctions ●

Shopping on the Web

Internet shopping is here to stay. *E-commerce*, the term commonly used for business on the Internet, is not a fad. Conservative estimates for retail sales by the end of 2000 top $50 billion dollars. By the end of 2003, retail sales are predicted to top $108 billion. That same year, Web commerce between Web businesses is expected to exceed $1.2 trillion.

Merchants, both big and small, are jumping on the Internet bandwagon. For one thing, the costs are lower because there are no expensive retail outlets or sales personnel. Expensive warehousing is a thing of the past. In fact, some Web merchants don't maintain any sizeable inventory and fill your order directly from the manufacturer or supplier.

If you haven't tried Internet shopping, there's no time like the present to begin. You can shop directly from your computer at any hour of the day or night. Want to buy Waterford crystal from Ireland or Belgian lace from Belgium? No problem. Your computer can whisk you to the site in a few seconds. Because you've got the world at your fingertips, you can compare prices on any merchandise and find where you'll get the best deal.

You can't go there

Although Amazon.com bills itself as providing the Earth's biggest selection, you couldn't physically go to the Amazon store to shop. Like many other Web merchants, Amazon.com does not have an actual retail establishment.

Shopping Tips

Internet shopping opens a whole new world of opportunities. However, before you max out your credit card, take a few minutes to get prepared. Shoppers need to be just as cautious in cyberspace as they are with any offline personal or telephone credit card purchase. An impressive-looking Internet site does not necessarily mean the company is legitimate.

Before you decide to purchase anything, consider the following points:

- Use the same common sense you would use when purchasing items in a store, by mail, or over the telephone. If you're buying from a company you don't know, be sure to ask about the company's refund and exchange policy before you buy anything. If the item is expensive, ask about a guarantee or warranty. Get a

clear picture of when and how the item will be shipped.
(Christmas presents that arrive in March aren't a great deal!)

- Protect your personal financial information. Order from secure
sites. Read the privacy policy posted at the site. Always print out
a copy of your order and confirmation number for your records.
If something doesn't feel right about the transaction, click the
Back button and move on.

SEE ALSO

➤ *You'll find how to pay for Web purchases on page 442*

- Think security. Con artists have found a ready outlet on the
Internet. Be wary of bait-and-switch techniques. Never reveal
your passwords or any information used to install your online
service. Make sure you're comfortable with a company before
doing business with it. If you want, check out the company with
the Better Business Bureau before you order.

- Remind yourself that if a deal sounds too good to be true, it
probably is. This old adage holds as true with e-commerce as
it does with other transactions you make. A fraudulent company's Internet Web site can look just as professional as that of
a legitimate company. Always know whom you are dealing with.

Going to the CyberMall

Start your Web shopping trip at a *CyberMall*. Instead of having to
search for each store you want to visit, CyberMalls enable you to
find a collection of merchants in the same location. When you're
through looking at one shop, you can use your browser's **Back**
button to get back to the mall's home page.

An online mall can range from an unadorned page of links to a well-
designed full-service shopping environment, complete with three-
dimensional plants and a food court. CyberMalls are fun to visit if
you're in the mood to window shop for the latest trends or when
you're ready for some serious shopping. (My favorite CyberMall is
shown in Figure 18.1.)

Stamps for all

If you're like most people,
a trip to the post office
means long lines and
wasted time. Visit the
online store at www.
stampsonline.com
for a great stamp shopping
experience. Shopping at
the site is like going to a
mall that's devoted to
stamps. You'll find regular
U.S. postage stamps, col-
lector's items, and other
stamp accessories. Best of
all, there are no lines and
the stamps are delivered
to you.

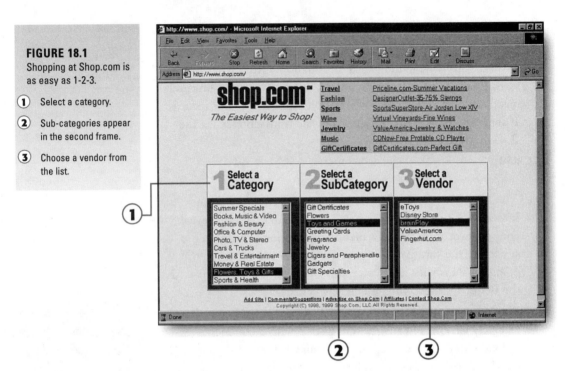

Table 18.1 shows some of the best CyberMalls on the Web.
However, don't stop with my list. Use the malls shown here as a
starting point—you're sure to find many more you like.

Table 18.1   Some great places to shop

Mall Name	URL	Order Method	Comments
Internet Plaza	internet-plaza.net/	online, email, fax, or phone	More than 200 establishments are located under one cyber-roof! The mall is broken down by streets, like Fashion Boulevard and Gourmet Lane. The Internet Plaza features a window shopping link that enables you to isolate specific products and services.

Mall Name	URL	Order Method	Comments
Web Warehouse	www.webware house.com	online, email, fax, or phone	In addition to hip brands such as The Armani Exchange, you can buy insurance, tickets to events in your local area, and even look at real-estate for sale. The site is easy to move through, because it's arranged by a series of links.
Shops.Net	shops.net	online, email, fax, or phone	Although Shops.Net is just made up of links to other sites, you'll find big-name shops such as Levi Strauss, The Sharper Image, and Toys-R-Us mixed in with a broad variety of goods and services.
eMall	emall.com/	online, email, fax, or phone	Find mainly specialty gourmet and garden items at this small shopping site.
MSN Shopping	www.eshop.com	online, email, and phone	A collection of the same stores you'll find at most upscale malls, including Godiva Chocolates, GAP, The Sharper Image, and The Disney Store. Try out one of their shopping services.
Brands4Less	www.brands4less.com	online	A giant collection of stores, all featuring brand names. Some of the prices are very reasonable.
Shop.com	www.shop.com	online, purchase order, phone, fax, or mail	Shopping at Shop.com is as easy as 1-2-3. First, choose a category, select a sub-category, and choose a vendor from the list. Like magic, you're whisked to the merchant's site.

continues...

Table 18.1	Continued		
Mall Name	URL	Order Method	Comments
iMall	www.imall.com	online	The iMall is so big that it has a sister mall in Korea! Take advantage of the iMall's unique search tool that enables you to look through each merchant's inventory for a specific item. Finish up with a Moonlite Raspberry Chocolate Cheesecake from Virtual Vineyards.

Search for What You Want

Another great place to find Web merchants is right on the pages of your favorite search tool. Search engines like HotBot and Infoseek have links to the Web sites of many of your favorite merchants. As shown in Figure 18.2, the search tool finds the best shopping sites for you and makes it easy to get from site to site.

SEE ALSO

➤ *Review information about HotBot on page 165*
➤ *Review how to set up an effective search query on page 173*

You can also use your favorite search engine to set up a search query detailing what you want to find. There's a good chance that you'll locate a Web merchant who can provide what you're looking for without having to try too many times. Remember to start with a broad-based query and then narrow it down.

Compare and Contrast with a Shopping Bot

At the end of a long day of shopping, your feet burn, you're hot and thirsty and, worse, everything looks alike. You've been there—so have I. Wouldn't it be great if you had a personal shopper to find the items you wanted and, even better, got you the best price possible?

Web shoppers can turn to a *bot* any time they need help. Shopping bots are software programs that are programmed to root out the best deals on the Internet. Fortunately, the services of a bot are generally free of charge.

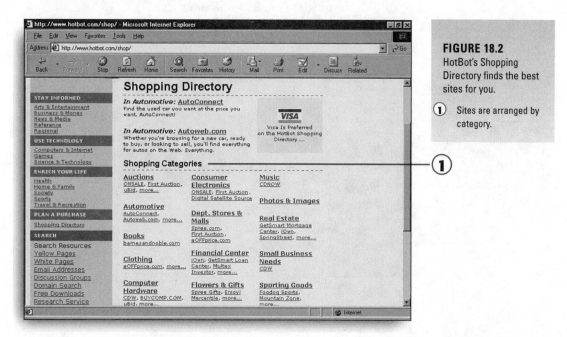

FIGURE 18.2
HotBot's Shopping Directory finds the best sites for you.

① Sites are arranged by category.

Links to shopping bots can be found on several of the major search-engine pages, such as Excite and AltaVista. You can also use some of these shopping bots:

- DealTime at `www.dealtime.com` has a unique tracking service. Pick a product such as computer hardware or software, consumer electronics, and items for the home and garden, and specify a price range. DealTime will search for the best deal based within the timeframe you set. DealTime brings you instant search results and also continues to look for late-breaking deals that meet your individual requirements. They alert you to these new deals in three ways: via email, pager, or their Desktop Notifier (which you'll need to download).

- Simon, an animated character, is just dying to help you at `www.mysimon.com`. (See Figure 18.3.) Simon's cute antics make you forget that mySimon uses Virtual Learning Agent technology, and looks through more than one thousand merchants for

Agent Bot, at your service

The term bot has become interchangeable with agent, to indicate that the software can be sent out on a mission, usually to find information and report back. Strictly speaking, an agent is a bot that goes out on a mission. The shopping bot's mission is clear; to find you the best deals on the Web.

everything from computer hardware to gourmet chocolate. You will also find a great newsletter and links to other e-commerce information on the mySimon page.

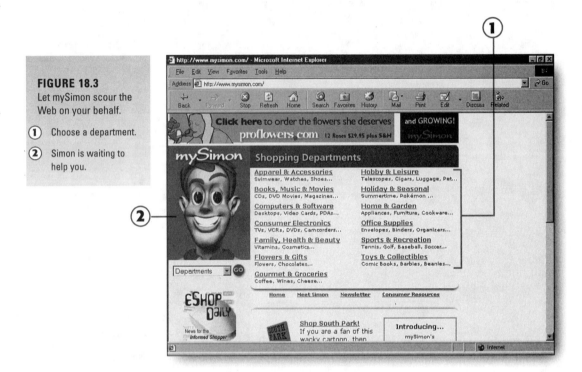

- With more than 3,000,000 items in their database, Stuff.com at www.stuff.com is sure to help you find what you need. Along with the standard links to categories, Stuff.com features an advanced search that enables you to combine words and phrases and use some Boolean logic.

SEE ALSO

➤ *Need help with Boolean logic? Turn to page 173*

- The Jango/Excite Product Finder at www.jango.com is actually part of the Excite family of products and services. Jango searches all major consumer categories quicker and easier than most shopping bots. Depending on the category, Jango also searches auctions and classifieds. Use the "Find Reviews" section to get information on the products you're looking for.

- CompareNet at www.comparenet.com is a recent Microsoft acquisition and has the power of Microsoft behind its service. CompareNet's greatest strengths are in the areas of office hardware, furniture, and supplies. It also does a great job comparing home electronics, automobiles, home appliances, sports equipment, and baby-care items.

Brand Names on the Web

Web shoppers are generally a pretty savvy bunch of consumers. Most Internet consumers turn to brand names when it comes to plunking down their hard-earned dollars. Why? Because brand names spell name recognition and consumer trust to most people. Branded stores and products turn shoppers into buyers.

Customers who might feel uneasy about buying on the Web have no problem when a recognized name is involved in the transaction. Computer hardware companies such as Compaq, Gateway, and Hewlett-Packard enjoy great name recognition on the Internet. In fact, the Dell Computer site, pictured in Figure 18.4, generates almost as much business from home users as it does from businesses. Microsoft, another leading technology company, is a name that makes products fly off Web shelves. In addition to their success in the software market, Microsoft also has interests in sites that sell cars, trips, and even homes.

Some Web merchants have a presence in both the real and cyber-market. Consumers can visit a Barnes and Noble bookstore, for example, or shop at barnesandnoble.com. JCPenney has a foot in both the retail and *e-tail* (Internet) markets. Other merchants, like Cdnow, are Web-only merchants with no physical location.

FIGURE 18.4
Buy your next computer from Dell.

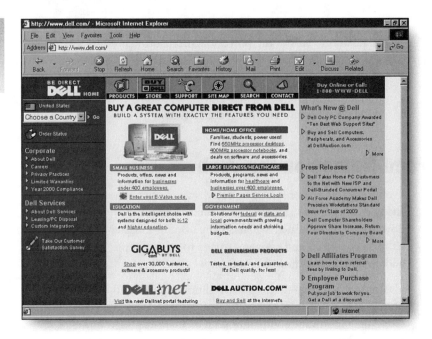

Table 18.2 shows some of the top sites known by brand recognition.

Table 18.2 Some great places to shop

Name	URL	Comments
Amazon.com	www.amazon.com	Everyone's heard of Amazon! In fact, Amazon.com has become synonymous with the new Web economy. Shopping at Amazon is a treat.
Barnesandnoble.com	www.barnesandnoble.com	Shopping at the online version of Barnes and Noble for books means no crowds or long lines at the checkout. The biggest drawback, though, is there's no groovy café.
JCPenney	www.jcpenney.com	The site is like an online catalog. You can spend hours browsing through the many pages that make up the site.

Name	URL	Comments
Gateway Computer	`www.gateway.com`	Gateway made a name for itself in the mail-order computer business. The Gateway Web site showcases the computer products with just the right amount of *kitsch*.
Dell Computer	`www.dell.com`	Through their Web presence, Dell sells high-quality computer equipment. Dell sells mainly to businesses but is reaching out to the home market.
Hewlett-Packard	`www.hp.com`	Hewlett-Packard has parlayed its excellent reputation for printers into computers and scanners. The HP Web site is tops for convenience and ease-of-use.
Gap Online	`www.gap.com`	Cool kids know that shopping at the Gap is hip. The Gap brand looks as good on the Web as it does in person.
Cdnow	`www.cdnow.com`	Cdnow sells more music than any other place on the Web.
Columbia House Online	`www.columbiahouse.com`	More than 15 million members shop here. Choose from CDs, videos, DVD's, and more.
1-800-flowers.com	`www.1800flowers.com`	Send a bouquet from the folks you know. Flowers are just the beginning at this extensive site.

Going to an Online Department Store

If you're like me, you can't walk out of a department store without buying many more items than originally planned. There's always a gadget or two that catches your eye or a gizmo you can't live without. You're sure to find the same is true at the online version of some popular discount department stores listed here:

- Target at www.targetstores.com has something for everyone. The site has links to several children's departments. If you're a new bride, sign up at the Club Wedd bridal registry. Babies can be registered at Target's Lullaby Club. Sign up for a Target credit card with Target's secure online application. If you feel the need to walk the aisles and push a cart, you'll find a store locator at the site.

- Kmart.com at www.kmart.com is a fun place to visit. The site is designed for easy navigation (you'll never get hung up in frames). You can click a link to see the weekly sale circular. If you're a television commercial junkie, be sure and visit Kmart's Real Video Theatre to download the latest Kmart ads to your computer.

SEE ALSO

➤ *If you need help downloading files, review page 188*

- Wal-Mart Online at www.wal-mart.com is almost as good as going to the store. The friendly Wal-Mart greeter stands on the home page to greet you. The site is set up as a navigational guide. You can click department links to move through the online store, or you can search for a product. As you move through the store, you're provided with a virtual shopping basket. At check out, you can review the items in your basket before you pay. The payment procedure is easy and secure.

Online Consumer Resources

Although online transactions generally work out satisfactorily, sometimes things go wrong. The item you purchased could arrive damaged or broken. The quality of the item might be a lot lower in reality than the way it appeared on the Web. Fortunately, there are a few online consumer resources that exist to help you.

SEE ALSO

➤ *In addition to the resources shown in this section, read about the Better Business Bureau (www.bbbonline.org) and the National Fraud Information Center (www.fraud.org) on page 107*

The webwatchdog, located at www.webwatchdog.com, tracks Web businesses. Web merchants are encouraged to register and place a link back to webwatchdog on their sites. Although not all legitimate merchants are registered with the webwatchdog, use the registry, illustrated in Figure 18.5, to search for merchants about which you're unsure. You can search the database for a specific business or search by category to find a list of companies that provide specific goods or services. If a consumer has filed a valid complaint about a Web business, you'll find the company in the webwatchdog doghouse.

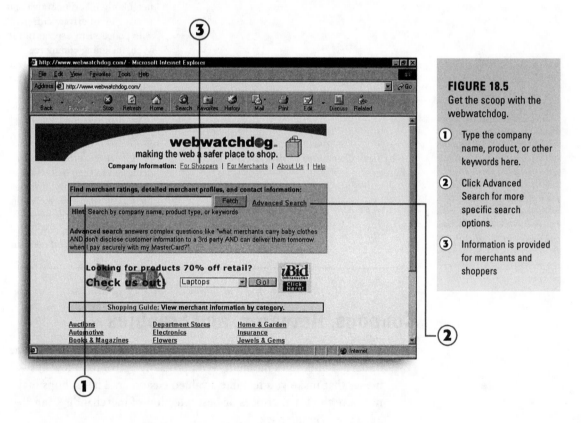

FIGURE 18.5
Get the scoop with the webwatchdog.

① Type the company name, product, or other keywords here.

② Click Advanced Search for more specific search options.

③ Information is provided for merchants and shoppers

In addition to webwatchdog, other services are waiting to help you. Table 18.3 shows some of the best consumer resources on the Web.

Table 18.3 Consumer resources on the Web

Name	URL	Comments
Federal Trade Commission Consumer Protection	`www.ftc.gov/ftc/consumer.htm`	Under the auspices of the U.S. government, this FTC site has links to many helpful sites. There's a 1-800 number to call if you need help.
CyberCops	`www.cybercops.org`	CyberCops is organized like a neighborhood crime watch and is made up of private citizens who police many aspects of the Web, including commerce. If you have a complaint against a Web merchant, CyberCops can probably help resolve it. You can read about some of the disputes that have been resolved by CyberCops at their site.
NetCheck Commerce Bureau	`www.netcheck.com`	NetCheck is a private agency dedicated to the goals of assisting consumers on the Internet. NetCheck works to resolve disputes and complaints between consumer and company, company to company, and company to consumer.

Coupons, Rewards, and Freebies

Merchants have known for years that loyal customers mean revenue dollars. Think for a moment—you probably patronize a few businesses that make you feel like a valued customer. These shops may not have the lowest prices or best selection of merchandise, but they keep you coming back.

Web marketers recognize that customer loyalty is important. However, it's harder for a Web-based emporium to show customers how important they are. Thoughtful touches, such as free hard candy, match books, and other small perks don't work on the Web. Instead, Web merchants are turning to *e-centives* to keep their customers happy.

E-centives can take several forms. You might be offered a coupon for dollars off in a future purchase. Or, you might get a reward that's proportional to the amount of money you spent. Other times, you might get a free perk for visiting or patronizing a site. No matter what you're offered, the underlying reason for the e-centive is to get you to come back and buy again.

Click and Win

Clicking banner ads, those pesky messages that flash across the top of many Web pages, is the most obvious place to find Web perks. *Click-throughs*, the term given to responding to banner ads, tells the advertiser that you've got an interest in the product. Generally, when you click a banner ad such as the one shown in Figure 18.6, you're directed to another site and presented with information about the product. You might even be offered a sweepstakes, special discount, or a free sample to try the product.

FIGURE 18.6
The banner ad at Yahoo! offers a chance to win.

① Click the ad for more details.

Many Web advertisers track the demographics of the people who click their ads. Information such as your geographic region or the referring domain name (generally your ISP) might be recorded and analyzed by the advertiser later on. If you're concerned about privacy, you might want to skip any banner ads.

SEE ALSO

➤ *When you visit a page on the Web, that site can record a lot of information about you, including your name, your company name, your location, the type of computer you're using, your operating system, the type and version of your browser, and what Web pages you've looked at. This exchange of information is called a cookie. Read about cookies on page 89*

In addition to banner ads, several Web sites offer premiums to anyone who will view their straight-out, unabashed advertising. Sometimes these sites are worth your while. If you don't mind a hard-sell approach, many of the products displayed are discounted heavily.

- **Prizepoint** at www.prizepoint.com gives prizes for its online games and trivia contests. You'll need to register before you can play.

- **MyPoints** at www.mypoints.com, operates on the points system. By visiting certain Web sites and responding to advertiser's email, subscribers earn points that can be cashed in for goods and services. Registration is mandatory.

- **ClickRewards** at www.clickrewards.com gives frequent flyer miles, called *click miles*, as a reward for visiting their advertisers.

Paying by Credit Card

Most of the purchases you make on the Web require payment by credit card. (It's rare to find a Web merchant who accepts COD terms.) Chances are, you're a little uncomfortable about providing your credit card information across the Internet. Many people don't take advantage of e-commerce because they share this concern.

Transaction security is the number one concern on every Web shopper's mind. Credit card fraud on the Internet is a frightening thought. Can some hacker see your credit card information and use it for criminal purposes? Although Internet credit card fraud can happen, you're more likely to have a problem if an unscrupulous restaurant server or salesclerk gets hold of your credit card and makes a copy of the card, or writes down the number and expiration date. (Think how long a server is out of sight with your card when you pay for dinner at a restaurant.)

SEE ALSO

➤ *Read all about transaction security starting on page 100*

Fortunately, technology has kept up with the need for transaction security. Several different methods are used to ensure that the Web merchant with whom you've placed the order will be the only one to see your payment information. But you still need to remember that you can't be too careful. Don't order from an unknown Web merchant who has posted an offer that's too good to be true. You probably don't duck into back alleys and deal with shady merchants on your real buying trips, so don't order from the Web equivalents.

Other Ways to Pay for Web Purchases

In addition to submitting your credit card information each time you make a purchase, you can choose another way to pay. Some Web merchants now accept *digital cash*.

The concept of digital cash is simple—you transmit information to the merchant who then uses the information to get the real cash from your account. The use of digital cash has been slow to catch on.

However, one product called CyberCash, has been instrumental in developing a model digital-cash system. Before you can use CyberCash, you need to install special client software onto your computer. When the software is installed, you open an account in a participating bank. Using the CyberCash software, you move money from your checking account into your CyberCash account. When you make a purchase with a merchant who uses the CyberCash system, the payment is made out of your CyberCash account. Because the merchant only sees your CyberCash account number, there's no danger that your real bank account or credit card numbers can be misused. Read more about the CyberCash system at www.cybercash.com/index2.html, shown in Figure 18.7.

Using a Digital Wallet

Digital wallets represent another way to pay for online transactions. Several companies have marketed digital wallets, including Microsoft. Although different companies offered various features with their wallets, the basic concept was always the same. Your payment and address information was stored within the wallet. When you made a purchase, your payment information was sent from the wallet. You didn't need to retype the same information again and again. Your payment information was secured by password, so you didn't need to worry that someone else could access your confidential information.

Microsoft Wallet

The Microsoft Wallet is still available. Users of Internet Explorer and Navigator can use it. You can read more about Microsoft Wallet at www.microsoft.com/wallet.

443

FIGURE 18.7
CyberCash is changing
e-commerce.

① Click the picture for
related details.

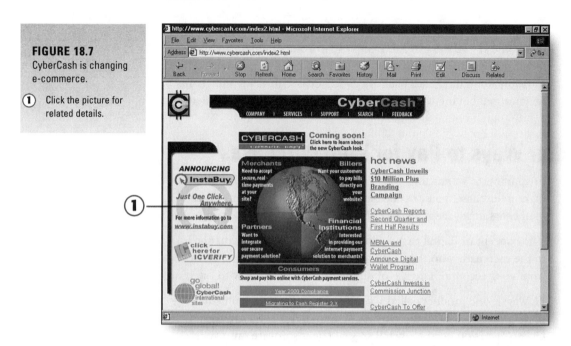

The best-known digital wallet was the Microsoft Wallet, an add-on
to Internet Explorer. While the concept was sound, the actual use
of the wallet was small. Merchants needed to register with Microsoft
and then enable Wallet payments on their sites. Only a handful of
merchants signed up to use the service.

Recently, a consortium of e-commerce giants, including America
Online, IBM, Microsoft, Mastercard, and Visa endorsed a new digital
wallet standard. The new technology is called *electronic commerce
modeling language* or ECML for short.

It may take a while for ECML to catch on. However, after the
ECML standard is firmly in place, more and more vendors will
accept digital wallet payments at their sites. Buying on the Web will
become even easier and more convenient.

Going Once, Going Twice, Sold at the Online Auction

Online auctions are the hottest way to shop on the Web. You can
buy anything at an online auction from antique salt and pepper
shakers to computers. Sometimes you can get a great deal at an
auction; other times you realize you paid too much.

Online auctions generally follow a simple formula. The seller puts an item up for bids for a pre-set time period. Some items have minimum selling prices. Buyers post bids on the item during the time the item is for sale. Sometimes the bidding gets fast and furious; it's not unusual for two buyers to try to outbid each other on a hot item. When the bidding closes, the highest bidder gets the item. Depending on the auction site, the buyer and seller might arrange for payment or the site acts as the intermediary for the transaction.

Buying anything from an auction involves some risk. You can't see the merchandise first-hand and must rely on a picture or other description provided by the seller. (Read my personal experience with a seller's description in the next section of this chapter.) If you're bidding on a designer item, you have no way of knowing whether the item is genuine or whether it is a forgery or fake.

Best Auction Sites on the Web

There are literally thousands of auction sites on the Web. Table 18.4 shows my top 10.

Table 18.4   Consumer Resources on the Web

Auction Site	URL	Comments	Payment
eBay	www.ebay.com	eBay's pages are accessed 1.5 billion times per month. With more than 2 million items in 1,600 categories, you're sure to find something to bid on.	Money order or cashier's check
uBid Online Auction	www.ubid.com	Owned by America Online, uBid has some great name-brand merchandise up for sale.	

continues...

Table 18.4 Continued

Auction Site	URL	Comments	Payment
Amazon.com	www.amazon.com	The Amazon auction is an addition to their regular business of books, CD's, and videos. Check for some rock-bottom prices on an eclectic collection of stuff.	
Collecting Nation	www.collecting nation.com	Mainly bears, Beanies, and other collectibles are available at this site.	Credit card, money order, cashiers check, or personal check
SportsAuction	www.sports auction.com	SportsAuction sells quality sports and autographed memorabilia.	Credit card or Invoicing
Cigarbid.com	www.cigarbid. cigar.com	Cigars and accessories are up for bids here.	Credit card
Haggle Online	www.haggle.com	Rock-bottom prices on computers and related equipment.	Check or money order

My Personal Auction Experience

Because I'm usually a cautious shopper, I was reluctant to join in the auction fray. However, one night my son and I paid a visit to eBay. We each found items that we couldn't live without. I followed the instructions to sign up as a registered buyer and we started bidding.

My first bid on a designer handbag was quickly topped. I raised my bid three more times, but the other bidders soon had the bag priced way beyond my budget. I also entered several bids on an automatic kitty litter box. My son Richard placed bids on several model cars and a digital camera. Like me, he was outbid on most of the items.

A few days later, I was notified that we had been the highest bidders on the cat litter machine and a model car. I sent cashier's checks to the two sellers and anxiously awaited our merchandise.

The cat litter changer came first. It was in perfect condition but had no instruction manual or assembly instructions. Was it a good deal? No! Between the cost of the item and the shipping charges, I could have gone to our local discount store and paid the same amount for a brand new one.

The model car arrived a few days later. Instead of the car we'd been expecting, the package contained a toy car that we could have purchased at the supermarket for under a dollar. (We paid $10.)

We were at fault in both cases. I realized that I should have priced the cat litter machine before I started bidding on one at the auction. Re-reading the description of the model car showed that the seller had never made any false statements. The description never claimed that it was anything more than a cheap toy. We assumed, incorrectly, that the car was a more expensive model.

Winning-Bid Strategies

With a little practice you can make some incredible deals on everything under the sun at an online auction. Successful auction bidders have a few tricks up their sleeves. Prepare yourself before you start bidding.

- Research the market value of the item you want to bid on. It's easy to overestimate an item's value or to get caught up in the heat of bidding.
- Timing is everything. Watch the opening and closing dates on the items you want. Check an item an hour or so before bids close and see whether you can swing a good deal.

- Read the description carefully. Often a seller uses the most glowing terms possible to describe an item, while leaving out some of the item's flaws. If you're not sure the item is right for you, don't bid.

- Be prepared to buy what you bid on. It's easy to place bids on more items than you can afford. After all, you reason, most times you'll be outbid. However, what if you're not outbid? Make sure you have enough money to pay for all the items you're bidding on.

- Check out the site's policies on fraud and privacy before you bid. Most auction sites have a policy against deceitful sellers. Is the site going to sell your personal information or make it public? Find out both policies before you sign up to bid.

- Find out about shipping charges and other hidden costs. Check to see whether the shipping charges are reasonable before you bid. If they seem excessive, if the auction charges surcharges, or other fees are too much, move on.

Bigger and Better

There's something for everyone when you shop online. You can buy knick-knacks, kitchen accessories, or appliances—all from the comfort of your computer. You can even get a mortgage or buy a car on the Internet. From the smallest accessory to a big-ticket item, you'll find it on the Web. In Chapter 19, "Big Ticket Purchases on the Internet," you'll have the fun of shopping for some bigger items on the Internet.

Big Ticket Purchases on the Internet

Buy a car online

Look for real-estate on the Internet

Learn how to make home repairs

Arrange for the vacation of
your dreams

Buying a Car Online

Maybe you enjoy going around to car dealers and spending hours speaking with slick-talking salesmen. Or, you're a real gearhead, who knows all about slip differentials, torque, horsepower, and gear ratios. If so, you needn't look to the Internet for help when you're buying a car! However, the rest of us can use the Internet for everything from model and invoice information, to the actual purchase of those dream wheels.

The Internet is a treasure trove of information about cars. In a recent survey, more than 40% of new car buyers said they'd used the Internet for some aspect of the purchase. Choosing the right car at the right price is never easy. Before you make a purchase you might regret later, do your research online.

Start with these three sites:

- *Auto Site, the Ultimate Automotive Buyer's Guide*, at www.autosite.com is a great starting point for your research. From prices on new and used cars to model specs to reviews of cars, the free service provided by the 30,000-page *Automotive Information Center* (AIC) is a good place for the consumer to do the necessary homework. The AIC acts as a clearinghouse for automobile information.

- *AutoWeb.com* (www.autoweb.com) is another good place to get the low-down on cars. The site offers extensive information on cars, plus a loan calculator and a place called AutoTalk, a bulletin-board area where buyers can exchange war stories and ask other consumers for advice. There's also an Autos Wanted section, where you can see whether anyone wants to buy the car you're replacing.

- *AutoVantage*, at www.autovantage.com, is a comprehensive site that offers information about new and used cars, classifieds, and a section for price quotes. If you join the AutoVantage Club, you can take advantage of their car-care discounts, savings on travel, free trip routing, and roadside assistance. Figure 19.1 shows the AutoVantage home page.

Buy or lease?

The decision to buy or lease should be based on your needs, the lease price, and the terms of the lease. If you drive 125,000 miles a year, leasing a car with a limit of annual 12,000 would be a mistake. A shareware program called Buy It or Lease It might help you decide what's best. You can obtain the program from ZDNet at www.zdnet.com/swlib.

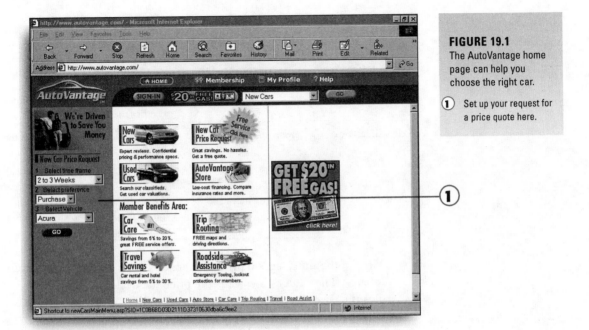

FIGURE 19.1
The AutoVantage home
page can help you
choose the right car.

① Set up your request for
a price quote here.

Finding the Best Price

The newspaper is full of dealers advertising one-price deals.
However, even if you hate to haggle, most times it doesn't make
sense to point at a car and say "I'll take it." The price of one car can
change for from buyer to buyer. The sticker price may not be the
price you'll pay.

Before you head to the dealership, take the time to do your car-price
homework. Even inexpensive cars take a big chunk of money. If you
spend too much, you're going to have to live with your mistake for a
long time.

Table 19.1 shows you some of the sites on the Web to get the scoop
on car prices.

Table 19.1	Car prices on the Web	
URL	Name	Comments
Microsoft Car Point	www.carpoint.com	Fill in a form to get a report that includes invoice price, retail price, destination charges, and even notes whether the luxury tax applies.
Kelley Blue Book	www.kbb.com	The Kelley Blue Book has been the car-buyers Bible for a long time. The online version is no less awesome.
Edmunds	www.edmunds.com	Wholesale and retail prices for new and used cars are shown here. Each option is individually priced.

Most of the time, a good price is expressed as an amount "over *dealer invoice*." The dealer's invoice is the price the dealer paid for the car, plus the cost of whatever accessories were added at the showroom. That price, however, can vary from month to month.

Besides learning the dealer's cost, a smart buyer needs to be aware of factory-to-consumer incentives, such as an offer of $1,000 cash-back. There also may be factory-to-dealer incentives (which the dealer won't reveal to you). The dealer also may have the option of offering low dealer-financing interest rates, which are often offered on cars that are not selling well.

Knowing the dealer's invoice price is the first number you need to work with. If you're planning to finance the car, you'll also need to take the interest rate of the car loan into account. Is there any advantage to buying an extended warranty? Will the cost of an upgrade, such as a moonroof or CD player, make the car more attractive to the next buyer? Consider all the angles before you sign on the dotted line.

Other traditional advice also holds. You might find that you're offered a better deal at the end of a month if a dealer has quotas to meet. Naturally, one year's models will be cheaper when dealers are anxious to clear space in their showrooms for next year's models. Unless you have to be the first on your block to get the newest model, hold out for a while before you buy a car that's just been introduced.

Buying the Car Online

Even in today's cyberworld, most people feel better about taking a test drive and kicking the tires. However, some excellent sites on the Web take the headache out of car buying for you.

One of the oldest auto sales operations on the Web is Auto-by-Tel at www.autobytel.com, shown in Figure 19.2. If you're using the latest versions of Internet Explorer or Netscape Navigator, you can click the link to the **Virtual Showroom** for an exciting experience. (You'll need a few plug-ins to proceed.)

SEE ALSO
➤ *Need help with plug-ins? Turn to page 199*

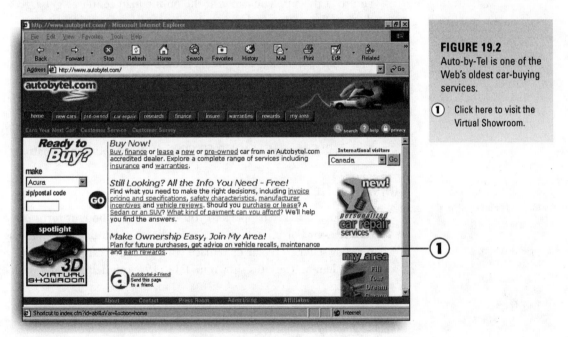

FIGURE 19.2
Auto-by-Tel is one of the Web's oldest car-buying services.

① Click here to visit the Virtual Showroom.

Using about 1,500 accredited dealers that pay a fee to participate, Auto-by-Tel says the consumer reaps the savings that dealers realize from the lower marketing costs associated with selling cars over the Internet. After a quote request is made via email, the dealer contacts the would-be buyer by telephone.

Buy a car at Wal-Mart

Through Wal-Mart's Sam's Club Auto and Recreation Program (www.samscarclub.com), you can get a discount on many new cars and trucks. The program is open to members of the club. You submit a request to the club, which is forwarded to a dealer who contacts you directly. If you're not already a member, sign up at Sam's Club Online at www.samsclub.com.

The service urges its dealers to create a separate department to handle sales from the site, and recommends that commission payments to the salesperson be set up on a per-car basis rather than as a traditional percentage of the sale. Dealers pay Auto-by-Tel a one-time sign-up fee of between $2,500 and $4,500 plus a monthly fee of between $500 and $2,000 depending on the location of the dealer and the type of cars it sells. Auto-by-Tel then trains its dealers to work with Internet customers.

General Motors is so excited about online buyers that they've put together an exciting site at www.gmbuyer.com. Simply complete a purchase request and get a low, Internet price quote from a GM dealer in your area on any car you want. The service is fast and easy. While you're at the site, you can visit the online loan center to get a great deal on financing.

Some car-buying services offer a different angle. Stoneage at www.stoneage.com lets consumers choose the dealer or dealers who will receive their price-quote request. Stoneage generates money from the dealerships, and also from people looking to sell their used cars. For $19.95, much less than the cost of a classified ad in your local newspaper, you can list your car on the Stoneage site until it is sold. Call Stoneage at 1-800-STONEAGE for more information.

Consumer Resources

Click and clack

If you're a fan of Car Talk, the famous show about cars that's broadcast on National Public Radio, drop by Tom and Ray's home on the Web. You'll find them at cartalk.cars.com.

Let's hope it never happens to you—the car you bought turns out to be a lemon. Fortunately *lemon laws* obligate an automobile manufacturer or seller to repair or replace your defective car. If you think you have a lemon, the sites shown in Table 19.2 can help you get back on track.

Table 19.2 Help for lemons

Name	URL	Comments
Autopedia:Auto Lemon Law Information	www.autopedia.com/ Lemon	Links to state statutes governing lemon laws; also some helpful hints on how to proceed.

Name	URL	Comments
The Lemon Car Page	`www.mindspring.com/~wf1`	Presented by an attorney, the site has links to sources of applicable laws for Lemon cars, consumer strategies in Lemon car cases, informal dispute resolution or arbitration, and Lemon links, Lemon lawyers, and other reading material.
National Highway Safety Administration	`www.nhtsa.dot.gov/cars/problems/complain/compmmy1.cfm`	Fill out an online form to complain about your car to the United States Department of Transportation.

Real Estate, Internet Style

Your living quarters represent one of your biggest cash outlays. Whether you're making mortgage payments or writing a rent check, your home represents one of your biggest cash outlays. Throw in a few repairs and it may seem like you'll never get out of the hole.

Relax! Turn to the Web for help. Whether you're buying, selling, or repairing your home, the Web can't help you win the lottery to pay off all your debts or make you a millionaire. However, you can find all sorts of information about real estate and homes.

Buying and Selling

Before you look for the perfect home online, be sure that you're familiar with the area in which you want to live. In some markets, property is selling almost as quickly as it's listed. To get the best deal, you might benefit from the combined services of a trained professional and your Web research.

Many sites on the Web provide listings that cover a wide geographic area. CyberHomes at `www.cyberhomes.com` is a good starting point. The mega-site has listings in most states. You can also get reports on the schools in a particular area. Realtor.com at `www.realtor.com` is another source of good information. The site caters to both consumers and realtors and has more than one million listings. You'll find an industry-specific glossary of terms you should understand if you're

Neighbor to the queen

Hightail it over to `www.uk-property.com` for a listing of properties for sale in the United Kingdom. You'll also find information on mortgages, auctions, and other areas of buying or selling a property in England.

Find the perfect rental apartment

Go to `www.apartment-life.com` for help in finding the perfect apartment. The site, sponsored by Apartments for Rent Online, has links to some great apartments. You'll also find some important information for renters at the site.

serious about buying. Homeseekers.com at `www.homeseekers.com` keeps a record of all homes listed with the Multi-List Service. If you know a home's MLS number, you can find detailed information about the property at the site.

The major real estate companies also have sites featuring their own listings. Re/Max (`www.remax.com`), Century 21 (`www.century21.com`), Coldwell Banker (`www.coldwellbanker.com`), and many others have extensive sites that cover the entire nation. Additionally, many local realtors have Web sites that can provide you with a wealth of information. Use the guide at LookSmart at `www.looksmart.com`, pictured in Figure 19.3, to find a realtor in your area.

FIGURE 19.3
Use LookSmart to find a local realtor.

① Select these sub-categories in the Finance category.

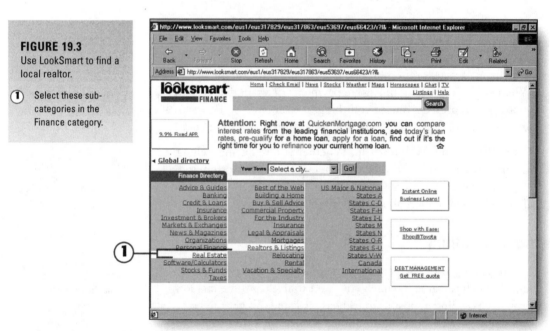

SEE ALSO

➤ *Review how to use LookSmart on page 161*

If you're selling your home, the Web can give your property some added exposure. Consider taking pictures of your home with a digital camera and posting them to the Web. Create a *virtual brochure* that showcases your property. If you don't have a Web site yet, check with your ISP to see whether you get free space for your own page. If not, sign up with one of the many communities that offer free space. You can also visit the folks at Websuite.com (`www.websuite.com`) for help. Websuite.com will host your site for around $10 per month; in return, they'll let you use their Online Mastermind system to create a Virtual tour of your home.

Financing Your New House

Can you afford a new home? Let's face it, it's unlikely that you can pay cash for your home. The average price of a new house is around $150,000. You'll probably need to finance at least some portion of your purchase.

Arranging financing can seem like a daunting task. Interest rates change all the time and then there's talk of points, prepayment penalties, and other financing terms. Fortunately, you can do some advance work on the Web. You might even find a Web broker who can handle the mortgage details for you. Table 19.3 shows you some of the best sources of financing on the Web.

Table 19.3 Mortgages on the Web

Name	URL	Comments
The Best Loans Online	`iown.com`	Fill out a form to prequalify for your home loan. If you prequalify, you can apply for a mortgage at the site.
Best Home Loan -Florida	`www.besthomeloan.com`	Best Home Loan specializes in hard-to-do mortgages. A bad or uneven credit history is not considered to be a risk. Although business is done primarily in Florida, the company has branches in many other states.
E-Loan	`www.eloan.com`	Apply to several lenders at the same time. New home purchases and home refinancing are considered here.
Associated Lenders	`www.mortgageloan.com`	National network of more than 120 lenders with 600 loan programs to choose from.

continues...

Table 19.3 Continued		
Name	URL	Comments
Crestar Mortgage Corporation	`www.crestarmortgage.com`	Prequalify for a mortgage from the comfort of home. Helps you calculate what you can afford and what the best terms are.

Fixing Up Your House

Feng Shui

Feng Shui, an ancient Chinese tradition that helps you to modify your home to enhance your life and good fortune, may be what your home needs. The term Feng Shui comes from the Chinese words for wind and water and embraces the idea that your living environment should be arranged so that it's in harmony with nature. You can learn more about Feng Shui at `www.3dglobe.com/fs`.

Every house can use a little sprucing up. Look at your house objectively and decide what it needs. Try to view your house as others see it, it's easy to become conditioned to peeling paint or a few sagging steps. If your house is more than a few years old, budget for one big project a year. That way, you won't be hit with crippling expenses if you decide to sell your home sometime in the future.

A licensed general contractor should handle major home repairs. Check out the contractor's license and be sure he's bonded and insured. Don't be embarrassed about asking to see your contractor's credentials. A good contractor will be proud to show them to you. Don't ever pay for a job in advance. Reserve the final payment until the job has been completed and, if necessary, inspected by the local building authorities.

If the repairs are small, or you want to try your hand as a do-it-yourselfer, several sites on the Web are just waiting to assist you with your repairs.

- Visit the Ask the Builder site at `www.askbuild.com` for information on home building or remodeling problems. Tim Carter, a nationally syndicated newspaper columnist and an expert in the building field, runs the site.

- Plumbing problems are no fun, messy to clean up, and usually cost a small fortune to fix. Stop your plumbing problems before they begin with a visit to the Ask the Master Plumber site at `www.clickit.com/bizwiz/homepage/plumber.htm`.

- Get a wide range of remodeling, decorating, and home care advice at Home Tips at `www.hometips.com`.

- You'll find a feast of home repair help, information, humor, and encouragement at the Natural Handyman site at www.naturalhandyman.com.

Don't stop with these sites. Search the Web using your favorite search tool for specific projects such as installing a skylight or putting in a hot tub. Check out the `alt.tools.repair+advice` and `misc.consumers.house` newsgroups. Who knows, you might even find that you like working around the house so much that you're willing to try it as a new career!

SEE ALSO

➤ *You'll find information on newsgroups on page 256*

Planning a Trip Online

A vacation can be the focal point of your year. Preparing for the trip can be almost as much fun as the trip itself. Selecting your final destination is the fun part—will it be a trip to the Australian Outback, the American West, or a few days at a rejuvenating spa? Even if you're just going home to see your family, you can get lost in the anticipation of how much fun you're going to have.

Most resorts, hotels, and tourist destinations have their own Web sites. If you're undecided where to go, use your favorite search tool to help you find the ultimate destination. For example, if you want to take a golfing vacation, start with Yahoo!. From the main Yahoo! page, click the link to **Travel**, choose **Resorts** from the list of subcategories and then chose **Golf Resorts**. As shown in Figure 19.4, you're sure to find the perfect place to stay.

Arranging for airline tickets, hotel stays, and car rentals is easy to take care of on the Web because choices are usually simple. More complicated vacation options, such as tours with extra nights and cruises with nonstandard destinations, are harder to arrange online. If you're planning a complex itinerary, realize that you might not be able to complete all the arrangements on the Web. However, it's a great place to start your plans.

Where are those newsgroups?

Each ISP decides which newsgroups to carry. If you can't find a newsgroup, check it out at Deja.com (www.deja.com). If you like the group, contact your ISP and ask for the group to be included on the list of newsgroups to which you can subscribe.

Live for danger

If you're looking for a different vacation this year—one with a little danger, visit the Fielding's Danger Finder at www.fieldintravel.com/df/advguide.htm. You'll find links to all types of adventurous vacations.

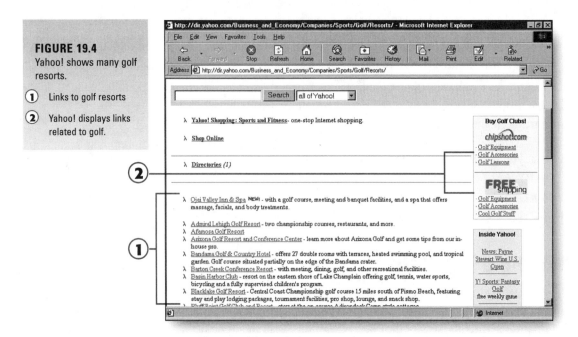

FIGURE 19.4
Yahoo! shows many golf resorts.

① Links to golf resorts

② Yahoo! displays links related to golf.

Internet Travel Agencies

If you're planing your trip from scratch, you'll need complete, current information on destinations, special offers, and promotions. Making air, car, and hotel reservations online can save you a lot of time and expensive phone calls. Table 19.4 shows you some of the best travel agencies on the Web.

Table 19.4 Internet travel agencies

Name	URL	Comments
Preview Travel	www.previewtravel.com	Find detailed information about airline flights, including the safety rating of the listed aircraft. Set up a profile for future bookings.
Travelocity	www.travelocity.com	The service is powered by SABRE, the reservation system used by many professional travel agents. You'll need to register with the service and call or fax your credit card information before you can purchase tickets. Travelocity provides sections for Today's Lowest Fares and Last Minute Deals.

Name	URL	Comments
Internet Travel Agency	www.itn.net	Subscribe to the service to get the best air deals, driving directions, and great deals on complete vacation packages. You'll also get a free subscription to *Webflyer* magazine.
Internet Travel Mall	thirdrock.com/itm	Internet Travel Mall is a navigational guide to hundreds of travel-related links. You'll find links to airlines, cruises, motor-coach travel, and more. You can even find links to travel agencies in out-of-the- way locations like Belize or Antarctica.
Travel Discounters	www.travel discounters.com	Use this site to find the lowest airline fares available. The site also features monthly specials and tips for finding the lowest fares.

Using Microsoft's Expedia Travel

The Microsoft Expedia.com site at www.expedia.msn.com is the premier travel site on the Web (see Figure 19.5). Collected in Expedia's pages is everything you'll need to plan the perfect vacation. You can visit the site on the Web or, if you're using Internet Explorer, you can add it to your active channels. The Expedia service is free. However, Expedia requires you to register to access their travel planning services. The registration is accomplished with a Registration Wizard that asks you to fill in some basic information about yourself. The information you submit is processed over a secure connection.

After you've registered with Expedia, you can use their Reservations service, look for a airline tickets with the Roundtrip Fare Finder, book a complete vacation with Vacation Packages, or find late-breaking vacation discounts. If you need help with any of your travel plans, a live travel agent is only a quick click away. Using the secure payment system, you can even pay for your vacation online.

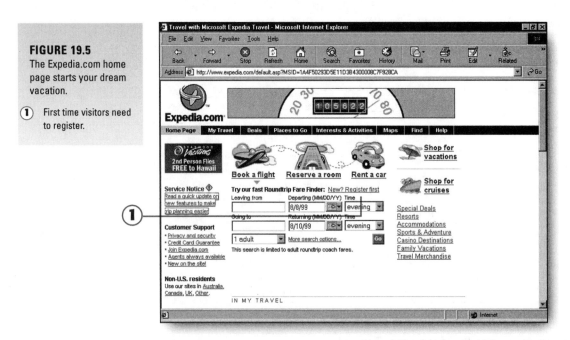

FIGURE 19.5
The Expedia.com home page starts your dream vacation.

(1) First time visitors need to register.

Short Notice-Cheap Flights

If you're footloose and fancy-free, you can get some incredible deals on airfare. Most of the airlines make these fares available only to Internet customers. Your travel agent probably can't get you a deal like this. However, if you want to take advantage of the low fares, you might have to wait until the last minute. Most of the sites shown here release their discounted fares on Wednesday, so be sure you check back then. If you wait until later in the week, the tickets will probably be sold.

- AmericaWest at `www.americawest.com`, as shown in Figure 19.6, calls their special Internet fare program Surf and Go. After you've registered, you can click the link to take advantage of the savings.

- Canadian Airlines at `www.cdnair.ca` offers great bargains on airfares, vacation packages, car rentals, and hotels for the upcoming weekend. New destinations are added every Wednesday and these special rates are available only at the Web site and must be reserved by calling Canadian Airlines (airfares only); in Canada at 1-800-665-1177 or in the US at 1-800-426-7000.

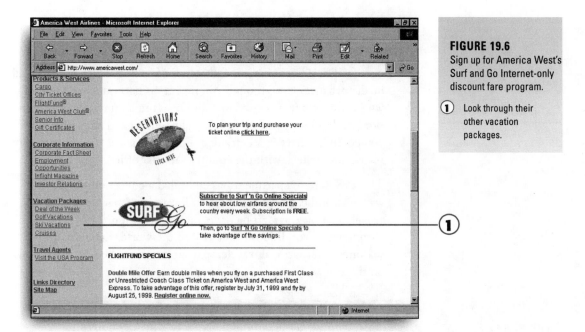

FIGURE 19.6
Sign up for America West's
Surf and Go Internet-only
discount fare program.

(1) Look through their
other vacation
packages.

- US Airways at www.usairways.com has E-Saver fares that offer dramatic discounts for last-minute weekend get-away travelers. After you subscribe to the E-Saver program, you'll receive an email notification each time special fares are available from your city.

- WebFlyer at www.webflyer.com offers a Deal Watch section that collects all the Internet-only weekend fares from both domestic and international airlines and displays them together, listed by originating city.

Tips for International Travel

Traveling outside your home country is not without risk. When you visit a foreign country, you are subject to its laws. Learn about local laws and regulations and obey them. Avoid areas of unrest and disturbance. Deal only with authorized outlets when exchanging money or buying airline tickets and travelers checks. Never deliver a package for anyone—unless you know the person well and are certain the package does not contain drugs or other contraband.

Currency converter

Foreign currency can look like play money if you're not used to dealing with it. Use the currency converter at www.oanda.com to figure out what you're really spending.

Some countries are particularly sensitive about photographs. In general, refrain from photographing police and military installations and personnel; industrial structures including harbor, rail, and airport facilities; border areas; and scenes of civil disorder or other public disturbance. Even though you meant no harm, taking pictures where you're not supposed to could result in an unexpected detention. Additionally, you could lose your camera and film, and worse, you could be charged a hefty fine. For information on photography restrictions, check with the country's tourist office.

The U.S State Department has compiled a collection of travel warnings and consular information located at `travel.state.gov/travel_warnings.html`. The page, pictured in Figure 19.7, is a good barometer to conditions in the rest of the world. Even if you're a seasoned international traveler, pay attention to the warnings shown on the site.

FIGURE 19.7
Check for warnings before you travel internationally.

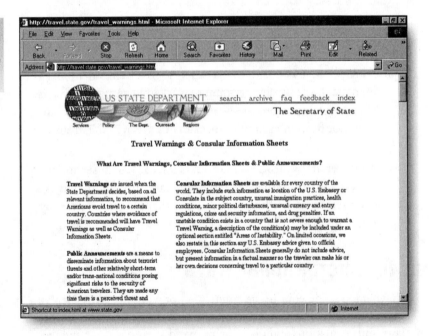

Additionally, use common sense when you're traveling out of your home country. Stay away from volatile situations, civil war, or unrest, or any place with severe disease or health problems. Your safety comes first. You want to be able to travel again, next year.

chapter 20

Hot Tunes and Games Galore

Learning about MP3 files •

Finding a player •

Listening to MP3 •

Playing games on the Internet •

What's an MP3?

Top 10 search term

MP3 is one of the hottest terms on the Web. In fact, most of the search tools on the Web report that the term "MP3" is one of the 10 most popular searches performed by users.

MP3s are small files that contain compressed sound. With this relatively new file format, incredible sounds that you can't tell apart from a CD come out your speakers. You'll be amazed, and will never again look at your computer the same way.

MP3 files are different than other sound files you can play on your computer (such as *.wav files*). Because of their unique qualities, MP3s have attracted the attention of the recording industry and people who love music. Some people think that the MP3 format will change the way music is recorded and sold.

More horsepower

To handle MP3 files successfully, your computer needs high horsepower. If you're planning to download and save MP3 files, you'll need lots of hard drive space (a typical MP3 file is around 4 megabytes in size). The time it takes for the file to play has a definite correlation with the speed of your processor and the amount of RAM that's installed in your computer. The higher the number of each, the faster the file will play.

For openers, your computer needs to have a sound card and a good set of speakers to play MP3 files. Your computer also needs a special player that's designed to handle MP3 files. (We'll talk about specific MP3 players later in this chapter.) MP3s are so popular, that you can obtain a portable MP3 player, or one that's designed to be used in your car.

The Birth of MP3

The history of the idea of downloadable digitized music occurred back in 1987 in Erlangen, Germany. A computer scientist named Dieter Sietzer, working with Germany's *Fraunhofer Institut Integriete Schaltungen*, attempted to devise a method for broadcasting sound in a compressed, digitized form. Their combined efforts resulted in a new mathematical algorithm, called a *codec*, an acronym for COmpression/DECompression. The codec was able to compress the size of a sound file without reducing its audio quality.

The Moving Picture Experts Group, (MPEG) approved the standard in 1992. The new files, alternatively called MPEG-1 or MP3, were revolutionary. However, even though the new files were relatively small, downloading an MP3 file with a slow modem could take an incredible amount of time—sometimes several hours. However, when modems hit speeds of 56K and computer processors got faster, the download process became faster.

College students were the first to embrace the MP3 format. Using somewhat crude recording equipment, students were able to *rip* songs from expensive CD's and make them available for free on the

Web. Soon everyone was listening to MP3. The record industry was quick to respond, with warnings and lawsuits about copyright infringements.

Right now, digital music rules the Web. Thousands of downloads are available for free. The recording industry is planning to market MP3s, with various payment schemes. Soon, you'll be able to create your own custom jukebox by downloading your favorite songs.

Are MP3s Legal?

MP3 files are legal if the song's copyright holder has granted permission to download and play the song. It is also legal to make copies of songs from CDs that you own for personal use.

It is illegal to make or download MP3 files without permission from the copyright holder, usually the artist or the record company, if the files are going to be distributed in any way. Of course, it is also illegal to encode music on CD's to MP3 format and then sell the encoded files.

Grabbing a Good MP3 Player

Just as every record collection needs a record player, the most important part of listening to MP3s is getting the right software program that can handle them. If your computer already has the latest version of the Windows Media Player or RealPlayer G2 installed, you'll be able to listen to MP3s. However, figuring out if you've got the latest and greatest versions of either media player can be difficult.

Your best bet is to download and install a media player designed to work with the MP3 format. Fortunately, you'll only have to do this one time. There are many different players that are available. The programs shown here will work with either browser and are all excellent choices.

SEE ALSO

➤ *You can review how to download files on page 188*

Hooked on MP3

If you find that you love MP3s, consider getting yourself a freestanding player that can be used at home or in your car. The Saehan MP-F20 uses flash cards and 32 megabytes of built-in memory to provide an hour's worth of music. Visit www.mpman.com for more information on the MP-F20 and other Saehan players. If you want MP3 music in your car, visit www.empeg.com for more information about the Empeg Car player. The Empeg sits on your dashboard and holds up to 35 hours of music (about 5,000 MP3 songs).

- RealJukebox, available at www.real.com/welcome/realjukebox, is made by the same folks that produce the RealPlayer G2. RealJukebox is considered by many people to be the best MP3 player. In addition to playing digitized music files that are stored on your computer or have been saved from the Web, use RealJukebox to search the Web for MP3 files or even purchase MP3s online. One of the best features offered by RealJukebox is the ability to create your own MP3 files from an audio CD that's loaded into the CD-ROM drive of your computer. RealJukebox, like RealPlayer G2, can be used for free. You can upgrade to a better model with more bells and whistles for around $29. (See Figure 20.1.)

FIGURE 20.1
Learn about the exciting RealJukebox software.

① Click the link for detailed instructions on setting up the player.

- Winamp, available at www.winamp.com, is a media player that handles MP3s and all of your sound needs. The program is easy to install and use, and comes with some neat visual add-on—like the frequency analysis display. Winamp is a shareware program. You can try Winamp for free. If you like it, registering your copy of Winamp will cost you around $10.

- The MusicMatch Jukebox lets you manage CD-quality music downloaded from the Web or from audio CDs. Advanced options include fade control. The stripped down version with lower audio quality is free. The full package runs around $30. Visit the MusicMatch home page at www.musicmatch.com.

Setting Up Your Player

Once the download is complete, you'll need to set up your player to work with your browser. Navigate to the folder where you saved the installation file and then double-click the file to begin the setup process. Installation is usually straightforward. Follow the onscreen prompts to complete the installation. Depending on the player you select, you might be asked to close your browser, disconnect from the Internet, or even reboot your computer.

During the installation process, one piece of information is key. You'll be asked into which folder you want to download the MP3 files you save from the Web. You can choose a particular folder, or you can accept the default folder, as shown in Figure 20.2.

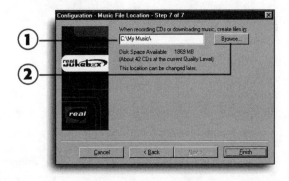

FIGURE 20.2
The RealJukebox specifies a folder for downloads.

① Downloaded music will be saved in the folder shown here.

② Click the Browse button to select another folder.

Make sure that you make a note of where the music files will be saved. If you want to send the file to a friend, or listen to it later on, you'll need to know in which folder it is saved.

As with any file you download and save to your hard drive, you need to delete the MP3 files that you don't want. Even the roomiest hard drive can get filled up with old files. Don't wait until you're out of space to get rid of the unwanted files.

Finding the Tunes

Only one

Be careful about downloading and installing more than one MP3 player. When you install a player, information is added to your Windows Registry as part of the installation process. If you install another player, most likely the information about the new player will overwrite the one you installed previously, making the new player the default.

Once the software for your MP3 player has been set up, you're ready to find some music. You can purchase CDs that contain MP3s at Amazon.com (www.amazon.com) and play them through the MP3 player you downloaded and set up. You can also turn to other sites on the Web. There are thousands of sites on the Web that feature MP3 music. Some of the sites offer free MP3 files, while others charge a nominal fee per tack. Table 20.1 shows you some of the best sites on the Web for finding MP3s to download to your computer.

Table 20.1   MP3 music sites on the Web

Name	URL	Cost Per Track	Comments
Liquid Audio	www.liquid audio.com	Free to $1.99	Browse through a catalog of over 5,400 tracks broken down into 23 categories. Both major and independent artists are represented. There's even a free downloadable player available at the site.
eatsleepmusic.com	www.eatsleep	Free	The site has over 1,500 MP3s for you to download. If you're into singing along, buy the $49.95 karaoke package.
MusicMatch	www.music match.com	Free tracks subscription to 25 new tracks is $4.99 monthly	Features recordings by mostly unknown artists. Also has links to many other sites.
MP3.com	www.mp3.com	Free	Music is divided by genre or region. You could spend a day here and not come close to listening to every song that's available at this massive site.

Name	URL	Cost Per Track	Comments
World Wide Bands	`www.worldwide bands.com`	Free	Alternative, jazz, blues, and hip hop from artists around the globe.
MP3Spy	`www.mp3spy. com`	Free	Listen to MP3s, search the Web for more, and get the latest MP3 news here.
EMusic.com	`www.emusic. com`	Around $1.00 per track	10,000 high-quality MP3 tracks with tunes ranging from alternative rock to gospel.
UBL.com	`www.ubl.com`	Free	UBL.com features five new MP3 files a week from alternative and pop artists who authorize free distribution. While you're here, visit the Advance Listening Station to hear music before it's released.
MP3now	`www.mp3now. com`	Free	In addition to loads of music available for download, you'll find technical information and links to the best MP3 players. Search the site by artist or lyric if you're looking for a special song.

If you can't find the song or type of tune you're looking for, use your favorite search tool, like Yahoo! or HotBot, to find the music you like. As shown in Figure 20.3, you can make your query as specific as you like.

FIGURE 20.3
A Boolean search at
HotBot finds just what
you're looking for.

(1) Original query

(2) Result

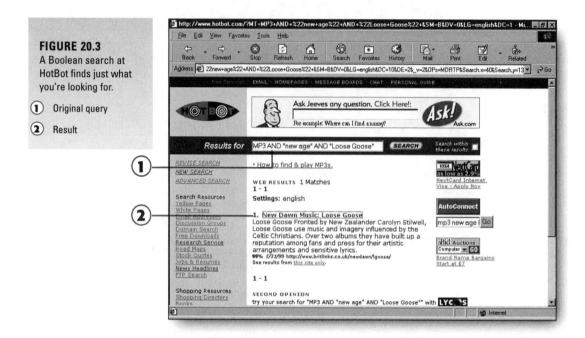

FIGURE 20.3
A Boolean search at
HotBot finds just what
you're looking for.

(1) Original query

(2) Result

Playing MP3s from the Web

MP3 files appear as links on Web pages. You can click an MP3 link
to play it, or you can specify that you want to save the file and play
it later.

When you click a link on a Web page to play an MP3 file, a
three-step process begins on your computer. First, the MP3 file
is copied (downloaded) from the Web to your computer. As the
download progresses, Internet Explorer users see a dialog box,
advising them of the progress of the download (see Figure 20.4).
Navigator users can track the progress of the download in the
Viewing Location dialog box.

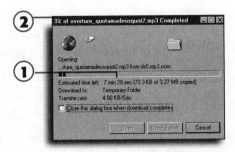

FIGURE 20.4
The Internet Explorer
File Download box
appears as the file is
downloading.

(1) Estimated time left

(2) Percentage of
completeness

When the download is complete, your MP3 player opens and loads
the file. To complete the process, the MP3 player plays the file for
your enjoyment. Figure 20.5 shows RealJukebox, playing a song that
was downloaded from the Web.

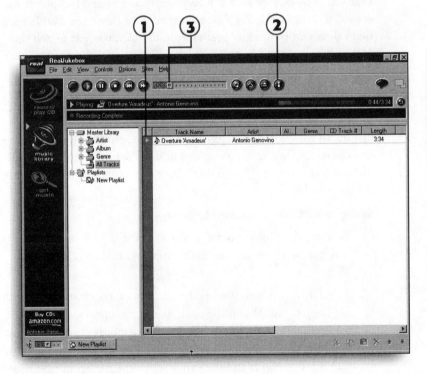

FIGURE 20.5
RealJukebox plays the
downloaded song.

(1) Arrow indicates the
song is being played

(2) Control buttons

(3) Drag the slider to
advance the play.

You can continue downloading and playing MP3s as you work on your computer. The songs you download will be added to your *playlist* and can be replayed again and again.

When you choose to save an MP3 file, the file is saved to your computer hard drive. When you want to play the file, open your MP3 player and load the file to hear the music.

Is it better to click **Play** or **Save** when you're downloading an MP3 file from the Web? The answer is complex, because it depends on what you're trying to accomplish. If you want to hear one MP3 at a time, then opt to play the file. If you're working on an important project and you don't want to listen to music now, save the file and listen to it when it's convenient.

Files that you play or save can be played from your MP3 player or copied to a *Superdisk*, *Zip disk*, or *cartridge*, or other removable media that's designed to hold large files. Additionally, you can attach the MP3 file to an email message and send it to a friend or colleague.

Saving an MP3

Saving an MP3 file can be accomplished up with a little Windows magic. To complete the steps of the exercise, connect to the Internet and open your browser. Cruise through MP3 sites and find the MP3 file you want to save. (If you don't have your own favorite site, visit www.mp3now.com.)

Saving an MP3 file with Internet Explorer

1. Position the mouse pointer on the MP3 file you want to save and right-click. A pop-up menu appears, as shown in Figure 20.6.

2. The File Download box appears briefly as information about the file is gathered. When the Save As dialog appears, the name of the song followed by an MP3 extension appears in the File name text box. (If the file has another extension, such as .htm or .cgi, wait a few seconds and then right-click the file again.) Navigate to the folder where you'd like to store the music file.

3. When the folder name you selected appears in the Save in text box, click **Save**.

Play or save

Whether you choose to play or save an MP3, the file is saved to the hard drive of your computer. When you choose **Play**, the file is saved to a temporary folder on your computer before you hear the tune. Make a note of the filename so you can search for it and then delete the file later on. Otherwise, your hard drive will be filled with old MP3 files that you played one time.

FIGURE 20.6
Use the shortcut menu to
save the MP3 file to disk.

① Choose Save
Target As.

4. The File Download box appears as the file is saved to your computer. Make a note of both the folder name to which the file is being saved and the name of the file. You'll need this information later on, if you want to play the file or work with it in any other way.

Like their Internet Explorer counterparts, Navigator users can save MP3 files with a few mouse clicks. Before you begin the steps of the exercise, make sure you know to which folder you want to save the MP3 files. It's a lot easier to figure this out ahead of time, instead of when you're saving the actual files.

You'll need to be connected to the Internet. Use Navigator to browse to an MP3 file you want to save. (If you're not sure of any sites yet, visit MP3.com at www.mp3.com.)

Saving MP3 files with Netscape Navigator

1. Place the mouse pointer on the music file you want to save and right-click.

2. When the menu appears, select **Save Link As**.

3. The Save As box appears with the filename displayed in the **File name** text box.

4. Navigate to the folder where you want to store the file. To begin the process, click the drop-down arrow next to the **Save in** box and choose a drive (such as C:, as displayed in Figure 20.7). After you select a drive, the contents of the drive appear in the Contents box. If necessary, use the scrollbar to find the folder you're planning to store the MP3 files in. When you find the folder, double-click to open it and then click **Save**.

5. The Saving Location dialog box appears as the file is being saved. Depending on the size of the file, the save process can take a while.

   That's it! You can open your MP3 player and play the file at any time.

Recording Your Own MP3 Files

Creating MP3 files is not for novices! Although in theory it's easy to record your own MP3 files, in practice it's a little harder to accomplish the task. Generally, MP3 files are created from sound files on your computer, or from CDs loaded into your CD-ROM drive. Special software, including a *ripper* and an *encoder*, is required.

Your MP3 player might contain the necessary components and be able to handle the recording process. Check the **Help** menu on your player to make sure. However, even if your MP3 player can record MP3 files, your CD-ROM drive may be an older model that's not compatible.

If you want more information on creating your own MP3 files, visit the MP3 for Beginners-Making MP3s page at www.mp3.com/faq/making.html. In addition to how-to information, you'll find links to articles and a CD-ROM compatibility list.

Playing Games

There are many different types of games on the Internet. You can play by yourself, test your skills with others, or even get involved in interactive role-playing. You can even play online versions of your favorite television games shows.

In addition to playing games, you can talk about your favorite game in a chat session or join a newsgroup or mailing list that's devoted to discussing games-related topics (see Figure 20.8). You can even download an endless supply of games software that will keep you tied to your computer and off the streets. Whatever your taste in games, there's a good chance that you'll find a game or two that you enjoy on the Web.

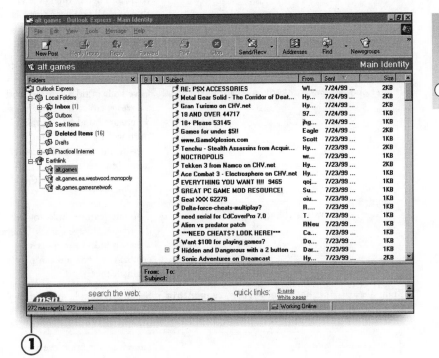

FIGURE 20.8
The alt.games newsgroup has people talking.

① Number of postings

Brain Games

Games that make you think are good for your brain. They give you a chance to be creative and expand your mind. If you're tired or stressed, taking a quick break with a brain game or two might actually improve your job performance.

Table 20.2 shows you some great spots for brain teasers.

Table 20.2 Food for your mind

Name	URL	Comments
Madlibs	www.webcomics.com/madlib/	Remember playing with Madlibs as a kid? Well, they are back, and better then ever at this site. All you have to do is fill in a form with silly nouns, adjectives, and more. You'll laugh when you see Madlibs other players have created.
Brain Food	www.rinkworks.com/brainfood/	Give your mind a workout with a devious collection of puzzles. There are hundreds, ranging from word games to logic problems to riddles. Some are tricky. Some require innovation. All require thinking power. Good luck!
Cribbage	www.cribbage.org	This site features links to several different cribbage games. There are even links to interactive cribbage, where you can play against others.
Brain Teaser	highballmedia.com/teaser.htm	Seemingly simple questions will keep you guessing for a long time.
duJour.com	www.dujour.com	Exercise your brain every day at duJour.com. After you take a moment or two to register, you can play several brain games that require some concentration.
The Case.com	www.thecase.com	Solve a new mini-mystery every day.

Playing Games with Others on the Web

Playing by yourself is fun at times but it can get awfully lonely. How about playing a game or two with people from all over the world? With the Web as a backdrop, you can make new friends and have fun at game sites all over the Web.

Playing interactive games can be done for free at many sites. Most times you'll need to register before you can jump into the game. The busiest connection times are during weekday evenings and weekends. If you're new to the game, try connecting during off-peak hours to see if you like it. You'll encounter much less traffic and find that the play proceeds at a slower pace.

If you're connecting to the Internet from work or school, check with your network administrator before you visit a game site. Many corporations use firewalls that won't allow you to connect to interactive game sites. Additionally, some companies can (and do) track the Internet travels of their employees. Playing Internet games could get you in serious hot water.

Perfectly polite, normal people sometimes turn into lunatics when they play online games. Try to keep yourself under control. Follow these simple rules of courtesy. The fact that you're playing the game on your computer never gives you a license to be rude or uncouth.

- Don't type nasty or sarcastic comments if your opponent loses or makes a mistake. It's tempting, sometimes, to zing a scorching comment at someone whom you consider to be an idiot. Remember that you could be the idiot next time in someone else's eyes!

- Don't disconnect or leave the game simply because you're losing. Once you start the game, stick it out until the finish. If you're really getting skunked, watch your opponent's tactics so you can use them the next time you play.

- Don't type messages to your fellow competitors in uppercase letters. Just like the rules of newsgroups and chat, capital letters indicate SHOUTING and are considered rude.

- Don't enter an Advanced room or site unless you really are a whiz. Play in the lower levels for a few times so you can learn the rules

Use your alias

If you're not sure that you want to leave your personal email address at an online gaming site, register with your free email address instead of the one you normally use. That way, you can try out the site anonymously. (Learn more about obtaining a free email account in Chapter 9, "Starting Out with Email.")

of the road. Most people who play advanced games really are advanced and they won't appreciate your fumbling around.

- Don't take the game so seriously that you forget the main reason you're there—to have fun.

Where can you go to play? Start out with the game sites at the Web's best search tools. Yahoo!'s game site, pictured in Figure 20.9, at `games.yahoo.com` brings you the chance to play challenging games against people from all over the world.

FIGURE 20.9
There are lots of games to keep you busy at Yahoo! Games.

① This many people are playing

② Name of the game

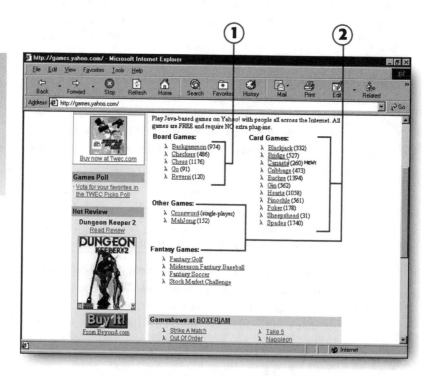

When you click a link to a game at the Yahoo! Games site, you're moved into a waiting area where you can choose the room in which you'd like to play. The rooms are labeled according to their proficiency level, so pay attention to which one you select.

Search engine games

Check out the interactive games at Lycos (`www.lycos.com`) and Excite (`www.excite.com`).

Join a Gaming Service

If you're really an avid gamer, you can join a gaming service on the Web. Many of the gaming services are free, although some services charge a membership fee. Joining a service is a good way to play your favorite games. You'll have a better chance of being paired with opponents whose skill level and interests match your own.

Depending on the game, you might have to download and install software on your computer before you can play. Don't be so caught up in the excitement of the moment that you forget to find out the system requirements for the software. If your computer is running Windows and the software will only work on a Mac, you've wasted time and, quite possibly, money.

Table 20.3 provides you with information about some of the gaming services you can join on the Web.

Table 20.3	Multi-player gaming services on the Web			
Name	URL	Cost	Games	Comments
2AM	www.2am.com	Free	Various, including Chain of Command, Total War, Poker, Chess, and Backgammon	2AM is part of the AltaVista network. You'll need to obtain the software and register before you can play.
HEAT	www.heat.net	Free for perimeter service, $5.95 for Premium	Various action games	A must for the serious action gamer. Superfast Internet connection makes the games live. Tech support is available seven days a week.

continues...

Table 20.3 Continued

Name	URL	Cost	Games	Comments
Imagic	www.imagic games.com	Free for basic service with other pricing plans available	Free for players of Backgammon, Checkers, Chess, and a scaled-back version of the Kingdoms of Drakkar	One stop gaming for everyone. Emphasis is on action games that require installation of software.
NTN	www.ntn.com	Free	Sports games, trivia	The Web-based version of the games on this network is similar to the NTN games played in restaurants and bars. Sample games are available at the site.
Vibes.com	www.vibes.com	Free	Mankind	Interactively participate in the ongoing sci-fi game called Mankind. Although there's no charge for playing, a full-blown version of Mankind software will set you back a few dollars.
The Station	www.station. sony.com	Free	Jeopardy, Wheel of Fortune, Trivia, and others	Play your favorite TV games online. Choose between 1 or multi-player options.

One of the biggest free gaming sites on the Web is called the Microsoft Zone. The site, located at zone.microsoft.com, is massive. You can play online games, purchase retail games, and get helpful hints about how to proceed. The site, pictured in Figure 20.10, is well ordered and easy to navigate.

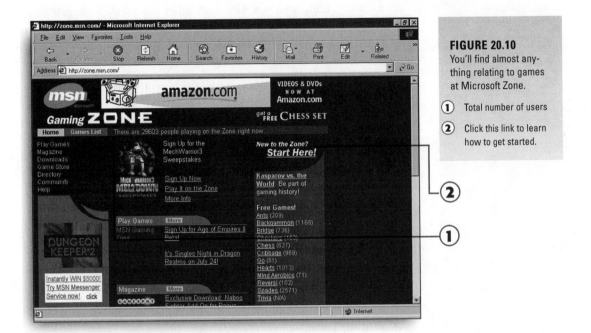

FIGURE 20.10
You'll find almost anything relating to games at Microsoft Zone.

① Total number of users

② Click this link to learn how to get started.

Playacting on the Internet

If you have a flair for drama and even the tiniest spark of imagination, you might enjoy a role-playing game. You've probably played some roles as a child (every kid plays "Let's Pretend" or "House" at one point or another). Maybe you've even acted in a play as an adult, or even been thrust into a real-life situation where you had to act a certain way. You're probably a good role-player right now.

In a role-playing game on the Internet, you assume the identity of a character and create a story around that character. The other game players also create stories around their characters. In a role-playing game, or *RPG* for short, the stories are blended together by an overseer called the *game-master*.

One person in an Internet role-playing game plays the role of gamemaster. The game begins when the editor sets the scene. He describes a world or setting and the situation on which the game is based. RPGs are based on the information and action provided by each player. An RPG story evolves over time.

Is it a MUD?

Back in the Internet's infancy, people played role-playing games called *MUD*'s (short for Multi-User Dungeon). MUDs, and similar games called MOOs and MUCKs, use a telnet connection to string their computers together. Although some folks are still passionate about their MUDs, most people enjoy the convenience of role-playing games using their regular Internet connection and their browser.

Listen to master

The gamemaster will tell you how your character should act in a situation. If you choose to ignore the instruction, the master is allowed to cancel your action, and make you do it the right way.

As the game progresses, each player takes a different character, and each character interacts with each other character. Role-playing, in this sense, is very much play-acting in the mind. You base your character's actions on information provided by the gamemaster. In turn, the other characters do the same.

Most of the time, RPG characters are involved in swashbuckling adventures or science fiction or fantasy settings. In one game, you might play the role of a King Arthur-like character, trying to rescue a sword or a lady. In another RPG, you might be a crew member, piloting an out-of-control spaceship. Your real gender isn't relative to the character you play; men play women and vice versa all the time.

RPGs Have Structure

RPGs have rules—very strict rules, in fact—about how the game should proceed. In every situation, your character cannot act in a manner that doesn't match the character's personality or physical appearance. For example, if your character, a one-legged dwarf, encounters a 30-foot rock wall, you can't just climb it and get on with the game.

Assume an Active Role

A great place for non-experienced RPG players to begin is the WebRPG home page (www.webrpg.com), shown in Figure 20.11. Read through the online manual that's posted at the site and find out what you'll need to get started. Most role-playing games are free but you'll need certain software installed on your computer. You'll find links to download the software, and find a group at the site. You can also look through some information for newbies.

Newsgroups about RPG playing can help you meet new friends. You'll find newsgroups, like the ones shown in Figure 20.12, that talk about almost every role-playing game. If you're looking for some information, or want to make some RPG contacts, lurk in some newsgroups for awhile and then post a message.

SEE ALSO

➤ *You can find more information about posting to newsgroups on page 272*

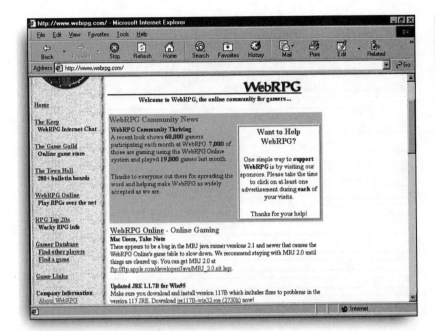

FIGURE 20.11
The WebRPG page shows you how to get started.

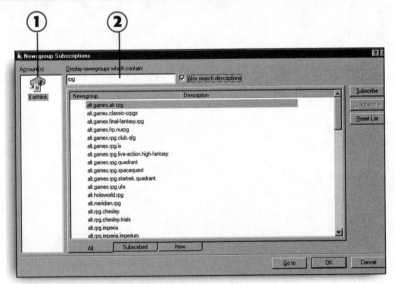

FIGURE 20.12
Click a group and then click Go to review the postings.

① The listing of the newsgroups that talk about RPG that are available on the Earthlink server

② Search criteria is rpg

chapter
21

Creating Your Own Web Site

Why Should You Build a Web Site?

Why should you build a Web site? Why not! Actually, there are as many reasons for building Web pages as there are people. Pages on the Web range from corporate sites to pages proclaiming an individual's likes and dislikes. For many people, creating Web pages is simply a hobby and a way to tell the world about themselves. The phrase "15 minutes of fame" translates to "15 megabytes of fame" on the Web.

Creating your own Web pages is a fun and educational process. Learning about Web site design may also be a boon to your career. Maybe you'll be the one assigned to update your company's Web site. You might even find that you have a flair for design and want to learn more so you can make Web site design your new vocation.

Web Page Elements

Web pages are created using HyperText Markup Language, usually called *HTML*. HTML isn't a language that you can speak. Instead, it consists of *tags* that tell your Web browser how to display text, images, links, and other aspects of a Web page. At first glance, HTML code might be intimidating. Relax! Many *WYSIWYG* (What You See Is What You Get) programs enable you to design Web pages without forcing you to learn about how to write HTML. In fact, if you're using Internet Explorer or Netscape Communicator, you probably already have a Web design program on your computer.

Although Web pages can take many forms, most Web pages contain common elements. Table 21.1 lists some of those elements and explains what they do.

Table 21.1 Common elements on a Web page

Table Element	Function
Page Title	Appears in the browser title bar. Many search engines index pages based on the words in the page title.
Headings	Break the page into sections, which add organization and visual interest. Headings range from size 6, the smallest, to size 1, the largest.

Table Element	Function
Text	The text on a Web page is the "meat," because generally it provides the information.
Graphics	Pictures tell a story. Graphics images on the page need to be added separately. Some designers add graphics images to the background of a page.
Lists	Web pages lend themselves to list format. By using lists, information can be presented in a clear, concise manner. Lists generally appear with bullets or numbers before each point.
Hyperlinks	Hyperlinks on a Web page provide jumps to other locations. Each link is actually made up of two parts. The *anchor*, which is the portion you click, is usually text but can be a graphic. The URL portion shows the location that the user moves to when the anchor is clicked.
Contact Information	Most pages display the name and email address of the page owner.

In addition to the elements shown in the table, the use of frames, tables, multimedia files, and *Javascript* are common.

SEE ALSO

➤ You can review how to navigate through frames on page 130

WYSIWYG Editors Do the Work

Unless you're an accomplished HTML writer, creating pages in HTML can get frustrating. For one thing, you probably don't know all of the codes and tags you need to make a Web page appear just the way you want it.

Happily, several WYSIWYG HTML editor programs take the guesswork out of Web page creation. All you need to do is type the text and add graphic images and maybe some multimedia effects. As you edit the page and move things around, the changes are automatically shown on the screen. During this time, your HTML editor is working in the background to generate all the necessary code.

Several good WYSIWYG programs are available for you to use. Fortunately, if you're using either the Internet Explorer or Netscape Communicator suite, you probably already have one installed on your computer.

Look at the code

Anytime you're viewing a Web page in your browser, you can view the HTML *source code*. In Internet Explorer, click **View**, and then select **Source**. Navigator users click **View**, and then **Page Source**. Your browser launches another window that contains the HTML code. Close the browser window when you're finished viewing its code to return to the page you were viewing previously.

Easy Page Building

One of the newest trends on the Web is the use of *Web page builders*—software that lets you point and click and build a credible page without too much effort. Many free services offer the services of Web page builders and then let you store your creation at no charge. If you're a member of My Yahoo!, for example, you can build a fabulous page with the Yahoo! GeoBuilder. The GeoBuilder, shown in Figure 21.1, lets you select your page from 35 templates and provides cool effects, like graphics and Web counters.

FIGURE 21.1
Use the GeoBuilder to make Web page building a snap.

(1) GeoBuilder opens in its own Window.

(2) This template is selected.

(3) Preview appears here.

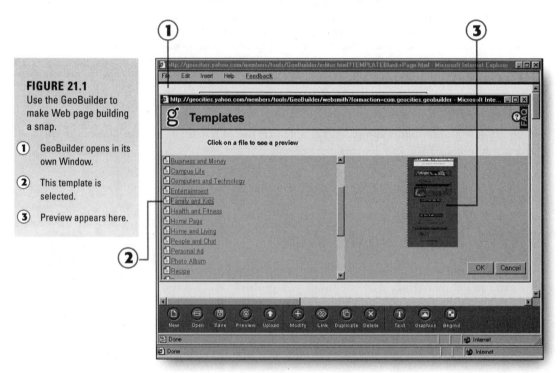

Introducing Microsoft FrontPage Express

Microsoft's FrontPage Express is a great Web page design program provided with the Internet Explorer suite. FrontPage Express is a scaled-down version of Microsoft's full-blown, commercial HTML editor called FrontPage. FrontPage Express makes it easy to build some very exciting Web pages without prior HTML experience.

FrontPage Express can help you create a simple page or one with some flair. You can add fonts, tables, Java applets, and sounds. A page designed in FrontPage Express can rival one created with a more expensive, harder-to-use WYSIWYG HTML editor.

Building your very first Web page

1. Click the **Start** button, choose **Programs**, and then select **Internet Explorer**, and then **FrontPage Express**. FrontPage Express opens with a blank page, as shown in Figure 21.2.

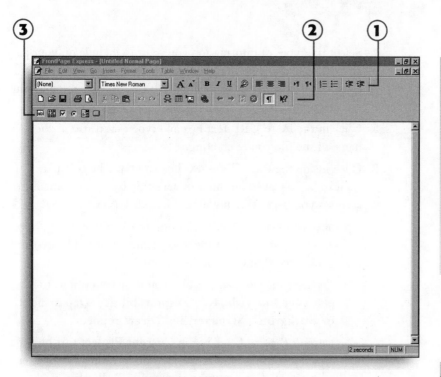

FIGURE 21.2
The FrontPage Express window.

(1) Formatting toolbar buttons change the appearance of text.

(2) Standard toolbar provides the most common commands and options.

(3) Forms toolbar is used for designing forms.

2. Click the **File** menu and choose **New**. The New Page dialog box appears.

3. Select **Personal Home Page Wizard** and click **OK**. The Personal Home Page Wizard dialog box appears, as shown in Figure 21.3. Several categories of information are already chosen for your page.

Upgrade to FrontPage

FrontPage Express is designed for individuals and small companies. If you want to add some really snazzy effects, or you're planning on hosting your own page, consider upgrading to Microsoft FrontPage.

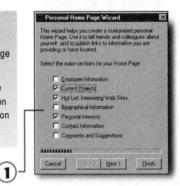

FIGURE 21.3
The Personal Home Page
Wizard.

① Checked boxes show
the type of information
that will be included on
your page.

①

Can't find the program?

If you can't find FrontPage
Express on your Windows
Start menu, or the program
doesn't open correctly,
you'll need to install it
again. If you installed
Internet Explorer from a
CD, insert the CD into your
CD-ROM drive and follow
the instructions to install
Internet Explorer add-on
components. Or, while
you're connected to the
Internet and using Internet
Explorer, click **Tools** and
Windows Update.
You'll be directed to the
Microsoft Windows Update
page. Scroll down the page
to the Internet Authoring
section, and follow the
instructions to download
and install the program.

4. Select the types of information you want to include on your page
   and click **Next>**. The next dialog box asks for a Page URL and a
   Page Title. (Uncheck one of the default boxes if you don't want
   its category to appear on your page.)

5. Click in the **Page URL** text box and type `index.html` as the
   name of the file you're creating.

6. Click inside the **Page Title** text box and type the title that you
   want to be displayed on the browser's title bar when someone
   accesses you page. When you're done, click **Next>**.

7. The next set of dialog boxes ask questions based on the options
   you chose in step 4. Fill in the information (as listed below) and
   click **Next>** to advance from box to box.

   - *Employee Information.* Enables you to select options to dis-
     play your **Job Title**, **Key Responsibilities**, **Department
     or workgroup**, **Manager**, and **Direct reports**.

   - *Current Projects.* Click in the **Current Project** text box and
     type a few things you're working on, pressing **Enter** after
     each one. Select a presentation style—**Bullet list**,
     Numbered list, or **Definition list**.

   - *Hot List of Interesting Web Sites.* Choose how to display the
     list of sites you like. You can display them as a **Bullet list**,
     Numbered list, **Definition list**, or **Import from Web
     page**. If you select **Import from Web page**, type the page's
     URL in the **File** text box.

   - *Biographical Information.* Select from **Academic**,
     Professional, or **Personal** format.

- *Personal Interests.* Type a few of your interests and choose how you want them to be displayed (see Figure 21.4).

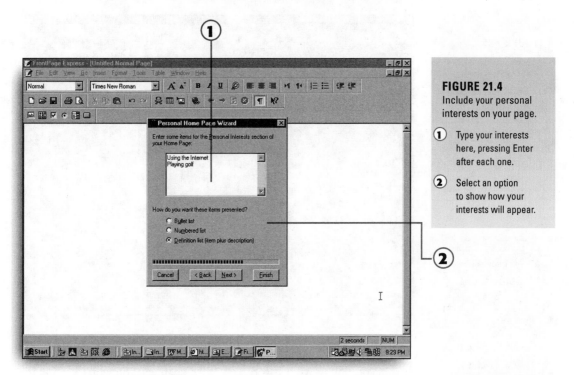

FIGURE 21.4
Include your personal interests on your page.

① Type your interests here, pressing Enter after each one.

② Select an option to show how your interests will appear.

- *Contact Information.* You can include as much or as little contact information as you'd like. Check the box next to **Postal Address, E-mail address, URL address, Office phone, FAX number,** and **Home phone** and type the information in the text box.

- *Comments and Suggestions.* People who visit your page will be able to tell you what they think of it. Unless you're planning to publish your Web page with the Microsoft Internet Information Server, choose the **Use Link, send e-mail to this address** option and type your email address in the text box.

8. When you've completed the boxes that ask for information on the sections you selected, a new dialog box appears showing your sections and asking in what order you'd like them organized. To move an item, click it and then click **Up** or **Down**. When the list is organized properly, click **Next>**.

Index is the first page

Web sites can consist of many pages. Many Web servers display a file called index.html as the first, or home page, of the site.

9. That's all you need for now! Click **Finish** for FrontPage Express to build the page, as illustrated in Figure 21.5.

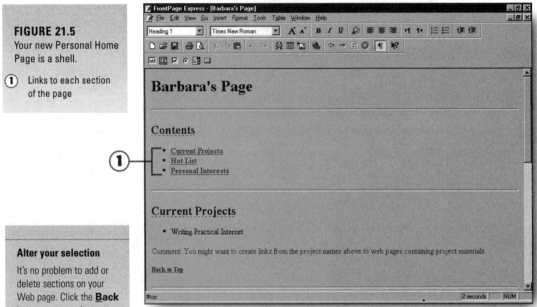

Now that you've created your page, take a moment and save it. If you don't save it before you make changes, you won't be able to return to the page's current shell format. Worse, you run the risk of losing all your work if you exit from FrontPage Express without saving the page. Saving takes only a few seconds and preserves your hard work.

Saving your new Web page

1. With the page you created on the screen, click the FrontPage Express **File** menu and choose **Save**. The Save As dialog box appears.

2. By default, the FrontPage Express defaults to saving your page onto a Web server. Change the default and save the page to the hard drive of your computer by clicking the **As File** button.

3. The standard Windows Save As dialog box appears. Navigate to the folder where you want to save the file. Click in the **File name** text box and type the same name that you assigned the file

in step 6 of the previous Step-by-Step exercise. (You probably named the file **index.html**.) It's not necessary to type the file extension—html—because it will be automatically assigned.

4. Click **Save**. Now you're ready to make changes to your page.

Not done yet

Don't close the page just yet. In the next few Step-by-Step exercises, you transform your page from a shell to a masterpiece!

Editing Your FrontPage Express Web Page

In essence, you created a shell when you set up your Personal Web Page with the Wizard. Now it's time to fill in the blanks and enter some information on the sections you selected. Before you begin, you need to understand a few basics about FrontPage Express.

First, working in FrontPage Express is a lot like working in your favorite word processing program. For example, as you reach the end of a line, FrontPage Express wraps the text to the next line, so you needn't press Enter. Adding formatting options like bold, italic, and underline to existing text is accomplished by highlighting the text and clicking the appropriate button on the Formatting toolbar. Most other Windows editing commands work as well.

Paragraph Styles Are Important

Keep in mind that the text you enter is always part of a paragraph style. Table 21.2 displays the name of the available styles and provides information about each one.

Table 21.2 FrontPage Express paragraph styles

Style Name	What It Does
Normal	Used for entering regular text without any text attributes.
Address	Used to create the name and email address of the owner of the page. The Address style is generally seen at the bottom of a page.
Bulleted List	Creates a list of items, with each item preceded by a bullet character. When the Bulleted List style is selected, pressing **Enter** adds another bullet to the list.
Defined Term	Items controlled by the Defined Term style appear lined up against the left margin.

continues...

495

Table 21.2   Continued

Style Name	What It Does
Definition	Used in conjunction with the Defined Term style, items using this style are formatted with an indent.
Directory List	When the Directory List style is selected, the resulting text appears to be formatted like a Bulleted List. However, both Internet Explorer and Navigator display text formatted with the Directory List style differently. Play it safe and use Bulleted List instead.
Formatted	Recognizes multiple blank spaces inserted with the keyboard spacebar. (Normal HTML code won't use more than one space between characters.)
Headings 1–6	The higher the number, the larger the font and darker the text.
Menu List	Like Directory List style, choosing Menu List will format text like the Bulleted List style. Don't use this style because it is handled differently by browsers; use Bulleted List instead.
Numbered List	When this item is selected, each line is preceded by a number.

Beware of fancy fonts

Even though you might be tempted to use some of the more dramatic fonts you have installed on your computer, restrict your choices to common fonts such as Arial, Times New Roman, Comic Sans, or Courier. A page that looks great on your computer won't display properly on another computer unless the same font is installed. By choosing a standard font, you'll be sure that your page always appears correctly—no matter who's looking at it.

If you want to select a style before you type text, click the **down arrow** on the **Change Style** button on the Formatting toolbar and choose the style you want. To change the style of existing text, highlight the text and then choose the style you want from the list of available styles.

Formatting and editing text

1. The page you created and then saved should be on the screen now. (If you accidentally closed the page, click the **File** menu from with FrontPage Express, and choose **Open**. When the Open File dialog box appears, click in the **From File** text box and click **Browse** to move to the folder where you saved the page. Select the file and click **Open**.)

2. The page title appears at the top of the page. Select the title and click the **Center** button 〔≣ ≣ ≣〕 on the Formatting toolbar. The title, still highlighted, appears centered on the page.

3. Click the **Increase Text Size** button 〔A〕 once to make the text bigger.

4. Click the **down arrow** next to the **Change Font** button, and choose another font from the list. You'll be able to choose a font that's installed on your computer.

5. Click the **Text Color** button ⌐. When the color dialog box appears, click a new color for the text and click **OK**. Make sure that you don't choose the same color for your background, because this will render the text invisible. (The text won't appear in the new color until you deselect it.)

6. Deselect the text by pressing the **right arrow** key.

7. Move down through your page and select some text you'd like to change. When the text appears highlighted, type the new text.

8. Continue replacing text by repeating step 7.

9. Add text anywhere on the page. Click the spot where you'd like the text to begin and start typing. Because FrontPage Express is a WYSIWYG editor, the text you add appears exactly as it will when you view the page in your browser.

10. To change the bland background, click **Format** and then **Background**. The Page properties dialog box appears with the Background tab selected, as shown in Figure 21.6.

11. Click the **down arrow** next to the **Background** that's currently selected and choose a color from the list. Don't choose the color that's the same as your text. Click **OK** to close the Page Properties dialog box and see the new color on your page.

12. Save the page by clicking **File** and then **Save**.

Adding a Link to Another Web Site

If you included a section for Hot Links on your Personal Web Page, FrontPage Express added some sample links that you can modify. You need to point these links to your favorite Web sites. Before you begin, make a note of a URL or two that you'd like to add.

A hyperlink is actually made up of two parts. The first part, called the *anchor*, is the text that appears in the Web page.

Replace placeholders

If you included a section for biographical information or another section for which you need to input your own personal data, you'll see some words that hold the space open. For example, instead of a calendar date, you might see the word "Date." Replace all the placeholders with real information.

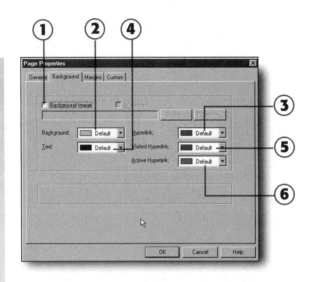

FIGURE 21.6
The Page Properties dialog box enables you to change the look of your page.

① Check this box to insert an image file for the background.

② Changes the background color

③ Changes the color of links

④ Changes the color of the text

⑤ Changes the color of links you've visited

⑥ Changes the color of the link that's being clicked

Other protocols

A hyperlink doesn't need to point to a Web page. In addition to the http protocol you selected, you can point a link to other Web protocols, including a *file, ftp, gopher, https, mailto, news, telnet,* and *wais*.

Adding working links

1. Scroll down the page to the Hot List section. Highlight the first sample link (**Sample Site 1**) and type the text you want to use as the anchor. (Since the text will be used as a hyperlink, it should indicate where the link will lead.) As you begin typing, the highlighted text is replaced by the characters you type.

2. Select the anchor text you just typed and click the **Create or Edit Hyperlink** button 🔘 on the Standard toolbar. The Edit Hyperlink window appears with the World Wide Web tab chosen, as shown in Figure 21.7.

3. Make sure that the **Hyperlink type** reads http:. If it doesn't, click the **down arrow** and choose **http://** from the list. Highlight the sample URL that appears in the **URL** text box and type another URL. (If you can't think of one, use **www. census.gov**, the address of the U.S. Census Bureau.) Check your typing to make sure you didn't make a typing mistake and click **OK**. The link appears on your page.

4. (Optional) Use an existing hyperlink on a page displayed in Internet Explorer to create a quick link. Open **Internet Explorer** (you need to be connected to the Internet) and move to the page that contains the link that you want to use. Click that link and drag it into the FrontPage Express window. When

the mouse pointer is positioned where you'd like the link to appear, release the mouse button. The link appears in your page, along with its anchor.

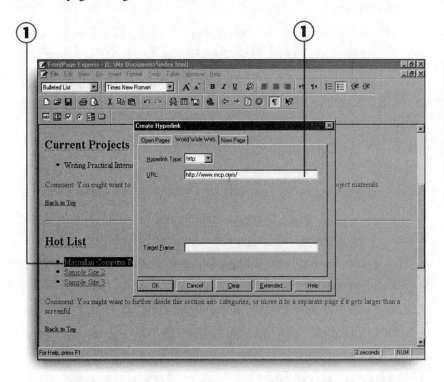

FIGURE 21.7
You can point a link to another site on the Web.

① Type the URL of the link.

② The highlighted text will be the link.

5. When you've added a few links, test them before you publish your page. If you're not already connected, connect to the Internet. Position the mouse pointer over the link and view the URL of the link in the status bar.

6. Edit a link by selecting the anchor and clicking the **Create or Edit Hyperlink** button on the Standard toolbar. When the Edit Hyperlink dialog box appears, make your changes and click **OK**.

Creating a Page with Netscape Composer

Netscape Composer is the component of the Communicator suite that enables you to create some great looking Web pages. Composer is a wonderful WYSIWYG editor. You can create a Web page from

A page is a terrible thing to waste

When you're making changes to your page in FrontPage Express, remember to save your work often. If you exit without saving, or your computer shuts down, your efforts will have been in vain. Saving takes a few seconds and preserves your changes.

Composer isn't installed

If you can't find Composer on your Windows Start menu, or you're sure you didn't install it, you can download Composer from the Netscape site in only a few minutes. From within Navigator, click **Help** and then **Software Updates** to get to the SmartUpdate page. Follow the onscreen prompts to download and set up Composer, and any other program in the Netscape Communicator suite.

scratch, or you can take the easy route and visit Netscape's Web site to access the Page Wizard or Netscape Templates. If you use a Wizard or Template, you can make editing changes later on in Composer.

Composer provides in-depth support for basic HTML elements, like links, images, and tables. The editing screen looks a lot like Navigator's browsing window, with a similar menu structure and two toolbars. The Composition toolbar is used for adding standard HTML features, and the Formatting toolbar takes care of character and paragraph formatting. The program works best when it's used to design a few individual pages or a small site. Composer doesn't offer support for frames or forms.

Composer offers the following features to make your Web page creation easier:

- Supports rich formatting, including fonts, styles, paragraph alignment, and bulleted and numbered lists.
- Includes built-in spelling checker.
- Supports drag-and-drop images, links, and Java applets.
- Includes Page Wizard and page templates.
- Enables easy table creation and editing.

Working with Netscape's Wizards and Templates

Creating a page with the Netscape Page Wizard or Templates is fast and easy. Best of all, you can create a dynamite-looking page without needing to know anything about HTML. Because you'll be visiting the Netscape Web site when you set up your page using the Wizard or Templates, you need to be connected to the Internet.

Beginning your page with the Netscape Page Wizard

1. Open **Navigator**. Click the **File** menu, choose **New**, and then select **Page From Wizard**. Navigator appears on the screen and the Netscape Page Wizard page loads in one frame of a three-framed page.

2. Scroll down the Page Wizard page and read the instructions. When you're ready to begin creating your page, click the **Start** button. The Instructions frame displays instructions for building your page while a preview of the page you're building appears in the right (Preview) frame.

3. Click the **give your page a title** link in the Instructions frame. The **Choices** text box appears in the Choices frame, located across the bottom of the page, as illustrated in Figure 21.8.

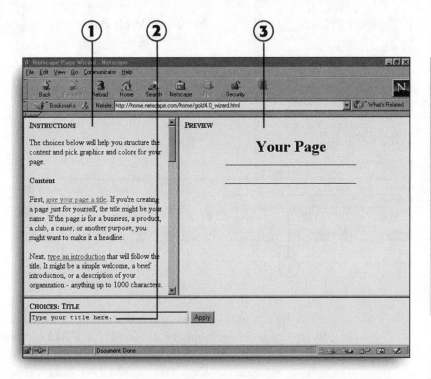

FIGURE 21.8
All the action takes place in the Netscape Page Wizard.

① Instructions frame contains links and information about building your page.

② Preview pane will be updated with your choices.

③ Highlight the text in the Choices text box and type the title for your page.

4. Highlight the text in the **Choices** text box and type your page title. When you're done typing, click the **Apply** button. Your title now appears in the Preview pane.

5. Click the **type an introduction** link. A new text box appears in the Choices pane. Highlight the text that appears in the box and type in a brief introduction to your page. When you're done, click the **Apply** button. Your Introduction text is added to your new page in the Preview pane.

Skip a category

Click the links and type text only for the sections you want on your page. If you don't want to include a section, such as an introduction or a conclusion, skip the link on the list in the Instructions frame.

6. Add a favorite link or two to your new page by scrolling down in the Instructions pane and clicking the **add some hot links to other Web pages** link (see Figure 21.9). Two new text boxes appear in the Choices pane.

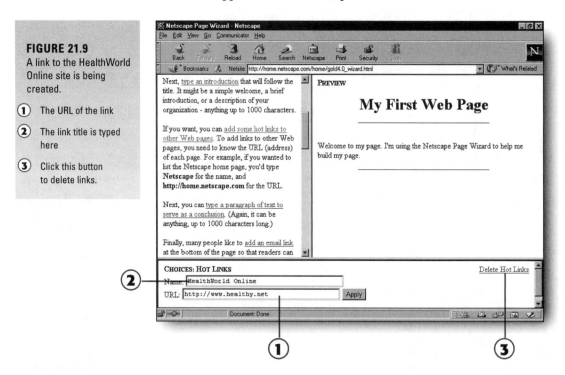

FIGURE 21.9
A link to the HealthWorld Online site is being created.

(1) The URL of the link

(2) The link title is typed here

(3) Click this button to delete links.

7. Highlight the text in the **Name:** text box and type in the name of a favorite page. Next, highlight the text in the **URL:** text box and type in the URL for the favorite page. (The HealthWorld Online page is located at www.healthy.net.) Check your typing carefully; if you've made an error, viewers will get an error message or the wrong page when they click the link on the finished page. After you're done, click the **Apply** button. Your link appears in the Preview pane.

8. Repeat steps 6 and 7 for each link you'd like to add.

9. Add some conclusion text to your page by scrolling down in the Instructions pane and clicking the **type a paragraph of text to serve as a conclusion** link. When the conclusion text box

appears in the Choices pane, highlight the text and type your conclusion text, taking care not to get long-winded and type something over 1,000 characters long. Click the **Apply** button when you're done to move your conclusion text to the Preview pane.

10. People can give you some feedback if you add an email link to yourself. Click the link to **add an email link**. When the email link box appears in the Choices pane, highlight the sample text and type your email address. Click **Apply**. An email link is added to the page, but you might need to scroll down in the Preview pane to see it.

11. Look over your page in the Preview pane. If you want to change anything you've added so far, click the link in the Instructions frame to the section you want to change. The text box that contains the text you typed for that section appears. Make the changes you want to the text in the box and click **Apply** to update the text in the Preview pane.

Dressing up your page with the Page Wizard

1. The page you created in the last Step by Step is visible on the screen. Scroll down the Instructions frame to the Looks section.

2. Choose one of the preset Netscape color schemes by scrolling down in the Instructions pane and clicking the **a preset color combination...** link. A sample of 18 different color schemes appears in the Choices pane, as shown in Figure 21.10.

3. Click one of color schemes that you like, and see how it looks in the Preview pane. If you want, try a few of the color combinations and choose the one you like best.

4. (Optional) If you'd rather add your own touch to the color scheme, do so by clicking the links below the link to the preset color combinations. One at a time, click the links to background color, background pattern, text color, link color, and visited link color, and choose a color from the palette displayed in the Choices frame.

5. Click the **choose a bullet style** link and pick the style of bullet you want to use to set off the lists on your page from the Choices frame. You'll be able to pick from simple bullets to animated squares.

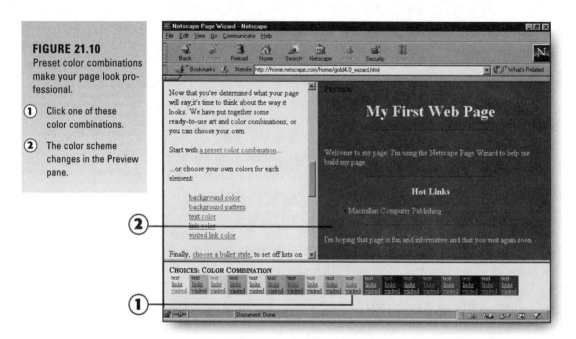

FIGURE 21.10
Preset color combinations make your page look professional.

① Click one of these color combinations.

② The color scheme changes in the Preview pane.

6. Choose a custom separator bar or horizontal line by clicking the **choose a horizontal rule style** link. Eighteen different line styles appear in the Choices pane. Scroll through and click the one you like.

7. You're done! Look at the completed page in the Preview pane and make any corrections now.

Saving the page to your computer

1. Even though you might not be aware of it, all the work you've done so far is up on the Netscape Web site. Before you go on, you need to save the page to your computer. Scroll down the Instruction pane and click the **Build** button. Your new page appears in a Navigator window, as shown in Figure 21.11.

2. Click the Navigator **File** menu and select **Edit Page**. The page now appears in Netscape Composer.

3. Save the page to your computer by clicking **File**, and then **Save**. When the Save As dialog box appears, navigate to the location where you want to save the page. The filename `yourpage.html` appears as the default name of the page. To change the default

name, click in the **File name** text box and replace the default name with whatever you'd like. Click **Save**.

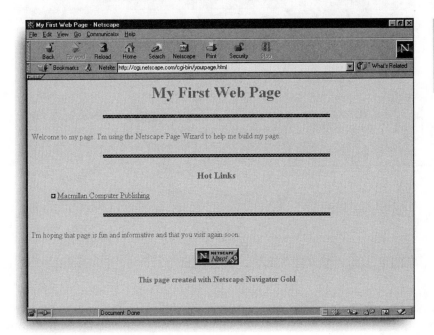

FIGURE 21.11
The completed page appears in Navigator.

Using some neat link tricks in Composer

1. Don't quit quite yet! First, add a link to a site on the Web that you've set as a bookmark. Click the **Communicator** menu and select **Bookmarks** and then **Edit Bookmarks**. The Bookmarks window layers over Composer.

2. Click a bookmark that you'd like to use as a link and drag it onto the Composer window. As you drag, your mouse pointer displays a small box attached to the tip (see Figure 21.12). When the pointer is located on the position you'd like the link to appear on page in Composer, release the mouse button.

3. Repeat step 2 to copy additional bookmarks to use as links. When you're done, close the **Bookmarks** window by clicking the **Close** box on its title bar.

SEE ALSO
➤ *Review how to set and work with Navigator Bookmarks on page 147*

Edit the page in Composer

Because Navigator and Composer look so much like one another, it's easy to forget which program you're using. Pages are edited in Composer and then previewed in Navigator.

FIGURE 21.12
The bookmark will become a link.

1. This bookmark is selected.

2. Mouse pointer has a box attached

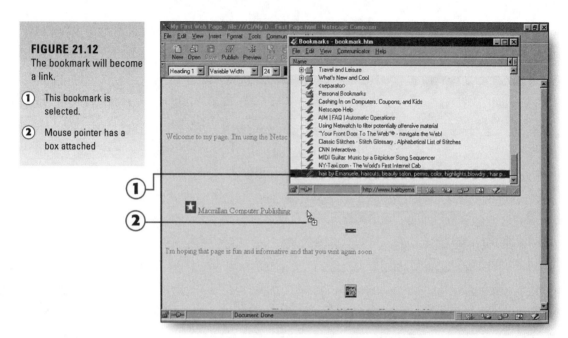

Composer distorts the graphics

Remember that you're working in Composer, not Navigator. The Netscape icon that was automatically inserted into your page might look distorted or squashed. Don't worry; it'll look fine when you view it in Navigator.

4. Some Web pages get quite lengthy. Make it easy for your viewers to get from the bottom to the top of your page with a mouse click. Press **Ctrl+Home** to move to the top of the page. When the insertion point is flashing at the top-left corner of the page, click the **Insert Target** button 🎯 on the Composition toolbar. Type `Top` in the resulting **Target Properties** text box. A target icon appears.

5. Press **Ctrl+End** to move to the very bottom of the page. Press the **Enter** key to move to the insertion point to a blank spot and click the **Insert Link** button. The Character Properties dialog box appears with the Link tab selected. The tab is divided into two sections.

6. In the first section, **Link source**, click inside the **Enter text to display for new link** text box and type `Return to top`.

   Move down to the second section, titled **Link to**. First, click the option button next to **Current page** and click **Top** in the **Select a named target in current page** text box. **#Top** appears in the **Link to a page location or local file** text box, as displayed in Figure 21.13.

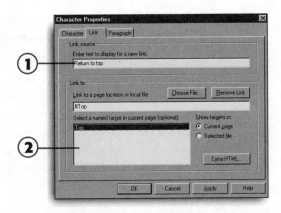

FIGURE 21.13
You control what happens when someone clicks a link on your page.

① Type the text for the link.

② The target shows the location to which the link leads.

7. Click **OK**. The Character Properties dialog box closes and you're returned to the Composer screen. The words `Return to top` appear at the end of the page.

8. Test your links by previewing your page in Navigator. Click the **Preview in Navigator** button. If you're informed you need to save the changes to the file before you can preview it, click **Y**es to save the file.

9. The page appears in Navigator. Click each of your links to make sure that they're working properly. If not, switch back to Composer. Highlight a non-working link and then click the **Insert Link** button. When the Character Properties dialog box appears, correct the error and click **OK**.

10. Remove a link on your page in Composer by highlighting it and selecting **E**dit, and then **D**elete. The link disappears from the page.

11. Save your page by clicking the **Save** button. (If you exit Composer without saving your page, all your work will be lost!)

SEE ALSO
➤ *You might have already created a résumé with the Netscape résumé template on page 387*

Pictures Tell a Story

Graphic images add appeal to most Web pages. Pictures draw the eyes of your viewers and catch their interest. Adding a few graphics to a personal Web page is a sure way to make sure that people stay and read you information when they land on your page.

There are only two types of images commonly used on Web pages—*GIF* (Graphic Interchange Format) and *JPEG* (Joint Photographic Experts Group) files. Both of these file types work well on Web pages because they offer good compression ratios. Compression is important on the Web because the smaller the image file size, the faster it will download and appear on your viewer's browser screen. (Don't you hate waiting while a picture slowly unfolds before your eyes?)

Getting Images for Your Page

Images for your Web page can be obtained in many different ways. One great way is to design them yourself. If you're the artistic type, you can use one of the many available computer graphics programs, such as Adobe PhotoShop or Corel Graphics to create your own images.

Another way to obtain images for your Web pages is to create them with a scanner or digital camera. In fact, the images created with a scanner or digital camera can be used in other electronic documents created with the latest versions of other computer software, like Microsoft Word.

All in one

If you're in the market for a scanner and a printer, consider getting a scanner/printer combination. The combination hardware, often called all-in-ones, can be used as a printer, scanner, and on the high-end machines, a copier and a fax machine. Visit the Hewlett-Packard site at www.hp.com for more information on their all-in-one products.

Scanners take a picture of the image and then convert the image to a graphics file. You can scan photographs, artwork, or even text documents. The most popular scanners come in two styles—flatbed and sheet feeder. A flatbed scanner looks like a desktop copy machine. A sheet-fed scanner takes up less space than a flatbed model. Some sheet-feeder scanners are small enough to sit behind your computer keyboard, making them handy to use as you work. Most scanners are easy to set up and install. Additionally, the price of scanners has dropped significantly in the last few years, making them affordable to most computer users.

If you're going to need a good number of photographs for your Web pages, consider purchasing a digital camera. Digital cameras bypass the paper stage because they store the images on your computer instead of negatives. You take photographs with a digital camera like you would with your regular camera. The resulting pictures must be downloaded to your computer with a serial cable that's part of the initial camera equipment. The images can be used on Web pages or other electronic documents. Digital cameras involve some cutting-edge technology. Although the price of the cameras has decreased in the last year or so, they are still expensive. Additionally, your computer needs a large hard drive and lots of RAM to work efficiently with the images.

In addition to creating, scanning, or photographing your own graphics, there are plenty of sources available that can supply you with images others have designed. You can purchase clip art packages that contain thousands of uncopyrighted images for your use, or you can find images the fun and easy way—on the Web!

Thousands of images are available on the Web for free. In fact, many Web sites are devoted strictly to the task of providing you with these images. Run a quick search for *clip art* in Yahoo! or your favorite search engine to find many sources of great images for your page.

SEE ALSO
➤ *For information on using Yahoo!, turn to page 161*

Table 21.3 lists some excellent places to begin exploring Web clip art.

Table 21.3 Great clip art for free		
Title	URL	Description
Clipart Directory	www.clipart.com	A listing of clip artsites.
Andy's Art Attack	www.andyart.com	A great source for free, original artwork and graphic design tips.
Barry's Clipart Server	www.barrysclipart.com	Thousands of clip art images you can use.
The Clipart Connection	www.clipart connection.com	Another large collection of free graphics connections.
The Mousepad	www.vikimouse.com	A neat collection of graphics drawn by a mouse. You can take any of the images, except those on the first page.

Inserting an Image in Your Web Page

Both FrontPage Express and Composer make inserting an image a snap. Both programs support drag and drop. If your image is open in one program like Corel Photoshop or a shareware program like Paint Shop Pro, and FrontPage Express or Composer is also open, you can click the image you want to use and drag it into your Web page. You can also insert an image that's stored on the hard drive of your computer by using the FrontPage Express or Composer menu.

Inserting an image on your page

1. Open FrontPage Express or Composer and open your Web page file.

2. Click the **Insert** menu and choose **Image**.

3. Type the folder path and file location of the image in the resulting **From File** text box (FrontPage Express) or the **Image Location** text box (Composer), and click **OK**.

   The graphic is inserted into your Web page document, placed with the program default size and layout options.

Publishing Your Page

Now that you've created a page, you need to get it posted where people can see it. Unfortunately, there's no set way to publish your page. Most Web hosting sites offer different instructions for getting your page online. Fortunately, many Web hosts are designed to be user-friendly and provide detailed instructions for getting your page online.

SEE ALSO

➤ *See information about posting pages to the Web on page 491*

Contact your ISP and find out if your contract includes free personal space. If so, find out from your ISP what you need to do to *upload* the page. You might need to use special FTP software. Another option for a Web home for your page might be a Web community. These communities are springing up all over the Web. You can post your page in a "neighborhood" for free and have fun with your virtual neighbors. Two great examples of Web communities are Yahoo!'s

> **Know the filename**
>
> Although the instructions for posting your page vary from Web host to host, make sure you know the filename and folder location of the page and graphics files (if any) before you begin. You'll save yourself time and grief if you know where the page and all the images are stored.

GeoCities at www.geocities.com and Lycos' Tripod at www.tripod.com. (I've been a resident of GeoCities for years, and I've become great friends with several other GeoCities dwellers.) Xoom at www.xoom.com is another Web community that seems to appeal to a younger crowd. Both GeoCities and Tripod offer easy upload directions for placing your pages on their servers.

Other Commercial HTML Editors

Although FrontPage Express and Composer offer a great way to create Web pages, both programs have some limitations. After you've practiced a little, consider moving up to an HTML editor that offers more features than either of the two browser suite components. Table 21.4 lists some other HTML editors you might want to try. Most of them are shareware, so you'll have a chance to try them out before you buy.

SEE ALSO

➤ *Learn about shareware on page 180*

Table 21.4	A sampling of commercial HTML Editors		
Program Name	URL	Cost	Comments
Microsoft FrontPage 2000	www.microsoft. com/frontpage	$149 new user $59.95 upgrade	FrontPage 2000 is included with the Microsoft Office 2000 suite, although it can be purchased separately. The best WYSIWYG HTML Editor on the market. With a Microsoft Office suite look and feel, FrontPage creates simple pages as well as complex sites with ease. Place page elements like graphics and text anywhere on your pages—even layer content with absolute and relative positioning. Place graphics within a block of text and the text will automatically wrap around the image appropriately.

continues...

Your own URL

Your URL may not be straightforward if you join a Web community. For example, if you have a page on the Xoom server, your friends will find you at members.xoom.com/ username. Visit Homepage.com at www.homepage.com for an easier name for your free page. Mailbank.com at mailbank.com is worthy of a look if you want a URL that makes sense to you. Mailbank.com hosts over 12,000 domains and you're likely to be able to get a URL that matches your name or company.

Table 21.4 Continued

Program Name	URL	Cost	Comments
HotMetal Pro 5.0	www.softquad.com/products/hotmetal/	$129	Provides three views for easy editing, advanced graphics editing, and loads of free software.
Namo Web Editor 3.0	www.namo.com	$79	A Visual Web authoring tool for novices and professionals. Includes DHTML, a JavaScript wizard, equation editing, Microsoft Word file import, additional graphics utilities, and WYSIWYG source-code editing.
HotDog Express	www.sausage.com	$49	If HTML resembles a Black Hole, then this program is for you. Without knowing or even wanting to know HTML, HotDog Express will, in four easy steps, help you to build and upload your very first Web page. Simply drag-and-drop "Web blocks" to construct a page of headings, images, paragraphs, lines, links, and even email addresses.

Beyond HTML

Just a few years ago, HTML was considered "the language" to know if you wanted to create a Web page. HTML is still an important component of Web pages. However HTML has a few limitations. First, some of the codes that work with one browser don't necessarily work with the other. Second, pages written with HTML are flat. The 3D effects and exciting animation we've come to expect on so many pages isn't possible with HTML alone.

Several other technologies are used to bring life and excitement to pages that you view on the Web:

■ *Plug-ins and Helper Apps* extend the functionality of a Web page by launching related applications. For example, Shockwave brings exciting multimedia effects to Web pages.

SEE ALSO

➤ *Review information about plug-ins and helper applications on page 199*

■ *DHTML* or Dynamic Hypertext Markup Language is a collective term for a combination of new HTML tags and options, style sheets, and programming that will let you create Web pages more animated and more responsive to user interaction than previous versions of HTML. Pages written in DHTML can look and behave like desktop applications, rather than standard Web documents.

■ *Javascripts* are small programs embedded into HTML documents that can make Web pages more exciting. For example, Javascripts can automatically change a formatted date on a Web page, cause a linked-to page to appear in a pop-up window, or change the appearance of a text or graphic when a mouse passes over it.

■ *Java programs*, different than Java scripts, communicate with the server that's storing the page and provide interactivity. Java might be used on e-commerce pages or on pages that feature Webcam shots, for example. If you're accessing the Internet at work, you might not be able to see Java applications. Many network administrators view Java as a potential security threat and don't allow Java-enabled applications.

■ *XML*, short for Extensible Markup Language, is viewed by many Web designers as the language of the future. XML is based on the HTML, but is much easier to work with. XML is a flexible way to create common information formats and share both the format and the data across the Internet. Proponents of XML say that it will fundamentally change publishing on the Web and then publishing in general.

Java on the street

Want to see Java in action? Ride around the streets with a New York taxi driver at www. ny-taxi.com. The pictures taken from the taxi are brought to you courtesy of a Java application.

APPENDIXES

GLOSSARY

128-bit encryption   Set up for use by users in North America, browsers enabled with 128-bit encryption provide increased security for information that's transmitted over the Internet, making it almost impossible for the information to be read or diverted.

ASCII format   A format for electronic files that uses only text and allows text attributes or graphics images.

audio streaming   Sound that's sent in compressed format over the Web, so that the listener can hear the portion of the transmission that's already downloaded as the remainder is downloaded. Radio broadcasts over the Web are sent in streaming audio format.

authentication   A process that occurs behind the scenes during an SSL transaction and checks to make sure that your identity matches that shown in your digital certificate.

Autocomplete   A browser feature that finishes typing URLs, based on sites you've visited previously.

Autocorrect   A browser that automatically corrects typographical errors in the URLs you type.

Autosearch   A special browser feature that allows you to type a simple search query directly into the Address box.

banner ad   A flashing image that contains information and links to an advertiser's Web site. Advertisers sometimes count banner "views," or the number of times the banner was clicked over a period of time.

binary files   Files that don't contain text. Program files and zipped files are examples of binary files.

bookmark   A site that's been listed by Navigator so that you can return to it quickly. Navigator provides a list of bookmarks to which you can add sites you want to revisit.

Bot   Short for robot, a bot is a software tool that digs for data. You can use a shopping bot to find the best merchandise at the best price.

browser   A program used to navigate the World Wide Web.

517

The browser controls the look of the Web documents and provides tools to move from one location to another. Internet Explorer and Netscape Navigators are Web browsers.

cache   An area on your hard drive where Web pages that you've already viewed are stored temporarily.

client/server   The relationship between two computer programs in which one program, the client, makes a service request from another program, the server, which fulfills the request.

closed mailing list   A mailing list where informative messages are sent to subscribers.

codec   Made up of an acronym for *compression/decompression*, a codec is an algorithm, or specialized computer program, that reduces the number of bytes consumed by large files and programs.

compressed files   Multiple files that are packed into one file for easy downloading and copying. Com-pressed files may need a program like Winzip to be unpacked.

Computer microphone   A hardware device that plugs into the sound card of your computer and enables you to talk over the Internet.

computer virus   A computer virus is a malicious program that hides inside another file. When you use the file, the virus can cause harm to your computer by destroying data and making your system inoperable.

Content Advisor   An Netscape Navigator feature which enables parents and other adults "supervisors" to limit access to sites viewed by children.

cookie   The exchange of information between your browser and the site you're visiting. A cookie can contain your name, your company name, your location, the type of computer you're using, your operating system, the type and version of your browser, and what Web pages you've looked at. Cookies are stored on the hard drive of your computer.

crawler   An electronic tool that searches through the Web and adds new Web sites to a database or index. Crawlers are sometimes called electronic spiders, worms, or robots.

crosspost   One posting that has been sent to multiple newsgroups or mailing lists.

cross-posting   The practice of posting the same message simultaneously to a number of newsgroups.

Cybercolleges   Universities and colleges which offer online college level classes.

Cybermall   A Web site that contains an online collection of merchants.

decompressed files   Multiple files that have been unpacked from a compressed file.

digest   A batch of email messages generated by an Internet mailing list.

Digital certificates   A personal certificate that identifies you or the vendor and is used during secure business transactions. Because digital certificates add an extra layer of security, they are not required for most Web transactions.

directory tree   The arrangement of drives, folders, and files on your computer.

domain   A set of network addresses that are organized in levels. The top level identifies geographic or purpose commonality (for example, the nation that the domain covers or a category such as "com"). The second level identifies a unique place within the top level domain. Lower levels of domain may also be used.

domain name   Also known as the hostname, the domain name is a unique identification for a Web site. Each computer on the Web has a domain name that identifies it from the others.

dot   The period character that separates portions of a URL, newsgroup name, or email address.

download   To copy a file from another computer (usually a server on the Web) to your computer.

drivers   Software that sets up some hardware that's connected to your computer. Printer drivers, for example, are needed by your computer so that it can successfully "talk" to the attached printer when you send a Web page or other document to print.

dumb terminal   A computer that's attached to a server and can only run programs through that server. When you attach to a telnet server, for example, you can only use the keyboard and monitor since the program on the server is in control.

E-centives   Incentives like coupons or discounts offered by Web merchants.

E-commerce   The term generally applied to business transactions on the Web.

e-résumé   An electronic copy of a résumé that's designed to be stored on a computer.

e-trading   The practice of buying stocks, bonds, and other securities over the Internet. You need to have an account set up with an online broker before you can e-trade.

e-zine   An online publication that usually contains original, sometimes offbeat or unusual content. Most e-zines are not commercial and don't contain advertising.

ECML   Short for electronic commerce modeling language, ECML is a new digital payment standard endorsed by e-commerce giants, including America Online, IBM, Microsoft, Mastercard, and Visa.

Emoticons Symbols used to express emotions during Internet communications.

encoder Special software that is needed in the process to create MP3 files from audio CDs. Some of the popular MP3 players, like RealJukebox, include the necessary software to create MP3s as part of the player package.

Explorer bar A feature in Internet Explorer that enables you to split the screen between the onscreen Web page and several different views, including your browsing History, a Search tool, and Favorites.

extranet An intranet to which access has been granted to users outside the company. Many companies grant customers access to selected pages on their intranets.

Favorites A list of marked sites in Internet Explorer that you can return to quickly.

firewall A program, usually an Internet gateway server, that protects an intranet from users from other networks. Firewalls can also limit what sites users who are acessing the Internet from their company's connection can access.

frames A browser feature that allows a Web page to be split into separate, scrollable windows.

Freenet A system that provides free, public-access to the Internet. Freenets are often sponsored or supported by local library systems. Although they don't usually offer all the tools provided by an ISP, Freenets give email services and limited access to the World Wide Web.

freeware Software programs that you can download and use for free.

FTP Short for File Transfer Protocol, a set of rules that controls the transfer of files between computers.

Game-master The overseer or editor of a role playing game. The game master is charged with the responsibility of making sure the participants perform within the confines of their characters. The game-master also makes sure that the role-playing game progresses to its conclusion.

GIF file Pronounced "jiff file" or "giff file," it's a graphics file that's used in many Web pages. GIF is short for Graphics Interchange Format and was developed by CompuServe. GIF files are great for storing lots of graphic information while maintaining a small file size.

Gopher An older Internet program that is based on a hierarchy of menus and sub-menus.

Gopher server   The physical server that holds the file or document you request from a Gopher menu.

GUI   Pronounced "gooey", A graphical user interface that allows you to easily interact with a computer via pictures and menu driven options for performing tasks. Typically, you use your mouse or other pointing device to make choices in a GUI program.

hash   A mathematically designed digest of a message that's sent during the authentication process of a secure Web transaction. Each hash is unique. When the receiving computer receives your message, it runs the same hash function you used. If both hashes aren't identical, the message is rejected. See *authentication*.

helper application   A computer program that's installed on your computer that works in tandem with your browser. For example, if you click a link to a Word document that's embedded in a Web page, your browser will open Word and display the linked document.

hit   A successful match in a search tool's database search. See *search query*.

Home page   The first page of a Web site that serves as an index or table of contents for the rest of the site.

HTML   Short for HyperText Markup Language, the set of "markup" symbols or codes placed in a file that's designed for display on a Web browser program. Pages you see on the Web are written in HTML.

Hyperlinks   A word, picture, or other element that you click to move from one Internet location to another. Hyperlinks, usually called links, can jump you to a different location on the same Web page or to a different site.

HyperText Markup Language   The set of "markup" symbols or codes placed in a file that's designed for display on a Web browser program. Pages you see on the Web are written in HTML.

IMAP   Short for Internet Message Access Protocol. IMAP is the most current standard protocol for receiving email messages from the mail server. It provides options such as viewing only the header or storing the messages you've read on the mail server.

Intellisense   Originally introduced with Microsoft Office 97, a feature of Internet Explorer that expands automation during Web searches.

Internet service provider   Often called an ISP, the company that provides individuals and other companies access to the Internet. Unless you have a direct Internet connection, you need to have an account with an ISP to get to the Internet.

intranet   A company's private internal Web site that lets only the people inside that company exchange and access information. An intranet usually looks much like any other site on the World Wide Web.

IP Address   The unique number that's assigned to each computer that's connected to the Internet. IP addresses are written as a series of four numbers, separated by periods.

IRC   An Internet system for chatting that involves a set of rules and conventions and client/server software.

IRC channel   Similar to a chat room, a chat group of Internet users that can be accessed using IRC software. See *IRC*.

IRC Network   A collection of IRC servers that are banded together (connected) and share chat rooms and individual chatters.

IRC server   A computer on the Internet that houses chat rooms.

JavaScript   Used in Web pages, JavaScripts bring interactivity to Web pages. There are thousands of uses for JavaScripts on Web pages. Some of the more common JavaScripts change the display date, show different graphics or text when a mouse passes over a pre-set area of the page, or launches a new window in the browser.

JPEG file   Prounounced "jay-peg," this file type is used for storing graphics files commonly used on Web pages. JPEG is an acronym for Joint Photographics Expert Group.

Keywords   Words that highlight or describe. In a search query, the Keywords are what you're looking for. In an e-résumé, Keywords are the nouns that highlight your special talents, skills, and experience.

LAN   Short for Local Area Network, a group of computers that are connected together.

LDAP   An email protocol that stores and retrieves directory information. Generally, LDAP enables you to search through Internet directories from your Personal Address Book.

link anchor   The part of a hyperlink that causes the mouse arrow to take the shape of a hand. See *hyperlinks*.

lurking   Hanging back and reading the postings of a newsgroup without replying or submitting any new postings.

mail servers   Electronic postal agents that send, sort, and deliver email messages using special mail protocols.

mailing list   A forum for discussion about a particular topic whose postings are sent to members through email. The messages can be sent individually or combined daily and sent in a digest format.

media player The software that's necessary to convert the streaming audio or video to sound or pictures and play them on a computer.

meta-engine A powerful search tool that looks through multiple search tools to match your search query.

Modem Short for MOdulator-DEModulator, a device that translates computer information into sound and sends or receives those sounds over telephone lines.

modulation protocol A standard used by all modem manufacturers that enables different modems, such as your modem and the modem to which you connect your ISP, to communicate with one another.

MP3 A file format in which a sound sequence is compressed into a very small file (about 1/12 the size of the original file) while preserving the original level of sound quality when it is played.

MP3 files Compressed sound files that have near-CD quality when they're played back.

MUD Short for Multi-User Dungeon, the first type of interactive role-playing games played on the computer, the term now indicates any type of RPG. See *RPG*.

multimedia files Files that contain text, sound or motion, like animation or movie formats.

Name resolution The behind-the-scenes process that converts text addresses, such as an email address or URL, to numbered IP addresses.

Net safe Keeping away from snoopers, strangers, or violent, lewd, or lascivious Web sites. The term is generally used in conjunction with children.

Net split A communication break between IRC servers, giving the appearance that everyone's left the chat room.

netiquette The conventions of politeness recognized for and expected by Internet users. Although netiquette technically covers the use of the Internet, it's most often referred to in conjunction with newsgroups.

NetWatch An Internet Explorer feature which enables parents and other adults to limit access to sites viewed by children.

Network News Transfer Protocol Often called NNTP, the server your Internet service provider uses for news.

newsgroups Themed Internet bulletin boards for users who share a common interest. Messages are posted to a newsgroup and can be read and replied to by all members of the group.

newsreader A special software program that enables you to read and reply to Internet newsgroup postings. Both the Internet Explorer and Netscape Communicator suites feature newsreaders or you can choose from a number of third-party newsreader programs.

nickname A name you use in chat programs instead of your real name.

OCR software Computer programs what are designed to convert scanned graphics images into text documents.

open mailing list A discussion group that takes place via email messages.

Page designer A professional company or individual who designs Web pages for a fee.

patch A software program designed to correct problems or errors or extend the power of the initial program. For example, a patch for Internet Explorer was designed to correct security errors in the original release of the program.

PICS Platform for Internet Content Selection, a group of people from all walks of life who screen Internet sites and rate the content.

playlist A collection of MP3 files that can be played in succession.

plug-in A program that is linked to your browser and extends its capability.

POP3 Short for Post Office Protocol 3, the POP3 deals with the way incoming messages are handled on the mail server. Generally, after you read a message that's been stored on a POP3 server, the message is deleted from the server (although it can be stored on your computer).

portal A World Wide Web site that is or proposes to be a major starting site for users when they get connected to the Web or that users tend to visit as an anchor site.

postings Messages posted to a newsgroup.

private key Used in secure business transactions, the private key is a random number that's known by one party or the other—the merchant or the browser.

proxy server a computer server that acts as an intermediary between a workstation user and the Internet so that the enterprise can ensure security, administrative control, and caching service. A proxy server is generally used by corporations and schools to separate their internal network from outside networks like the Internet.

public key Used in secure business transactions, the public key is a random number that's known only by your browser and the merchant.

résumé bank A Web site that stores electronic résumés. Prospective employers look through résumé banks or select candidates for positions within their companies.

rip   Create an MP3 file from an audio CD. See *ripper*.

ripper   Special software that creates MP3 files from audio CDs. After a song has been ripped, it needs to be encoded to complete the process of making an MP3 file. Some of the popular MP3 players, like RealJukebox, include the necessary software to create MP3s as part of the player package.

RPG   Role playing games in which the participants are assigned characters. Each character has a set personality and must carry out his/her action in a prescribed way.

RSAC   Short for Recreational Software Advisory Council, this independent, non-profit organization based in Washington, D.C, uses a content advisory system to help parents and educators rate Web sites that may be viewed by children.

scannable   A document that's ready to be fed through an electronic device. After a document is scanned, the resulting image file is read by an OCR program and converted to text. See *OCR software*.

Screen tip   A pop-up explanation of a toolbar button's function that appears when the mouse pointer passes over the button.

search engines   Search tools that index new pages by the use of electronic tools (see *crawler*) and enable you to search through the list of results for the sites you want to see.

search query   A keyword or phrase used by the Internet search tool to find matching documents on the Web.

Server Gated Cryptography   128-bit encryption offered by certain banks and merchants (usually outside of the United States or Canada) who have been pre-approved to provide the highest level of encryption.

shareware   Computer programs that you can use for free on an evaluation basis and then pay for if you decide to continue using them.

signature file   A file that's attached to outgoing email messages and newsgroup postings. Called a *sig*, a signature file can contain address information, a funny or philosophical comment, or a picture drawn with text characters.

site directories   Search tools, usually arranged by categories, that index new pages by Web sites that have been submitted to the directory.

Smart Browsing   A special browser feature that allows you to type a simple search query directly into the Address box of Navigator.

SMTP   Short for Simple Mail Transfer Protocol, SMTP is the protocol that processes outgoing email messages.

sniffer   A diagnostic tool that's used to solve data problems. Used illegally, a sniffer can intercept data that's being transmitted across the Internet, such as email addresses or credit card numbers.

source code   The underlying HTML code that's instructs your browser to display a Web page.

spam   Unsolicited junk email you receive via the Internet.

SSL   An acronym for Secure Sockets Layer, SSL was developed by Netscape to provide security to buyers and sellers during an online transaction.

Standalone chat programs Independent programs that allow you to participate in real-time communication with others on the Internet.

Start Page   The page that appears when you first launch your browser. The Start Page can be changed at any time.

subscribe   The action of joining a newsgroup or mailing list. Newsgroup names are added to your regular newsgroup list so that the newest postings are downloaded to your computer. The messages associated with a mailing list are sent through email.

Superdisk   A disk that's designed to hold up to 120 megabytes. To read the disk, your computer needs a disk drive that can read the disk.

TCP/IP   An acronym for Transmission Control Ptotocol/Internet Protocol, TCP/IP is the preferred way for data to be transferred over the Internet. The sending computer places the data in packets and then sends the packets out. The receiving computer removes the data from the packets and reassembles the data into its original form.

telnet   A system that enables you to connect to a server and run programs as if you were sitting at its keyboard.

Thread   The original posting and collection of related responses in a Usenet newsgroup.

unsubscribe   Removing the name of a newsgroup from your regular newsgroup list. When you unsubscribe to a group, you no longer receive its postings.

upload   The transmission of a file from one computer system to another, usually to a larger computer system.

URL   Pronounced "you-are-el," the Uniform Resource Locator is the address of a file or other resource you access on the Internet.

Usenet   A collection of over 32,000 Internet discussion groups that post messages to Internet newsgroups. Your ISP may not carry all of the Usenet newsgroups.

V.90   The current standard for 56K modems. See *Modem*.

virtual bank   A bank that conducts all its business on the Internet and does not have a physical location.

virtual brochure   An electronic brochure that includes graphics, photos, and text. The virtual brochure is posted to the Web so that everyone can see it.

Wave file   An audio file format, created by Microsoft, that has become a standard PC audio file format for everything from system and game sounds to CD-quality audio.

Web sites   Related collection of Web files that include a beginning file called a home page.

Web-based chat   Web pages that contain chat rooms you can enter and use to communicate with others.

Webcast   A radio or television transmission that's broadcast over the World Wide Web.

WebRing   A group of Web sites that are interlinked so that you can visit each site one after the other, eventually returning to the first Web site.

Webzine   The online version of a commercial magazine.

WYSIWWG   Pronounced "wiz-ee-wig," the letters stand for What You See Is What You Get. WYSIWYG Web page design programs show you what the end result will look like as the page is created.

Yahooligans!   The section of Yahoo!, the popular Web site directory, that's designed for kids.

Zip drive or cartridge   An external storage device that extends the storage capacity of your computer.

527

Employer Sites from A to Z

If you are really serious about looking for a new career, why not visit some companies on the Web. You save valuable time and shoe leather. Additionally, with a Web visit, you never need to hear "No thanks" or other platitudes.

The companies shown here make up a cross-section of employers who display employment information on their Web pages. Most of the companies are large and might have an office or branch near your home. The advantage to visiting a company's employment or career page is that it generally offers up-to-the-minute opportunities. By the time an ad for the available position appears in the Classified section of the newspaper, some Web-ready soul (like you) might have snagged the job.

If you don't see the company you want to work for here, search for that company's URL and visit the site. The job market is volatile; positions open and are filled quickly. A position that was open when this book was written might not be available today.

The following listings are broken down by the following:

- The name of the company
- The URL of the company's employment page or job listing
- A brief description of the typical employment opportunities offered by the company

AT&T

www.att.com/hr

AT&T has jobs available in many of their divisions, including AT&T Business Multimedia Services, AT&T Information Solutions, and AT&T Wireless. Positions range from sales and marketing jobs, to administrative positions in Human Resources, Accounting, and Finance.

Bristol-Myers Squibb Company

www.bms.com/joinus/

Bristol-Myers Squibb Company, a diversified worldwide health and personal care company, has many opportunities, including positions in chemical research and account executives. The site provides information on employee corporate benefits.

Club Med

www.cooljobs.com/clubmed

Club Med manages resorts in many countries and operates tours and cruises. Advertised positions include Resort Administration, Arts and Crafts, Maintenance, and Retail Sales. The site is available in French or English.

DuPont

www.dupont.com/careers

DuPont, a research and technology company, produces chemicals, polymers, and fibers. Their career site features an ever-changing list of available positions, including jobs that range from technical and scientific to sales associates.

Ethan Allen

www.ethanallen.com/about/

Ethan Allen is a retailer and manufacturer of fine home furnishings. Listings of all available opportunities in retail positions as well as in the corporate and manufacturing fields are displayed at the site.

Family Golf Centers

www.familygolf.com/employ.htm

The Family Golf Centers are a chain of driving ranges, batting cages, and miniature golf courses. The site features listings of the employment opportunities, as well as an address to reach the corporate Human Resources Department.

Greyhound Lines Inc.

www.greyhound.com/Company/jobs.html

Greyhound Lines Inc. is a large intercity bus company. Available positions include Driver Operations, Customer Service Representatives, and Information Technology professionals.

Hewlett-Packard

www.jobs.hp.com/

The Hewlett-Packard site is a comprehensive site that enables you to search for jobs in Canada, the U.S., Europe, Latin America, and Asia Pacific. Hewlett-Packard aggressively recruits employees and offers pages for college recruiting, job search, and recruiting events.

Intel

www.intel.com/intel/oppty/

If you've heard of a Pentium computer chip, you've heard of Intel. The site provides links to Intel's Hot Jobs, in addition to links to Intel recruiting events and college programs. Job categories include technical positions like Integrated Circuit Engineering and Manufacturing as well as positions in Marketing and Sales.

Janus

ww3.janus.com/welcome/jobs.htm

Janus, the international investment banking firm, offers many opportunities to people looking to work in the investment banking field. The Web site gives information about company benefits, specific jobs, and corporate opportunities.

Komag, Incorporated

www.komag.com/career/career.html

Komag, one of Silicon Valley's largest employers, is a supplier of thin-film media for computer hard drives. Click one of Komag's locations on the world map at their site to view that region's opportunities. Komag's available positions are primarily technical, although clerical and administrative jobs are posted at the site as well.

Lowe's Companies, Inc.

content030e.advantis.com/frames/empopps/findex.htm

Lowe's, a prominent building materials/specialty retailer, plans to have 600 stores open by the year 2000. Positions are available at the General Office as well as at the retail store level.

Microsoft Corporation

www.microsoft.com/jobs/

If you're using Windows, you know something about Microsoft Corporation. Microsoft actively recruits recent MBA graduates and has available positions in both technical and non-technical areas. The Microsoft career site offers a link to a calendar of dates, places, and times that Microsoft will be recruiting locally.

Nabisco

www.nabisco.com

Start your visit to Nabisco at their Main Street page. Click the link to **Town Hall** and then find employment possibilities by clicking the **Job Opportunities** link. Because Nabisco is a global company producing packaged food, you can pick from available positions in the Headquarters, Data Center, or Bakeries and Field divisions.

OmniPoint

www.omnipoint.com/

OmniPoint, the cellular phone service provider, offers a comprehensive employment Web page. There are listings of all employment possibilities available, in 24 different categories.

Procter and Gamble

http://www.pg.com/careers/us/career.htm

Procter and Gamble sells over 300 brands in over 140 countries. They offer entry-level career advice and internships. You can also search for and apply for one of their worldwide positions.

Quantum Corporation

www.quantum.com/hr/hr.html

Quantum makes computer storage products. Their Employment Opportunities page contains links to pages for College Relations, Current Job Openings, and Benefits, in addition to a page with instructions for applying for a job at Quantum. Choose a Quantum location to view the available positions. Jobs cover a wide range of areas, including positions in finance, administration, marketing, and sales.

Rubbermaid Incorporated

www.rubbermaid.com/corp/careers/rj2main.htm

Rubbermaid, a manufacturer and marketer of consumer products, lists career opportunities at their corporate headquarters in Wooster, Ohio and several other divisions. Positions run the gamut from Auditor to a Technical Facilitator.

Sears

www.sears.com/company/hr/jobpost.htm

Sears, a major retailer, offers positions in Automotive, Information Systems, Mall Management, Store Support, and Staff Support. Additionally, Sears' College Relations Department features a National Management Training program, designed to teach college students many aspects of the retailing business.

Tribune

www.tribune.com/employment/

The jobs listed on the Tribune Opportunities page include jobs located in Chicago, Orlando, and other Tribune sites. The Tribune is a provider of information and entertainment, and its jobs reflect the company's diversity. Available positions include jobs in journalism, accounting and payroll, and sales. Other jobs require expertise or experience in computer technology.

Unisys

www.corp.unisys.com/unisys/jobs.nsf

Unisys is a leader in the information management industry. View available positions broken down by geographic location or search for a job title. Most positions at Unisys are technically oriented and require experience or education in the computer industry.

Vanguard

www.vanguard.com/cgi-bin/Employ

Vanguard is a large company, dealing in mutual funds. Available openings are listed by geographic location and then broken down further into categories such as Customer Service and Management/Executive.

Wal-Mart

careers.wal-mart.com/

The Wal-Mart career site, called Careers@Wal-Mart, features information about the company and links to positions in its Retail Division and Information Systems departments. Also included on the page is a link to Wal-Mart's College Recruiting page.

Xicor

www.xicor.com/

Xicor is pioneering the application of field alterable technologies in new markets such as linear and microcontroller peripherals. To get to the Career Opportunity frame, click the link on the menu at the left side of the main page. Although most of the positions require technical expertise, jobs like Material Specialist Stores, that require mailroom and shipping and handling experience, appear from time to time.

Yahoo! Inc.

www.yahoo.com/docs/hr

Yahoo! Inc. is an Internet media company with an intuitive, up-to-date and efficient guide to the Internet. Yahoo! calls their employees "Yahoo!s." Their Employment Opportunities page lists positions in technical areas, like Engineering and Graphic Arts, and non-technical areas like Sales. Also included are positions for Surfing Yahoo!s, people who review Web sites for inclusion into Yahoo's giant Internet index.

ZAC Technologies

www.zac.com/jobs.html

ZAC Technologies is a company based out of Hoboken, New Jersey that specializes in Web-related jobs. Fill out an online résumé for immediate consideration.

Appendix

B

The Best Buying Sites on the Web

E-commerce is changing the way we shop. Visit the sites listed here to find a wide variety of goods and services.

The listings are broken down first by category, and then by the following:

- The name of the company
- The URL
- A brief description of the how the site is organized or what you can expect to find

Apparel

Abercrombie and Fitch

www.abercrombie.com/anf/onlinestore

Abercrombie and Fitch used to be a world leader in camping and outdoor goods, but now they're hot among anyone under 21. Shop in either the men's or women's departments. Make shopping easier by making up a personal profile.

The Gap

www.gap.com

The Gap, the clothing store famed for its ads for khakis, offers online shopping for hip and happening clothing. Choose from six categories. Snag a good deal and save big bucks at the sale area.

L.L. Bean

www.llbean.com

L.L. Bean offers over 600 of its most popular products on a Web site that's easy to navigate. The merchandise is categorized into clearly defined categories and is accompanied by photographs and descriptions. If you don't want to order online, you can request a snail mail catalogue.

Land's End

www.landsend.com

The Land's End site is more like a community than a store. In addition to providing clothing, shoes, and luggage, you can arrange a vacation or tour through the online travel service. Land's End also features a virtual model, which you customize to your own sizes, so you can try on clothes and other accessories for sale on their site. Sign up to receive a monthly Land's End newsletter or visit Dodgeville, Land's End's online community. Kids can enter a poetry contest and compete for prizes for themselves and their school.

Fredericks of Hollyweb

www.viamall.com/fredholly

The famous lingerie catalog of Frederick's of Hollywood makes online sizzle. You can find lingerie, shoes, wigs, and gifts at this hot site. There's even a special plus-size collection of fashions.

Eddie Bauer

www.ebauer.com

Shop EB, Eddie Bauer's online catalogue, is one of the best shopping sites on the Web. If you plan to shop at the site again, register for EB Exclusive, which stores your personal information such as important gift-giving dates. You can also set up email reminders of important dates.

American Eagle Outfitters

http://www.ae-outfitters.com/line.htm

"Shop in your Underwear" begs American Eagle Outfitters online establishment. In addition to trendy clothes, apply for a credit card, read the AE-Zine, and sign up for free email.

Victoria's Secret

```
http://www.victoriassecret.com/vsc/html/catalogue
```

Who hasn't heard of the Victoria's Secret catalogue? The entire catalogue (and more) is here at the internationally known lingerie store. Victoria's Secret recently added an online shopping area, where you can buy everything in their sexy online emporium.

Bedding and Bath Accessories

Pacific Coast

```
www.pacificcoast.com
```

Pacific Coast features natural, allergy-free, down pillows and comforters. After a hard day on the Internet, you can fall asleep in comfort and style with products from this site. Shop securely in Pacific Coast's online store, or find a retail store near you that carries their products.

Victoria's Secret

```
http://www.victoriassecret.com/vsc/html/os/bedindex.html
```

Victoria's Secret, the lingerie shop, recently added bedding to its seductive line. The online bedding collection shop features such great pictures that you can imagine yourself relaxing in one of their well-appointed beds. Just about every fabric, texture, and style of bedding is available, including jersey and satin as well as soft textured fabrics.

Chadder & Co.

```
www.chadder.com
```

How about luxurious bathroom fittings from one of England's suppliers of fine bathrooms? The prices are in British currency and don't include tax, duties, or shipping costs. Still, it's fun to look at the pictures of elegant fixtures and imagine them in your dream house.

Books

Amazon.com

www.amazon.com

A trip to Amazon.com, the leading online bookseller, can take hours. Books at this site are usually discounted. Search the site by author, title, or subject for any book in the extensive catalogue. Amazon offers some great personalization features for repeat customers. Book prices are discounted.

Macmillan Computer Publishing

www.mcp.com

The Macmillan online bookstore features more than 2,000 books and software products from some of the best names in the business: Adobe, Borland, Lycos, Netscape, Que, Sams, Ziff-Davis Press, and others. You can use the search function to search for the right computing book. Visit the Software SuperStore for products designed to help you use your computer.

Barnes and Noble

www.barnesandnoble.com

A visit to the Barnes and Noble site is more than a trip to a book store. You can participate in a literary forum, read live online interviews, or search their extensive catalogue. Barnes and Noble's Personalized Book Recommendations suggests books just for you, based on your answers on a brief questionnaire.

Bargain Book Warehouse

www.1bookstreet.com/1bargainbookstreet/Bargain_Home.asp

You'll find savings up to 80% on all kinds of popular fiction and non-fiction books, both in and out of print. The site is designed for easy navigation. Although the catalogue of available books is not as extensive as either Amazon or Barnes and Noble, there's a good chance you'll find the book you want.

Cars

Microsoft CarPoint

carpoint.msn.com

Although you might not want to buy a car online, you can do all of the preliminary shopping at Microsoft CarPoint. CarPoint's Surround Video feature enables you to explore the interiors of most of the cars on the market. You can also use the CarPoint loan calculator to find out if you can afford the car you want.

Online Auto

www.onlineauto.com

If you've got an idea of the model and make of the car you'd like to buy, visit Online Auto to confirm your choices. Online Auto features links to car dealers which can be sorted by state or vehicle. Online Auto also features free used car ads.

Computers

Computer Discount Warehouse

www.cdw.com

A no-frills site for the serious computer shopper. The Search, Browse, and Compose features help you find the best deal. If you want to be notified of specials and special deals, sign up for the Buyer's Edge newsletter. Reviews and tips on the latest and greatest equipment are maintained on the site, so you can read about a product before you buy.

Dell Computers

www.dell.com

Although Dell is known as a giant for business computers, they are making big inroads in the home market as well. Browse the various

computers to find the model that suits your needs and order it
online.

CompUSA

www.compusa.com

The computer superstore scores an online hit. Products are accompanied by detailed descriptions, so you're sure you're getting exactly
what you want. While you're at the site, you can enter a trivia contest. A children's department has its own outer-space design. PC
Modem, the online computer expert, answers any technical questions
you might have.

Insight

www.insight.com

Hardware, software, and online technical support are packed into
this great site. You can find daily specials on the latest and greatest
computer equipment. Click a link to visit the Hard Drive-In Theatre
for help picking the right hard drive for your computer. For amuse-
ment, visit the Insight Cybertainment center.

Entertainment

Reel

www.reel.com

Reel is the largest video store on the Web. With more than 35,000
videos for rent and 80,000 for sale, you're sure to find a movie you
want to see. Searching for movies with Reel's advanced search tools
is almost more fun than seeing the movie itself. For something different, sign up for Reel's virtual classes in film theory at their online
Cinema U.

Tower

www.towerrecords.com

The Tower Records online music store is one of the Web's hot spots. In addition to a great collection of CDs, you'll find special promotions and giveaways. If you need to search the catalogue of CD titles, the Quick Search feature makes it easy to find just what you want.

Music Boulevard

www.musicblvd.com

Visiting this site of over 185,000 CDs and tapes is almost like watching MTV. Listen to selected tracks before you buy. The site is organized into seven departments. Browse through all of them and look at the collection of cover art.

CD Now

www.cdnow.com

CD Now is the world's largest online music store. Together, with Music Boulevard, another online music giant, they bring you one of the most comprehensive music collections available on the Web.

Flowers

Virtual Florist

www.virtualflorist.com

Send beautiful bouquets from this Canadian-based florist anywhere. Also, as an added twist, send a floral image with a personalized greeting for free. Virtual Florist sends an email to the recipient, with a special URL. The virtual bouquets are easy to send and everyone loves getting one.

1-800-Flowers

www.1800flowers.com

With over 150 floral arrangements and gifts to look through, it's easy to send someone a special gift. Read the online magazine, called Fresh Thoughts, for tips on caring for your flowers, the proper type of arrangement to send for a specific reason, and even the appropriate message to write on the card. If you want 1-800-Flowers to help you out, sign up for the Gift Reminder Service that alerts you five days before you need to send a bouquet.

Great Flowers

www.greatflowers.com

Great Flowers is a comprehensive site for everything floral. The site features wonderful pictures of bouquets and floral arrangements. Also available from Great Flowers is a reminder service, a Flowers Every Month service, a tracking device, and an affiliate network.

Food

NetGrocer

www.netgrocer.com

Shop with NetGrocer and receive your groceries by Federal Express the next day. NetGrocer, the first online grocery store, is a site to take seriously. A cash register keeps a running tab of your purchases as you add things to your virtual shopping basket. Items are sorted by 14 categories, including brand name, price, calories, and fat content.

Candyland Warehouse

www.candylandwarehouse.com

Like hard candy? Many varieties are available at this online confectionery, including low calorie and sugarless flavors. The prices are better than you'll find locally. Enter the contest to win free candy.

Wilderness Coffee House

www.wilderness-coffee.com

The Web version of a famous Minnesota coffee store is designed so well that you'll swear you can smell coffee brewing when you visit the site. The prices of all items are clearly marked. You'll also learn the origin and history of the coffee beans. For online orders, the beans are roasted every Wednesday to ensure that you'll get fresh coffee.

Fragrances

Perfumania

www.perfumania.com

Perfumania is the ultimate choice for quality brand name perfumes, colognes, and fragrances. You'll also find gifts, kids fragrances, and aromatherapy items at this great site. Prices are great. Check out the sale prices on the Red Tag specials.

Perfume Web

www.perfumeweb.com

Order online or call a toll-free number for perfume at discount prices. Prices are usually around 40% lower than what you'd pay in a department store. Delivery is fast and reliable.

Pets

The Dog House Online Emporium

www.thedogbakery.com

The site features gourmet foods for dogs. Treat your pet to a special goodie from the Gourmet Pet Bakery. Or buy your pooch some special beef taffy or a basted turkey foot. There's even a section to buy yourself a cute, non-edible gift.

Aardvark Pet

www.aardvarkpet.com

Featured as a site with gifts for pets and the people who love them, you're sure to find something for your favorite two or four-footed friend at Aardvark. The inventory is extensive and fun. In addition to the standard cat and dog supplies, you can find reasonably priced supplies for hamsters and birds. The Gifts for People section includes apparel, software, jewelry, and toys.

The Puppy Cam Network

www.thepuppycam.com/

The Puppy Cam Network is an online shelter for puppies and kittens, in which you can donate or adopt. You'll find the Puppy Cam Network in over 12 cities, with 28 more cities coming online soon. Visit the site to sponsor a pet, ask an expert about pet care, or even see what animals are available for adoption in local shelters.

Sewing and Needlework

Sarah Howard Stone Online Sewing Catalogue

www.sarahhowardstone.com

There's something for anyone who enjoys sewing at Sarah Howard Stone. Choose from patterns, notions, fabrics, ribbons, and lace. You can even buy gifts and jewelry from the site. Visit the gallery to see some finished projects.

Vermillion Stitchery

www.vsccs.com

The site is a counted cross-stitcher's dream. Charts with all different types of designs are available at the site. You can even send away for a free flower chart that changes monthly.

Crafts Galore

www.craftsgalore.com

With a catalogue of over 19,000 craft items, Crafts Galore has everything for the Webcrafter. The site is designed with buttons (that look like buttons) and lots of cute touches. You'll feel like you're visiting with old friends when you tour the site.

Toys

FAO Schwarz

www.faoschwarz.com

The ultimate online toy store has products for kids and grownups. The site features challenging contests and great giveaways, as well as the best collection of toys in the world. You can shop at the site or send for a catalogue.

Toys-R-Us

www.toysrus.com

Shopping at Toys-R-Us online is almost as exciting as shopping at one of their superstores. Toys are arranged by categories and by brand name, making it easy to find exactly what you want. If you want to find that perfect toy quickly, use the Toy Finder. Prices at the site are reasonable and their shopping policies are explained clearly.

E-Toys

www.etoys.com

E-Toys is one of the largest online toy stores on the Web. You can search for toys there by age, price range, brand, other stores, or other areas of the Internet. E-Toys also has many other toys that aren't available anywhere else.

INDEX

555

S

*site directories, 158,
160-163*
smart features, 153-154
WebRings, 159, 174-175
secure Web sites, 102-103
spoofers, 88
URLs, 26, 112
country codes, 114-115
domain names, 113-114
domains, 113-116
dot (.) character, 113
entering, 112, 116-118
history lists, 122-130
http://, 112-113
name portion, 113
www, 113
Web pages, 26
Web sites, 25

**World's Radio Station Web
site, 319**

worms, 157-159

Worth Online, 356

www (URLs), 113

WWW. *See* World Wide
Web.

**WYSIWYG HTML edi-
tors, 489**
Hot Dog Express, 512
HotMetal Pro 5.0, 512
Microsoft FrontPage
2000, 511
Microsoft FrontPage
Express, 490-499
Namo Web Editor 3.0,
512
Netscape Composer,
499-500, 505-507

X - Z

X.2 modems, 37
Xicor Web site, 536
XML, 513

Yahoo!, 157, 160-163, 471
building custom start
pages, 139-141
career opportunities, 536
Chat, 287
games, 480
GeoBuilder, 490
Geocities
kids-only pages, 406
publishing Web sites, 511
resume postings, 386
Messenger, 292-294
New icon, 315
newspaper directory,
315-316
People Search, 310
reference desk, 362
scrolling news tickers, 313
sports, 325
Travel, 459-460
Yahooligans!, 365,
406-409

YMMV, 272

**Yuckiest Site on the
Internet, 424**

za.ads.jobs newsgroup, 402

**ZAC Technologies Web
site, 536**

**ZDNet Buy It or Lease It
program, 450**

Zeen e-zine, 410